Guardians of the Arsenal

GUARDIANS
OF THE
ARSENAL

The Politics of Nuclear Strategy

JANNE E. NOLAN

A NEW REPUBLIC BOOK

Basic Books, Inc., Publishers   New York

Library of Congress Cataloging-in-Publication Data

Nolan, Janne E.
    Guardians of the arsenal: the politics of nuclear strategy/
Janne E. Nolan
    p. cm.
    "A New Republic Book."
    Bibliography: p. 287.
    Includes index.
    ISBN 0-465-09802-9
    1. United States—Military policy. 2. Nuclear warfare. 3. United
States—Politics and government—1945-   . I. Title.
UA23.N65   1989   89-42524
355'.033573—dc20   CIP

To Barry, Jenny, and Ali

CONTENTS

ABBREVIATIONS

ABM	antiballistic missile
ACDA	Arms Control and Disarmament Agency
AEC	Atomic Energy Commission
ALCM	air-launched cruise missile
ALPS	accidental launch protection system
ATB	advanced-technology bomber
BAMBI	ballistic missile boost intercepts
BMD	ballistic missile defense
BMDC	Ballistic Missile Defense Command
CIA	Central Intelligence Agency
CINC	commander in chief
CINCSAC	commander in chief, Strategic Air Command
CTB	Comprehensive Test Ban
DARPA	Defense Advanced Research Projects Agency
DGZ	desired ground zero
DIA	Defense Intelligence Agency
DoD	Department of Defense
DPM	Draft Presidential Memorandum
DR & E	Defense Research and Engineering
ERIS	exoatmospheric reentry vehicle interception system
FAS	Federation of American Scientists
ICBM	intercontinental ballistic missile
INF	intermediate-range nuclear forces
JCS	Joint Chiefs of Staff
JSCP	Joint Strategic Capabilities Plan
JSPD	Joint Strategic Planning Document
JSTPS	Joint Strategic Target Planning Staff
MAD	mutual assured destruction
MIRVs	multiple independently targeted reentry vehicles

MPS	multiple protective shelter
NASA	National Aeronautics and Space Administration
NATO	North Atlantic Treaty Organization
NEACP	National Emergency Airborne Command Post
NIE	National Intelligence Estimate
NORAD	North American Air Defense Command
NSAM	National Security Action Memorandum
NSC	National Security Council
NSDD	National Security Decision Directive
NSDM	National Security Decision Memorandum
NSSD	National Security Study Directive
N-STAP	National Nuclear Strategic Targeting and Attack Plan
NUWEP	Policy Guidance for the Employment of Nuclear Weapons
OTA	Office of Technology Assessment
PD	Presidential Directive
PRM	Presidential Review Memorandum
R & D	research and development
RDF	Rapid Deployment Force
SAC	Strategic Air Command
SALT	Strategic Arms Limitation Talks
SBI	space-based interceptor
SBL	space-based laser
SDI	Strategic Defense Initiative
SDIO	Strategic Defense Initiative Office
SIOP	Single Integrated Operational Plan
START	Strategic Arms Reduction Talks
UCS	Union of Concerned Scientists

ACKNOWLEDGMENTS

THIS BOOK is first and most importantly the result of the intellectual and financial support given by the Carnegie Corporation of New York, which funded the project *The Politics of Nuclear Doctrine;* and of the work of Defense Forecasts, Inc., which managed the Carnegie project and allowed me to participate in research that led to the writing of this book. I am particularly grateful to Frederic (Fritz) Mosher, chair of Carnegie's program on Avoiding Nuclear War, who contributed directly to the project's conception, understood fully its complexities, and provided insight and encouragement throughout.

I would not have been able to conduct this study without the extraordinary generosity of the Brookings Institution, which has sanctioned my continued presence on its premises. As my residency has been extended from an initial arrangement for one year to now more than two, everyone has been kind enough not to point out that visiting fellows, like any other visitors, are not supposed to overstay their welcome. Brookings is an incredible place, a unique combination of scholarly privacy and genuine collegiality. Its image as a bastion of staidness is a great cover for what really goes on there.

I am especially indebted to John Steinbruner, the director of the Foreign Policy Studies Program, both for his personal kindness and for his critical work on nuclear strategy, which proved invaluable to my effort to understand this subject. Bill Quandt, the acting director of the program in 1986 who first brought me to Brookings, deserves very special thanks. I also want to thank Susan Stewart, despite her periodic veiled threats to divest me of my office, and Charlotte Brady, who, with Susan, keeps me constantly entertained. Other colleagues, including Bruce Blair, Marty Binkin, Josh Epstein, Paul Stares, Dick Betts, Ray Garthoff, Michael MccGwire, Ethan Gutmann, and others too numerous to list, account for the convivial and intellectually challenging environment at Brookings. Those who were forced to cope with the telephone traffic I inflicted on them, including Kathryn Ho and Ann Ziegler, should be credited for their indulgence.

I initially came to Brookings with the support of the Council on Foreign Relations, which awarded me an International Affairs Fellowship in 1986. I began to study some of the issues covered in this book under the council's auspices, and benefited tremendously from the contacts and experiences I was afforded as a council fellow. Tony Dunn, director of the fellowship program, was extremely supportive, as was Alton Frye. I had some memorable times using the elegant offices on the top floor of the Pratt house, made even more memorable by the presence of my distinguished air force colleague Donald Loranger. The council provides special opportunities to younger scholars with this fellowship, a privilege I am honored to have received.

Much of this book is based on personal interviews. I conducted dozens of interviews with individuals from a wide spectrum of backgrounds, political orientations, and expertise. What was perhaps most fulfilling in the conduct of this research was encountering so many dedicated people whose interest in effective national policy supercedes personal ambitions or biases. The sensitivity of the subject necessitates anonymity for many of the individuals who gave generously of their time and insights. You know who you are: I hope this book lives up to your standards, reflects your insights fairly, and adds to the debate in a way you find helpful.

There are many individuals who could speak on the record. At the risk of egregious omissions, I want to thank David Aaron, Martin Anderson, Bruce Blair, Harold Brown, Sid Drell, Greg Fossedal, Alton Frye, Bill Furniss, General Robert Herres, Bill Hoehn, Bruce Jackson, Bill Kauffman, General Jack Merritt, Paul Nitze, Bill Perry, John Pike, Ted Postol, Condi Rice, James Rubin, Leon Sloss, Larry Smith, R. Jeffrey Smith, Strobe Talbott, Richard Wagner, Douglas Waller, Ted Warner, Bruce Weinrod, General Jasper Welch, and Pete Worden.

It should also be noted that much of the historical material used in this book would not have been available without the painstaking effort of scholars who have worked to identify and declassify government documents and, in turn, made them available for others to use. Among the pioneers in this field are David Rosenberg, Fred Kaplan, and Des Ball. The National Security Archives, under the capable leadership of Scott Armstrong, has managed to collect and organize hundreds of documents and provide future scholars with an extraordinary resource.

Acknowledgments

I also want to thank those who read and commented on drafts of this manuscript, including Strobe Talbott, John Steinbruner, Bruce Jackson, and Roger Duter. The anonymous readers, some of whom went over each page in painful detail, have to be thanked privately.

The manuscript would not exist without the research assistance of David Boren, Margaret Sullivan, and Mary Umberger. Margaret Sullivan proved that there is no such thing as an unavailable document if you use your talents creatively. Matthew Bunn answered even the most obscure questions about sources quickly and patiently. Mary Umberger deserves special praise for her dedicated and competent assistance in the final stages of preparing this manuscript. Her recent death was tragic. I miss her.

The New Republic editor from Basic Books, Bill Newlin, was an inspired influence, a man born to the craft. He has seen this book through from its original embryonic chapters, and exuded enthusiasm quite beyond his job description. So too for the project editor, Suzanne Wagner, and the copyeditor, Otto Sonntag, whom I know only telephonically, but their work speaks for itself.

Leon Wieseltier, who has undertaken far nobler causes, made me a direct beneficiary of his unswerving commitment to the integrity of books, for which he deserves special thanks.

Finally, I am indebted in countless ways to Barry Blechman. My collaborator in this endeavor from the beginning, he helped conceive the idea, raised the money for a project that sustained me while I wrote this book, commented on every draft, and is still speaking to me. If this were a movie, Barry would be listed as the producer. As it is, he is the continued inspiration for all things.

Guardians of the Arsenal

CHAPTER 1

The Politics of
Strategic Defenses:
The Reagan Legacy

IN THE EARLY YEARS of the postwar era, nuclear policy was largely protected from the adversarial politics of democracy. Closeted in secret think tanks and in obscure areas of the Pentagon, a handful of individuals designed the nation's nuclear forces far from the public eye. Although the public's fear of nuclear war prompted periodic outbursts of citizen opposition, the day-to-day conduct of national security enjoyed a special status in American political thought. Defense was widely agreed to be the rightful business of the president and the military, not of ordinary Americans.

The steadily growing influence of public opinion in the last two decades has altered fundamentally the calculations of political leaders in designing nuclear policy. With the escalation of congressional and media interest, the public now routinely brings its influence to bear on defense decisions through elections, legislation, and headlines. The invocation of "national security" no longer prompts tacit public acquiescence in national policies. "[The public] want[s] to be included in the fateful decisions that are being made," argues Flora Lewis, "to know enough of the details not to be bullied or frightened by people who put them off with 'just trust me, I know what's best.' "[1]

3

Today, even freshmen congressmen or congressional candidates regularly play to their constituents and to the press by challenging the president and the Pentagon on defense issues. The peace vote, as it has come to be known, is courted actively in congressional races and even influences the way in which some local candidates frame their electoral platforms. And it is now routine for presidential candidates to dedicate much of their campaigns to the discussion of war and peace, engaging in protracted debates over what were once considered arcane issues of nuclear weaponry. National defense, in short, has been absorbed into grass-roots politics and mass culture.

The politicization of national defense helps explain both how one key element of the Reagan agenda—the Strategic Defense Initiative (SDI), or Star Wars, as it is more popularly known—originated and why it was able to capture such a disproportionate amount of public and media attention relative to its immediate budgetary, or even military, significance. Initially conceived as a research program for defensive technology slated to cost less than 2 percent of the defense budget—a budget that was to exceed $1.5 trillion between 1982 and 1987—the SDI nevertheless quickly moved to the center of partisan political disputes about administration policy.

Americans have an intrinsic faith in the value of debate and public involvement as means of ensuring sound and accountable government decisions. Public interest in national security is inspired by the belief that war is too important to be left to generals and certainly too dangerous to be left to elected officials. If the public can be educated sufficiently to question defense policy, peace activists argue, nuclear weapons will be recognized for the horror they threaten and be abolished.

The SDI suggests another by-product of the popularization of the nuclear debate, however: the potential for mass delusion. Driven by pressures to appeal to an anxious electorate, the SDI became an overtly politicized caricature of nuclear strategy, far removed from the technological and strategic realities that constitute the American nuclear arsenal. In the effort to assuage the fear of nuclear war, it focused the public's attention on a futuristic concept of an American defense posture, which, whether welcome or feared, had little to do with the actual trends in U.S. military capabilities or even the internal objectives of the initiative itself. The debate over the SDI may seem to have created a more attentive electorate, but it also reveals the extent to which heightened public attention can help catalyze severe policy distortions, challenging politicians to devise ever more brilliant public strategies, increasingly and deliberately designed to obscure reality.

Radical a turn in American nuclear doctrine as it may have seemed, however, the SDI is in two key respects not fundamentally different from half a dozen other such episodes in the forty-plus years of the nuclear era.

First, although no other doctrinal change has ever been presented as dramatically as the SDI, the publicly declared basis for U.S. force planning—the cosmetic rationale that overlay concrete plans to use nuclear weapons in war—has always been subject to political calculations. Changes in nuclear doctrine have been fueled primarily by domestic political impulses, with every new administration perceiving the need to alter, often to reverse, the policies of its predecessor. These changes reflect the desire felt by new presidents to demonstrate their authority and to show concern for reducing the threat of nuclear devastation with conscious efforts to forge positive, peaceful historical legacies of their own. Typically tempered over the course of incumbency, such efforts nevertheless do have profound influence on the direction and content of American politics.

Second, the SDI is consistent with the long-standing schism between public declarations about nuclear forces and the reality of plans to develop and use those forces for military objectives. Advances in the capabilities of nuclear forces have always been pursued for the purpose of fighting wars, should deterrence fail. Every postwar American administration has sought to develop technologies and plans to make nuclear weapons usable for military objectives. For obvious reasons, this is not a goal that political leaders like to publicize. It is the task of politicians to present the public with a more consoling picture of national policy.

This means that the periodic formal shifts in doctrine have always affected domestic politics far beyond the largely secret realms in the executive branch where decisions about nuclear weapons are actually taken. Even as defense issues become exposed more and more frequently to public discussion, serving as subjects for political stump speeches, television, and best-sellers, those charged with the design of operational plans for nuclear war have remained largely unaffected by public sentiment or political tides. Whether the doctrine has been called "massive retaliation," "assured destruction," "flexible response," or "defense dominance," the sweeping changes implied in the political sphere have had only an indirect consequence for the men at the Strategic Air Command (SAC) or the national weapons laboratories, whose enduring challenge has not changed: to translate the awesome power of nuclear weapons into credible military options.

Publicly revealed changes in nuclear doctrine, in short, have always been superimposed, with modest effect, on a consistent, largely secret effort to design weapons and related systems to make nuclear war militarily credible. Whereas the public activity has been episodic and usually polemical, the secret effort has been continuous, and largely removed from the ups and downs of electoral politics and the public mood.

The Speech

The SDI offers as dramatic an illustration of the schism between public policy and operational war plans as has ever come along. Unabashedly formulated as a political device, it was the logical product of a media-concious administration, which understood that it is more effective politically to design policies that appeal to the public's sentiment than to try to confront issues directly. In an age of media "sound bites" and policies expressed by bumper stickers, even nuclear doctrine could be a subject for mass popularization, the Reagan administration concluded—by galvanizing favorable public opinion to preempt and overwhelm skepticism. In the words of one administration official, the SDI reflected "a uniquely Southern California mentality," far removed from the professional elitism of the East Coast establishment that had long dominated the formulation of nuclear strategy.

Intended as a rhetorical palliative to the prevailing public fears of nuclear war, the president's televised announcement, on March 23, 1983, of a new American strategic doctrine was a remarkable tactic of public diplomacy. As portrayed in President Reagan's speech, the SDI promised a "peace shield," a space-based umbrella of benign technologies that would deliver Americans from the threat of nuclear apocalypse. Challenging the most fundamental orthodoxies that had guided American security policy throughout the postwar decade—in a moving address punctuated with vivid moral denunciations of the policy of nuclear deterrence—the president spoke over the heads of the defense "establishment" and called on the public to join him in his vision.

"The human spirit must be capable of rising above dealing with other nations and human beings by threatening their existence," the president said, denouncing the idea of deterring war by threatening nuclear retaliation against aggressors. The president offered instead "a vision of the future which offers hope. It is that we embark on a program to counter the awesome Soviet missile threat with measures that are defensive. . . . [This program] could free the world from the threat of nuclear war." Nuclear weapons, said the president, can be "rendered impotent and obsolete."[2]

Only a handful of individuals were involved in the drafting of the final version of the speech. Most officials reacted with genuine astonishment, including Reagan's most senior advisers and Cabinet members. Drafts had not been cleared by either Secretary of Defense Caspar Weinberger, who was reduced to making frantic midnight phone calls to the White House from a conference he was attending in Lisbon, or Secretary of State George Shultz, who had received a copy only the night before "as a courtesy." The Joint Chiefs of Staff (JCS), ordinarily the architects of any alterations in the nuclear posture, had not been formally notified. Even the assistant secretary of defense for policy, Richard Perle, known widely as the preeminent proselytizer of strategic defenses in the administration, played no formal role in drafting the statement; he was in Europe.[3]

Watching the address on television at home, the two midlevel officials responsible for much of the original speech draft, Kathleen Troia, one of Secretary Weinberger's principal speech writers, and the director of strategic forces policy, Franklin Miller, were stunned. Their draft had set out the broad objectives of the Reagan defense budget, emphasizing the need for increases in defense spending and for deployment of a new, land-based strategic missile, the MX. This was to be the traditional presidential appeal for defense programs given early in the year, before the Congress begins its annual deliberations on funding for the Defense Department. It was a key speech for an administration that had pledged to expand American military forces drastically, the opening salvo of what State Department officials dubbed the "Year of the Missile," in reference to impending deployments of new nuclear missiles in both the United States and Europe.[4]

The speech had been returned by the White House to the Pentagon the day before, largely unchanged except for a blank section marked "insert." The authors had no warning of what this insert would be but were not especially concerned—probably an inspirational presidential anecdote, Miller assumed, a little homily adding the personal touch favored by the "Great Communicator." Similarly, in the daily meeting of the National Security Council (NSC), in the White House Situation Room on the morning of March 23, Deputy National Security Adviser Robert McFarlane mentioned that there would be an "additional section" in the president's speech that night, but, according to a participant, no one paid much attention. White House staff had by now become used to these "afterthoughts" inserted by domestic advisers or even the president himself, typically a harmless rhetorical flourish "like an encomium to Sally Ride," the first woman astronaut.[5]

Instead, the president announced plans for a new nuclear doctrine—a sweeping change in American security policy—absent even the most embryonic technical plans for its implementation. Confusion was the order of the day, especially among defense officials who thought they were responsible for nuclear policy. Frank Miller's young deputy, William Furniss, watching the speech on television in a hotel room in Wyoming just before he was to debate the noted arms control advocate Herbert Scoville, said, "I was appalled; this is crazy." That afternoon, Major General Donald L. Lamberson, the official who was then coordinating the Pentagon's directed-energy weapons programs—a technology central to strategic defenses—had told the Senate Subcommittee on Strategic and Theater Nuclear Forces that such systems were insufficiently promising to warrant additional funding.[6]

Even Alexander Haig, President Reagan's former secretary of state who had resigned at the end of 1982, later decried the timing and content of the announcement:

> The White House guys said, "Hey, boss, come on. You're going to make a big splash. Big P.R. You're going to look like the greatest leader in America. Get out there and give that speech." And he did. . . . But the preparation had not been made. I know the aftermath the next day in the

Pentagon, where they were all rushing around saying, "What the hell is strategic defense?"[7]

It was quite clear that the speech was aimed at a domestic audience. Political advisers, including the President's assistant for policy development, Martin Anderson—known as the father of Reaganomics—had been struggling for some time to come up with a tactic to overcome political liabilities arising from the perception of Ronald Reagan as a hard-line Cold Warrior, without alienating the conservative constituencies that had helped bring the incumbent to power.

The public was primed for change, Anderson argued. Americans were fed up with the failure of past administrations to allay their fears of nuclear war. They were confused and frustrated by the endless bickering among experts about what to do, by those deadly debates about incremental limits on nuclear weapons that had brought nothing but failure for the Carter administration. They wanted the president to stand up to the Soviets and restore confidence in American security.

But something also had to be done to stem the growing criticism of the administration's rejection of any negotiations with the Soviets to reduce nuclear weapons. The idea that nuclear forces had to be strengthened first to allow the United States "to negotiate from a position of strength" was losing ground in the media and the polls. "There has to be a switch from the false perception that Reagan sees complex foreign policy issues in black and white," Anderson had argued during the campaign, "that he is only concerned with relatively narrow ... defense policy issues such as ... stockpiling nuclear weapons to blast the Soviet Union."[8]

Key White House advisers, including White House Counselor Edwin Meese and National Security Adviser William Clark, agreed. The prevailing public pessimism over foreign and defense policy was a legacy of the Carter administration. Important administration priorities were already in jeopardy, including the ten-warhead MX missile, then foundering in congressional controversy over its proposed basing mode, and the impending deployments of new nuclear missiles in Europe, which drew intense opposition on both sides of the Atlantic. Even the Joint Chiefs were gloomy about the prospects for getting congressional funding for their nuclear modernization plans. What was needed was a "new framework" that dispelled public pessimism and helped clear the way for the Reagan defense buildup.

Not coincidentally, some of these advisers and the president himself had been briefed on strategic defense concepts by a number of different advocates. A lobby for defenses had begun to emerge even before the 1980 election campaign, a loose coalition of politicians, scientists, and defense theorists who saw promise in emerging defensive technologies. A number of them had actively supported the Reagan campaign, and some were Reagan's personal friends. One key adviser, the deputy director of the Defense Intelligence Agency (DIA) until 1976 and an avid enthusiast of defenses, Lieutenant General Daniel Graham, first began promoting the idea during Reagan's unsuccessful presidential campaign in 1976, secretly providing advice to Reagan advisers despite his sensitive government job and legal strictures prohibiting political activity.[9]

Although divided in their views, the advocates agreed that the current configuration of U.S. nuclear forces was being steadily outstripped by Soviet military developments. They strongly rejected the concept of "nuclear parity" put forward by arms control experts and officials in former administrations, Democratic and Republican. The Soviets were moving with determination, the Reagan advisers believed, while the United States was deluded by a belief that it could maintain some form of equilibrium in the U.S.-Soviet nuclear rivalry. By the same token, some of these advisers argued that new technologies, ranging from X-ray lasers to space-based battle stations, could be exploited to overwhelm Soviet advances, catching the Soviets off guard in the one area where the United States continued to have advantages—high technology.

The growth in Soviet nuclear capabilities since the late 1960s had resulted in heightened concerns for "stability"—the absence of incentives for either side to strike first in a crisis. In traditional deterrence theory, stability is assured through mutual vulnerability: as long as both sides know they can inflict unacceptable damage on their adversary, even after a first strike, then neither side can imagine gaining military advantage from a preemptive attack. As enshrined in the 1972 Antiballistic Missile (ABM) Treaty, moreover, defenses were explicitly rejected, not only because they were technologically elusive but also because they would disrupt the stable balance of forces assured by credible retaliatory capabilities.

Scientific advances in the 1970s, however, coinciding with the dramatic growth in Soviet nuclear forces, which seemed to be endangering the survival of the American strategic "triad"—the air-, sea-, and land-based weapons that form the U.S. deterrent—had rekindled interest in defenses. Unlike the defense systems discussed in the 1950s and the 1960s that were designed to intercept missiles just prior to impact (like the ballistic missile boost intercepts, or BAMBI), the new concepts suggested that defenses could be far more technologically robust, providing for several space- and ground-based "layers," each adding an increment of protection.

The ABM Treaty prohibited development or deployment of all but a nominal ground-based defense, although both sides continued to pursue research on many kinds of defense systems, to hedge against unilateral abrogation or "breakout" by their adversary. Research was already being conducted in all the technologies that were to become relevant to the SDI, although "exotic" space weapons, like lasers and particle beams, received far less attention than more conventional concepts useful for protecting missile silos. And almost none but the most iconoclastic experts ever discussed the defending of cities, understood to be a technological pipe dream in the face of a global nuclear arsenal with more than 50,000 weapons. Even the exaggerated technical fantasy of a 90 percent leakproof astrodome defense would mean millions of casualties in the event of war—nowhere near the level of acceptability that would warrant public support for the billions of dollars it would cost.

Defenses were an incendiary topic among defense intellectuals. The bitter scientific and political disputes over the ABM Treaty had left permanent divisions among colleagues. Most arms control experts associated defense advocates with hard-line and bellicose views, intent on destabilizing the nuclear balance in the chimerical quest for military superiority. But the idea of defenses had always played a role in conservative debates, and, for many, the repudiation of defenses was a mistaken and inevitably temporary aberration in American policy. For example, the pledge to build defenses was included as a priority in the 1980 Republican party platform, which urged the development of "an effective anti-ballistic missile system, which is already at hand in the Soviet Union, as well as more modern Anti-Ballistic Missile technologies." This plank of the platform was written by the Reagan campaign strategist Richard Allen, who was to become Reagan's first national security adviser.

According to Anderson, all of Reagan's senior campaign aides—Ed Meese, Peter Hannaford, Richard Allen, Michael Deaver, and Anderson himself—believed as a philosophical matter that "we should have had ABM, a shield to stop missiles, years ago." Anderson had hoped to make defenses a campaign issue in late 1979 but was over-ruled by more-senior political strategists, including Deaver, for being too radical. "No way, said the political guys," Anderson recalled. "They were afraid some smart Democrat could destroy it, and we couldn't answer effectively. It was like the brilliant papers [the for-mer chief of the Council of Economic Advisers] Alan Greenspan did on how to get rid of agricultural subsidies or how to improve Social Security—too controversial to be campaign issues."[10]

Once in power, however, a number of key individuals considered missile defenses to be a critical priority for the new administration. Some newly appointed defense officials had been fighting a passion-ate rearguard action against the "assured destruction" creeds in U.S. doctrine for years and wanted to terminate the 1972 ABM Treaty and move to deployment of defenses. Among them were the former Boe-ing engineer T. K. Jones, who became the deputy under secretary of defense for research and engineering, and Richard Perle, a former staff aide to Senator Henry ("Scoop") Jackson, Democrat of Washing-ton, who was appointed assistant secretary of defense for interna-tional security policy.

T. K. Jones, an eccentric loner who had for years proselytized on behalf of a national civil defense program—shelters to protect citi-zens in the event of nuclear war—was awarded a permanent place in nuclear folklore because of a remark he made to the *Los Angeles Times* reporter Robert Scheer in 1981. Asked how Americans could survive a Soviet nuclear attack, Jones explained that everyone could have his or her own homemade civil defense by digging a hole and getting in before the missiles hit. "If there are enough shovels, every one's going to make it," he said. "It's the dirt that does it."[11]

Richard Perle, known to the press and colleagues as the Prince of Darkness for his strident anticommunism and often vicious bureau-cratic maneuvers, had come to Washington in the late 1960s to lobby in favor of the "Safeguard" antimissile system, which was later can-celed, and against the ABM Treaty, and then served as an aide to the conservative Democratic senator Jackson. Considered the architect of Jackson's numerous anti-Soviet and anti–arms control initiatives in the 1970s, Perle came to see in the SDI his opportunity to achieve the goal of his life's crusade: burying the ABM Treaty once and for all.

But strategic defenses were still considered a "fringe" issue in the larger defense community, rife with technical and political liabilities. Beginning in the Kennedy administration, defenses had been debated exhaustively, developed temporarily, and finally repudiated. The rejection of a defensive strategy, legalized in the ABM Treaty, had been reified in the establishment's defense literature, which treated the subject as virtually taboo. Space defense, in particular, had an image problem. Beam weapons and space war were portrayed as subjects for science fiction and cranks. One former congressional aide, Douglas Waller, remarked, "The only people I ever heard arguing for space defense before March 1983 were those guys in the airport who think Kissinger is a Communist."[12]

To the president, however, strategic defense seemed like an attractive solution to several problems. First of all, it was different—a key requirement for all new administrations trying to establish an agenda—and a genuine personal yearning for Reagan as well. As a high-tech venture, it could be a bold way to challenge the Soviets, appealing to conservative supporters. But since it was "defensive" and might be shown as deflecting war from earth to space, it could divert attention from the nuclear buildup, the subject of widespread public fears. It was potentially the conservative's version of global disarmament, the technological fulfillment of "peace through strength."

This convergence of motives led to a decision in early February of 1983 to investigate the idea of defenses, in the form of a study undertaken by three NSC staff members working in secret under instructions from Deputy National Adviser Robert McFarlane. The study was conducted without anyone else's knowledge. Everyone involved recognized that the idea of a radical change in nuclear strategy was very controversial and could easily be derailed by the "traditionalists"—defense and foreign policy professionals—if known more widely in the bureaucracy. "The normal way to proceed would have been to talk to the Defense Department, have them study the problem, and give the president their recommendations," said Anderson. "That option was never suggested, perhaps because we all knew it would not work. Put before the bureaucracy, we knew the idea would be murdered in its crib."[13]

The decision to add the new strategy to the March speech was apparently a genuine afterthought, the result of a conversation McFarlane and National Security Adviser William Clark had with the president at Camp David on March 18. The president complained of his reluctance to give the hard-line speech, scheduled for the evening of March 23, as drafted. It was full of rhetoric about the Soviet threat, all doom and fear. Just ten days earlier, the president had received a cool reception to a speech he had given in Orlando, Florida, when he referred to the Soviet Union as an "evil empire." The president wished the new speech could have some kind of upbeat promise of a better future instead of just "this Soviet threat stuff."[14]

Accordingly, McFarlane and his staff immediately began adapting their work on strategic defenses into language for the speech insert, a section they referred to as the annex. Since the original mandate of the study, "to look into the possibility of defenses," was so vague, the staff were not sure what they were supposed to be doing. The first draft of the annex was quite specific and pledged to build defense systems "such as lasers and particle beams." In response to a uniformly negative reaction from those few individuals consulted outside the McFarlane group, however, specifics were dropped at the last minute in favor of a more abstract challenge to the nation's scientific community: "those who gave us nuclear weapons, to turn their great talents now to the cause of mankind and world peace." Several years later, McFarlane claimed he never had the slightest intention of sanctioning a sweeping change in nuclear strategy, but thought of defenses against ballistic missiles as a possible bargaining chip to get limits on Soviet offensive forces.[15]

The president's science adviser, George Keyworth, the only putative expert on defensive technology on the White House staff, was not brought into the net at all until Saturday, March 19, apparently because McFarlane realized it would be embarrassing if it was revealed that the White House's chief scientist had been deliberately excluded. Keyworth had presided over a study on strategic defenses submitted to the White House in January by the White House Science Council, which had been extremely negative in its assessment of emerging defense technologies as a basis for a shift in U.S. strategy. Keyworth had never shared the report with his superiors, perhaps because of an awareness of his limited authority. Keyworth had been chosen for his job as part of the new administration's conscious effort to redefine—some would say downgrade—the role of the White House science adviser, something Keyworth clearly understood.

According to Anderson, administration advisers had picked Keyworth, an unknown figure from the Los Alamos nuclear laboratory who had the support of Edward Teller, because he was neither a major figure in the scientific community nor beholden to it. "During my years on Nixon's White House staff in the late 1960s I watched the role of the science adviser move away from being a representative of the president to the scientific community . . . to being the representative of the scientific community as just one more powerful special interest group," said Anderson, who claims to have played the key role in selecting Keyworth. What was needed was a loyalist, "not the envoy of the scientific community . . . blessed by the reigning mandarins of science." According to Anderson, "Keyworth fit those specifications precisely and, as a bonus, he came from a weapons laboratory and was not hostile to using science to help defend the country."[16]

Apparently overwhelmed by the White House momentum, Keyworth gave his full approval to the insert. He, McFarlane, and the president himself are widely recognized as the three authors of America's sweeping new doctrine. Keyworth reportedly typed the text on a manual typewriter to keep it out of the White House computer system, which could be accessed by other officials. He was rewarded for his efforts with the privilege of bringing the news to the handful of State Department and Defense Department officials who were informed in the two days remaining before the speech.

Richard DeLauer, under secretary for defense, research, and engineering, the senior Pentagon official in charge of new-weapons research and development, found out about the insert on the morning of March 23. He "went ballistic," according to a participant in the meeting, infuriated that nuclear policy could be the subject of "such a half-baked political travesty." To his further embarrassment, the news was delivered during a meeting with Lieutenant General Brent Scowcroft, national security adviser to President Ford, who was heading a major administration study on the future of U.S. strategic forces.[17]

The "Scowcroft commission," a high-level bipartisan panel of experts that was to determine the fate of the administration's key strategic priority, the MX missile, was just going into the delicate final stages of negotiations on carefully brokered recommendations on the future of U.S. nuclear forces. Scowcroft reportedly commented that the speech would kill not only the commission but also the MX. Although the consequences were not so dire, critical administration objectives were clearly at odds. A month later, the Scowcroft report stated categorically that existing technology offered "no real promise of being able to defend the United States against massive nuclear attack in this century." One of the panel's three principal recommendations—to deploy a single-warhead, mobile, land-based missile—may never see the light of day, partly as a result of attacks by newly converted congressional enthusiasts of defenses.[18]

Only Shultz and Perle had any success at all in eleventh-hour damage limitation, changing one part of the speech to indicate that defenses would be built against Soviet ballistic missiles—not against cruise missiles or manned bombers—and adding an awkward nod to the potential danger of having both defenses and offenses as elements of the U.S. nuclear posture, potentially provocative to the Soviet Union. The first change, intended to add a touch of realism, created a fundamental contradiction: how can nuclear weapons be impotent and obsolete if air-delivered weapons are not included? The second change, which resulted in the sentence "If paired with offensive systems, [defenses] can be viewed as fostering an aggressive policy, and no-one wants that," dismissed in a quick polemical flourish decades of debate about the offense-defense relationship and the foundations of strategic stability. But the changes were better than nothing.[19]

It was the president himself, according to a close adviser, who insisted that the speech promise the elimination of all nuclear weapons and who denied the requests of Shultz and others to temper further its rhetoric. In stark contrast to President Carter's disastrous speech in 1979 depicting Americans as victims of "malaise" and as sufferers of a "crisis in self-confidence," President Reagan's SDI speech was designed to appeal to the most inspirational principles of the American ethos, sweeping away complications and doubts.

The SDI was to spark a revolution born of American technological ingenuity, bringing peace through national will. Although the speech embodied the administration's profound skepticism about the value of negotiating with the Soviet Union, this was revealed only in the most positive light—in a reascendancy of hope for military security achieved unilaterally, with American technology. It was a paean to the good old American know-how heralded in more innocent times, and appealed to Americans' nationalistic, even isolationist, instinct. Not only could America become secure, but it could more or less "go it alone," unimpeded by the demands of outsiders. Moreover, by issuing a challenge to move American horizons to the last great frontier—space—the speech tapped another profound source of patriotism in American political culture.

The Aftermath

As a political gambit, the president's bold stroke initially succeeded. The debate over nuclear policies was instantly intensified by a massive infusion of popular support. Simply bringing the attention of Americans to the absence of protection from nuclear war provoked a profound emotional response, as if the reality of four decades of nuclear vulnerability were being discovered for the first time. An engineer in Kansas noted, "Finally, a president has the courage to do something to save American lives."

The speech transformed the political significance of strategic defense and nuclear strategy by turning a long-standing but relatively obscure dispute among strategists into a barometer of values and political allegiance. Within months, even highly technical questions about the relative feasibility and desirability of defensive technologies became tests of support for a popular administration and, implicitly, for competing ideas of world order. Absent a concrete technical framework, the debate became a war of theology and speculation.

Skeptical defense and arms control experts who argued that no technological breakthroughs capable of creating a hermetic seal over the United States would ever exist or that the president's plan could start a new round of expensive and dangerous arms competition were suddenly outflanked. Their arguments sounded negative and trivial, opposing a patriotic revolution supported by a visionary president determined to change the course of history. Members of Congress, who understood the announcement to be a political tour de force without any sound empirical groundings, were left with the unenviable challenge of explaining to constituents why they opposed a program to protect American civilians and accepted a world in which vulnerability to nuclear attack is somehow a better foundation for security.

Not for the last time, the hard-line conservative president had moved far to the left of his critics, denouncing not just nuclear weapons but even the entire strategy upon which the American security paradigm relied. In light of the president's political popularity, and the obvious public appeal of his vision, simply ridiculing the concept of a space-based, multilayered "Maginot Line" was not an effective option. Ultimately, the real genius of the SDI speech was that it forced its opponents to expound the virtues of the status quo.

In what was to become a voluminous literature of speeches, articles, books, pamphlets, and congressional testimony, the establishment ceded the terms of the debate to the president. Despite the virtual technological vacuum surrounding the SDI program, and its patently misleading bromides, dozens upon dozens of experts offered detailed analyses of the promises or dangers of strategic defenses, devising models to demonstrate how a "transition to defenses" would prove stabilizing or destabilizing. Since there was nothing definitive about the emerging concept, there was no limit to the theorizing about possible outcomes. It was a heyday for physicists who knew something about weaponry and a boon to the "view-graph community," the dozens of consulting firms around the country that vie for government contracts to analyze military problems.

As a basis for policy, however, the speech proved to be an invitation to highly politicized chaos. The former director of the U.S. Arms Control and Disarmament Agency during the Carter administration, Paul Warnke, argued in 1985,

> [The SDI] is all things to all people. To the president, it is saving people's lives. To Defense Secretary Weinberger, it is a technological steppingstone from missile defense to the president's larger conception of immaculate defense. To others, it is simply a means of defending missiles. To some, it is a bargaining chip in arms control negotiations, while to others, including the president, it is untouchable.[20]

The schismatic goals laid out in the president's speech plagued the SDI from the outset: Is it to protect populations or military forces? Is it to be a "perfect shield" or just a partial defense against ballistic missiles? Is it a research program or a commitment to deployment? Is it space defense or more conventional terminal defense? Will it eliminate all nuclear weapons? Will it violate the ABM Treaty? Will the nation defend its allies or retreat into "Fortress America"? Are Americans aiming at military superiority over the Soviets, or will the

SDI be bargained away in arms control negotiations? How much will it cost?

As officials, scientists, and politicians moved to fill in the details of this policy vacuum, the SDI transformed a previously prosaic quest for advances in defensive technologies into a political lightning rod, giving administration critics a key target to attack. Its shifting objectives and vague goals created the broad impression that the administration did not have a coherent policy, infuriating opponents and disappointing proponents.

Under attack from all sides, the SDI induced among its official advocates a siege mentality that over time turned the debate into one between either "true believers" or "enemies." In such an atmosphere, those who raised even modest questions about goals soon found their voices muffled. But since many of the officials in charge had very different views about the purpose of the program, public statements were soon at odds, and pro- and anti-SDI factions exploited the divisions for their own ends. The program's high political profile encouraged individuals to settle their policy disagreements in public, in the press, and before the Congress. Before long, the main task of officials working to establish a coherent direction for the SDI was not in the realm of strategy or technology but in that of public relations.

Over six years, the SDI has served as a kind of intellectual superconductor for a national debate about American security. The SDI was both the product of the highly charged political environment prevalent before 1983 and an agent of its intensification. The unorthodox nature of the public appeal for a radically new doctrine, before the foundations for even modest change were in place, engendered new and even sharper divisions throughout the policy community and the electorate. The political fury resulting from this "top-down" strategy is likely to be remembered as one of the enduring legacies of the Reagan administration. And it is still an open question whether the political gambit helped or harmed the goal of strategic defense.

The SDI has also served as a persistent source of conflict in executive-congressional relations, including a protracted confrontation over the Senate's constitutional authority to make treaties. It posed serious complications in U.S. relations with allies, led to the near abrogation of the ABM Treaty—the linchpin of U.S.-Soviet nuclear agreements—and, in a dramatic moment in Reykjavik, Iceland, in October of 1986, preempted the most comprehensive and radical proposal ever considered to reduce U.S. and Soviet nuclear arsenals. These are remarkably significant effects for an initiative that has yet to produce one concrete change in America's nuclear posture, a policy that former secretary of state Henry Kissinger called "a slogan in search of a program."[21]

Clearly, one impetus for the SDI—the wish to defuse public controversy over nuclear weapons—appears to have backfired, and badly so. Partisan disputes have never been absent during major shifts in nuclear policy—quite the contrary. From the 1950s through the 1970s, controversies over nuclear policies, from the testing of weapons in the atmosphere to the creation of civil and ballistic missile defense, provoked bitter public opposition, transforming many citizens into political activists. But these debates seem, in retrospect, modest compared with what developed after 1983.

Since the president's speech, thousands of American citizens, from virtually all walks of life, have become advocates or critics of SDI concepts: technicians working in weapons laboratories, citizens' lobbies with such unlikely names as Mothers Embracing Nuclear Disarmament, the Gray Panthers, or Women for a Secure Future, university students and faculty who have publicly welcomed or repudiated participation in SDI-related research, local and state politicians who a decade ago would not have been expected to express opinions on defense policy, and leaders of all major religions. As of 1988, over 110 national organizations actively opposed the SDI. Even the Vatican launched a study in 1985 assaulting the SDI's technological and strategic merits, although Pope John Paul II refused to make an explicit statement on the subject. Phyllis Schlafly, the strident antifeminist who believes women belong in the kitchen, nevertheless took time from her own domestic chores to become an SDI supporter, excoriating Soviet defensive programs in an article in the *New York City Tribune*. Scientists examining the SDI pursued their disputes over principles of physics in acrimonious press releases and congressional testimony. Senators and their aides were forced to affect knowledge of astrophysics, rocket propulsion, and computer software as they struggle to follow the contradictory arguments of experts in countless hearings. It was a good time for scientists and engineers to get jobs on Capitol Hill—the "geek contingent," as Mark Steitz, a former Senate aide, uncharitably described the sudden addition of technical experts to congressional staffs.[22]

The public cacophony aside, the SDI debate represents an extreme example of the fundamental phenomenon explored in this book—the dissonance between public perceptions of nuclear issues and the actual operational implications of publicly articulated policies. While the electorate has for the most part focused on the president's dream—America under an astrodome of defenses, for good or ill—the actual objectives of the SDI moved programmatically and, to all intents and purposes, strategically into a research and potential deployment effort aimed at developing ways to improve the capabilities of offensive nuclear forces.

Except for a very few remaining advocates, the promise of population defense, which inspired great hopes in the public in 1983, has evaporated in official circles. Not that population defense has been officially repudiated. It is simply acknowledged to be a very distant goal, achievable in the foreseeable future only as a by-product of enhanced deterrence. Administration officials now openly admit that only a tiny minority of them—the president among them—ever thought seriously that the goal of defending populations was more than a political gambit to gain public support for modernizing the American strategic triad, for dispensing with the restrictions of the ABM Treaty, and for encouraging American military developments in space. Indeed, the vagueness of SDI objectives has left deep divisions among various proponents who are struggling to promote competing definitions of the goals being pursued.

At the same time, the drastic changes in the U.S. nuclear posture that preoccupied many SDI critics, some of whom believed that the intiative presaged a revolution in American plans to achieve the capability to wage and win a nuclear war, have also proved vastly exaggerated, since defensive technologies are commonly recognized as too embryonic to alter decisively our military capabilities and as likely to remain so for many years. The president's efforts did succeed in reinstating defenses as a respectable subject for analysis and the pursuit of military options in space as a worthy subject of establishment research. But the goal of altering U.S. nuclear doctrine remains elusive.

The publicly enunciated doctrine of the SDI—a radical shift in the U.S. nuclear posture, to "defense dominance" and "assured survival"—has had no demonstrable impact on actual operational plans. The SDI has coexisted with, but has had no effect on, the policies guiding the acquisition, deployment, and targeting of nuclear forces. The Department of Defense's new Nuclear Weapons Employment

Policy (NUWEP), signed in late 1987, which provides the policy guidance to the Joint Chiefs and the nuclear commands for the use of nuclear weapons in war, makes scant reference to defenses. There have been alterations in nuclear planning to accommodate the goal of greater "flexibility" in forces and additions to U.S. capabilities to destroy various types of Soviet military targets; but these have had nothing to do with the SDI. It is as if there were two separate Departments of Defense, one hyping strategic defense as the highest national priority and the other conducting the real business of national security while studiously ignoring defenses.

The administration also tried to reinterpret the meaning of the ABM Treaty to pave the way for the development and deployment of defenses. Thwarted by congressional opposition, however, its treaty reinterpretation has not yet resulted in any alterations in force planning. The formal shift of the SDI program in late 1986 from the "research" category to "acquisition" to permit potential deployment of some existing defense systems in the next decade is primarily a political, not a military, decision: it represents an effort to demonstrate to critics that the SDI is real. Foundering in confusion over its genuine intent with respect to the ABM Treaty, over negotiations with the Soviets on offensive force reductions, which depend on agreement about the future of the defenses, and over the technologies in question, however, the administration never created enough momentum for significant force changes.

Formal declaratory policy also remains largely unchanged. According to the most-senior officials who have authority for U.S. nuclear planning, U.S. doctrine was, and remains, "flexible response"— the ability to launch measured strikes in order to halt a war short of an all-out nuclear exchange. Current doctrinal goals now ascribed to the SDI are very much in line with traditional rationales of deterrence—heightening an attacker's uncertainty, protecting retaliatory options, and limiting damage to the United States, should deterrence fail.

It is often forgotten that in his speech the president pledged to "remain constant in preserving the nuclear deterrent and maintaining a solid capability for flexible response." Richard Perle said in congressional testimony in 1985, "SDI, whether it proves to be capable of defending the population or not, would greatly improve the credibility of our deterrent, and I think it is worth pursuing for that reason alone." This is a far cry from the denunciation of the immorality of deterrence that informed earlier administration rhetoric and seized the nation in a frenzy of advocacy and recrimination.[23]

Many argue that the SDI forced the Soviet Union to take the United States seriously in Geneva "for the first time," by making the Soviets fear a technological race they would inevitably lose. However correct, this view is difficult to validate. After eight years of a Reagan presidency, there was only one agreement, limiting European-based and not strategic systems. By eliminating entire classes of nuclear missiles—an important precedent—the agreement seems to bear out the president's belief that reductions, not modest limits, are the real and achievable goals of arms control, the result of America's "hanging tough." Yet "hanging tough" has meant refusal to negotiate any limits on defensive systems, even though that position has led to our reaching no agreement on strategic offensive weapons.

Most important, the grand debate on the SDI and its promise to eliminate nuclear weapons was carried out against the backdrop of a huge expansion of nuclear forces, a development that, ironically enough, received far less public attention. The irony is that the SDI program distracted defense critics in the Congress and the public from the enormous appropriations given the air force and navy to modernize their nuclear capabilities. As one senior air force official said, "If we hadn't had the SDI, we would have had to invent some other distraction to get all this gravy."

The navy, which has played the most modest role in the SDI, received funds not only to modernize and expand its retaliatory forces with the *Ohio*-class submarine and the highly accurate eight-warhead D-5 ("Trident II") missile but also to make major advances in plans to deploy long-range cruise missiles, of which 758 will be nuclear armed. To be deployed on battleships, cruisers, and attack submarines, the nuclear cruise missile will permit the navy to shift "from fifteen offensive strike platforms (aircraft carriers) to more than 195 strike platforms," according to the director of the cruise missile program, Rear Admiral Larry Bose. Once potentially highly controversial, both the Trident II and the cruise missile programs have moved through Congress with a minimum of controversy.[24]

The air force has received congressional support for a wide range of offensive nuclear programs, including two new strategic bombers, the B-1 and the advanced-technology "Stealth" bomber, a new generation of air-launched cruise missiles, and other types of missiles to equip those aircraft. Even though the MX has been attacked in Congress, it continues to be funded, "capped" by law at a total of fifty missiles, pending the identification of a compelling basing mode. The air force has also received funds to develop a new land-based missile, the "Midgetman," which was originally intended to be a single-warhead system but which is under increasing pressure to be designed to accommodate multiple warheads. Major budgetary increases were also granted to improve the command and control of nuclear forces, "to ensure that our deterrent forces remain strong and durable over extended periods," as a Department of Defense statement put it in 1986.[25]

The services, especially the air force, also gained explicit acceptance of their promotion of space as an arena for military operations, institutionalized through the new Space Command, whose activities and objectives have been neglected, compared with those of the SDI astrodome. Although the Congress impeded operational tests of anti-satellite weapons, considerable funding has gone into the examination of different potential antisatellite systems. Long before any strategic defense concept can become operational, many of the technologies being pursued under the SDI may prove useful for attacking satellites and carrying out offensive missions in space.

At a time of intense competition for budgetary resources, the Congress's continued willingness to fund such a robust modernization of U.S. strategic forces shows just how seriously the president's goal of "rendering nuclear weapons impotent and obsolete" was taken. Without question, these modernization programs will determine the future of American defense capabilities far more than anything envisioned or pursued as part of the SDI. Ironically, the SDI has served to paralyze its critics in exaggerated polemics over what *might* happen, while the real future of nuclear forces was being determined elsewhere. Appropriating the vocabulary of the strident advocate of nuclear disarmament to smooth the way for massive infusions of new weapons into the American arsenal required quite a rhetorical tour de force, but Reagan was up to it. Patently at odds with the nuclear-free world promised in the SDI, the administration's ambitious plans to expand American offensive nuclear forces should be of no concern, the president suggested, because these weapons would soon be rendered irrelevant by perfect defenses.

As in all former shifts in nuclear doctrine, latent recognition of obsolescing weapons—in this case, intercontinental ballistic missiles (ICBMs)—has lent impetus to the effort to discover new ways to thwart adversaries. As one official put it simply, the competition with the Soviet Union over ICBMs faces inexorably diminishing returns, "so we have to compete somewhere else." The current environment is ripe for technological change. Within the government, though, it is still not one in which major reductions in war-fighting capabilities—which would hinder the United States's ability to target the Soviet Union—is ever considered seriously by planners. The schism between the high polemics of the "nonnuclear world" heralded by the president and the realities of nuclear force planning has never been wider.

The Evolution of Nuclear Doctrine

Because U.S. nuclear doctrine implies the design of military options for using nuclear weapons in combat—in short, nuclear war plans, from targeting strategy to the evacuation of leaders in a nuclear attack—it is not a subject that officials like to discuss in public. However cautious, doctrinal debates in the nuclear age serve to remind Americans that deterrence, and thus their security, is based on plans to use nuclear weapons in warfare.

Since the detonation of atomic bombs over Hiroshima and Nagasaki during World War II, American nuclear doctrine has rested on the difficult and counterintuitive logic that the more powerful the nuclear arsenal, the less likely the need for its use. Defending this tortured logic has never been easy, and that is one reason why a formal distinction is made among the four elements of strategic doctrine, separating declaratory policy—what is said publicly—from the employment, acquisition, and deployment policies that make up the actual, highly classified plans for conducting nuclear operations.

Politically motivated swings in public expressions of doctrine belie the bedrock quality of the "planning community"—the individuals in the office of the Joint Chiefs of Staff and the military services, at SAC and the European and Pacific Commands, Space Command, and in the intelligence services—that actually plans how the United States will launch its nuclear weapons so as to prevail in war. Originally thought of as the "ultimate" weapon, so terrifying that the existence of even a few would end all war, nuclear weapons have since 1950 instead preoccupied thousands of scientists, war planners, and officials with one fundamental problem: How can we make nuclear weapons accurate enough, precise enough, small enough, and flexible enough that their effects can be "contained" for use in combat? How can we attack our opponent's military forces so perfectly as to disarm him before he can retaliate? These "scientific" challenges of war planning make up the structural reality of nuclear forces, for which the public debate about nuclear doctrine, arms control, and particular weapons has served as a political sideshow.

In a steady evolution, from the Eisenhower administration's policy of massive retaliation to the Carter administration's deliberate leak of its "countervailing strategy" in 1979—in the apparent effort to shore up electoral support for the president against critics charging that he was "soft on defense"—doctrine has become more exposed to partisan political debates.

During the Reagan administration, the Right and the Left converged in their belief that the growth of public attention to nuclear matters is a salutary development, but for startlingly different ends. As a matter of deliberate policy, those who crafted the SDI were intent on turning nuclear doctrine into an electoral cause célèbre, actually capitalizing on the antinuclear sentiment that disarmament advocates helped inspire. Like his critics, the president deliberately galvanized public sensitivities regarding nuclear weapons in order to expose and discredit the fragile intellectual calculus of his predecessors' policies.

Ronald Reagan was certainly not the first to attack the idea of mutually assured destruction (MAD). Ever since its introduction by Secretary of Defense Robert McNamara in 1964, MAD has been vilified by almost everybody, from SAC to the United World Federalists. The policy is denounced for its reliance on the slaughter of millions of civilians as the basis for deterring war, alternatively because of its unprecedented savagery or because of its lack of military credibility. The promise of mutual suicide in the event "deterrence fails," the basic tenet of MAD, is no more comforting to military commanders than to pacifists.

At the same time, every innovation in nuclear doctrine suggesting the intent to deviate from this posture has met with profound resistance in the American body politic. MAD may be repugnant, but that is its virtue. Anything that suggests that nuclear war might fall short of mutual annihilation—whether such a policy is called "limited options," "damage limitation," or "countervailing strategy"—suggests sinister and misguided plans to engage in actual nuclear combat. With the arguable exception of the SDI, any hint of change from the doctrine of MAD has been greeted with genuine shock in the American public and the Congress, provoking the grotesque thought that nuclear weapons could be seen as acceptable instruments of politics and war.

As Senator Edmund Muskie said to Secretary of Defense James R. Schlesinger in 1974, in reaction to the new Nixon policy of "limited options," the idea of limiting the scope of nuclear wars was not compelling, because it minimized the intrinsic horror of nuclear weapons, portraying them as if they were legitimate arms for battle:

> Whether or not this new strategy is designed to lower the nuclear threshold, it seems to me at the very least to reflect the fact that perhaps the nuclear threshold has already been lowered; that both sides now are less horrified by the prospect of nuclear war; that both sides are now more willing to consider the use of tactical nuclear weapons.[26]

In other words, if MAD is bad, limited counterforce is worse. Thinking the unthinkable automatically raises the risk of war by the very act of making it thinkable. Moreover, it is a contemptible exercise. Armageddon is one thing, but trying to tinker with its details is truly satanic. The belief that nuclear war can only be a sudden, fatal spasm is somehow crucial to public reassurance, a stubborn denial of the reality of war planning.

Yet, despite grudging public acceptance of its premises, the strategy implied by MAD has seldom borne any relation to operational reality. As a practical matter, the history of American nuclear doctrine is quite the opposite of apocalyptic visions. It is the history of the quest, however chimerical, for nuclear forces that can disarm adversaries, avoiding the level of civilian casualties that might cause a president to hesitate to act in crisis. It is the history of a continuing effort to escape the imperative of "total war" implied by the power of nuclear weapons and the pressures for disarmament from a public fearful of global holocaust. It is the history of a calculated effort to deter Soviet military aggression by threatening the use of nuclear weapons but avoiding any actions that could lead to nuclear provocation. It is the history, too, of a steadily burgeoning intellectual, technological, and bureaucratic infrastructure charged with the implementation of "the unthinkable"—how to deploy nuclear weapons to deter war, how to use these weapons for political objectives, how to contain their effects for military advantage, and how to avoid suicide.

Usually seen as the antithesis of MAD, concepts of "limited counterforce"—the ability to attack Soviet military targets selectively in the event of provocation—had their genesis in the defense think tanks of the 1950s and came of age as an element of official doctrine under President Kennedy. The first integrated plan for nuclear war operations, called SIOP-62 and inherited from the last days of the Eisenhower administration, consisted of an overwhelming number of counterforce targets, although it was an inflexible plan more appropriate for a preemptive first strike rather than for retaliation.[27]

Every doctrinal shift since that time has emphasized the need for greater selectivity, flexibility, and precision in targeting to attack an adversary's military forces and the development of "options" that withhold weapons while carrying out limited attacks. Nuclear war is envisioned as a series of graduated military responses, permitting leaders to control escalation while trying to end the war on terms favorable to the West. Strategies for engaging in a "protracted nuclear exchange," with pauses for negotiations, are not a science fiction fantasy for those in charge of nuclear operations.

The emphasis on limited war in American doctrine is the result of an instinctual reaction by political leaders and their advisers to the absence of choice. If nuclear war seems inconceivable, it is equally inconceivable to an American president that the nation be hostage to its own technology, caught in a trap of immutable vulnerability and political stalemate. Each successive administration has tried to escape from this dilemma with new weapons and new declaratory doctrines; each has essentially failed.

However well intended, the elegant models of limited warfare advanced by the "wizards of Armageddon" in the 1950s and refined in subsequent decades have served in fact as the engine for a steady improvement of nuclear capability. Once credibility was defined as the ability to exert control over the way in which nuclear weapons would be used, the only practical measure of deterrence had to be more forces targeted flexibly against military targets. This has meant that every president since Kennedy has presided over the design of nuclear forces and operational plans that emphasize ways to destroy military targets selectively, controlling escalation and exacting calculable political and military victories from nuclear conflict. This is the crux of credible deterrence, the pragmatic anatomy of a military abstraction.

Over time, the orthodoxies of politicians and war planners have become ever more divergent. The arms control community, from left to center, stresses the need for "assured retaliatory capabilities" as the basis for deterrence, for survivable forces that discourage either side from perceiving advantages in attacking preemptively. Neither side should have forces whose vulnerability or capability could encourage a first strike in a crisis. (Arms control, it is believed, can help formalize mechanisms for mutual restraint to encourage both sides to develop such forces and reduce their arsenals.)

In contrast, the dominant ethos of military planners emphasizes deterrence based on a credible capacity to fight wars. As SAC's former commander in chief, General Russell Dougherty, stated, the task is "to convince and motivate [SAC personnel] that the better they are at their war-making skills, the less likely they are to have to fight."[28] Since the days of Curtis LeMay, it has been seen as SAC's imperative to prepare for war: "With atomic weapons and the type of warfare that we're going to have to fight, we had to be ready to go to war not next week, not tomorrow, but this afternoon, today. . . ."[29]

From the operational perspective, deterrence derives from the ability to destroy the "Soviet target base," especially those targets that the Soviets hold most valuable—their strategic offensive weapons. Such targeting requires very accurate, "prompt, hard-target kill" weapons, which can destroy missiles and bombers even when they are in hardened shelters or mobile. SAC certainly does not publicly subscribe to a preemptive strategy, and the potential effectiveness of a disarming first strike in the face of over 10,000 Soviet strategic weapons is highly questionable. But notions of destroying Soviet weapons before they are launched have been included in U.S. nuclear war plans from the earliest days. With the growth of Soviet strategic capabilities, moreover, many newer U.S. strategic weapons make military sense only if used under time pressures so extreme that political notions of "assured retaliation" are tested severely.

The enduring schism between political and operational assumptions about what constitutes nuclear deterrence has meant that the political process has lagged far behind in its influence over, or understanding of, nuclear policy. Without a clear grasp of the linkages between the plans for using nuclear weapons and political objectives, or, put differently, between the character of weapons and the implied employment policy, there is no set procedure for defining what is needed to achieve "deterrence." Protracted congressional and public controversies over particular nuclear weapons systems notwithstanding, political energies have been largely absorbed in debating abstractions, instead of in determining what kinds of plans and forces are needed to advance national policy. To paraphrase General Dougherty, civilians' disputes about such issues as the morality of nuclear war, the desirability of "first use" of nuclear weapons, the credibility of limited nuclear engagements, and other "positions held with almost theological intensity" in the political sphere "are interesting dichotomies, but . . . not helpful to a military commander."[30]

In short, arms control analysts and military planners have created distinct languages and conceptual frameworks for grappling with the ineffables of nuclear war. If not exactly a dialogue of the deaf, it could be seen as one of the hearing impaired. General Thomas D. White, air force chief of staff under President Kennedy, went further than Dougherty on this score. In 1963, he expressed scorn for the effete language and euphemistic jargon of the "defense intellectuals" in the McNamara Pentagon, men whom he believed to be deliberately misleading the American public about the real purpose of nuclear weapons. He argued, "Such relatively reassuring terms as 'mutual deterrence,' 'stability,' 'no-cities counterforce,' 'second-strike counterforce capability,' and other quasi-military shibboleths . . . have created an atmosphere and mislanguage which is dangerously deceptive." To General White, it was the defense intellectuals, living in a "weightless dreamland," who set about to create public smoke screens about the reality of nuclear war plans.[31]

It is generally assumed that responsible political authorities, beginning with the president, are fully aware of the plans for nuclear war fighting that underlie U.S. policy. More pointedly, most Americans probably believe that nuclear weapons are designed and deployed in a manner consistent with national goals and that the president and his deputies are kept informed regularly about how these policies are being implemented, including how nuclear weapons would be launched.

But this view belies the far more complicated decision-making process that constitutes what comes to be known as American nuclear doctrine. From the elevated policy announcements of political leaders to decisions about missions and forces and to the preparation of plans for wartime operations, the actual implementation of nuclear policy involves many competing actors with rather distinct bureaucratic interests. The procedures for ensuring coherence between the political and the planning spheres have been, until very recently, negligible, and civilian oversight only sporadic.

Paradoxically, the plans put in place since the time of McNamara to guarantee that nuclear war could be limited and controlled by civilian authorities also contributed to a vastly complex network of command centers and planning apparatus whose day-to-day operations are managed by the military and a small number of civilian experts. The sheer complexity of the infrastructure assures a certain degree of autonomy from the less "expert" appointed officials, who tend to hold short tenures in the government. From the procedures established for instant global communication in crisis to the methods used to develop target lists, the structure of the command is largely beyond the expertise of elected officials and their deputies. This is partly because access is strictly controlled by the military and intervention by "outsiders" actively discouraged. More fundamentally, it is because time or interest is lacking.

Although the president retains ultimate authority for launching nuclear weapons, most presidents and senior aides would be hard-pressed to describe what is really in the war plans or how "flexible" options would actually be executed. Absent even a rudimentary understanding of these realities, a president's actual ability to be decisive about what to launch, against what, and for what purpose, especially in an environment of crisis, is a subject of some controversy.

This was stated starkly by an officer who served as the director of the White House Military Office from the Johnson to the Carter administrations and had charge of the "football"—the briefcase carrying the nuclear launch codes that is supposed to be accessible to the president at all times:

> No new President in my time ever had more than one briefing on the contents of the Football, and that was before each one took office, when it was one briefing among dozens. Not one President, to my knowledge, and I know because it was in my care, ever got an update on the contents of the Football, although material changed in it constantly. Not one Presi-

dent could open the Football—only the warrant officers, the military aides and the Director of the Military Office have the combination. If the guy with the Football has a heart attack, they'd have to blow the damn thing open.[32]

The disjuncture between political beliefs and military imperatives could prove a prescription for disaster in wartime. The renunciation of a first-strike posture at the political level suggests the frictions that might occur in crisis as military commanders and civilians discover fundamental disparities in expectations. With only a few minutes of warning time, there will be no opportunity carefully to work out philosophical differences about what "retaliation" means.

The difference between military and political beliefs about nuclear weapons also affects the levels and types of weapons that make up "requirements" in peacetime. It should not be surprising, for example, that there is usually strong resistance in the military to arms control proposals that would force a reduction in weapons sufficient to alter target coverage. Whether they result from arms control or unilateral measures, like President Carter's cancellation of the B-1 bomber, decisions to reduce high-priority forces are usually resisted forcefully by the Joint Chiefs, however compelling the strategic logic may seem at the political level.

The remarkable difference between the rhetoric of stated policy and the actual plans and options for nuclear war are not well understood. The elegant notions of doctrine that academics describe, coherent paradigms guiding the acquisition, deployment, and targeting of forces, have little bureaucratic meaning. By the same token, targeting plans are among the areas of policy that are of least interest to civilians, and very few individuals have demonstrated a willingness to learn their arcane details.

In part, this situation is the product of fatalism. The idea that nuclear war plans would ever be tested is seen by most officials as so dreadful, and the challenges of nuclear war fighting so overwhelming, that it has proved preferable to shove the whole subject to the bottom of the in-box.

Moreover, it is not clear what payoff there could be from this kind of exercise. "Mr. President, you now can choose any kind of Armageddon you want," is what one former Carter official said he would write in a memo after battling the military to make sure the official doctrine of "flexible options" was really being implemented. Coherence in nuclear planning is certainly not the stuff of press releases and good headlines, and no president, other than Jimmy Carter, has ever found it interesting to engage in the brain-numbing exercise of examining war plans.

It is axiomatic that as long as politicians resist thinking beyond the superficial explanation that nuclear weapons are for "deterrence" undefined, they cede the ability to engage in an effective examination of how deterrence can best be achieved. The actual character of the nuclear arsenal will be left to those who are less squeamish. The result is a largely unquestioned system of "guardianship." In the words of Robert Dahl, "We have in fact turned over to a small group of people decisions of incalculable importance to ourselves and mankind, and it is very far from clear how, if at all, we could recapture a control that in fact we have never had."[33]

CHAPTER 2

The Politics of
Nuclear Superiority:
From Forrestal to McNamara

T HE DIVERGENCES between operational and political beliefs about nuclear weapons were set early in the nuclear age. By the end of the Eisenhower administration, they were already firmly entrenched. Indeed, the divergence between the public and political dialogue on nuclear weapons and the official and usually secret decision making on nuclear plans and policies took less than four years to emerge, after the detonation of the first atomic bomb. Within months of the use of atomic weapons in Hiroshima and Nagasaki to compel Japan's surrender, President Harry Truman stated unequivocally that nuclear weapons would serve no useful political or military purpose ever again. He even announced a radical plan to create an international system for the control of atomic arms. But despite avid public support, by the fall of 1949 Truman no longer took the possibility of international control seriously. Instead, he came reluctantly to accept the view that nuclear arms should form the backbone of U.S. military strategy. In the three years following this turnaround, he not only approved three major increases in U.S. capabilities to produce weapons-grade nuclear material, permitting the arsenal to grow from several hundred weapons in 1949 to twelve thousand in 1959, but also set in motion the technology development programs that created the hydrogen bomb and advanced strategic bombers. Truman, moreover, bears the greatest responsibility for initiating the system of "guardianship," taking the initial steps to give control of nuclear weapons to the armed forces and authorizing them, in turn, to plan for the employment of these weapons in war.

President Dwight David Eisenhower accelerated these trends. Maintaining an active interest in bringing the nuclear arms competition under international control, he nonetheless expanded the production of bombers and initiated the development of nuclear ballistic and cruise missiles. Although he managed to resist pressures to expand the nuclear materials production system for many years, toward the end of his term he, like all of his successors, gave in. Eisenhower presided over the development of an arsenal that resulted in more than thirty thousand weapons by the late 1960s. Despite his strong belief that a nuclear war would be an unimaginable catastrophe, he relied on the threat of massive nuclear retaliation as the basis of American military strategy. And he encouraged the armed forces to develop more elaborate plans for nuclear warfare on both the strategic and the tactical levels.

Truman and Eisenhower: The Origins

American and world opinion has never shaken the searing image of the consequences of atomic warfare brought home by the destruction of two Japanese cities in 1945. For all the horror and suffering inflicted by the nuclear explosions, they left one positive permanent legacy: every president, regardless of any indifference or inattention, has had to make the control of nuclear weapons central to American policy. What little progress there has been toward the control of nuclear weapons, we owe primarily to the memory of the terror they caused in this one instance of their use.

President Truman spoke rarely in public about nuclear policy and never about nuclear doctrine. Nor does he appear to have participated in such discussions in the privacy of government offices. He simply denied the military utility of nuclear forces and urged that they be subject to strict international control. He talked about controlling atomic weapons as early as his 1946 State of the Union Message and created a State Department committee, cochaired by Dean Acheson and David Lilienthal, to give substance to the proposal in April of that year. Announced publicly in June by Bernard Baruch, a political confidant of the president, the plan called for the establishment of an international atomic development authority to bring all aspects of nuclear energy under international control and to ensure that atomic weapons would never again be used in war.

Truman maintained his support of the Baruch plan to the last day of his term. But whatever sincere hope there might have been for its success, and one doubts that there was ever very much within the government, it had clearly faded within two years of the announcement. In May 1948, the U.S. Atomic Energy Commission acknowledged in its third annual report that the negotiations had reached a stalemate. The Soviet Union refused to consider granting the international agency the right to carry out on-site inspections to enforce its decisions. And it demanded that the United States divulge the secrets of the bomb prior to the establishment of the control system. Neither condition was acceptable, of course, and the idea languished along with its rhetoric of exaggerated optimism.

These discussions took place against a background of rapidly deteriorating relations between the United States and the Soviet Union, setting early precedents for the two-track policies of peaceful rhetoric and military investment that have continued through the 1980s. Even as the public President Truman steadfastly pursued nuclear arms control and loudly denied the utility of nuclear weapons, his administration was quietly beginning to come to grips with the military and the political potential of these powerful weapons—planning how they might be used in war and, symbolically, in support of American diplomacy.

It was always Europe that impelled a reliance on nuclear weapons. As American hopes for a peaceful settlement in Europe withered in the face of the Soviet occupation of Eastern Europe and internal Communist agitation against democratic governments in France, Italy, and other nations, American officials began to see the threat of atomic warfare as the necessary counter to the USSR's huge armies and military ambitions. This perception, which remains the basis of American nuclear policy today, has required the United States to resist any actions that might be seen as leading to the denuclearization of Europe. It also has been the primary factor in the persistent efforts of successive American administrations to develop nuclear weapons with sufficient accuracy and targeting flexibility to be used against maneuvering military forces on the battlefield. To some observers, the entire history of the American quest for "credible" nuclear forces stems from the peculiar dynamic of the U.S. commitment to the security of Europe, framed largely around the failure to deploy conventional defenses equal to the Soviet threat.

American and British air force officials apparently discussed basing U.S. bombers in Britain as early as 1945. In 1946, a detachment of B-29 bombers—the type of aircraft used to bomb Japan—was deployed temporarily to bases in Germany following the shooting down of an American reconnaissance aircraft near Yugoslavia.

In 1948, the Cold War intensified. In response to Soviet pressures on Berlin, B-29 bombers were deployed twice to Germany on a temporary basis. In August, they were deployed to Britain as well and placed under the direction of General Curtis LeMay, then the commander of U.S. air forces in Europe. American nuclear forces have remained in Europe as part of the European command ever since.

Officially, it was announced that the B-29's were not carrying nuclear bombs. It is now known that the aircraft sent to Britain had not even been modified to enable them to deliver atomic weapons. But the signal intended by dispatching these "atomic" bombers was received loudly and clearly by both the Soviet and the European leaders. Defense Secretary James Forrestal, the administration's leading proponent of a policy of American "nuclear commitment" to Europe, wrote in his diary, "Throughout my recent trip in Europe I was increasingly impressed by the fact that the only balance that we have against the overwhelming manpower of the Russians, and therefore the chief deterrent to war, is the threat of the immediate retaliation with the atomic bomb."[1]

There is no firm evidence that the United States actually committed itself to using atomic weapons to defend Europe before the deployments of B-29's in Britain, but Forrestal's (and others') hints of the time—bolstered by the significance of the implied threat of B-29's operating in Germany—suggest that the concept of "extended deterrence" was already being articulated. In the fall of 1948, the first explicit nuclear commitment was made. Following discussions between Secretary of State George Marshall and the British military chiefs in September, Truman for the first time told his top advisers that he would, in fact, authorize the use of nuclear weapons if Europe were under attack. In November, Forrestal conveyed the message to Winston Churchill. The commitment was formalized and heralded in the North Atlantic Treaty in April 1949, two months before the Soviet blockade against Berlin was finally lifted.

This first break in Truman's reluctance to consider the military uses of nuclear weapons was soon followed by a progressive change in his attitudes and policies. Faced with heightening Cold War tensions and, in September 1949, the detonation of the first Soviet atomic weapon, the Truman administration initiated the first formal efforts to translate the power of the American nuclear arsenal into an effective instrument in its rivalry with the Soviet Union.

It was not until the Eisenhower administration, however, that nuclear weapons gained a central position in American policy. President Eisenhower maintained consistently that nuclear weapons would be used to defend America's security and that of its allies, if necessary. Although he emphasized that nuclear weapons were most likely to be used against a major power, he refused to rule out the possibility of their use in *any* circumstances, and officials at the highest levels of his administration on several occasions seriously considered the use of nuclear weapons.

Eisenhower's highest priority was to contain federal spending, because of his fervent belief that deficit spending posed the greatest long-term threat to the nation's security. All other goals were subordinate. He was willing to curb defense expenditures, domestic programs, and any other area of government spending to avoid incurring deficits. He viewed atomic weapons as the means of achieving effective defense capabilities on the cheap. U.S. conventional-force levels and budgets were cut sharply following the end of the Korean War, particularly those of the army and the air force's tactical components. But the air force's strategic-bombing capabilities were augmented, as were the navy's nuclear attack aircraft based on carriers. The smaller army was restructured into "Pentomic" divisions and equipped to fight on atomic battlefields.

This "New Look" in defense made possible the policy of "massive retaliation." Articulated in the earliest days of the administration by the new secretary of state, John Foster Dulles, the policy pledged that the United States would retaliate massively with atomic weapons in response to any attack against it or its treaty partners. Dulles signaled the new policy prior to the election. In *Life* magazine in May 1952, he said,

Nuclear Superiority: From Forrestal to McNamara

> There is one solution and only one: That is for the free world to develop the will and organize the means to retaliate instantly against open aggression by the Red armies so that, if it occurred anywhere, we could and would strike back where it hurts by means of our own choosing.[2]

The new secretary was to spend much of his first term attempting to live down the word "anywhere" in this preelection statement. He tried to articulate the doctrine more carefully in a speech to the Council on Foreign Relations in January 1954 and in an article in the council's journal, *Foreign Affairs,* later that year. He backtracked from his original remarks in another *Foreign Affairs* article two years later. The United States could not rely "solely" on nuclear weapons for its security, he held, trying to temper his suggestion of nuclear recklessness. The seeming pervasiveness of Dulles's nuclear enthusiasm continued to haunt the secretary, however, providing fodder for Democratic attacks on the administration. When "brush-fire wars"—in Vietnam, Malaya, and elsewhere—proved impervious to the administration's policy of nuclear threats, the Democrats redoubled their attacks, denouncing it as not only dangerous but also ineffectual.

President Eisenhower, by contrast, had a deep appreciation of the consequences of nuclear war, particularly following the development of thermonuclear weapons (H-bombs). A commission chaired by James Killian, the provost of the Massachusetts Institute of Technology, was instrumental in 1954 in conveying a grim picture of the consequences of a U.S.-Soviet thermonuclear exchange. One of the commission's members, John von Neumann, a renowned mathematician from Princeton, demonstrated how H-bombs could be mated with intercontinental ballistic missiles for "strategic" nuclear war, painting a vivid picture of the devastation that could result.

These images of nuclear holocaust had profound effects on Eisenhower. He came to believe that a thermonuclear exchange would be an "absurdity," according to General Andrew Goodpaster, the president's military assistant. In the eyes of the president, the new weapons really changed "the scale of things." For years, he resisted pressures from the military and from the Right to expand the size of the air force and to increase nuclear materials production. He argued passionately that nuclear superiority was an illusion and that "nuclear sufficiency" should be the objective of force planning. And he came to believe that U.S.-Soviet relations had to be shifted from a confrontational to a cooperative posture: if there was a nuclear exchange, it would result from a political failure to manage relations with the USSR.[3]

Eisenhower initiated the search for practical means of controlling nuclear arms and hired Harold Stassen to head the new Disarmament Office within the White House. Early results of these policies included a summit conference in Geneva in 1955 and the Soviet premier Nikita Khrushchev's subsequent visit to the United States. The United States also offered bold arms control proposals, including "Open Skies" in 1955, calling for a full exchange of information on the two sides' military establishments, verified by aerial inspection. This was intended to lessen the probability of surprise attack, a subject treated at length in a conference in 1958. Some of the ideas discussed there have since become part of U.S.-Soviet negotiations, including the concept of verification of agreements by "national technical means."

Eisenhower never resolved the issue of nuclear utility in his own mind or as a matter of policy, however. Even as he pursued political accommodation and agreements to control nuclear weapons, he authorized the development of nuclear war plans and weapons development programs that greatly multiplied America's nuclear capabilities. His inconsistency is revealed in his memoirs:

> From the moment that the Soviets exploded their first atomic bomb and built airplanes capable of carrying them over great distances, Americans realized that, as never before in history, they must thenceforth live under the specter of wholesale destruction. But multimegaton bombs and long-range missiles do not necessarily mean that we must live forever in disabling fear. . . . Though we know that there is a constant possibility, however remote, of an unprecedented holocaust, we still must be wise and courageous enough to live fully, confident . . . that we shall always be ready to defend liberty no matter what the price.[4]

More than any of his successors, President Eisenhower seriously contemplated using nuclear weapons in specific situations and actually threatened to use them in order to bolster U.S. leverage in several crises. Determined to end the war in Korea, for example, the new president decided, in his own words,

> to let the Communist authorities understand that, in the absence of satisfactory progress, we intended to move decisively without inhibition in our use of weapons, and would no longer be responsible for confining hostili-

ties to the Korean Peninsula. . . . In India and in the Formosa Straits area, and at the truce negotiations in Panmunjom, we dropped the word, discreetly, of our intention.[5]

Recently declassified government documents suggest that the president's advisers were divided about the wisdom of using nuclear weapons in Korea and were greatly concerned about the effect of such an action on the European allies, especially on the British. The actual threat that was passed to China through the Indian government, moreover, according to Dulles's reporting cable, appears to have been only that if the war did not end soon, the United States might extend the conflict geographically. The Chinese were assumed to have understood that warning to mean that the United States might strike, possibly with nuclear arms, against airfields in Manchuria. We do not know whether the threat worked. The Chinese did make a key concession soon thereafter, but other factors, particularly the death of Stalin, had given Chinese leaders greater flexibility, and they themselves had had enough of the war.[6]

China was again seriously threatened with nuclear attacks in 1958 during the offshore-islands crisis. This time, verbal hints about nuclear use were bolstered by the movement of nuclear armaments to the region. Again, Eisenhower officials thought the threat had the desired impact; indeed, in this instance, the impact seems to have been profound. Nikita Khrushchev apparently warned the Chinese leader Mao Tse-tung not to press the United States too hard in the crisis and, understanding the stakes, refused to provide weapons to offset the U.S. threat. When Mao called the United States a paper tiger, Khrushchev pointed out that, even so, it was a tiger with nuclear teeth. Mao eventually backed down from his threat to invade the islands. But the incident apparently convinced him that the USSR was an unreliable ally, and it had the unintended consequence of encouraging China to develop its own nuclear weapons and to pursue a course more independent of the USSR.

The Eisenhower administration's nuclear diplomacy focused on Europe. By mid-1953, it had become evident that the NATO allies would not fulfill the goals for the size of conventional forces that they had set for themselves only the year before, at Lisbon. It became clear that, without adequate conventional forces, U.S. nuclear weapons would have to serve as a "make-weight," in General Goodpaster's term, for conventional military capabilities.

A special multinational committee of the organization's military staff (Supreme Headquarters Allied Powers, Europe, or SHAPE) began to study how to make use of tactical nuclear weapons in a conflict on the Continent. Called the "New Approach," the study group's recommendations reflected the "New Look" in the overall U.S. military posture, consistent with the Eisenhower administration's emphasis on the role of nuclear weapons. Approved in 1955 by the alliance's political organization, the plan became known as MC 14/2—to be replaced ten years later by Robert McNamara's flexible response strategy. The alliance's official strategy has not been changed since.

The plan for using tactical nuclear weapons in Europe had been approved by President Eisenhower in 1954. General Goodpaster, who participated in the study group and briefed the president on it, believes that he would have followed the plan had war broken out in Europe. Most important was the recognition of nuclear weapons as political instruments: the mere existence of the plan was intended to act as a deterrent. According to Goodpaster, NATO organizations and allied governments were so thoroughly penetrated by Soviet agents that it was assumed that the planning for using nuclear weapons would become known to the Soviets and cause them to take U.S. nuclear threats seriously.[7]

This theory was tested during the Berlin crisis of 1958–59. The crisis originated in November 1958 when Khrushchev, in a formal diplomatic note, placed a six-month deadline on efforts to resolve the Berlin situation. The Western allies feared that the USSR might impose a new blockade on the city if they failed to comply with terms favorable to the Russians. Harassment of Western convoys on the autobahns to Berlin heightened American concerns that this was a real threat. Coming against a background of highly visible Soviet ICBM tests, the launch of the first Russian space satellite, and a stepped-up program of nuclear weapons tests, the crisis had a nuclear tinge to it from the beginning. Lest Soviet willingness to stand up to American nuclear threats be underestimated, Khrushchev's note left little to the imagination:

> Methods of blackmail and reckless threats of force will be least of all appropriate in such a problem as the Berlin question. . . . Only madmen can go to the depth of unleashing another world war over the preservation of privileges of occupiers in West Berlin. If such madmen should

really appear, there is no doubt that straight jackets could be found for them. . . .[8]

Given the very limited conventional military capabilities of the United States and its allies in Europe at the time, the West apparently would have had few options, apart from capitulation or initiating nuclear war, in the event of a blockade. Although Eisenhower expressed skepticism in public, he appeared almost sanguine in private about the possibility of confronting Khrushchev with nuclear force if the Soviets continued their actions in Berlin. Following an NSC meeting in December, for example, he said, "In this gamble, we are not going to be betting white chips, building up the pot gradually and fearfully. Khrushchev should know that when we decide to act, our whole stack will be in the pot."[9]

Eisenhower backed up his words with the unprecedented action of prohibiting planning for conventional responses to a blockade. He wanted to avoid signaling any willingness to fight at lower levels of conflict, thereby weakening the putative impact of the nuclear threat. Eisenhower's plan was apparently to test any intention of blockade with a small convoy and to suspend all traffic to Berlin if the convoy was stopped. He also planned to turn to the United Nations and direct diplomatic contacts to resolve the situation. If these political means failed, military—presumably, nuclear—options would be considered.

To everyone's relief, Khrushchev lifted the deadline in March, and tensions subsided accordingly. The real Berlin crisis was delayed from coming to a head until after Eisenhower had left office. Whether Eisenhower would indeed have turned to nuclear options if the scenario had played itself out is a matter of speculation. One will never know for certain if the willingness to take the issue right to the brink helped persuade Khrushchev to back off.

Nuclear Force Planning

In July 1949, a report prepared for Truman's secretary of defense Louis Johnson concluded that even if delivered with perfect precision, the entire U.S. nuclear stockpile—then consisting of only 133 weapons—would destroy less than half the Soviet Union's industrial capacity and thus would not be sufficient to force the USSR to surrender in the event of a conflict. Prepared by General Hubert R. Harmon, the report concluded that every effort should be made to deliver the greatest number of bombs to the greatest number of Soviet targets.

With the explosion of the first Soviet atomic bomb, in September 1949, the report was quickly endorsed by Johnson, Secretary of State Acheson, and David Lilienthal, chairman of the Atomic Energy Commission. Truman approved the proposal one week later. At that point, Truman had yet to be briefed on the military's plans on how atomic weapons might be used in war and had declined several efforts to involve him in such discussions. Nor did he ever actually see the Harmon report. Secretary Johnson refused two requests from the White House for the report, stating that it was of "limited value" and that an oral briefing would be quite sufficient. In fact, the secretary concealed the report because its conclusions were at odds with his own. It favored the navy's arguments for a role in atomic warfare by building "supercarriers," a position that Johnson had disallowed in the department's continuing budget debates.[10]

As radical a departure in policy as it may have seemed, however, General Harmon's study was only a sideshow in the nuclear developments of the Truman administration. The key decision in the fall of 1949 concerned the hydrogen bomb, known affectionately as the "super," a weapon with an explosive potential of almost unimaginable magnitude. When it was first considered by a committee of the NSC, in November 1949, officials were deeply divided over whether the United States should build the weapon, even if it proved technically possible. Johnson was firmly in favor and Lilienthal equally opposed. Dean Acheson, the third member, proposed a compromise, suggested to him by his new director of policy planning, Paul Nitze.

Paul Nitze is the individual who, more than anyone else, has influenced both the policies guiding the development of U.S. nuclear weapons and the halting progress toward their control. Never a principal cabinet officer, Nitze nevertheless managed to place himself at the center of the action in almost every postwar administration and, even when out of office, typically found a place at the heart of the debate. In the Truman years, Nitze was at Acheson's side; in the early 1960s, he was a key aide to Robert McNamara. During the Nixon administration, he was a principal negotiator in the talks that led to the 1972 ABM Treaty. In the late 1970s, he joined the opposition to the SALT negotiations and was a decisive force in preventing the SALT II Treaty from being put forward for ratification. In the 1980s, he served Secretary of State George Shultz, first as negotiator for intermediate-range nuclear forces and then as special adviser on arms control to President Reagan. For forty years, if the issue concerned nuclear weapons, Nitze was there.[11]

Nitze proposed a compromise to the H-bomb decision in 1949, which Truman accepted, that recommended that the question of technical feasibility be explored and be accompanied by a major review of U.S. political-military strategy. The decision on the super could then be based rationally on technical as well as political considerations.

The technical issue was resolved in only a few months; H-bombs could and would be built. The review of strategy proved far more complex. It marked, in fact, a watershed in American history. Drafted largely by Nitze, NSC-68, as the study became known, drew a vivid picture of the threat the Soviet Union posed to the United States, identifying 1954 as the year of "maximum danger." According to Fred Kaplan, the document scared Truman's domestic adviser Charles Murphy "so much, that he didn't go to the office the next day, but just sat at home, reading the memorandum over and over."[12]

NSC-68 essentially defined the policy of containment, which dominated the U.S. approach to the USSR for the next twenty years. It was a categorical assertion of the need for major improvements in U.S. and allied military capabilities and for an aggressive political, economic, and psychological strategy to create unrest in Soviet "satellites," in order to keep the Soviets off balance. Nitze doubted that nuclear weapons would be useful in limited wars and decisive in even a major U.S.-Soviet conflict. But the study recommended a sharp expansion of the U.S. nuclear stockpile to prevent the Soviets from surpassing the United States in nuclear capabilities.

So began what has been the enduring rationale for continual nuclear innovation. Regardless of the nature of beliefs about the potential utility of nuclear weapons or about the manner of their use, avoiding the *perception* of a future Soviet nuclear advantage has been the driving imperative behind decisions to expand nuclear weapons, from the time of Harry Truman to that of Ronald Reagan. Any time the United States has failed to act in this manner, the political costs have been enormous: the most important instance was when it decided not to match the USSR's fledgling antimissile system in the early 1960s—a decision reversed six years later, and the focus of protracted controversy in the 1980s.

This divergence between military need and political rationale is an essential explanation of why the public justification for force levels has little to do with operational planning. Administration after administration has justified nuclear modernization programs not on the basis of "requirements" to fight nuclear wars, which would never pass public scrutiny, but on the basis of potential inferiority to Soviet nuclear forces.

Approved formally by President Truman on September 1950, NSC-68 was to have profound effects on U.S. nuclear planning for decades. Two days after Truman's decision, the Atomic Energy Commission, now chaired by Gordon Dean, proposed a second expansion of nuclear production capabilities. The proposal had the full support of the armed services. This time, capabilities were to double by 1953, at a cost of $1.4 billion (perhaps $4 billion in current terms).

The military—SAC and the air force, in particular—had gained firm control of nuclear force planning by 1952. A new request for an increase in nuclear production that year originated with SAC and was linked to "targeting requirements." When the AEC was notified, Gordon Dean held that he needed a more adequate explanation of the requirements before he could support the request.

At a meeting with Truman and his top advisers, however, Dean's concerns received scant attention. General Arthur Vandenberg, the air force chief of staff, argued simply that it was necessary for American security to increase the number of Soviet targets the United States could destroy. Acheson supported him. And Truman, in his usual manner, expressed no interest in learning how the additional weapons might be used; he merely acquiesced in the position of his military adviser.[13]

Throughout the Truman and Eisenhower administrations, there was a mutually reinforcing relation between proponents of larger bomber (and, later, missile) forces and proponents of expanded nuclear stockpiles. The air force's highest priority, shared by the air force's friends on Capitol Hill, was in bombers. "Requirements" to deliver more nuclear weapons to more targets served as a good justification for a growing bomber force. For public consumption, however, the political discourse on bombers appealed to rather different criteria.

Nuclear Superiority: From Forrestal to McNamara

The promotion of strategic air power began as early as 1947 with the appointment, by President Truman, of the five-member Air Policy Commission, supervised by Thomas Finletter of New York. After months of hearings, and more than 140 witnesses, the commission concluded that U.S. air capabilities were already inadequate for the period before the Soviet Union developed nuclear weapons, expected by 1953, and "hopelessly wanting" for the period after this occurred. It recommended that the air force be expanded accordingly, from fifty-five to seventy air groups.[14]

President Truman rejected the Finletter commission's proposals, however, and so Congress pursued the issue on its own. The president and Congress sparred over the size of the air force for the next three years. Neither the Berlin blockade nor the detonation of the Soviet atomic bomb shook the president's refusal to accept more than fifty-eight air groups in the near term or his conviction that modernization programs would permit a reduction to forty-eight groups in five years. It took NSC-68 and the Korean War, which seemed to confirm Paul Nitze's dire prophecy of unrelenting Soviet aggression, to permit the air force finally to achieve its objectives.[15]

The debate on bomber force levels resumed in 1955 with the appearance of the so-called bomber gap. A national intelligence estimate in May of that year predicted that the USSR would have seven hundred intercontinental bombers by 1959. Reported sightings of large numbers of a new class of Soviet bombers with intercontinental range before the annual May Day parade, and a deliberate Soviet deception to exaggerate the number of operational bombers during a ceremonial fly-by, seemed to confirm the forecasts. Supporters of a larger air force were vindicated. The Democrats exploited the issue for all it was worth, charging Defense Secretary Charles Wilson with jeopardizing U.S. security for economic purposes. Wilson's retort that Congress's complaints were "phony" only riled the legislature further.

In 1956, Senator Stuart Symington, a Democrat of Missouri, chairman of the Air Force Subcommittee of the Armed Services Committee, held hearings on U.S. airpower. During the course of these hearings, air force spokesmen, in direct contradiction of Secretary Wilson, charged that B-52 production rates were being restrained by inadequate funding. Without an increase in the air force's budget, they argued, Soviet strategic bombers would outnumber those of SAC between the years 1958 and 1960. Again, the comparison between

U.S. and Soviet capabilities was the decisive element in the public political discourse. Little, if any, attention was paid to the operational significance of additional U.S. strategic bombers.[16]

In fact, planning for a different kind of expansion of U.S. nuclear delivery capabilities had begun early in 1955. Reporting to President Eisenhower secretly in February, the Killian commission had identified ballistic missiles as the greatest future threat to American security. This group of prominent scientists and foreign policy experts, with a staff of forty scientists and engineers, was charged with examining U.S. technological capabilities to handle prospective security problems. In response, Eisenhower declared the development of these new weapons a top national priority; in his memoirs, he compared the accelerated missile program to the Manhattan Project. The air force's existing Atlas missile program was assigned "highest national priority"; the air force was also authorized to develop two additional types of missiles, the Thor and the Titan. And the army and the navy were each permitted to begin developing intermediate-range missiles, the Jupiter and the Polaris, respectively.[17]

Notwithstanding the grim prognostications of the Killian commission, however, Eisenhower was not about to yield his primary security objective—the preservation of fiscal responsibility. For all the rhetoric about a Manhattan Project, he actually held missile development funds well below the level being urged by the new weapons' most fervent supporters. He also expressed outright skepticism about the military utility of the new missiles. If both sides possess large missile forces, he said at a press conference in February 1956, military conflict will "no longer [be] war, because war is a contest, and you finally get to a point where you are talking about race suicide, nothing else."[18]

Asked at a press conference in March 1955 if the Soviet Union would challenge U.S. nuclear superiority within the next three years, Eisenhower responded acidly, "If you get enough of a particular type of weapon, I doubt that it is particularly important to have a lot more of it."[19]

By August, Air Force Secretary Donald Quarles was beginning to challenge the orthodox view that Soviet actions were the determinant of increases in the size of U.S. forces. His predecessor, by contrast, had resigned earlier in the year to protest the president's refusal to expand bomber forces. In an address to the Air Force Association,

Quarles said, "There comes a time in the course of increasing our air power when we must make a determination of sufficiency." The secretary defined "sufficiency" as an absolute power to inflict damage, not as the calculation of the relative strength of two nations' forces. He explained, "The build-up of atomic power in the hands of two opposed alliances of nations makes total war an unthinkable catastrophe for both sides."[20]

Even John Foster Dulles began to modify his position, admitting for the first time in February 1956 that the possession of large numbers of nuclear weapons by both sides was leading to a situation of "mutual deterrence."[21] But the administration's efforts to restrict strategic forces kept running into political pressures created by invidious comparisons with projections of Soviet military forces. While the "bomber gap" had been more or less debunked by the end of 1956, it was soon replaced with a "missile gap." In 1957, Soviet ICBM flight tests and the launch of the first Earth satellite by the USSR created an atmosphere of panic in the United States that even a president as popular as Eisenhower was unable to dispel. Public clamor for "crash" missile programs to counter Soviet actions was fueled by leaks of the report of yet another commission—this one chaired by H. Rowan Gaither, an analyst at the Rand Corporation.

Charged with examining proposals for civil defense programs, the Gaither commission decided to define its task more broadly and to analyze the entire issue of national defense in the missile age. It painted an even grimmer picture than did the commissions that had preceded it. Its report, entitled "Deterrence and Survival in the Nuclear Age," recommended at $25 billion blast shelter program, in addition to immediate measures to permit SAC to survive a surprise attack, the acceleration of missile production, and the development of capabilities to fight "limited" wars.

Eisenhower was briefed by Gaither on November 4, 1957, one month after *Sputnik 1* and only three days after the Russians had launched their second satellite. He was unimpressed, telling Goodpaster, "Hell, they didn't tell me anything I didn't know already." Recognizing the potential political liabilities of the report, Eisenhower sought to keep it secret, even to the point of invoking executive privilege to prevent a secret background briefing to Senator Lyndon Johnson, a Texas Democrat, in January 1958. As usually happens with hot political properties, however, the president's efforts were in vain, and Gaither's recommendations found their way to the press within weeks, adding to the administration's discomfort and making more difficult its efforts to continue to restrain defense spending.[22]

Unable to control the public and congressional outcry, the president grudgingly acquiesced and requested a $1.4 billion supplementary appropriation to speed up the dispersal of SAC aircraft in 1958, placing a greater fraction of SAC's bombers on fifteen-minute alert and accelerating the missile programs. He requested a second $1.5 billion supplemental in April. These steps signaled the end of even a token posture of strategic sufficiency and, with it, the demise of Eisenhower's efforts to base forces on criteria other than overreaction to Soviet developments.

Nuclear Guardianship

Harry Truman maintained strict civilian custody of the fledgling nuclear arsenal from the end of the war until May 1950. He was assisted in this task, and reinforced in his views, by David Lilienthal, the first chairman of the Atomic Energy Commission.

When the Joint Chiefs of Staff finally succeeded, in 1952, in gaining control of the stockpile, it marked the formal establishment of the current "guardianship" system, whereby the president retains authority for decisions to use nuclear weapons, but all operational aspects of weapons planning are controlled by the armed forces. The president is the only individual authorized to release the weapons for use, but the armed forces—under only the broadest guidance of the civilian secretary of defense—establish the plans for their use, determine "requirements," and maintain operational control from the moment they leave the production line.

The Joint Chiefs first attempted to wrest authority for the stockpile from the AEC in December 1946. At that time, the Military Liaison Committee to the AEC, created by the Joint Chiefs to articulate the military's requirements, urged that the armed forces be granted greater authority on the grounds that it was necessary to enhance military flexibility. Truman rejected the argument outright; he saw the issue of civilian control as a fundamental policy question, unaffected by any technical considerations.

Nuclear Superiority: From Forrestal to McNamara

With the support of Secretary of Defense Forrestal, however, the Joint Chiefs persisted. A second attempt was made during the Berlin blockade, when U.S. strategic bombers were being deployed to Europe and the United States was beginning to extend nuclear commitments to its allies. Appearing before the AEC in June 1948, Forrestal requested that complete control be granted to the "National Military Establishment." Turned down peremptorily by Lilienthal and the other two commissioners, Forrestal appealed personally to Truman, questioning "the wisdom of relying upon an agency other than the user of such a weapon, to assure the integrity and usability of such a weapon."[23]

The issue was joined at a Cabinet meeting on July 21, 1948. The chairman of the Military Liaison Committee, Donald Carpenter, a former executive of the Remington Arms Company, held that military custody was in the interest of a coherent command structure and requisite military flexibility. Lilienthal countered that a transfer of authority would imply that Truman was relinquishing his constitutional right to retain sole responsibility for any decision to use the bomb. The president sided with Lilienthal. Later that year, in the AEC's annual report, he reaffirmed his support for civilian control, stating that he regarded "the continued control of all aspects of the atomic energy program, including research, development, and the custody of atomic weapons, as the proper functions of the civil authorities."[24] Two days after the key Cabinet meeting, Truman told Forrestal that he would be willing to examine the issue again following the November election, but nothing apparently came of it. A good politician, the president was probably just giving the disappointed adviser some reed to hold on to.[25]

But Truman's attitude toward atomic weapons changed substantially during the period 1949–50. Although his views on civilian control were among the last to change, when they did, it was a rapid transformation. Two events were crucial: the outbreak of the Korean War, which brought an atmosphere of crisis that made it more difficult to resist the military's arguments for more autonomy, and the retirement of David Lilienthal. Lilienthal had long been the president's sole ally on the issue of civilian control. On July 10, 1950, two weeks after Lilienthal was replaced by Gordon Dean, representatives of the Military Liaison Committee renewed their efforts. This time they were smart enough to use "salami tactics," requesting only that some of the nonnuclear components of the bombs be stored secretly under military control in Great Britain, in order to facilitate transfers of the weapons, should their use in Europe become necessary. The AEC approved the request and proposed it to Truman, who acceded to their recommendation.

Later that month, the Joint Chiefs, through the Military Liaison Committee, asked that nonnuclear components of additional weapons be similarly transferred and stored secretly under military control in the Pacific area. Unable to reach the president, Dean approved the request himself, with the authorization of Defense Secretary Louis Johnson. Nine months later, in April 1951, General Arthur Vandenberg asked the president to approve the transfer of a few complete nuclear weapons to military control, and the president agreed without consulting the AEC. Slowly but surely, the transfer of authority was becoming irrevocable.

The final step occurred near the end of Truman's term, in September 1952. A special committee consisting of Dean Acheson, Secretary of Defense Robert Lovett, and Gordon Dean reconsidered the roles of the various agencies in the operational and the policy aspects of nuclear weapons. Its recommendations, which Truman accepted, granted custody of operational nuclear weapons to the National Military Establishment. The committee also laid out procedures for regulating nuclear production. The Joint Chiefs received authority to determine weapon "requirements" because of their legislated role as the president's principal military adviser. The AEC's role was reduced to safeguarding weapons in development and to determining the rate of materials production necessary to fulfill military "needs." This marked the culmination of the process in which nuclear weapons changed from being seen as extraordinary devices to being considered an integral element of the nation's arsenal—different in degree from other weapons, but still just weapons. In effect, Truman made the armed forces his custodians of military strategy, a role they retain to this day.[26]

The National Military Establishment took over physical custody of the nation's nuclear weapons and worked out procedures for command and control during the early years of President Eisenhower's administration. In August 1953, nuclear weapons were first allocated to U.S. commands, meaning that complete weapons were now in the hands of American field commanders overseas. The Joint Chiefs established an "atomic weapons reserve," however, and retained direct control of 25 to 30 percent of the arsenals allocated to the military commanders.[27]

By December 1954, Eisenhower had directed the new chairman of the AEC, Lewis Strauss, to turn over, for overseas deployment, a third of all hydrogen bombs and almost half of all atomic weapons. The Joint Chiefs pressed to accelerate the pace of transfers, arguing that their custody of the entire arsenal was essential to ensure the weapons' survival in the event of an attack as well as their readiness for use.

By the end of 1956, physical control of virtually all operational weapons was in the military's hands. Once this occurred, guidance for the physical protection, dispersal, and all routine operational matters came directly from the Joint Chiefs. A memorandum in July 1954, for example, empowered "higher commanders," at their discretion, to "allocate or suballocate atomic weapons" to subordinate commanders. Even subordinates of foreign nationalities, as in NATO channels, were to be given command of nuclear weapons in wartime, so long as the weapons remained in U.S. physical custody for transportation, handling, and delivery. In November 1955, for instance, the Joint Chiefs decided that any commander with the high-yield weapons would "have the authority to declare an emergency which would permit weapons to be loaded in bomb bays for dispersal." While this step was taken ostensibly to increase military readiness, it also permitted the commanders to decide when the AEC would relinquish custody of the nuclear component, which had to be inserted before the weapon was placed on the aircraft.[28]

The military was also granted greater authority to plan the use of nuclear weapons. Although it is not clear to what extent President Eisenhower actually predelegated authority to release nuclear weapons, it is apparent that under certain conditions, such as the need to use air defense missiles to defend the continental United States, the authority to initiate a nuclear conflict would have resided in the military's hands.[29]

In the spring of 1956, the State Department and the Defense Department drafted a document entitled "Authorization for the Expenditure of Atomic Weapons." Its purpose was "to provide for immediate defensive readiness of U.S. military forces against major hostile assault wherein the time or damage factors would preclude normal presidential consideration and decision upon the expenditure of nuclear weapons." The document was approved in May 1957, although Eisenhower did not approve the implementing instructions until May 1959.[30]

The final draft of the authorization document remains classified, but early drafts indicate that the armed forces were probably granted the authority to use nuclear weapons under a variety of emergency circumstances. As submitted to the Joint Chiefs, the draft provided advance authority for the use of nuclear weapons to defend U.S. territory and "friendly territory adjacent to the United States," to defend U.S. forces outside American territory if they were attacked with atomic weapons, and to retaliate for an atomic assault on the United States if "the president or other person authorized by law to act in his stead" was not available. But the Joint Chiefs found even these permissive conditions insufficient. They added atomic attacks on U.S. forces in international waters as grounds for authorizing a U.S. response with nuclear weapons. Most important, the Joint Chiefs stressed that they should be authorized to respond with nuclear weapons to protect U.S. forces overseas when attacked "by Sino-Soviet Bloc forces with or without atomic weapons."[31]

Operational Nuclear Planning

Despite the rich public political dialogue on nuclear weapons, such questions of operational planning and use have received little attention, although one would expect them to be in the forefront of the public's concerns. Like most other operational matters, however, questions of nuclear release are guarded closely within professional military circles, with some guidance from appointed officials and virtually no participation by the nation's elected officials.[32]

During the Truman years, nuclear war planning was based on a rather rudimentary system of ad hoc decision making. The small size of the nuclear arsenal, the extreme secrecy that surrounded anything to do with atomic energy, and a general lack of interest on the part of the president all contributed to the decentralization.

Truman's attitude was fairly cynical. Since he thought nuclear weapons had little political or military utility, being solely "terror" weapons of last resort, he was unwilling to participate in providing guidance to the military planners and was uninterested in their plans. On one occasion in 1949, an effort was made to arrange a briefing for the president on plans for nuclear war, but something came up and the meeting was cancelled. In Truman's view, the military's plans were largely irrelevant. In the unlikely event it ever came to his having actually to contemplate using nuclear weapons again, he would simply decide what targets they would be used against, on the basis of whatever criteria he considered essential at the time. He would rely on the advice of the few men he trusted—probably all civilians—just as he had decided how the atomic bombs should be used against Japan.

The military planners thus proceeded more or less alone, relying on their own concepts, with rare inputs from the secretary of defense. The first list of atomic targets was drawn up in 1947 and incorporated in the early JCS war plan BROILER. Similar plans succeeded it, known by the colorful names of FROLIC and HALFMOON. These plans, which envisioned atomic attacks on Soviet cities, were drawn up without the benefit of *any* political guidance. Questions about the tactical or political purposes of the attacks and about the types of targets to be emphasized (or spared) were left solely to the target planners. The only formal guidance ever prepared during the Truman administration, NSC-20/4, was based on a State Department document requested by Secretary of Defense Forrestal. It laid out broad U.S. objectives in the event of war with the Soviet Union, calling for the reduction or elimination of "Bolshevik" control inside and outside the Soviet Union. The purpose was to demonstrate how to conduct war without having to force an unconditional surrender or to occupy Soviet territory. That was about it; all other war-fighting concepts and implicit political objectives were left to the military to decide.[33]

The military planners drew their lessons from their experiences in World War II, focusing on the targeting of the Soviet transportation system, the petroleum industry, and the electric power grid as a means of crippling the Soviet "will to wage war." In the earliest days, when there were only tens or at most hundreds of weapons, the plans stressed the destruction of cities, because these contained the heaviest concentration of the vital war-making targets sought by the planners. The accuracy of any bombing, moreover, was expected to be very poor. BROILER called for dropping 34 bombs on 24 cities, while another joint war plan, OFFTACKLE (approved in October 1949), called for attacks on 104 urban targets with 220 atomic bombs.

By August 1950, planners had begun to pay attention to military targets, giving primary importance to "the destruction of known targets affecting the Soviet capability to deliver atomic bombs." This was the genesis of many of the concepts that guide modern "counterforce" targeting plans. The plans in 1950 demonstrate unequivocally that, even at this early date, military planning was not based solely on the "wholesale slaughter of civilians," as Ronald Reagan depicted the basis of all nuclear strategy prior to that of his own administration.

There were three main categories of targets. First priority was assigned to *blunting* any Soviet atomic offensive—what today are called "counterforce" targets, such as the enemy's nuclear forces and command and control facilities. This raised the issue of the importance of preemptive attacks in effective strategy, a question debated by military planners ever since 1945 but not yet addressed by political authorities. From a military standpoint, if Soviet bombers were to be prevented from making nuclear strikes on the United States, they had to be destroyed at their airfields, prior to taking off for the attack. As a political matter, however, a preemptive strategy was extremely controversial.

Second priority was assigned to *retarding* the Soviet offensive against Western Europe. This class of targets included railroads, petroleum refineries, and electric power plants. Attacking the USSR's economic infrastructure, it was believed, would stall its industrial capacity to support war, although it would clearly have been preferable to be able to attack Soviet military forces themselves. The desire to have weapons with the speed, accuracy, and targeting flexibility to be used against maneuvering Soviet ground formations has been a key motivation of U.S. nuclear development programs ever since.

Third priority was assigned to *disrupting* the Soviets' will to wage war, that is, their industrial capacity. In practice, the distinction between the second and the third categories was never clear. This problem continued to haunt U.S. planners as late as the Ford administration, when U.S. targeting criteria were altered to include plans to disrupt the USSR's ability to "recover" economically after a war.[34]

Throughout this period, the target lists were drawn up by the Air Staff in Washington, which adapted the more general war plans approved by the Joint Chiefs. This procedure changed significantly in

1951, when the plans came under severe criticism from General Curtis LeMay, the commander of SAC. LeMay, a war hero and former commander of the U.S. bombing campaign against Japan, charged that the Air Staff's planners paid no attention to how difficult it was actually to carry out the missions they specified in their target lists. After a contentious meeting in January, the Air Staff's targeting panel agreed to submit all future plans to SAC for comment before submitting them to the Joint Chiefs for approval. Having gotten a foot in the door, LeMay and SAC soon took over the entire edifice.

Once the target list was drawn up, it was left to SAC to formulate the operational plan for its implementation. Clusters of individual targets had to be assigned to individual aircraft, the timing of attacks had to be coordinated so that one U.S. bomber would not be flying through the explosion detonated by a second bomber, second waves had to be planned in case key targets were missed the first time, bomber flights had to be coordinated with reconnaissance aircraft and tankers—all this was an incredibly complicated business, which came to be known as the Basic War Plan.

Beginning in 1951, LeMay suddenly quit submitting SAC's Basic War Plan to any higher authority, except when a briefing to the Joint Chiefs was demanded specifically by his superior, the air force chief of staff. With incredible chutzpah, LeMay claimed that submitting the plan for approval would jeopardize its security—that, in short, the Joint Chiefs (meaning the army and navy) were not to be trusted. Not only was neither the president nor his secretary of defense kept apprised of operational nuclear plans; even the highest-ranking military officials apparently were in the dark. LeMay remembered,

> As long as we [SAC] had the only atomic capability in the armed forces, things were fine. But pretty soon the Tactical people got into the outfit, the Navy got into the outfit, the Army got some artillery, etcetera, etcetera, and I can remember late in the game when we finally got it across that the situation as it existed made no sense because everybody was trying to get in.[35]

By the fall of 1955, SAC had achieved virtually complete control over target selection for most of the nuclear arsenal as well as over the Basic War Plan. As the size of the U.S. strategic bomber force and the nuclear arsenal grew, the task of strategic targeting became more and more complicated. In 1957, for instance, the target list included more than three thousand military and industrial targets. By the end of the decade, SAC targeters had designated more than twenty thousand separate potential "ground zeros."

To try to deal with the complexity, the JCS approved a procedure in which committees made up of army, navy, and air force officers would determine the criteria to guide target selection but in which the actual allocation of targets was left to the unified and specified commands. In other words, SAC would draw up the strategic-bombing list, which accounted for the largest portion of the weapons, while the navy commanders in the Atlantic and the Pacific, and the commander of U.S. forces in Europe, would draw up their own lists. All these lists were supposed to be submitted to the JCS for approval, but the Joint Staff lacked the resources to analyze the by now huge target lists. SAC's targeting task alone was so complicated that it could be accomplished only with the assistance of a brand-new IBM 704 computer, one of the first of its kind.

In March 1954, a new statement of U.S. objectives for general nuclear war was approved by the president to replace NSC-20/4. Although "preventive" war was ruled out as a matter of policy, preemptive strikes in the midst of a conventional conflict or upon receipt of warning that the Soviet Union was preparing an attack were not. Preemption was considered a particularly sound option because there was expected to be a relatively long period of strategic warning as the USSR prepared for war. Even after a first wave of Soviet attacks had reached the United States, counterstrikes on Soviet nuclear forces and facilities were expected to be able to reduce the damage that might be inflicted in the absence of preemption. Accordingly, SAC's operational plans put the highest priority on military targets, especially on airfields and other nuclear targets, and stressed the desirability of hitting the enemy before he could launch his attack. General LeMay was unequivocal about how this objective would be achieved. Writing to General Nathan Twining, his nominal superior as air force chief of staff, LeMay said, "If the U.S. is pushed in a corner far enough, we would not hesitate to strike first. . . ."[36]

As the size and composition of the Soviet nuclear arsenal changed, however—particularly after the USSR demonstrated that it could develop ballistic missiles—doubts began to arise about the United States's ability to disarm the enemy. Even the limiting of damage from a Soviet strike to "tolerable" levels might prove difficult. Pentagon analyses projecting that U.S. bombers could be vulnerable to a Soviet missile first strike raised further doubts about current strategy. Frustrated by the unrelenting pressures to increase the size of the bomber force and nuclear stockpile, Eisenhower finally spoke out against what he perceived to be the insane futility of SAC's activities. In January 1959, he exclaimed, "They are trying to get themselves into an incredible position of having enough to destroy every conceivable target all over the world, plus a three-fold reserve."[37]

Throughout Eisenhower's second term, there was a complicated and bitter bureaucratic struggle over the character and objectives of nuclear targeting. This dispute had serious implications for the kind of strategic forces that would be acquired in the future and for the manner in which the procedures for nuclear planning would be defined.

The essential struggle was between the navy and the air force. By the mid-1950s, it had become clear that it would be possible to deploy missiles on submarines, potentially providing a nuclear capability that, hidden under the seas, could be invulnerable. This development helped reinforce the notion that nuclear war might more realistically be *prevented* than waged. By deterring a Soviet first strike through the threat of devastating retaliation, rather than by seeking forces to limit the damage from a Soviet attack by destroying its strategic forces preemptively, the United States might have a more "stable" nuclear posture and reduce the risk of war. The competing concepts of "preemption" and "retaliation" had very different implications for the choice of targets as well as for the size and composition of the U.S. strategic forces necessary to carry out the strategy. "Preemption," by definition, would require large numbers of highly accurate counterforce weapons, while "retaliation" conceivably could be accomodated with a smaller force of less capable weapons targeted more selectively.

The possibility that the navy might be able to provide the mainspring of U.S. nuclear capabilities had at last brought an individual into the nuclear planning arena who was a match for LeMay—Admiral Arleigh Burke. Burke avidly promoted the notion of finite deterrence. A force of forty-five submarines, he maintained, of which twenty-nine would be kept at sea at all times, could destroy 232 Soviet targets. This "was sufficient to destroy all of Russia" and would deter any Soviet attack. The air force retorted that the threat of retaliation was insufficient and that it would be imprudent not to maintain capabilities to destroy Soviet nuclear forces and industrial capacity, preemptively if necessary. The air force even attempted a blatant power play in 1959 to gain control of the navy's new Polaris submarines: it proposed the establishment of a comprehensive structure called the Strategic Command. General Thomas Power, the air force chief of staff, stated that the "details" of the new command would be worked out by the commander of SAC, as the specified commander "who has responsibility for the mission area." But the ploy was a little too heavy-handed, and it failed. In the end, the United States did build a force of strategic submarines very much like that recommended by Burke, and kept them strictly under navy control. Even so, SAC was able to retain control of nuclear targeting and operational planning, including the targeting for the new Polaris missiles, through the creation of the Joint Strategic Target Planning System (JSTPS). As a sop to the navy, the vice-commander of JSTPS has always been an admiral, although never more senior than a three-star officer.

Even before deployment of the first Polaris submarine, when the navy's strategic forces consisted solely of aircraft based on carriers, it had become obvious that the navy's and the air force's target planning had to be coordinated. The dangers of separate targeting were apparent: in targeting the same Soviet targets, they were assuring "fratricide" of each other's aircraft or missiles, or at least making their plans useless by targeting already destroyed targets. The problem was becoming more acute as both services introduced new missiles. In July 1960, Secretary Gates told the president that in fifteen meetings with the Joint Chiefs over the preceding six months, he had been unable to resolve the problems. He and the chairman of the Joint Chiefs, Nathan Twining (an air force general), believed that an integrated target list and operational plan were essential and that the only practical option was to assign the task to SAC. The army and the navy, he complained, viewed this as air force aggrandizement and refused to give way.

Eisenhower was disgusted by these internecine disputes, and charged that "the original mistake in this whole business was our failure to create one single Service in 1947." He even mused about replacing the Joint Chiefs entirely if they did not come up with a solution. In the end, he decided to assign the job to SAC, but the SAC organization responsible for joint nuclear planning was to be augmented with personnel from the other services. The new organization was charged with creating a new national target list and a Single Integrated Operational Plan, or SIOP, combining the detailed planning for the air force and the navy. Resigned to the inevitable, Arleigh Burke sought to make the new system work, sending a detachment of capable naval officers out to staff the new organization at SAC's headquarters in Omaha. Burke urged the army chief of staff, General George Decker, to do the same, but the army had no role in strategic targeting and little interest in nuclear planning except at the tactical level. Greatly outnumbered in a hostile and competitive environment, the navy detachment had less influence than it had hoped. The organization, and the nation's strategic planning, remained dominated by SAC, JSTPS, and the air force, as they still are today.[38]

The JSTPS produced the first integrated target list, SIOP-62, within a few months. It was based neither solely on the navy's notion of finite deterrence through retaliation on industrial targets nor on the air force's concept of damage limitation through preemption against military and, especially, nuclear targets. Rather, it combined the two, envisioning first a massive strike against thousands of targets as early as possible upon receipt of strategic warning and then repeated waves of reattacks to ensure a high level of damage throughout the Soviet Union and allied nations. Although Burke had serious reservations about the plan, he saw little choice but to go along. He and the other members of the Joint Chiefs approved SIOP-62 in December 1960. Thus the nation's first integrated operational plan for nuclear war was left, along with its legacy of bureaucratic tensions, for Robert McNamara and the incoming Kennedy administration to take care of.

McNamara and Flexible Response

The period from 1961 to 1967 was one of unprecedented civilian intrusion in military planning. Having finally wrested control of nuclear forces from civilians in 1958, the military was suddenly confronted with a renewed assault on its prerogative. The services had fought valiantly during the preceding decade to get control over nuclear weapons away from civilians, and it was not about to relinquish the victory without a bloody fight.

Defense Secretary Robert McNamara's assertion of civilian control encompassed all aspects of military policy, from the most trivial budget details to the fundamentals of nuclear strategy. His crusade set off political firestorms not just in the Pentagon but also among traditional military supporters in the Congress and around the country. In the days before the Vietnam War and the Watergate scandal, the country was not used to interference by political appointees in matters affecting national security.

But McNamara was determined from the outset to force the services to obey political directives fully. He set about to dismantle the system by which the services planned force requirements. It was traditionally an interservice sparring match in which each branch virtually demanded that it be equipped to fight any war on its own. McNamara dismissed the whole system as anachronistic and at odds with the spirit of discipline and austerity he intended to instill in the Department of Defense.

By harnessing the budget and intelligence processes and putting them firmly under civilian control, McNamara believed, he could rationalize all areas of strategic policy. He established an elaborate system of Draft Presidential Memoranda (DPM) that imposed detailed justification for each element of the defense budget, policy, and doctrine. Defense planning and budgeting were to be conducted "against firm projections four or five years ahead" or longer if possible—an unprecedented degree of centralization. The whole system was to be rational, purged of the emotionalism of service loyalty and petty bureaucratic ambitions. If the Defense Department was to be a successful corporation—and McNamara an effective CEO—all employees would have to toe the line.

As early as February of 1960, General Tom White wrote to SAC Commander Thomas Power, warning, "While our experience with the new administration is brief, there is no question but that complete reappraisal will be made of our military strategy, force and weapon system requirements and current posture."[39] The reformist zeal that Secretary of Defense McNamara and his band of civilian technical analysts, the "whiz kids," brought to the task was particularly galling to the professional military. In 1961, William Beecher caricatured the dynamics between civilians and the military as "fuzzy-cheeked whiz kids with computers telling battle-scarred dogfaces how to fight and win wars."[40] General White was just as blunt: "In common with other military men," he wrote in 1963, "I am profoundly apprehensive of the pipe-smoking, tree-full-of-owls type of so-called 'defense intellectuals' who have been brought to this Nation's capital."[41]

The clash was more than merely cultural. It was over the primal question of who is rightfully in charge of conducting war. The McNamara years provide a rich illustration of the great divisions between civilians and the military in the struggle for authority for war fighting, and the very different approaches and values the two groups brought to the task of ensuring security.

In the end, the legacy of the McNamara years for political control of nuclear operations was mixed. McNamara forced the services to adhere to strict ceilings on the numbers of weapons purchased, and he questioned their judgment about the roles and missions of every weapons system. He presided over the first major civilian innovation in nuclear doctrine—the concept of "flexible response"—which was not popular among military planners. He won innumerable budget battles and managed to sustain a ceiling on the number of nuclear systems, and that was anathema to the Air Force.

Despite his fervent effort and the full support of President Kennedy, however, McNamara did not succeed in gaining control of nuclear operations. Like the annointed few in the Strategic Defense Initiative Office two decades later, the McNamara whiz kids left Washington chastened by the power of the bureaucratic status quo. Their attempt to revolutionize nuclear planning had some effect—a rhetorical commitment to the doctrine of flexible response among them—but in the end, the military retained its prerogative for the conduct of war fighting.

The Demise of Massive Retaliation

The Kennedy administration moved quickly to place its imprint on American nuclear strategy. As the experiences of the Berlin and Cuban crises underscored, the most urgent priority was to repudiate the policy of massive retaliation, a policy that the young president and his aides found not only incredible militarily but also morally repugnant. An all-out nuclear attack against Soviet civilians in response to any level of Soviet provocation did not square with the spirited humanism of the new administration. Given the growth of Soviet nuclear forces, moreover, the strategy seemed increasingly senseless. Even with American nuclear superiority, a first strike still was only a threat to create a global holocaust, hardly a credible response to a modest Soviet conventional incursion in Europe or Korea.

The contradictory impulses of the Kennedy administration, shifting between hardheaded military pragmatism and liberal humanism, are aptly illustrated in its attempts at nuclear innovation. The same president who successfully concluded the Limited Test Ban Treaty, pushed for a Comprehensive Test Ban (CTB), and refused to sanction the more bellicose actions urged by advisers during the Berlin and the Cuban missile crises presided over a major civil defense program, one clear instance of "brinksmanship" with the Soviet Union, a major expansion of U.S. offensive nuclear capabilities, and the introduction as official policy of "flexible counterforce."

In his campaign against Richard Nixon, Kennedy had effectively manipulated the "missile gap," an alleged Soviet advantage in nuclear missiles later admitted to have been a political fiction. Well before, as a young senator in the 1950s, Kennedy had sought the political limelight by attacking the complacency of the Republicans toward advances in Soviet military power. Many of the linguistic flourishes and Cold War themes used in the presidential campaign material had been honed earlier on the Senate floor. As president, Kennedy wanted to prove his mettle against the belligerent Soviet leader, Premier Nikita Khrushchev, to prove to domestic critics that a forty-three-year-old liberal was up to the challenge. But he also expressed a personal sense of horror about nuclear weapons and the dilemma they posed for U.S.-Soviet relations. Dean Rusk, Kennedy's secretary of state, remembers leaving a meeting with the president a few weeks after the inauguration. A few advisers had spent the day discussing the effects of nuclear war. As Rusk tells it, Kennedy looked to him as they left the Cabinet Room and said, "And we call ourselves the human race. . . ."[42]

Just a few weeks later, with the encouragement of his secretary of defense, Kennedy publicly renounced the policy of huge, preemptive nuclear strikes that was part of the Eisenhower strategy of massive retaliation. It was the first—and last—time an American president pledged never to strike first with nuclear weapons. As it turned out, however, the president's lofty rhetoric was far removed from the pragmatic theorizing about "preemptive counterforce strikes" that was going on among his new aides or from the reality of the plans themselves. Within a year, it was also at odds with the signal Kennedy sent to the Soviets during the Cuban missile crisis when he said, "Khrushchev must not be certain that, where its vital interests are threatened, the United States will never strike first."[43]

The Berlin Crisis

The Berlin crisis helped bring to the fore the contradictory impulses of the president and the new administration. As the crisis unfolded, Dean Acheson, the former secretary of state, was called in as a special adviser. Totally at odds with most other Kennedy advisers, he advanced hawkish views that even some Cold War veterans like Arthur Schlesinger, Jr., found frightening. Acheson's exposition of American options in Berlin, first revealed in April 1961, was "rather bloodcurdling," claimed Schlesinger. "Skipping over the possibilities of diplomatic and economic response, Acheson crisply offered a formidable catalogue of countermeasures, concluding tentatively in favor of sending a division down the Autobahn."[44]

As it turned out, this was only the beginning. Acheson subsequently sent Kennedy a memo recommending national military mobilization, an increase of $5 billion in the defense budget for new conventional forces, and a staunch refusal to negotiate with the Soviet government.[45] Kennedy agreed with Acheson that the situation required the United States to demonstrate that it would use nuclear weapons before it would accept Soviet expansion in Europe. In this assessment, Berlin was the ultimate test of the Cold War balance of power, a test the United States could not afford to fail.

However chilling Acheson's recommendations, they highlighted the limited number of military options the administration actually had at its disposal. The special group charged with managing the crisis, the Berlin task force—made up of Paul Nitze, then assistant secretary of defense for international security affairs, Foy Kohler, a former staffer of Acheson's, Abram Chayes, a State Department legal adviser, and Rusk—soon reinforced the message. Meeting daily beginning in June, the task force uncovered in detail the stark reality that American nuclear superiority did not accord commensurate political and military choices.

Various military plans were discussed over the course of the crisis, including firing an atomic warning shot over an isolated area of Russia. Earlier, NATO and JCS plans had reportedly suggested small conventional attacks down the Autobahn, escalating to nuclear weapons if these failed to force the Soviets to back down. It was clear to the civilians in the Pentagon, however, that the nuclear escalation the JCS had in mind could only be a form of "massive retaliation," the full execution of the Single Integrated Operational Plan. Carl Kaysen, an NSC assistant, had told McGeorge Bundy as early as June that the JCS plan was "exactly the one-sided response with all of our nuclear forces envisioned in SIOP-62."[46]

Just after the Soviets began building the Berlin wall in August, a small task force was set up in the Pentagon to analyze the possibility of a counterforce attack aimed at destroying the fledgling Soviet nuclear arsenal, "alternative limited target lists which might be relevant to Berlin," as Kaysen described the work of the task force. In part a reaction by senior aides to the inflexibility of the JCS plans, the new interest in examining these options also reflected the administration's growing awareness that there was no missile gap.

To the contrary, the former Yale professor William Kauffman had by this time analyzed the intelligence data coming from the photoreconnaissance satellite Discoverer, revealing the very limited number of Soviet nuclear weapons. Added to the new details about weaknesses in Soviet operational plans uncovered by CIA analysts, the evidence indicated a clear U.S. nuclear preeminence. By September, the gap was officially history: National Intelligence Estimate (NIE) 11-8/1-61 calculated that the Soviets had fewer than ten operational ICBMs.

This suggested to the civilian Pentagon analysts that there might be hope for finding a practical middle ground between "holocaust and humiliation," as Kennedy called it, which could be relevant to Berlin. Finished in September, the task force used mathematical models refined by the Rand Corporation to identify Soviet counterforce targets, calculate the U.S. forces needed to destroy them, and assess the number of Americans who might be killed by the surviving Soviet forces. The point of the exercise, according to Kaysen, was to develop "a first strike plan to show that we could have a successful clear first strike."[47]

Nevertheless, the study's calculated optimism was not enough to persuade the president of the utility of nuclear weapons. The Pentagon group's conclusions that only a few Soviet bombers were likely to survive a determined first strike—a military triumph—did not compensate for the JCS "assurance" to Kennedy that U.S. casualties could be kept to "below ten million."[48] Kennedy was viscerally opposed to any option, however "modest," that involved nuclear weapons: "We go immediately from a rather small military action to one where nuclear weapons are exchanged, which of course means . . . we are also destroying this country."[49]

Previously, in July, in a speech about Berlin, Kennedy had stressed his willingness to negotiate with the Soviets as one of the options for resolving the crisis. Reflecting the views of his more liberal advisers, he said, "In the thermonuclear age, any misjudgment on either side could rain more devastation in several hours than has been wrought in all the wars of human history."[50] Whatever the apparent "liberal" victory, however, the Berlin efforts had as their main legacy the building up of U.S. conventional forces and the enshrinement of limited counterforce as the basis for future U.S. nuclear strategy.

In the aftermath of Berlin, "flexibility" in both conventional and nuclear forces became the buzzword of the moment. A paper given to Kennedy in Hyannis Port on July 8, prepared by his special adviser Henry Kissinger, Chayes, and Schlesinger, criticized Acheson's "brinkmanship" and argued that "the Pentagon should be required to make an analysis of the possible implications of nuclear warfare and the possible gradations of our nuclear response."[51] The point was clear: there was insufficient understanding of the consequences of nuclear war for the current military posture to be credible. Overwhelming U.S. nuclear superiority did not compensate for paralyzing fears of the unknown.

One enduring legacy was the remarkable difference between the attitudes that motivated the president and his political advisers and the coldly scientific models of the Pentagon analysts who were called on to identify "options" for a military resolution of the crisis. The Pentagon task force study demonstrating that the United States could execute a successful first strike against the fledgling Soviet arsenal with "only" a few million American casualties was greeted with genuine revulsion, even by hard-liners like Paul Nitze. There was still too much uncertainty in the operation of a first strike, and the level of American casualties of the most optimistic estimates was profoundly disturbing.

Even the idea of a warning shot had been considered too dangerous. What if the trajectory gave the impression the shot was headed for the Kremlin? asked Bundy. What if the Soviets responded in kind, and there was an exchange of warnings that led to escalation? asked Nitze. The potential risk associated with the unleashing of nuclear forces had given concrete meaning to *self*-deterrence, hardly an acceptable military posture for the most powerful nation in the world.

Kennedy subsequently asked for more-flexible war plans, in the search for "credibility." The idea of discriminating and graduated nuclear response had been articulated by a number of technical analysts in the 1950s, and Paul Nitze had published an article on the subject in 1956 in the prestigious journal *Foreign Affairs.* But the Berlin crisis gave the subject a tangible urgency.

"The ideas [of flexible response] were annealed in the crucible of the 1961 crisis," argues Richard Betts. "The Berlin flexible response planning yielded complex options for the use of force, beginning with small-scale conventional actions and ranging upward." "Upward," in this case, was spelled out in National Security Action Memorandum 109 of 1961. From selective attacks for demonstration purposes to tactical uses of nuclear weapons, escalation continued up to a level referred to simply as general nuclear war.[52]

SIOP-63

For McNamara's new appointees in the Defense Department—many of them civilian analysts who had spent years "thinking the unthinkable"—the concern that massive retaliation was drastically out of date with the realities of the growing Soviet nuclear capacity, alliance politics, the fluidity of international alignments, and modern concepts of nuclear war operations had been an issue well before the Berlin crisis. If the Soviets had conventional superiority and enough nuclear forces to obliterate the United States, what possible credence would anyone give to the idea of an all-out strategic attack on the Soviet Union to deter their military adventures? The key was to figure out how "general nuclear war" could be managed, rationalized, made into a real military plan.

McNamara came to office with virtually no experience in either nuclear matters or politics. He admitted to having read only one book on national security. He was appointed because of his demonstrated intellectual and managerial skills as head of the Ford Motor Company. He was not President Kennedy's first choice; the job had first been offered to Robert Lovett, secretary of defense under Truman, but he declined for reasons of age and ill health.

McNamara had an innate belief in the primacy of logic and rationality; any problem could be solved, he liked to say, if you thought about it enough. Asking him to grapple with the cosmic uncertainty posed by nuclear weapons suggests a certain mismatch. Even more confusing was the Byzantine world of nuclear planning, an entrenched bureaucracy of experienced military men who loathed McNamara on sight and hated his whiz kids even more. Who were these under-forty geeks in suits who had never fought a war and who thought that their jobs entitled them to insult uniformed officers? They were intellectuals, men who had pursued the outer boundaries of policy questions with the aid of computer models and slide rules. LeMay referred scornfully to the work done at Rand as "pet projects unrelated to national defense," such as "the sex life of the polyp."

General Leighton Davis, former head of air force systems command, summarized the views of most military officers toward the approach to planning that McNamara's team used, the "systems analysis and cost effectiveness" criteria that were to supersede the "irrational" considerations in formulating policy. Referring to Alain Enthoven, the brilliant economist who became deputy assistant secretary of systems analysis—the "SA Guru"—Davis said, "What's missing [in his analysis] is the essence of military doctrine, if you want to call it, judgment and operational factors. He didn't weight those very highly compared with the other quantifiable terms in his equations."[53]

With an insatiable appetite for technical details, McNamara listened attentively to the young analysts who had been grappling for years with the ineffable question of military application of nuclear power. Since at least the mid-1950s, a group of strategists at the Rand Corporation, including William Kauffman, Enthoven, and Harry

Rowen, deputy assistant secretary of defense from 1961 to 1965, had tried to come to grips with the problems of nuclear strategy. Credited with the development of the "no-cities" approach, the basis of McNamara's first doctrinal innovation, Kauffman had briefed McNamara during his first week in office. His intellectual contribution was to demonstrate both the fatuousness of massive retaliation and the strategic utility of counterforce strikes that kept attacks on civilians to a minimum.[54]

Kauffman and his colleagues were not the first to argue that nuclear weapons were indeed weapons and that something short of the Apocalypse had to guide American strategic planning. They were, however, among the first "think tank" intellectuals to have such direct access to the inner sanctum of the government. "Intellectuals" played a role in the Eisenhower administration, and great scholars like Paul Nitze had risen to senior positions as advisers. But very few technical experts had ever found a place in the political limelight. Without McNamara, this situation might have remained unchanged. Few political appointees have ever welcomed detailed technical analyses of issues as arcane as nuclear war planning.

One reason that the whiz kids found the new secretary of defense to be receptive was his reaction to the military commanders who first briefed him on the SIOP on February 3, 1961. Accompanied by Deputy Secretary of Defense Roswell Gilpatrick, General Maxwell Taylor, chairman of the JCS, Charles Hitch, a budget analyst, and Herbert York, the director of Defense Research and Engineering (DR & E), who had been held over temporarily from the Eisenhower administration, McNamara went to SAC headquarters at Offutt Air Force Base, near Omaha, to learn about the plan.[55]

The briefing was a nightmare rendition of civilian-military relations, a bureaucratic catastrophe. Unimpressed by the whizbang SAC presentations of computer models and complex computations for nuclear targeting—a briefing style that persists at SAC today—McNamara criticized SIOP-62 on several counts. The methodology to calculate "damage-expectancy" was so badly skewed that it required four weapons for each target site—known as a Desired Ground Zero (DGZ)—and there was no accounting for the aftereffects of nuclear blasts, such as fallout. The resulting "overkill" was preposterous. York calculated that the plan called for almost half a megaton for a target similar to Hiroshima, a city devastated by a bomb one-fiftieth the size. McNamara openly accused the commanders of underestimating damage calculations to justify continued additions to the strategic arsenal. Their whole approach, he argued, was as fanciful as it was cynical.

SIOP-62 provided for a massive first strike against targets not just in the Soviet Union but in all of Eastern Europe and China as well. The plan included fourteen "options" that a president might consider in crisis, but all of them involved full execution of the strategic arsenal against an "optimum mix" of targets—military and urban-industrial targets. In truth, there was no practical distinction between them. The only "withhold" option was to launch 1,400 nuclear weapons kept on alert on short warning, with the rest—up to 3,500 weapons—launched within twenty-four hours. As Fred Kaplan described it, "That was the crux of the SIOP: a first-strike plan that held back nothing, that killed hundreds of millions of people just because they lived under Communist rule, without any Communist government's having so much as scratched a square inch of the United States."[56]

Shortly after returning from Omaha, McNamara issued a directive to the Joint Chiefs, the service secretaries, the director of DR & E, and the Pentagon's general counsel, listing ninety-six projects and questions he wanted answered. Drafted personally by McNamara, the thirteen-page directive issued tasks to particular individuals and in many cases imposed extraordinarily short deadlines. The one sent to the JCS chairman Lyman L. Lemnitzer said, "Prepare a doctrine which, if accepted, would permit controlled response and negotiating pauses in the event of a thermonuclear attack." The general was given just over six weeks to comply.[57]

A spirit of innovation permeates all new administrations, but the McNamara years set an unprecedented standard. His directive, quickly dubbed "96 Trombones," was generally loathed by careerists who assumed that the zeal of the newcomers would eventually dissipate. To the contrary, McNamara moved to revolutionize the entire military apparatus, including its most sacrosanct and jealously guarded area, "requirements."

The pre-McNamara practice of allowing the services to set their own requirements for forces and weapons was effectively demolished as policy as early as January 1961. A memorandum prepared by David Bell, director of the Bureau of the Budget, for an NSC meeting outlined the problems the new crowd was intent on fixing. The memo notes that rivalry among the services had been left untended to the point that the United States had three separate strategic doctrines (identified in an internal NSC memo in 1961 as "Air Force: counterforce deterrent; Navy: finite deterrent; Army: credible deterrent"). Still fiercely independent, the services also used separate intelligence estimates to assess "the threat." Since these were the bases for force planning, they were inevitably biased to justify service preferences and larger weapons inventories.[58]

Key to establishing civilian control of requirements, intelligence assessments would no longer be the responsibility of the services after 1961. A study conducted in 1960 had warned of the distortions in intelligence resulting from service competition and had recommended a national agency for intelligence collection. McNamara established the Defense Intelligence Agency (DIA) in November 1961 and gave it control of all Defense Department intelligence resources. The centralization of intelligence was to be another means of exerting control over service requirements. The air force, in particular, had already offended McNamara with its aggressive promotion of missile gaps and bomber gaps as the basis for its requests for new weapons.[59]

More important was the basic issue of who had the authority to launch nuclear weapons. The military had come a long way from President Truman's first, grudging release of atomic weapons from the custody of the AEC. SAC's perception of its independence was underscored colorfully by Curtis LeMay when he reportedly told Robert Sprague, deputy to Gaither and later co-chairman of the Gaither committee, that he didn't care about vulnerability and all the other handwringing issues that civilians were bringing to the attention of the Gaither committee in 1956: "I'm going to knock the shit out of them before they hit the ground."[60] Bundy had brought the issue of civilian control to the attention of the president in the early days of the administration, describing "a situation . . . in which a subordinate commander faced with a substantial Russian military action could start the thermonuclear holocaust on his own initiative if he could not reach" the president. McNamara was going to take care of that as well.[61]

One of McNamara's junior aides, Daniel Ellsberg, working under Nitze's aegis as the assistant secretary of defense for international security affairs, argued for what was to become the no-cities doctrine: "alternative options should include counterforce operations, carefully avoiding major enemy cities while retaining US ready residual forces to threaten those targets." The current plans based on inflicting maximum civilian casualties in the Soviet bloc "would fail to inhibit punitive retaliation by surviving enemy units, but would instead eliminate the possibility that enemy responses could be controlled or terminated to US advantage."[62] The thirty-year-old analyst's conclusions were signed as official guidance from the secretary of defense to the JCS in May of 1961 to revise SIOP-62.

The effort to reform the SIOP, however, proved that belief systems about nuclear weapons were more resilient than McNamara might have imagined. The dispute over nuclear plans was as much a philosophical as a policy clash, although officially it was fought as a battle over who should control the arsenal.

The military had the experience and was ultimately accountable, argued SAC, not these intellectuals whose fanciful concepts about nuclear doctrine showed how out of touch they were with the complexity of the task. Devising an integrated nuclear targeting plan required the coordination of flight times so that refueling tankers and bombers could hook up twice to permit the bombers to get to their targets and return home safely. The weapons themselves could not be allowed to "interfere" with one another, or a nuclear blast from one bomber might kill another pilot flying too close. Changing wind conditions and poor visibility could prove fatal to the entire architecture. As General Jasper Welch, a key architect of Nixon's nuclear planning, argued, "Putting together a well integrated plan was damn tough in those days, with antiquated command and control and unfriendly software. There was massive human involvement."[63]

Lemnitzer was blunt with McNamara in responding to his directive, rejecting any strategy in which nuclear force was measured or restrained. These notions totally ignored military logic: American forces might not survive sufficiently to retaliate effectively; it was highly unlikely that the Soviet Union could distinguish between a limited and a total counter-societal attack; millions of civilians would be killed anyway, so it was hardly "humanitarian"; and the idea of "riding out" a Soviet first strike could result in such a disruption of U.S. command and control systems that the surviving leadership would have to turn to a simple plan for massive retaliation in any case.

More fundamentally, the concept contradicted the whole point of nuclear weapons. The idea of "withholding" cast suspicion on the willingness of the United States to act in crisis, Lemnitzer argued; it also suggested that it would be possible to get the Soviets to withhold, "a degree of tacit [Soviet] cooperation which does not now appear realistic." His bottom line: "We do not now have adequate defenses, nor are our nuclear retaliatory forces sufficiently invulnerable, to permit us to risk withholding a substantial part of our efforts, once a major thermonuclear attack has been initiated." He did offer to study the matter for "more limited engagements," meaning war outside of the continental United States, in Asia or Europe.[64]

When he briefed Kennedy on the SIOP in September, Lemnitzer presented these arguments forcefully, aware that the planning for SIOP-63 was already well advanced and would include all of the crazy premises he had already rejected unless the president intervened. Lemnitzer's briefing hinged on the argument that the current "optimum mix" of target plans in SIOP-62 "should result in the US prevailing in nuclear war." He described the organizational reforms adopted since 1959, the results of study no. 2009 of 1960, which led to the existing SIOP, the objectives of guidance, and the range of operational concepts that informed planning. He concluded with the emphasis that the SIOP was *designed* for execution as a whole" and that, although there were some "flexible" features, "withholding a portion of the planned attack could degrade our plan and the forces committed to it to the point that the task essential to our national survival might not be fulfilled."[65]

Lemnitzer did not succeed in persuading the president, who had the highest regard for McNamara and a tendency to distrust the military. SIOP-63 was formally adopted in January 1962. The plan included five "primary attack options" designed to be executed under varying conditions of preemption or retaliation, to withhold attacks in a number of different ways, and to focus on the destruction of Soviet forces while holding "reserve forces capable of destroying the Soviet urban society, if necessary, in a controlled and deliberate way." The plan constituted the basis for a "second strike counterforce strategy," which has remained a part of official doctrine ever since.[66]

The Short Career of No-Cities

In early 1962, McNamara revealed the new U.S. strategy to the public; his sense of political timing for such a decision remains a mystery. McNamara's discussion of no-cities at a secret meeting of NATO ministers in Athens got quite a cold shoulder, especially from the French. De Gaulle had already ridiculed publicly the American strategic guarantee to defend Europe, scoffing at the idea that the United States would ever "sacrifice New York for Paris." The French, moreover, were clearly intending to develop a nuclear deterrent of their own, independent of U.S. nuclear capabilities. But like the small British nuclear force, this would squelch the whole logic of no-cities, because it would be capable only of attacking Soviet cities and would therefore implicate the United States in a strategy that was the antithesis of measured, countermilitary responses. What domestic political benefits were intended to result from public revelation of "counterforce/no-cities" is an also an enigma. Preoccupied with internal squabbles and the urge to send a clear message to enemies at home and abroad that the era of change had begun, McNamara and his Pentagon advisers seem simply to have been anxious to make the doctrine public. In a speech drafted by his special assistant Adam Yarmolinsky, no-cities began its short career as American declaratory doctrine as part of the 1962 commencement ceremony at the University of Michigan.

Just a month before the Cuban missile crisis, McNamara gave a speech stressing the military as well as the moral logic of the new doctrine:

> The United States has come to the conclusion that, to the extent feasible, basic military strategy should be approached in much the same way that conventional military operations have been regarded in the past. That is to say, principal military objectives, in the event of nuclear war, should be the destruction of the enemy's military forces, not his civilian population.

If retaliation could be directed against the Soviet Union's military machine, not its civilian innocents, and if this could prevent the Soviets from attacking American cities, lives could be saved.[67]

Above all, flexibility was enshrined as an ultimate objective of U.S. nuclear doctrine. Earlier that year in a speech in Chicago, McNamara had been even more explicit:

> Our forces can be used in several different ways. We may have to retaliate with a single massive attack. Or, we may be able to use our retaliatory forces to limit damage to ourselves, and our allies, by knocking out the enemy's bases before he has time to launch his second salvos. We may seek to terminate a war on favorable terms by using our forces as a

bargaining weapon—by threatening further attack. In any case our large reserve of protected firepower would give an enemy an incentive to avoid our cities and to stop a war. Our new policy gives us flexibility to choose among several different operational plans. . . .[68]

The Soviet response was immediate: McNamara was a craven warmonger. Across the country, the American public seemed to agree, recoiling from the blithe descriptions of how to fight a nuclear war. The speech sounded odd not just to the innocent audience of graduating college seniors but to everyone other than the handful of experts who had grown inured to the horror that nuclear weapons inspire in the average citizen. Perhaps the Joint Chiefs got the message, but the public was terrified.

McNamara's blunder was reminiscent of another palpable reminder of nuclear vulnerability. The Berlin crisis had sparked the greatest level of public fears about the nuclear menace in the history of the American psyche, exacerbated by Kennedy's televised address in the midst of the crisis, calling for a nationwide fallout shelter program.

Kennedy's civil defense initiative was the product of the president's personal attitudes, taken against the advice of key advisers like Carl Kaysen, who knew such plans to be expensive fantasies unrelated to effective nuclear strategy. The black-and-yellow signs that designate nuclear shelters are still in American government buildings and public high schools. Citizens also took to private shelters, deluging the Pentagon with calls about how best to construct shock-resistant basements or underground shelters. *Life* magazine ran a series of articles on the techniques of fallout shelter construction, accompanied by a letter from Kennedy urging all Americans to "read and consider seriously" its contents. Yarmolinsky spearheaded the effort to adapt the series into a government pamphlet, an effort that aroused extreme controversy. An unexpected convert to the cause who even built his own shelter, Yarmolinsky produced a draft that described the postattack environment as quite survivable and the shelter program as a boon to free enterprise.[69]

In the media and in public discussions, questions about "nuclear ethics" abounded. Do you have to take in neighbors and friends in the event of nuclear attack if you have a shelter? A columnist for the Catholic magazine *America,* the Reverend L. C. McHugh, advised his readers that it was consistent with the Catholic faith to shoot neighbors if they tried to force their way into your shelter. For schoolchildren, Bert the Turtle taught the techniques of hiding under desks—"Duck and cover." That was the first postwar precursor of the SDI.

This was the era not just of *Dr. Stangelove* and *On the Beach* but of an even more vivid expression of nuclear nightmares: movies about mutants. They included *The Blob, The Attack of the Crab Monsters,* and *Them!,* about an invasion of giant ants apparently escaped from the Los Alamos nuclear laboratory. Tom Lehrer sang about lovers walking arm in arm in arm. Atomic paranoia was born, a feature of mass culture that has profoundly influenced American politics.[70]

By November of 1961, Ted Sorensen, Kennedy's speech writer who had earlier insisted that civil defense be pursued, advised Kennedy that it was becoming "our number one political headache." Ironically, one of the fatal blows to the program was struck by none other than Edward Teller, later the godfather of the SDI. Kennedy's science adviser, Jerome Wiesner, seized the opportunity to expose the madness of civil defense to Kennedy by arranging a meeting with Teller, an avid proponent. Teller's scheme, which hinged on a $50 billion nationwide plan involving the construction of shelters whose depth would be increased progressively as the Soviets developed more-capable weapons, was so absurd that it helped the president see the whole idea as a political liability.[71]

The Cuban Missile Crisis

The fights over SIOP-63 and the no-cities doctrine were soon overshadowed by developments in Cuba, which forced the administration to consider tactical decisions of more immediate importance. The Cuban missile crisis required the young president to confront for the second time the most fundamental questions of the atomic age: Is there such a thing as a "tolerable" level of nuclear risk? How do you assess the importance of the objective against the possible risk to millions of American lives? Are the consequences of nuclear engagements calculable, and, if so, what is the upper limit of bloodshed and adversity the nation should be willing to face? Unlike conventional engagements, where the costs and consequences evolve over time and give leaders the opportunity to reevaluate the merit of the objectives being sought, the contemplated use of nuclear weapons offered no such consoling margin of time—or error.

By the time of the Cuban crisis, America's strategic superiority over the primitive Soviet nuclear arsenal had been well documented. But it gave President Kennedy only cold comfort. The very weakness of the Soviet Union, it was believed, might prompt an irrational or accidental launch of missiles and result in an "unacceptable" level of American casualties. McNamara's previous intellectual architecture had suggested an ability to use "flexible options" and "limit damage" in a nuclear exchange, but such formalistic theories of nuclear engagement bore no relevance to the frightened men charged with resolving a dangerous crisis. The elegance of the McNamara doctrine dissolved in the real-world terror of the moment, captured by Kennedy's comment "What difference does it make? They've got enough to blow us up anyway."[72]

The Kennedy administration's experience in the Cuban missile crisis highlights the disparity between nuclear doctrine and the actual sentiments of the civilian political leadership when tested in crisis. On the one hand, no Kennedy official had questioned that the policy of massive retaliation had to go. As an intellectual exercise and a political posture, this led naturally to consideration of limited-war strategies. On the other hand, when tested, no one in the Kennedy administration believed that nuclear war really could be contained. As a practical matter, limited nuclear war was not taken seriously as a credible military option, and any level of nuclear confrontation with the Soviet Union was deemed so dangerous that consensus on acceptable thresholds proved elusive.

In fact, the relation between doctrine and behavior was so slight that virtually no reference in the transcripts of the meetings suggests that anyone ever thought about flexible options during the week of the crisis. Recently declassified audiotapes of the proceedings of the executive committee charged with handling the crisis—which included all of Kennedy's most-senior advisers—reveal starkly the difference between paper war plans and crisis management.

General David Burchinal, the director of plans for the Air Staff, tells a revealing story. McNamara was with the Joints Chiefs in their classified meeting area, the "tank," and was brought the news that a U-2 spy plane had strayed into Soviet territory. "McNamara turned absolutely white and yelled hysterically 'This means war with the

Soviet Union. The President must get on the hot line to Moscow.' And he ran out of the room in a frenzy."[73]

To the military commanders who hated McNamara, his "emotionalism" was a source of cynical humor. Curtis LeMay has mocked the "panic" among civilians during the crisis:

> Everybody [was] scared to death around Washington here, particularly on the civilian side of the fence, that we were playing with the destruction of the world. This never entered my mind. I remember President Kennedy sent us all around a little silver calendar on a plaque with the dates shaded for about ten days during the Cuban missile crisis as being an earthshaking event. I didn't see any earthshaking event. . . . Of course, we were all prepared for it. The Air Force, particularly . . . SAC was completely a hundred percent on alert. . . .[74]

LeMay's statement reveals the fundamental difference between theory and practice. It was SAC's job to be prepared to fight, not to wring its hands over the fate of the earth. To LeMay, the fact that SAC was on alert was in itself politically significant. Had the decision to execute nuclear war plans gone forward, however limited in intention, SAC's behavior would not have revealed in the least that American doctrine had changed in 1962.

SAC "was prepared for it," but "it" was a war very different from any the civilian leadership could have sanctioned. Even the most limited of the "attack options" would have involved hundreds of weapons aimed at Soviet ICBMs, weapons that lacked the accuracy either to avoid inflicting major civilian casualties or to prevent a response from surviving Soviet missiles against American cities. In any case, McNamara today dismisses this prospect with his usual cold certainty. "We never conceived of using nuclear weapons," he stated categorically in 1986.[75]

The Cuban crisis also revealed how remarkably unsystematic the process for deciding to use nuclear weapons might be—personalities, timing, preconceptions, and physical and emotional frailties might all play a role. The discussions were frighteningly idiosyncratic and incoherent, marked by vast disparities in opinion about the state of the nuclear balance and the military options in hand. For example, Dean Rusk believed that the missiles in Cuba "would make it possible for them to knock out SAC bases with almost no warning." McNamara, by contrast, stated repeatedly that the missiles were a political problem, of no military significance. Neither opinion was based on empirical certainty. Arthur Schlesinger's description of the decision-making process—"this combination of toughness and restraint, of will, nerve and wisdom, so brilliantly controlled, so matchlessly calibrated"—is an artful description of an elegant fiction that has lived on in the public's mind. The transcripts and tapes of the meetings provide a rather different, more alarming picture.[76]

The Shift to Mutual Assured Destruction

There is a common misperception that the push for flexible counterforce options is a doomsday plot of a military bent on designing nuclear weapons for the battlefield. To the contrary, notions of limited options are still not popular in the armed services. Whereas Kissinger once asked rhetorically, "What in the hell is strategic superiority?" many commanders could still ask today, "What the hell is nuclear restraint?" Nuclear war is war. You do not punch someone in the nose who is armed with a submachine gun and wait to see what happens. Ideas of "restraint" belong to the realm of diplomatic, not military, tactics.

In general, military officials resist any policy that suggests interference with the execution of the full SIOP. The tendency is to view limited options as potentially drawing down forces from the SIOP for some half-baked response, or on behalf of some civilian notion of "restraint" or "assured second strike"—jeopardizing the execution of the central plan. As General Welch said, grinning, "People think SIOP stands for 'strategic,' but remember, it stands for 'single.' "[77]

To the extent that the military has accepted the concept of less than all-out nuclear encounters, it has tended to be as a justification for new weapons needed to execute the complex plans these intellectual abstractions have generated. This practice began with McNamara. It was the air force's way of demonstrating that no type of civilian intrusion would be allowed to interfere with the basic mission of SAC, to be prepared to fight nuclear wars.

After resisting SIOP-63 vociferously, the air force soon realized that the plan could be a blueprint for massive budget increases. Within a matter of months after its adoption, the air force embraced no-cities as a prescription for a first-strike counterforce strategy and asked for forces equal to the task. Since there are many more military than civilian targets and since military targets are more difficult to destroy, no-cities meant far larger weapons requirements. As presented to McNamara, the air force's ultimatum was essentially, If you want these unrealistic instructions operationalized, you're going to have to pay.

In 1962, the Joint Chiefs were calling for between 2,000 and 3,000 land-based missiles and 900 RS-70 bombers by 1970, orders of magnitude beyond what McNamara would approve. The SAC commander General Thomas Power argued that the country needed 10,000 missiles. During a visit by Kennedy to Vandenberg Air Force Base in May of 1962, Power had even tried to get around McNamara with a direct appeal to the president. McNamara recalled,

> The Commander of the Strategic Air Command met us when our plane landed. As we got into his car, he turned to the President and said, "When we get the 10,000 Minutemen, I . . ." At that moment, the President said "What did you say?" "Well, I started to say when we get the 10,000 Minutemen, we're going to do . . ." The President said "I thought that's what you said." And he turned to me and said "Bob, we're not going to get 10,000 Minutemen, are we?" I said, "No Mr. President, we're limiting it to 1000."[78]

Some members of Congress had encouraged the atmosphere of "first-strike mania" by interpreting McNamara's Ann Arbor speech as the basis for aggressive development of new weapons. No-cities was fine as long as it meant disarming first strikes against the Soviet nuclear arsenal. As one member of the House put it, "This Committee has been on record since 1961 in favor of a first strike posture under certain conditions. . . ."[79]

For the air force, McNamara's most searing decision was his frontal assault on bombers. In repeated memorandums, McNamara articulated his view to the president that the bomber, though not obsolete, was far inferior to the missile for carrying out nuclear operations. Missiles were not only more survivable and cheaper but also coincided more closely with flexible-response missions. He canceled the new RS-70 outright and cut funding requests for the B-52, which was already in production, in every subsequent budget.[80] To SAC, this really was goring the sacred cow. The manned bomber was the preeminent weapon, its war-fighting backbone—the nuclear version of the strategic-bombing mission that the air force thought so successful in World War II.

On the civilian side, however, some advisers, including Kaysen and Bundy, were arguing for even lower levels of forces than those approved by McNamara—600 instead of 800 Minutemen in 1962, and fewer Polaris submarines. In a rather sanctimonious memorandum to Bundy on November 14, 1962, Kaysen argued,

> On strategic retaliatory forces, I think McNamara has now come around to buying the arguments some of us were making last year. These arguments, however, are like the different arguments he himself made last year, justifying no particular numbers, and I still think it is true that he is buying more in the way of missiles than we need. *The real purpose of his paper* [the Draft Presidential Memorandum] *is more a defense against service demands for a bigger force than justification of the forces he has requested.*[81]

In other words, McNamara was being criticized for abandoning absolute logic and fiscal austerity of systems analysis in favor of bureaucratic compromise.

Faced with liberal budget pressures and service insurrection, McNamara began to repudiate counterforce in official declaratory doctrine, but he soon realized that new criteria would have to be developed to impose discipline on service requirements. In January 1963, he dispatched Kauffman to brief the air force and instruct it to stop using the declared strategy—flexible counterforce—as criteria for its requirements.[82] In its place came assured destruction.

The concept emphasized deterrence over war fighting; unlike no-cities, the new rationale could be quantified, and it could be operationalized with numbers and types of forces. According to McNamara, "assured destruction" meant having enough forces that would survive after a first strike to be able to destroy one-half of the Soviet Union's industrial capacity and one-fourth to one-fifth of its population in retaliation. This could be done with about four hundred megatons—the point at which a curve indicating targets destroyed for a given level of megatonnage "flattens out."

With the concept of assured destruction, McNamara tried to harmonize the acquisition of forces against a strategic rationale and finally to answer the question put by Enthoven in 1959, "How much is enough?" By buying Minutemen missiles in hardened launch facilities and Polaris submarines instead of bombers and more vulnerable missiles like the Titan, McNamara oriented the force structure toward survivability and a condition of assured retaliation. And by stressing the need to destroy urban-industrial targets rather than military forces, he could hold within strict limits the required number of weapons of any given type.

But despite McNamara's assertion of a new planning doctrine, the objective of limiting damage to the United States from a Soviet strike remained the key ingredient in *operational* doctrine and continued to drive requirements well beyond the criteria of assured destruction. As McNamara himself told Congress in 1963, "I do not believe it [MAD] is a change of strategy and plans. . . . It has been our policy to endeavor to target these [Soviet nuclear] weapons for destruction. . . ."[83]

In the fiscal year 1964 budget documents, counterforce was duly deemphasized as a strategic mission and the planned number of ICBMs to be procured reduced from 1,400 to 1,000. But the budget justification document also noted that urban-industrial targeting did not make optimal use of nuclear forces and, in a compromise with the air force, approved development of a new and more accurate ICBM, the Minuteman II. The whole purpose of the new missile was to provide greater accuracy to destroy "fully hardened targets," meaning Soviet missile silos.[84]

When McNamara approved the research program for development of multiple independently targetable reentry vehicles (MIRVs), moreover, he ensured that his enduring legacy would be counterforce. As he put it in 1964, "I intend to change the direction [of the MIRV program] to provide for the development of a capability for delivering three Mk12 A warheads to geographically separated targets. . . ." In 1965, he stressed the capability of the improved MIRVed Minuteman to increase the "single shot kill probability" against military targets. Although he claimed in public that MIRVs were directed at the Soviet ABM deployments, in the 1966 classified budget document, he specifically justified the number of MIRVed Minutemen as a counterforce system—without reference to Soviet ABMs.[85]

In retrospect, it is apparent that McNamara paid a high price for his fights with the air force over how many Minutemen to deploy: the development of MIRVs. The political cost of imposing cuts on the number of missiles the air force wanted was offset by the promise of a new technology. Limits on launchers were traded for a quantum increase in the number and quality of warheads. In the end, the MIRV decision was a triumph of McNamara's budgetary and strategic philosophies: counterforce on the cheap.

It is not clear that McNamara or any of his advisers really considered the long-term consequences of what might happen if the Soviet Union followed suit. The Soviets' technological inferiority seemed to make the Americans' MIRV decision prudent; any Soviet MIRV program was a more distant problem than the internal bureaucratic pressures coming from the Joint Chiefs and the specter of a Soviet ABM. Even as a prospective development, the Soviet MIRV threat was not a great worry to Kennedy advisers. An aide to Bundy, Spurgeon Keeny, wrote in a memorandum in 1965,

> I think the Bureau of the Budget's case against the MIRV is not very good ... based on the "worst threat" in which the Soviets put MIRVs on all of their strategic missiles.... If we thought that an all-out Soviet effort of this nature were developing ... we could change the firing doctrine for Minuteman so that they could be automatically launched in the face of attack or we could supply terminal defense at our Minuteman sites which would also radically change the exchange ratio.[86]

In fact, the Senate did note the danger of Soviet MIRV deployments. In a report prepared by the Preparedness Investigating Subcommittee of the Senate Armed Services Committee in September 1968, senators questioned the assumption advanced by McNamara that with the MIRV program "we will have achieved dramatically increased accuracies ... while the Soviets have made no such advances. ..." To the contrary, the report argued, "prudence surely dictates that we assume that [MIRVs are] ... also within the technological capability and resources of the Soviets. In addition, we must recognize that the greater throwweight which many of their missiles possess gives them greater flexibility to proceed with such warhead improvements as MIRVing. ..."[87]

One of the questions that will never be answered with certainty is whether McNamara's obsession with budgetary issues, holding down the number of launchers, clouded his judgment about MIRV technology. MIRVs offered a cheap way to buy off the services, declare victory on the launcher numbers, avert the ABM development that would have been a real budget buster, and still have counterforce. Had McNamara's relations with the Joint Chiefs been less hostile and had there not been a climate of urgency, would McNamara have had more time to consider the MIRV decision? Would he have chosen otherwise? His current views are not very revealing. He claims he never intended to deploy MIRVs at all: "It was assumed at the time we started research that we would never deploy it, if the Soviets agreed to stop deployment of ABM." This directly contradicts the arguments he made to the president on behalf of MIRVs as "hard-target kill" weapons.[88]

The Doctrinal Legacy

McNamara presided over a profound deepening of the division between declaratory doctrine and operational plans. Strategic doctrine became a device for trying to impose discipline on the bureaucracy and assuage the public, rather than a unifying framework for guiding nuclear planning. By permitting this schism to emerge, McNamara hoped to restrain force levels and impose fiscal discipline, while retaining damage limitation and counterforce objectives in actual plans. The military can plan all it wants, McNamara seemed to be arguing, but it will be limited in its strategic objectives by fiscal discipline. "You plan, but I'll buy," is how David Aaron, former deputy national security adviser in the Carter administration, described it.[89] In the end, McNamara's attitude was not that different from Truman's demonstrated indifference to the military's nuclear plans.

In fact, even the force levels eluded McNamara's initial drive for strict control. The strategic weapons approved by the McNamara Pentagon represented a large surplus, given the size of the existing Soviet arsenal, and were totally at odds with the forces that should have resulted from assured-destruction criteria. Although the number of launchers was restrained, continued adherence to damage limitation objectives placed upward pressures on requirements and permitted the air force to continue its quest for a first-strike, counterforce capability.

In the end, McNamara had won many of the budget fights but had lost the war over their operational significance. At the same time, his public reversal of doctrine from no-cities to assured destruction, by prompting a perception in Congress that he had abandoned the goal of American superiority, fueled congressional pressures for more weapons and higher budgets—the antithesis of what McNamara had hoped to achieve.

Though well developed in theory, moreover, the flexible options incorporated in operational plans were still large and indiscriminate. The SIOP remained the highest priority of SAC's missions, severely limiting the forces available for executing limited options quickly. For all of his efforts, the SIOP McNamara left behind in 1968 was largely unchanged from the one he had inherited in 1961. One Pentagon official said of McNamara's contribution in 1967,

> The SIOP remains essentially unchanged since then [McNamara's Ann Arbor speech of June 15, 1962]. . . . However . . . all public officials have learned to talk in public only about deterrence and city attacks. . . . Too many critics can make too much trouble (no-cities talk weakens deterrence, the argument goes) so public officials have run for cover. That included me when I was one of them. But the targeting philosophy, the options and the order of choice remain unchanged.[90]

To McNamara, the experience proved profoundly disillusioning. In 1967, Ivan Selin, the deputy for strategic systems in the Office of Systems Analysis, went to see McNamara to talk to him about how badly SAC had implemented his doctrine of flexible response. The idea of limited options was still a fiction in the current SIOP, Selin argued, especially in light of increases in Soviet forces. Execution of the first SIOP option, a limited counterforce attack, would now require so many weapons to destroy Soviet missiles and bombers that the Soviets would be very unlikely to perceive it as a limited strike.

The Lemnitzer argument in 1961 about the fallacy of limited options had become rooted in the reality of ongoing Soviet military deployments. Selin was trying to work it out with the JSTPS, but he needed the secretary's backing to make enough changes in the targeting plans to ensure that the SIOP reflected doctrine. "In principle I agree with you," McNamara responded, "but I just can't afford to spend the political capital." He had too many other fights on his hands and no longer had the stomach for this battle.[91]

McNamara has since repudiated his entire legacy of doctrinal reform. Plans, he argues, are meaningless, and nuclear weapons are "of no military value whatsoever." Kauffman is equally cynical. Nuclear strategy is "a bankrupt exercise, as bankrupt as the Penn Central railroad."[92]

Nuclear Superiority: From Forrestal to McNamara

The doctrine of assured destruction had a final legacy, one with tremendous political impact. It was blamed for the loss of America's nuclear superiority, and thus it earned permanent political disgrace.

By 1965, the U.S.-Soviet nuclear balance was a subject of great debate in Congress. The USSR had made major strides in its space program and was moving forward with an antiballistic missile system. However rudimentary, the Soviet ABM system was an important symbol, spurring concern in parts of the administration and Congress that the Soviets did not share the American "belief" in assured destruction. Although the United States enjoyed clear numerical and qualitative nuclear superiority, the Soviets were on the march. The rhetoric of America "asleep" and "falling behind," which Kennedy had intoned in his presidential campaign, was beginning to seem less empty.

The shift to assured destruction in declaratory doctrine had been duly criticized by American conservatives. By repudiating the first-strike option, the new doctrine seemed to be an abject acquiescence in the loss of America's nuclear preeminence. In a hearing of the House Appropriations Committee in 1963, for example, Congressman Gerald Ford, a Republican of Michigan, had challenged McNamara's assertion that we were approaching an era in which it would become "increasingly improbable" that either side could launch a successful first strike and avoid "a devastating retaliatory blow." Ford asked impatiently, "Are we so unimaginative, lacking in skill and diligence, to permit this to be upon us?" The very idea of mutual deterrence, from Ford's perspective, was no more than capitulation to the Soviets—the product, as Ford said in a subsequent debate in the House chamber, of "a wrong attitude, a bad frame of mind."

Reflecting an attitude that endures in the American ethos today, Ford stated angrily, "I refuse to concede that the ingenuity of 180-some million Americans cannot be channelled to preclude this grim prospect." In short, American know-how could overwhelm the Soviets if McNamara would just stop capitulating. More pointedly, the Republican congressman Harold Ostertag, of New York, questioned McNamara's new doctrine by referring to a recent newspaper headline that described the shift to MAD as "McNamara ... Rejects Effort at Force to Smash Red Missile Power." Congressman Melvin Laird, soon to become secretary of defense himself, accused McNamara of pushing the United States if not to a position of "underdogs" then to one of "equidogs."[93]

These exchanges set the tone of congressional confrontations with the secretary for the rest of his tenure. Repeated efforts to add funds to develop new technologies, however quixotic, were Congress's way of expressing its dismay at McNamara's failure to avert Soviet military gains. Egged on by high-ranking military officers, Congress put McNamara's entire approach to defense planning on trial. As Alton Frye summarized the mood, "The deep fears of Soviet aggression in a program for world domination sought relief in the kind of technological escapism represented by certain advanced weapons concepts." In light of the experience of the SDI, Frye's words have taken on a disturbingly clairvoyant quality.[94]

CHAPTER 3

The Politics of Parity: From Laird to Brown

ROBERT McNAMARA'S failure to bring nuclear plans into line with political objectives was the result not only of the technological difficulties of adapting nuclear weapons to the logic of limited war but also of the intractable resistance to his innovations from opponents in the military. By the mid-1960s, his frontal assaults on the "war fighters" had created a full-blown political backlash. Outraged military commanders sought solace in a sympathetic Congress, fueling an insurrection against the relentless intrusions of Pentagon civilians. In the end, McNamara's courage in taking on countless bureaucratic battles was counteracted by his lack of political finesse.

No one since has tried to attack the military's authority with such zeal. One lesson learned, it seems, is that the fight is not worth it. Every subsequent administration has nevertheless tried to rationalize nuclear plans and align the character of the nuclear arsenal with political objectives. None claims to have been successful.

Because of technological improvements in nuclear forces, flexible response, which remains the American strategy today, has become far more than the abstract concept it was under McNamara. Warfighting plans have evolved steadily and now include a wide array of nuclear options, from the massive to the highly selective. But flexible response still has a limited constituency in the military and the public. Many in the military continue to doubt its credibility as a

89

military strategy, while the public finds little comfort in the lexicon of limited nuclear engagements.

The fragile support for flexible response has made the managing of nuclear policy a taxing chore. Political leaders must fight a two-front war: ensuring that war planners are designing plans that actually support national objectives, while presenting the public with a compelling rationale for the nation's nuclear capabilities.

Over time, the two spheres have grown further and further apart. As the public has become more assertive about nuclear policy, the management of public opinion has inevitably taken precedence over scrutiny of the details of the SIOP in the priorities of political leaders. Public controversies have diverted the attention of high-level officials from the prosaic task of overseeing nuclear operations, an unrewarding one under the best of circumstances, to nuclear "public relations" and spin control. Allaying public fears and demonstrating authority over nuclear weapons is now a political challenge, met by designing new names for "declaratory" doctrines, giving reassuring speeches, and pursuing arms control negotiations. Planners, meanwhile, are left with the responsibility for translating vague political guidance into actual force plans, a task carried out with a minimum of political interference.

The evolution of nuclear doctrine from the late 1960s to 1980 represents a continual struggle to develop credible nuclear counterforce options to implement a strategy of flexible response. Major changes in targeting plans have taken place, and the apparatus for nuclear war fighting has grown far more complex. But the role of "outsiders" in the process is still remarkably modest. Despite four doctrinal innovations in the period 1968–80, always accompanied by a burst of high-level political attention to nuclear plans, the subject inevitably returned to political obscurity by the end of an administration.

In light of the schism in doctrine that evolved over the last two decades, the SDI seems less of an anomaly. President Reagan was more direct in his acceptance of doctrine as a domestic political instrument, unabashedly designing nuclear doctrine for maximum public appeal regardless of how disconnected it was from the reality of nuclear forces. But he was simply building on the legacy of his predecessors, using the rhetoric of declaratory doctrine for what it does best—marketing. Indeed, the SDI may seem no more out of sync with operational reality to some planners than the theory of limited nuclear options. These kinds of notions have always been peripheral to nuclear war fighting, they would argue, the pastime of civilian theorists. Indeed, if General White were around today, he might well find the "weightless dreamland" for which he denounced McNamara's strategists reincarnated in the fanciful notions of peace shields and layered defense.

Defenses, Round 1

The reluctance of Americans to accept the decline of American nuclear superiority was best demonstrated in the political struggle over strategic defenses in the period from the mid-1960s to 1972. The Laird Pentagon inherited the controversies from its predecessor. McNamara had left a legacy of partisan dispute about the growing Soviet nuclear capability, especially its deployment of antiballistic missiles. The Nixon administration had no interest in deploying nationwide defenses, something many in Congress were then urging, but it faced the immediate imperative of defusing congressional and public disputes over this issue.

For advocates of defenses, deploying American antiballistic missiles in the late 1960s was vital. A failure to rectify America's vulnerability to nuclear attack seemed like unprecedented abdication, the legacy of the MAD advocates willing to permit America to become a permanent nuclear hostage. For critics of ABMs, by contrast, the quest for defenses was quixotic and dangerous, a last-ditch effort to cling to the memory of a simpler age when the Soviets posed no real threat to American territory.

The defense debate had begun in earnest in 1965, when McNamara tried to convince President Johnson of the fallacy of a defensive strategy and to dissuade him from approving deployments of antiballistic systems. Building on work conducted in 1964 by the air force general Glenn Kent, then an aide to the director of DR & E, Harold Brown, McNamara expounded what was to become strategic creed— the inherent instability of an "offense-defense" competition. Defenses could be offset by an adversary adding offenses, and with existing technologies the offense could maintain its preeminence at lower cost. For now and the foreseeable future, the destruction the United States would suffer from a nuclear attack could not be limited in any meaningful way by building defenses, because the Soviets could simply deploy countermeasures to offset them—simpler, cheaper countermeasures, like additional warheads. Defenses could thus have the perverse effect of spurring the Soviets to move toward an offensive buildup that would make the United States more rather than less vulnerable.[1]

But the services supported defenses. A top-secret memorandum sent to McGeorge Bundy in November 1962 gave a preview of the incipient disputes over strategic defenses that were to dominate the debate by the end of the decade:

> The split . . . finds General Taylor joining the Chief of Staff of the Army and the Chief of Naval Operations in opposition to Secretary McNamara, with the Chief of Staff of the Air Force advocating a position essentially aligned with that of the Secretary of Defense. . . . General Taylor and the two JCS colleagues who join him feel that the most glaring deficiency in the US military posture is the lack of an anti-ballistic missile capability, especially in light of the growing evidence of a substantial Soviet effort in the same field.[2]

The pressure was not just from the Joint Chiefs, moreover. A top-secret memorandum from Dean Rusk to McNamara sent in November 1964, for instance, makes a fervent plea for ABM:

> I continue to feel that the possibility of developing a technologically feasible, as well as reasonably economic defense against ballistic missiles is a matter of immense political import. . . . This is one area . . . where we could achieve a significant neutralizing impact on any Soviet anti-missile successes. . . . Our effort must be large enough to manifestly provide for the survivability of our population. . . .[3]

McNamara essentially bought off his opponents by giving large amounts of money to a long-term research and development program for an antiballistic missile, the Nike-X, and gambling on its never being deployed. The tactic allowed him to tout the Nike-X's potential capabilities, superior to those of the existing Nike-Zeus, which the Joint Chiefs wanted to deploy.

However convincing McNamara may have been on the substance of ABM, President Johnson had a firm eye on the politics. A clamor for an ABM system had been growing in Congress for some time. Opponents of the Limited Test Ban Treaty in 1963, for example, including Senators Strom Thurmond, Republican of South Carolina, John Stennis, Democrat of Mississippi, and Frank Lausche, Republican of Ohio, had argued that the treaty would interfere with the development of an American ABM system. Johnson also faced an election in 1968, and one of his leading Republican opponents, Governor George Romney of Michigan, was already promising to attack him on the ABM issue.

By mid-1966, there had already been sufficient congressional support for ABM that $167 million could be added to the fiscal year 1967 defense budget. Johnson listened closely to congressional sentiment, particularly among the southern Democrats he counted as his closest allies. They generally were staunch defense advocates. With the help of such Senators as Richard Russell, Democrat of Georgia, then chairman of the powerful Armed Services Committee, Stennis, and Henry Jackson, the military had at last found a direct channel to the White House.[4]

In November of 1966, McNamara went twice to Austin to discuss the ABM question in private audiences with the president. After his second meeting, on the tenth, he held a press conference and revealed that the Soviet Union had deployed an ABM system; he did so apparently to preempt a news leak and to control the "spin" on the story. The Soviet deployment would have to be matched with enhanced U.S. offenses, he argued, including improved versions of the Poseidon and Minuteman missiles. Defenses were *not* the answer, he insisted. It might be desirable eventually to deploy a defense against China, because its forces would be much smaller, but it was still premature to consider such a response.

On December 6, McNamara again flew to Austin to meet with President Johnson, this time accompanied by Deputy Secretary of Defense Cyrus Vance, National Security Adviser Walt Rostow, and all the Joint Chiefs. The purpose of the meeting was to review the defense budget, but the dominant issue was what to do about ABM. McNamara had stood firm until that time, refusing to spend the funds appropriated by Congress; he had yet to be overruled, despite the Joint Chiefs' unanimous support for production and deployment of a nationwide defense.

Since most of the systems envisioned were ground based, the army's interest was significant, far more so than that of the other services. Under the McNamara reforms, strategic weapons competed with one another in the budget, rather than with the conventional

forces assigned to the services individually. A larger army appropriation for ABMs would therefore increase the army's share of the strategic pie—a long-standing goal—without jeopardizing other key priorities, like army divisions or new helicopters.

The Joint Chiefs had made a deal. In return for the other services'
support, the army pledged to back the navy's development of a new
sea-based ballistic missile system, and the air force was assured that
there would be no effort to have the army play a role in defending air
force missile silos. Their unanimity was a reflection of the new spirit
of cooperation among the Joint Chiefs, forged by their common opposition to McNamara.[5]

McNamara later described the December meeting as follows:

> The five Chiefs unanimously recommended to the President . . . the
> production and deployment of an anti-ballistic missile defense. The Presi-
> dent turned to me and asked me what my recommendation was. I said "Mr.
> President, that's absolutely wrong. I strongly recommend against it." He
> then turned to Walt Rostow. Walt joined with the Chiefs. He turned to Cy.
> Cy said "I strongly agree with Bob." So we had a situation where the five
> Chiefs of Staff and the nation's security adviser were taking one decision
> and the Secretary of Defense and his Deputy were taking another. That's
> a miserable position for a President. I did not like to push him too hard
> under those circumstances.[6]

According to McNamara's own accounts, he presented the president with two alternatives: either to move forward with the procurement of "long–lead time" items for the Joint Chiefs' preferred ABM
system, deferring any decision on deployment and initiating discussions with the Soviets to limit strategic armaments, or to begin deployment of an anti-Chinese system. Johnson agreed to instruct the
State Department to start looking into possible Soviet interest in arms
talks and to postpone the deployment decision.

To McNamara, the key objective was to prevent any irrevocable
action that could lead to the offense-defense instability described in
the Kent study. His assessment took into account that the president
was extremely vulnerable to the mounting criticism of the Vietnam
War from the Democratic Left and that, like all new presidents, he
was eager to demonstrate control of the nuclear threat. With this in
mind, McNamara could argue that "a dramatic act of restraint," like
forgoing ABM, could lay the basis for Johnson's peaceful legacy.
Funds would still be spent on predeployment activities for the

Nike-X, however, to defuse political pressure. In turn, McNamara reasoned, counterpressures against ABM could be activated by casting its deployment as threatening prospects for accommodation with the Soviet Union, increasingly a popular cause with the public.[7]

However clever McNamara's domestic political maneuvers, the Soviets were not cooperative. After an unsuccessful meeting with Premier Aleksei Kosygin in June at Glassboro, New Jersey, in which Kosygin emphatically rejected McNamara's concept of defenses as "destabilizing" and which was followed almost immediately by the announcement that the Chinese had detonated a hydrogen bomb, Johnson told McNamara that a deployment decision had to be announced by the following January. McNamara revealed the decision to move forward with a U.S. ABM in his now famous speech to a conference of newspaper editors on September 18, 1967, in San Francisco.

The speech confused all but a handful of insiders. Fourteen pages were dedicated to the futility of the strategic arms race. Three pages discussed the offense-defense dynamic and portrayed defenses as an inherently losing proposition. The final page returned to the themes of the "mad momentum intrinsic to the development of all new nuclear weaponry." But sandwiched between the last two sections was the announcement that the United States now had the capacity to defend against a Chinese nuclear attack and that it would "begin actual production of such a system at the end of this year." He called the system the Sentinel.[8]

McNamara's advisers have disagreed as to just how deliberately their former boss planned to sabotage the proposal by giving the ABM system such a limited mission. A few think it was just political "damage limitation"—choosing among the least onerous of several bad political compromises. Others believe that McNamara knew that the Chinese threat was so uncompelling as a strategic rationale that attaching the ABM decision to it would force the debate back to first principles: why bother?

In either case, McNamara ceded on the deployment to regain the terms of the strategic debate. He won Johnson's approval for repudiating the idea of ABM as the salvation of American nuclear superiority by separating it from both the Soviet threat and any politically popular promises for population defense, thereby setting in motion what was to become the architecture for negotiated, mutual arms restraint. In a political climate in which the only acceptable alternatives for dealing with the Soviet threat were considered to be nuclear superiority or complete disarmament, McNamara's ideas for incremental limits were truly "an unnatural act," as Paul Warnke later called arms control.[9]

Once attached to a limited mission and made concrete in the details of an actual deployment, defenses were demystified, relegated to prosaic debate over technical capabilities and costs. The progenitors of the current advocates of "terminal defense" who in 1967 read McNamara's speech as official sanction of a multibillion-dollar nationwide defense were proved wrong. Presaging a speech given by Senator Sam Nunn, a Democrat from Georgia, twenty years later (see chapter 6), McNamara yielded to his opponents on a dubious deployment scheme in order to restore the primacy of the strategic framework he favored—deterrence based on arms limitations negotiated with the Soviet Union.

Defenses, Round 2

McNamara left the Pentagon before the real controversy over his speech began. By the time of the presidential election in 1968, the political climate had changed dramatically. Dominated by the Vietnam War, the congressional mood had grown more critical of Pentagon policy and American citizens more assertive. Partly this was due to the strange psychology of defenses. Having made it clear that it was not possible to defend American lives or property, the ABM decisions of both the Johnson and the Nixon administrations had the perverse effect of reminding Americans of their vulnerability to nuclear attack.

When Richard Nixon moved into the White House in January 1969, the Sentinel ABM system envisioned by McNamara was almost immediately renamed the Safeguard. In the process, it gained a new mission—protecting U.S. nuclear forces from Soviet attack—but was redesigned to be cheaper than the increasingly costly system the Johnson administration had sanctioned.

The Congress had begun holding open hearings on the subject in November 1967. These discussions, which brought together administration witnesses and scientific critics, were helping to publicize the system's liabilities and to politicize the whole issue. This was unprecedented. Sensitive issues of national security had always been discussed behind closed doors, especially in the Joint Atomic Energy Committee, and only rarely had dissent from the administration's national security policies been given a hearing.[10]

A political coalition of congressional representatives, scientists, and public activists opposing ABM had been growing since the time of McNamara's speech. Americans who lived near sites where the army wanted to deploy ABM organized strident political opposition, convinced they were going to be "nuked" by the very systems intended to protect them. Distinguished scientists engaged in acrimonious denunciations of the system's technical limitations. Others argued that it was a strategic misstep, sending the wrong signal to the Soviet Union. Still others saw it as a needless diversion of scarce resources. Senator Walter Mondale, a Minnesota Democrat, argued,

> The uneasy deterrence balance is threatened by the deployment of the ... [ABM] system. This threat comes from uncertainties—the uncertainties as to whether an anti-ballistic-missile system can work ... the uncertainties which come with the inevitable introduction of offensive weapons to negate the effectiveness of an ABM defense ... the uncertainties about our intentions when the deployment of more weapons indicates a decision to spend on military materials rather than on peaceful and domestic needs.[11]

The decision to change the mission, and the name, of the planned ABM system was a deliberate effort to find a more compelling marketing strategy for it. Congressional debate on the Sentinel had made it clear that a defensive system whose mission was limited to protecting against the Chinese nuclear threat was too weak to sustain political support. Mistakenly, however, the reincarnation of the Sentinel as the Safeguard was taken as a sign of the administration's capitulation to the anti-ABM forces. A *New York Times* editorial commented, "The Congressional pressure that spurred the Nixon Administration to halt deployment of the Sentinel antiballistic missile system signals a healthy new disposition on Capitol Hill to challenge the military-industrial complex. . . ."[12] The limits the administration itself put on the program helped create the impression that it was a technological mongrel in search of a purpose. Marketed as an anti-Soviet system, Safeguard had no pretensions of protecting American lives. As Kissinger later maintained, the rejection of any promise of population defense "was a purely political decision," designed to allay the fears of arms control advocates who thought it would threaten the Soviets. But this undercut its popular appeal. "Our dilemma was that we could sell an ABM program to the Congress apparently only by depriving it of military effectiveness against our principal adversary," he complained.[13]

In any case, the Safeguard decision was espoused only halfheartedly by key administration advisers. It helped assuage conservatives. It even provided prudent "insurance" against other potential nuclear states. But its chief value, certainly for Kissinger, the key architect of the new administration's security policy, was as a bargaining chip. It was needed to counter the technology of the Soviets and indicate that Americans could beat them at the game. As Kissinger explained, "Offering to limit our ABM could become the major Soviet incentive for a SALT agreement."[14]

In a climate in which the Congress was pushing for cuts in both offensive and defensive forces, trading in the ABM for limitations on offenses was one way to protect American nuclear capabilities—buying off domestic critics and getting Soviet restraint into the bargain. Since a Strategic Arms Limitation Talks (SALT) agreement was central to the overall strategy for the administration's new policy of détente, enticing the Soviets into a new era of strategic accommodation made the bargaining chip especially important politically. As one fervent supporter of defenses noted bitterly, "The arms control process was even more of a pedagogic tool for the Nixon Administration than for its predecessor."[15] In other words, giving up a capability to defend themselves was part of the price Americans paid for the effort to re-create the Soviet Union in their own strategic image. Since the Soviets never really agreed with the logic of assured destruction and retained defenses as part of their strategy, critics argued, it was a very bad deal.

In the end, congressional opinion combined against the Safeguard system. Although the administration bought time by arguing that it was needed for negotiating leverage—implying that ABM opponents would be jeopardizing the SALT process—the Senate Armed Services Committee voted in mid-1971 to restrict Safeguard to two sites, down from the twelve originally requested.[16] On May 26, 1972, a limit of two sites on each side was enshrined in the ABM Treaty signed by President Nixon in Moscow. A 1974 protocol to the treaty further reduced the limit, to one site. As a final symbol of the irrelevance of defenses in American strategy, the United States unilaterally shut down its only site, at Grand Forks, North Dakota, two years later.

MAD Repudiated

Kissinger's strategy for ABM reflected a growing schism in the development of American nuclear doctrine. On the one hand, the restriction of Safeguard to the defense of missile silos was intended as a deliberate sop to arms control advocates who would have seen an effort to develop population defenses as a repudiation of the "doctrine" of assured destruction. By 1969, despite the doctrinal innovations brought about by no-cities and flexible response, assured destruction had earned its place as public creed. Whatever the reality of operational doctrine, the couching of policy as assured destruction had become essential to reassuring domestic political audiences. Declaratory doctrine had developed a life of its own.

At the same time, Kissinger saw the Soviet Union's continuing ABM deployment and Kosygin's behavior at Glassboro as clear indications that the Soviets did not share American views about assured destruction or about the destabilizing character of defenses—or that if they did, they just did not care. The Soviets had to be shown that the United States could respond on their level and then be induced to join in mutual repudiation of defensive technologies. "For Kissinger and Nixon," according to one critic, "the American ABM was to be at once a bargaining chip and a pedagogic tool in the service of MAD."[17]

While seemingly logical, this assessment is dead wrong. Although its handling of domestic critics and the Soviets indicates an artful manipulation of declaratory doctrine, the Nixon administration came into office determined to repudiate all vestiges of assured destruction in actual military planning. The first formal study charged with this objective, later the basis for National Security Study Memorandum (NSSM) 3, was intended to be the stake driven through the heart of assured destruction: "Up to now, the main criterion for evaluating US strategic forces has been their ability to deter the Soviet Union from all-out, aggressive attacks on the United States," argued the study. From now on, however, U.S. planning would emphasize early "war termination, avoiding attacks on cities, and selective response capabilities [which] might provide ways of limiting damage if deterrence fails."[18]

This was not a radical departure to anyone familiar with the efforts of the McNamara era; in fact, the principal author of the study was Ivan Selin, the Pentagon staffer who had implored McNamara to let him work with the JSTPS to create real flexible options in SIOP-63. But the new crew portrayed these principles to Nixon as a fundamental change, and he subsequently adapted them in a speech to Congress in February 1970. "Should a President, in the event of a nuclear attack, be left with the single option of ordering the mass destruction of enemy civilians, in the face of certainty that it would be followed by the mass slaughter of Americans?" Nixon asked.[19]

Here was a repudiation of massive retaliation with the added twist of a rejection of the suicide implied by assured destruction. Instead, Nixon told Congress, the United States would abide by principles of "strategic sufficiency," would rely on forces capable of deterring war by threatening unacceptable retaliation. No one probed how this was really different from assured destruction, except to note that it seemingly dispensed with the countersocietal retaliation on which assured destruction was supposedly based.

The speech was disingenuous, as are Kissinger's recollections of the legacy he inherited from McNamara. In his memoirs, Kissinger wrote,

> The first problem was to redefine the strategy for general nuclear war. According to the doctrine of "assured destruction," which had guided the previous Administration, we deterred Soviet attack by maintaining offensive forces capable of achieving a particular level of civilian deaths and industrial damage. The strategy did not aim at destroying the other side's missile or bomber forces. . . .[20]

Kissinger, an expert on nuclear strategy who had been working in the field since the 1950s, knew better. Assured destruction was not operational doctrine, and there were provisions in the SIOP, albeit limited, for something beyond just a reflexive act of massive retaliation against civilians. The new administration was merely building on the work done by predecessors, not altering policy radically. In any case, "strategic sufficiency" had no more operational meaning than assured destruction; it was the utterance of a new president putting his own spin on an old problem.

Kissinger was determined, along with the president, to recast doctrine in his own image and to claim the credit for it—the political impulse shown by every subsequent administration. As Nixon was telling the Congress about deterrence based on "sufficiency," Kissinger was energizing the executive branch to develop a more robust architecture for limited counterforce options.

MIRVs Eclipsed

Historians have pointed to the congressional defeat of the ABM system and to the subsequent signing of the ABM Treaty as the crowning achievements of domestic political pressure against an administration bent on nuclear excess. It is, in fact, the only time Congress has ever succeeded in defeating a major weapons system that had the support of the executive branch. The politics of the ABM debate are forever depicted by arms control supporters as a successful story of citizen activism, congressional courage, and the promise of future episodes in which arms control sentiment can roll back the inexorable power of the military-industrial complex.

Like the SDI debate just a decade later, however, the defeat of Safeguard has its own ironies. As Congress threw itself into paroxysms over the dangers of deploying defenses, the real future of the nuclear posture, limited options made possible by MIRVs, was being determined elsewhere. It is taken as an article of faith by arms control advocates that the reversal of the ABM deployment averted a dangerous arms race. It is rarely noted that it also absorbed political energies that might otherwise have been focused on the dramatic changes in the offensive arsenal taking place at the same time. Safeguard might well have collapsed of its own technological weaknesses, but that was not true of the MIRVs.

Alton Frye, who has written a brilliant and detailed account of the congressional actions of the time, observed that throughout the 1960s, as the ABM debate heated up, the American MIRV program had registered but slightly in Congress, the significance of the effort not at all. MIRV had reached the flight test stage with an invisibility scarcely imaginable for a program expected to cost upwards of $10 billion. . . . One finds hardly a mention of MIRV in the lengthy debates on ABM during 1968, despite the fact that MIRV was already closer to deployment than the defensive system and was potentially a comparably destabilizing system.[21]

The initiatives in 1969 and 1970 to halt both the MIRV program and the programs to improve the accuracy of land-based strategic missiles were the only deliberate attempts ever made in Congress to limit nuclear strategy through legislation. A number of moderate and liberal senators, supported by expert work from staffers who had formed a bipartisan coalition behind the scenes, took on the counterforce issue beginning in 1969. The staffers—including Frye, then an aide to the Massachusetts Republican senator Edward Brooke, and Larry Smith, aide to the New Hampshire Democratic senator Thomas McIntyre—had been well ahead of the curve, anticipating that MIRVs could prove far more destabilizing than ABM. But as long as ABM was *the* issue, the general feeling was that "the budding coalition against ABM should not change horses midstream by diverting its energies to MIRV."[22]

Like opponents of SDI in the 1980s, antinuclear groups during the early 1970s were so preoccupied with defenses that they had little time for or interest in other weapons developments. The coalition of grass-roots activists and scientists focused their energies on repudiating the Safeguard proposal technically—on demonstrating its inherent weakness as a system, its high cost, its lack of a real mission. As Frye has emphasized, there was no comparable "hook" for MIRVs. Absent a clear technical flaw that could be readily grasped, a strong anti-MIRV movement would have required an understanding of the arcane debates on nuclear strategy, and these could hardly create any fire in the political process.

The first effort to halt MIRVs in the Senate (Resolution 211) was introduced in June 1969 with forty sponsors. It urged the administration to negotiate a moratorium on MIRV testing as part of the SALT negotiations. On the House side, Congressmen John Anderson, Republican of Illinois, and Jeffrey Cohelan, Democrat of California, raised more than one hundred signatures for a similar measure, and Clement Zablocki, Democrat of Wisconsin, chairman of the Foreign Affairs Committee, convened hearings on the subject. At the same time, a number of more liberal members, including Congressman Jonathan Bingham, Democrat of New York, and Senator Clifford Case, Republican of New Jersey, pressed for a unilateral halt of tests. The latter proved to be a politically misguided venture, permitting defenders of the MIRV program to brand even the moderates' efforts as "unilateralist" clamors for restraint on U.S. nuclear modernization.

A number of external events coincided to weaken the prospects of the legislation: the testing of the first models of the Soviet SS-9, a land-based missile with multiple warheads (although not independently targetable) portrayed by hard-liners as a massive increase in Soviet counterforce capabilities; the Soviet negotiators' apparent lack of interest in the subject of MIRV bans (which would have codified Soviet technological inferiority); and the slow pace of the SALT process overall. In the absence of an agreement to get rid of the Soviet ABM, American MIRVs had a politically compelling strategic rationale.[23]

Many in the Congress had been heartened by Nixon's affirmation of strategic sufficiency as the basis for deterrence. Senator Brooke and others saw this as a sign of the president's understanding that stability required that neither side be able to threaten the other's retaliatory forces—a good basis on which to pursue limitations on counterforce capabilities.[24]

But there were enough contradictory statements by Nixon officials that it should have been obvious that sufficiency, like assured destruction, was not a binding operational doctrine. When General John Ryan, the air force chief of staff, testified before the Senate Armed Services Committee in October 1969, for example, he stressed the need for MIRVs to provide the United States with a highly accurate capability to destroy such hardened military targets as missile silos. Repeated Pentagon statements reaffirmed this mission. As Frye has noted without a trace of sarcasm, "If perfected, this kind of advanced MIRV system could reduce the President's policy to mere rhetoric."[25]

The disparity between the president's stated doctrine and Pentagon statements seems to have been interpreted in the Congress as a genuine error. Brooke brought these contradictions to the attention of the president in a lengthy letter in December and received reassurances from Nixon that the United States had no intention of "threatening a nation with a first strike." Nixon's letter emphasized that there was no "current US program to develop so-called 'hard-target'

MIRV capability" and claimed that the program to which Ryan had referred had been canceled. This was confirmed the following year by John Foster, the director of DR & E; "My purpose was to make it absolutely clear to the Congress and hopefully the Soviet Union that it is not the policy of the United States to threaten their deterrent capability," Foster testified to the House in June 1970.[26]

The comforting words were effective. Feeling they had won a victory—"cancellation of an actual program oriented toward counterforce," Frye exclaimed, as well as a presidential affirmation of "the exclusively retaliatory function of US strategic forces"—congressional critics were genuinely shocked when it was revealed in March 1970 that the first deployments of Minuteman III missiles, the MIRVed version of the U.S. ICBM, were going ahead on schedule. The combination of the SALT process and the political renunciation of counterforce had led critics to believe that the notion of restraint to strengthen deterrence had won the day.[27]

In fact, the Minuteman program had been humming along quite undisturbed by the political turbulence. In the fall of 1970, General Ryan, apparently unfazed by any of the preceding year's debate, gave a speech once more heralding the Minuteman III as "our best means of destroying time-urgent targets like the long range weapons of the enemy." Secretary of Defense Laird was hastily called upon to clarify the statement; he assured Brooke that the general was referring to a strike against "remaining weapons of an aggressor nation that had struck first."[28]

Even at the political level, Kissinger was not impressed by the anti-MIRV efforts. In his memoirs, he lumps Bingham's initiative together with Brooke's, characterizing both as unilateralist and misguided. He suggests that the effort was mostly inspired by sentiment: "In an emotional conversation with me on May 23 Brooke stressed that if the [MIRV] tests were completed, then indeed the 'genie' would be 'out of the bottle'; the whole issue was a matter of 'conscience.' "[29]

With a lot of controversy and parliamentary maneuvers, the Senate passed Resolution 211 on April 9, 1970, by a wide majority. It was nonbinding and honorific, but still an achievement: the first piece of legislation putting the Senate on record in favor of broad strategic restraint, with a specific recognition of counterforce capabilities as the most important area for negotiation. Brooke then set about developing binding legislative instruments that might force the administration to align its weapons programs with its rhetoric. A series of amendments proposed in the Senate Armed Services Committee in 1970 tried to limit programs intended to improve the accuracy of the missile force, including a modest funding cut for a key program—the Advanced Ballistic Reentry System—which was adopted in committee. A more controversial amendment, also sponsored by Brooke, would have prohibited the expenditure of funds to develop, test, or buy a MIRVed system capable of destroying hardened targets. It was instantly opposed by the secretary of defense on grounds of excessive congressional intrusion, however, and never put to a vote.[30]

The latter amendment was nevertheless an important harbinger of changes in the Congress. The product of an unprecedented staff effort, it tried to define and give political prominence to a sensitive and complex issue of nuclear strategy: the notion of "hard-target kill." The initiative had been devised after long discussions with Pentagon analysts about the arcane details of targeting calculations: circular error probable (CEP), pounds per square inch (psi), and probability of kill (Pk)—not the usual stuff of Senate debate. It was a new world: Senate staffers and Pentagon targeting experts trying to devise mutually acceptable limits on nuclear employment strategy.[31]

The amendment actually did include a working definition of hard-target kill: "that combination of warhead yield and accuracy required to generate the equivalent of one-third the level of blast overpressures and related effects considered necessary to enable a single warhead to neutralize a hardened missile silo." Its heroic effort at precision notwithstanding, the amendment got embroiled in partisan debate and never left the Armed Services Committee. It came to be seen as little more than a sign of opposition to the administration and "softness" toward the Soviet Union.[32]

Still, the "hard-target kill" amendment was an important event in the procedural history of congressional activism. As Larry Smith recalls, members were not used to the rigorous scrutiny of budget line items that the antiaccuracy amendments had required. For instance, jurisdiction over research and development, where funding for MIRVs and other strategic improvements could be found, resided in the Preparedness Subcommittee. Chaired by Stennis, the subcommittee had long been a rubber-stamp operation. R & D was not recognized as politically significant until after 1969 when the debate over

Safeguard, whose funds were in the R & D account, brought it political attention.

In the full committee, moreover, the younger senators who might challenge the Pentagon were largely overlooked. Seated at the bottom of the table in the hearing room, Senators Brooke and McIntyre would plead to their seniors, "Can you please speak up so we can hear what you're deciding?"[33]

According to David Aaron, then a staffer for Senator Mondale, the political problems for limits on improvements in missile accuracy were summed up by Senator Stennis's acid remark "Dammit, if I'm gonna get me a gun to shoot myself a rabbit, I'm gonna get one that shoots straight." That was the gist of the debate. The counterintuitive logic of accuracy restraint could not compete politically with the homespun common sense that if you're going to buy a weapon, it should be the best.[34]

In the end, the skirmishes between the Congress and the administration over nuclear doctrine and strategic weapons programs forced the White House to become more attuned to the political consequences of its rhetoric. They did not succeed, however, in imposing discipline on military operations or in obtaining decisions about forces. Brooke's pressures caused the administration to explain its policy in greater detail, and this in turn gave the Congress a better way to gauge force developments. But it was all to little effect on the operational side.

As a reminder that the refinements in doctrine being presented to the Congress were intended to affect the politics, not the operations, of nuclear strategy, the Pentagon submitted an urgent supplemental funding request just days after the successful conclusion of the SALT I agreement. This request included $20 million for improving further the capability of the new Minuteman III missile to destroy hardened military targets. It was the first of the "arms control sweeteners," force measures said by the Joint Chiefs of Staff to be "required" to compensate for what had been bargained away, and seen by political leaders as necessary to keep the Joint Chiefs behind the treaty.

Buoyed by the SALT agreement, the House passed the funding request without debate. Even the White House behaved as if it really did not know what was happening. According to Frye, when some senators asked about this sudden development, the White House privately acknowledged its chagrin over the contradiction between the program and stated policy, but for bureaucratic reasons had found it difficult to reverse the Secretary of Defense. Once the problem came to White House attention, the best hope of those closest to the President seemed to be that the Senate would quietly delete this offensive item.[35]

The Senate complied with the wish, but not without first engaging in a sharp debate in which many senators urged giving the Defense Department the funds anyway.

From N-STAP to NSDM-242

"When I entered office," Kissinger wrote in his memoirs, "former Defense Secretary Robert McNamara told me that he had tried for seven years to give the President more options. He had finally given up, he said, in the face of bureaucratic opposition. . . ." Kissinger was determined to do better.[36]

Between the time of President Nixon's first speech questioning the existing nuclear doctrine, in February 1970, and the formalization of the new doctrine, known as National Security Decision Memorandum (NSDM) 242 and signed in January 1974, Kissinger organized a number of interagency studies to examine the alternatives. The NSC was agitating to "get the bureaucracy to do something," according to one official involved.[37]

To work out the Pentagon's position, a group was established in January 1972. John Foster, of DR & E, was in charge, and its members included Gardner Tucker, the new director of Systems Analysis, Jim Martin, an operations research expert, and the retired colonel Archie Wood, then a civilian employee in Systems Analysis. Over time, this group became the main focus of the interagency effort and was expanded to include representatives from the State Department, the CIA, the NSC, and all the relevant bureaus of the Pentagon. The staff director was Brigadier General Jasper Welch, of the air force, a former weapons designer from Livermore National Laboratory, who was Foster's close friend.[38]

Foster was apparently not thrilled with the assignment. When he asked Welch to chair the group, he said, "I can't deal with the JCS and Omaha. They'll tear me apart." Aside from appreciating Welch's military background, the SAC officials were vastly relieved to have been liberated from McNamara's whiz kids. "They didn't want the whiz kids pushing buttons in the Pentagon, they didn't want to lose control, and they didn't want to be asked to do things they couldn't do. It's bad for deterrence to say, 'We can't do this,' " said Welch. This was key: the SAC planners had just been through seven years in which civilians had asked them repeatedly to create nuclear plans that they thought totally unrealistic.

The resulting study, known as the National Nuclear Strategic Targeting and Attack Plan, or N-STAP, was an eighteen-page document, which took the form of instructions from the secretary of defense to the JCS. It was to provide concrete instructions to SAC, written in a way, according to Welch, "so if it appeared verbatim in Omaha, it would be understandable, actionable, useful." For Welch, the goal was to avoid the abstractions of the McNamara heritage, to be realistic and practical. This was also a way of avoiding friction: the study process involved frequent interaction with SAC personnel, to get their views on what could and could not be done.[39]

One source of serious dispute between the military and the whiz kids had been the latter's refusal to understand the concern that analysis of American military weaknesses played into the hands of the enemy. This is dogma at SAC. It is the antithesis of the approach of the intellectuals, who believed that every problem should be identified, analyzed, and solved. To the whiz kids, the military was just reluctant to admit failures. To military men, it seemed the whiz kids thought they were still playing with computers in Santa Monica, not the nation's ultimate security. This was not going to happen with the N-STAP. Nothing was put on paper without the prior approval of Welch, who instructed the staff to prepare the documents in such a way that, if they were leaked, "it would help deterrence."[40]

In another effort to avoid the pitfalls of the McNamara era, there was an explicit decision not to criticize predecessors. Regardless of what individuals found in their investigation, they were prohibited from attacking agencies or accusing others of failures. The point was to build consensus and to preserve American credibility. "What were we going to say? 'You guys screwed up. We've been kidding, the deterrent wasn't good all along'?" asked Welch. This was a long way from the strident attacks on the competence of uniformed officers that characterized McNamara's unwelcome visits to Offutt.[41]

One of the first decisions that had to be made was whether the N-STAP was a "force-building exercise" (identifying the forces needed to carry out a new doctrine) or a "targeting exercise" (rearranging existing forces to meet the criteria of limited options). As a political compromise, it ended up being the latter. Welch recalls, "In order to get the systems analysis crowd, led by Arch Wood, I had to say we couldn't build forces. I maneuvered it so he could see it as a big concession. Johnny [Foster] and I had plenty of other places to work strategic modernization."

Two main question were being asked: (1) What can we destroy with certainty? (2) What would the Soviets fear to lose the most? The first question resulted in the grouping of high-quality weapons with high-priority targets according to exacting "damage expectancy" criteria. These so-called major attack options were expected to destroy valuable military assets with a high degree of certainty. The plan then moved down to successively less important targets, each of which could be destroyed with less effectiveness and efficiency, while still meeting the criteria of the plan. This was one way of making targeting efficient: ensuring that weapons on targets would actually do the job, with the explicit provision that some lesser-priority targets would not be covered as effectively.

Discussion of the second question—what targets were most valuable to the Soviets—focused largely on traditional criteria, including targets that contributed to the USSR's "ability to wage defense of the homeland," the continuity of its national command authority, and its overall military-industrial capability. But the Welch group also came up with an innovation: targets that made possible the continuation of the Soviet state as a modern, industrial society. The survival of that sector, the group reasoned, was what the Soviet government ultimately valued most, because of the nation's pride in having risen from the ruins of war and poverty to become an industrial giant. This was the basis of the subsequent decision to target "economic recovery" capabilities—ensuring that, in a war, it would take longer for the Soviets to recover than for the United States. The plans also called specifically for targeting the leadership of the Soviet Union—the party, the army, and the technocrats—to "make sure each of these groups finds itself *directly* vulnerable," said Welch, "down to and including the Oblast Communist Party Headquarters." It was a document dedicated to the psychology of deterrence.[42]

The study recommended four major targeting innovations that became the doctrine of NSDM-242 when it was first issued, in 1974: (1) the concept of "escalation control," which provided for limited options throughout a nuclear exchange and included the capability to stop short of general nuclear war; (2) the concept of withholds, targets that would be excluded entirely (such as population centers) to preserve bargaining leverage; (3) the targeting of industrial recovery capabilities; and (4) the idea that Soviet military forces, both nuclear and conventional, were to be targeted anywhere in the world. Taken as a whole, the targeting plan was a major triumph of technical precision and microanalysis.[43]

Welch's description is a little more colorful:

> We took people off the target list—explicitly. As much as anything, to keep targeting people from frittering good weapons. We could have options that you didn't treat every nuke as precious. If the ninth and tenth Poseidon warhead didn't have any place to go, that was okay. The notion of less than all-out options was nailed down. It could be a series of limited options and maybe never result in an all-out attack. That was a novelty. We got the China thing straightened out. We made sure the Soviets knew we could intervene in a Sino-Soviet war. And if [the plans] leaked, the East Europeans would have every reason to revolt: we would attack Soviet forces in their countries. Soviet forces were fair game anywhere in the world.[44]

The group continued to work on the development of techniques to hamper industrial recovery, now known as economic retardation, using analysts at the JSTPS and letting private contracts—to the Wharton School of Business and Dartmouth University, among others—to help define the problem. The various studies' conclusions are interesting as examples of the academics of nuclear targeting. The studies identify in detail different types of factories and industrial workers and their relative importance to the Soviet industrial base. They then estimate the "rate of recovery," using quantitative models to demonstrate how quickly a factory could be rebuilt and start functioning in the "trans-attack" environment. The whole idea is to figure out how much destruction you need to prevent workers from returning to their jobs after nuclear war or, put differently, to "retard significantly the ability of the USSR to recover from a nuclear exchange and regain the status of a 20th century military and industrial power more quickly than the United States."[45]

The accidental emission of radioactivity at a single power plant in the Soviet town of Chernobyl in 1986 resulted in the evacuation of entire communities and the poisoning for decades of agriculture and livestock throughout the region. Winds carried enough radioactivity released in the accident to kill or contaminate livestock in Scandinavia. That experience might suggest that dropping a nuclear bomb of a few megatons on a petrochemical plant in Leningrad would "retard" workers' productivity somewhat.

But Welch concluded from the complex econometric models that unless the Soviet state and government "crumbled" as well, the Soviet economy could not be prevented from recovering. Why not? "Because most factories operate on two shifts. According to the calculations of time needed to replace capital equipment (based on value added per year to capital cost to replace), if people survive, you can generate enough production in a year to rebuild factories," he recently explained.

What about fallout and radiation; how are those factors assessed? "All that chit-chat, it's not important. Even if a nuclear cloud falls on your garden, if you never washed your vegetables, you'd be okay. . . . All these flower children from the sixties have very weird ideas about what's livable."

The idea of retarding economic recovery was a triumph of traditional air force notions of targeting, consistent with the strategic-bombing campaigns of World War II that sought to destroy the German war support industries. For deterrence to work, from this perspective, targeting plans should inspire psychological devastation in the enemy leadership. The Communist party cell leader in Minsk should know he is on the list and should feel personally vulnerable. The head of Gosplan, the central apparatus for Soviet economic planning, should know that the USSR's industrial accomplishments could be wiped out at will by American power. And the satellite countries under Soviet domination should have yet another reason to think about insurrection once they realized that they would be unwitting victims in a U.S.-Soviet nuclear conflict.

The choice of criteria about what could be destroyed with certainty was comforting to SAC, for it was no longer being asked to do the impossible. These highest-priority targets included "soft" targets that did not require extreme accuracy. Targeting "economic recovery" was a good way of giving military value to what might otherwise have been construed as civilian targets. Moreover, given the supposed difficulty of impeding the rebuilding of industries, more weapons would be needed to achieve the goal of destroying "70 percent of the Soviet industry" in a general war.[46]

By the end of the Ford administration, four years later, the meaning of "economic recovery" seemed less clear. Drafting the last "posture statement" for Secretary of Defense Donald Rumsfeld in 1976, Kauffman inserted, he says, a few caveats about the utility of this mission for deterrence. "What's this?" asked Rumsfeld. Kauffman started to explain why he had doubts about whether this was an effective use of nuclear weapons, and how difficult it was to differentiate "recovery" from other economic or civilian targets. "No," Rumsfeld interrupted, "I mean, what are 'recovery' targets?"[47]

Once again, an innovation in doctrine, seemingly compelling at the beginning of an administration, had become an artifice. The innovation did affect the character of the targeting plans, by allocating "high quality" weapons to so-called countervalue targets. But the main objective of the innovation was to recast doctrine in a new way, demonstrating the appearance of political control, which, in the end, had only a marginal bearing on the real character of nuclear war fighting.

Kissinger and Limited Options

The N-STAP served as the basis for NSSM-169, the precursor of NSDM-242, and was approved formally by the president in the fall of 1973. Earlier that year, the NSC, with input from several other agencies, had taken over the work of the Foster panel. Phillip Odeen, a former Pentagon aide, was appointed by Kissinger to chair the group, which also included Colonel Jack Merritt, a military officer on detail to the NSC, Jan Lodal, a young former Pentagon analyst, and David Aaron, a staffer new to the NSC from ACDA.[48]

The task of revising nuclear options had been in the official NSC in-box since the beginning of the administration. It had been laid aside repeatedly because more pressing priorities, such as SALT I and the Vietnam War, occupied bureaucratic energies. Kissinger apparently assumed that his initial instructions from the preceding year were being obeyed.

He was mistaken. "No one wanted anything to do with it," Aaron recalls. "Since I was the first person from ACDA to work in the NSC and ACDA under [its former director] Gerard Smith was considered politically deviationist, they wouldn't let me work on arms control. So I got stuck with targeting. I sat on it for a year."[49]

Kissinger had paid one visit to SAC early in the administration, an experience that had underscored his frustration with the inflexibility of the existing plans. He wanted nuclear options that were useful for limited wars. Given the USSR's clear quantitative superiority in conventional forces in Europe and given signs of its growing capacity to project military force far from its borders, the United States had to be able to marshal its armed forces for global deterrence. With no prospect of defense budget increases in the aftermath of Vietnam, this necessarily meant finding a way to overcome limitations on conventional forces by means of nuclear weapons.

Political and security relations with NATO at the time Kissinger came to office were less than optimal. McNamara's European innovations, particularly the enshrining of flexible response as NATO's official doctrine in 1967, had not brought hoped-for increases in conventional forces or European political support. The new doctrine repudiated massive nuclear retaliation, calling for NATO to defend against Soviet conventional forces with its own conventional defense. It retained, however, a commitment to initiate the use of nuclear weapons if conventional defense failed.

The Nuclear Planning Group, a structural innovation of McNamara's intended to harmonize nuclear policies among the NATO countries, had instead highlighted fundamental divergences of opinion among them about the utility of nuclear weapons. Kissinger repeatedly expressed concerns about the lack of coherence in NATO strategy and the absence of proper plans for executing limited nuclear options. In what was to become the hardy perennial of NATO relations, the Europeans clearly saw flexible response as the U.S. commitment to engage in strategic nuclear war involving U.S. and Soviet strategic weapons in response to Soviet aggression, outside of European territory. This was the opposite of the objective of the United States, which saw the plan as escalating military responses in *Europe,* culminating in general nuclear war only if all else failed.[50]

Kissinger lamented the State Department's and the Pentagon's reluctance to looking seriously at plans for the *tactical* use of nuclear weapons around the world. A study completed in 1970 by the Pentagon had concluded that nuclear weapons had no decisive impact on the possibility of war in Europe. As Kissinger later wrote, "It was a counsel of defeat to abjure both strategic and tactical nuclear forces, for no NATO country—including ours—was prepared to undertake the massive buildup in conventional forces that was the sole alternative."[51]

He also was concerned about nuclear diplomacy in Asia. In light of his still secret demarches to China, it was of enormous importance to him to reform the SIOP in order to indicate to the Chinese that they were no longer part of the U.S. nuclear targeting plan. In February 1970, Kissinger had drafted a statement for Nixon to be delivered in the president's "state of the world" message, which declared, "The prospects for a coordinated two-front attack on our allies by Russia and China are low both because of the risks of nuclear war and the improbability of Sino-Soviet cooperation." Kissinger noted in his memoirs, "We had sent an important signal. . . . We would no longer treat a conflict with the USSR as automatically involving the People's Republic. . . . The Chinese had an option to move toward us."[52]

Kissinger continued on and off to look for ways in which demonstrations of preparedness to engage in limited nuclear encounters could help the United States against Soviet military adventurism. According to Aaron, Kissinger asked SAC in 1974 to devise a limited option that the president could use to threaten the Soviets if they invaded Iran. The Joint Chiefs returned with a plan to aim two hundred nuclear weapons at targets in the southern part of the Soviet Union—oilfields and airstrips. Kissinger was aghast. As one NSC official remembers it, "Kissinger bellowed, 'Are you out of your mind? This is global war.'"

Six months later, in a second try, the Joint Chiefs came back with a plan that called for placing one "atomic demolition" device on one of the main roads into Iran and then detonating two small nuclear weapons on the other main artery, to prevent Soviet troops from advancing. The Joint Chiefs had taken him at his word. This was certainly a limited option. Kissinger lost his temper again: "We go to nuclear escalation with three weapons, so the Soviets attack us with everything they've got? You call this a plan?" This was the last time Kissinger had direct interaction with the Joint Chiefs about limited-war plans. As it was, Kissinger himself did not know how to calculate a "limited" option, and the smallest options for nuclear attack ever included in the SIOP previously were so large they provided no useful basis for designing options consonant with Kissinger's instructions.[53]

It was not just the JCS who found Kissinger's nuclear ambitions hard to translate. It was also a problem for NSC analysts. The directives from Kissinger—the "criteria" for limited options to which he still refers proudly—were completely vague. Aaron remembers them as "more and more of these conceits, stuff from people who'd never been in a car accident, let alone a war."[54]

And it was not clear what the payoff would be. Aside from Kissinger's interest in demonstrating his personal authority, to "show we had our nuclear wits about us," as one participant put it, the issues dominating the headlines were not in this primordial backwater. The analysts turned to the task only under duress.

In early 1973, the group set to work to answer the question "If deterrence fails, what are our options?" There were two secondary objectives: to identify who would actually prepare "limited options," since SAC did not seem to want to, and to learn how to separate targeting plans from weapons acquisition decisions. The McNamara legacy, in the minds of the NSC study team, was a lot of weapons with counterforce capabilities, but no real targeting options other than massive retaliation. Clearly the planning apparatus was not working, and it had been a mistake to let SAC keep control of the operations. Despite increased civilian control of weapons buying decisions, SAC had simply adapted vague policy directives to fit its abiding interest in a large option for prompt launch.

The approach of the NSC staff was distinctly different from that of the Foster group. They were trying to operationalize political directives, which came from on high. The real question had to do with foreign policy. Their task was not to develop a war-fighting plan but to identify political and military options that would be available to the president if deterrence collapsed.

Without a capacity for limited options, the president would have only one choice, a massive nuclear attack, which would mean in peacetime that the condition of assured destruction would remain the real American nuclear doctrine. This was as untenable politically as it was dangerous militarily. From perspective of the NSC, nuclear weapons had to be able to deter at all levels of political and military challenges: against small nuclear attacks, against the threat of attack, and even against conventional incursions. Moreover, should it ever come to it, nuclear weapons had to be used in a manner that would permit political authorities to negotiate an end to the conflict at different points in the process of escalation. This was called intrawar deterrence.

The NSC staff were not about to ask SAC what it thought could and could not be done. Aaron, for one, was unimpressed with the Pentagon's contribution. "There were lots of studies," he remembers; "we just didn't read them." As far as Aaron was concerned, SAC would never accept the political objectives of limited options. "There's almost a clandestine relationship between the Right and Left when it comes to nuclear weapons. The JCS, like arms control advocates, know that when you pull the plug, you drain the tub."[55]

There was one point of clear consensus: the existing SIOP included no limited counterforce options. But beyond this recognition, the problems seemed intractable. Every small option, every "shot across the bow," seemed to suggest that the United States was afraid to use its nuclear capability. But every larger option the group examined risked provoking a general nuclear war. These problems were papered over with an agreement in the study group that even if the planned limited options could not be fully executed in fact, it was important for deterrence to have them in theory. The president, or at least Kissinger, had asked for it, and no one was willing to say it could not be done. The study concluded that nuclear weapons could bolster the achievement of international objectives and overall political confidence if targeting were made more flexible. It set out the guidelines for flexibility and the diplomatic objectives inherent in the targeting philosophy. The analysts also recommended some important procedures to increase civilian control over targeting and acquisition decisions.[56]

NSDM-242, containing the combined insights of the Foster and NSC-led interagency efforts, outlined three objectives for nuclear doctrine: (1) to deter nuclear attack on the United States or its allies; (2) to conduct "selected nuclear operations" and to seek "early war termination at the lowest level of conflict" if deterrence failed; and (3) if "escalation cannot be controlled," to destroy "the political, economic and military resources critical to the the enemy's . . . ability to recover . . . as a major power."[57]

As a practical matter, it is difficult to see how very different this was from flexible response: both envisioned a series of limited attacks primarily on Soviet military forces, culminating in the destruction of Soviet society if all else failed. The new policy did have an element of added flexibility, now more possible technically with the advent of more accurate MIRVs. It also placed greater emphasis on the *psychology* of deterrence, on holding at risk what U.S. planners believed the Soviets valued most. And it postulated a structure for negotiating pauses during war—"the anatomy of the endgame," as Welch put it.

The memorandum authorized the secretary of defense to put forward new policy guidance to implement the doctrine, incorporated into a document called Policy Guidance for the Employment of Nuclear Weapons (NUWEP). Far more specific than any guidance provided under McNamara, the NUWEP is still the primary document used today to provide instructions to the targeteers. It sets out planning assumptions, attack options, and targeting directives needed to carry out political objectives. The guidance is provided to the commanders of the Unified and Specified Command and to the director of the JSTPS. The JCS use it as the basis of their annual force planning, the Joint Strategic Capabilities Plan (JSCP).[58]

The completion of the first SIOP based on NUWEP-1, SIOP-5, took almost two years from the time NSDM-242 was announced. The changes required to be made in the SIOP were significant in two respects. First, SIOP-5 options could be smaller. Until SIOP-5, the smallest option in the SIOP planned for 2,500 nuclear weapons to be launched against the Soviet Union. Second, partly because the new SIOP was designed to impede the USSR's economic recovery but also because the intelligence community revised official estimates of the size of Soviet forces, the target list for SIOP-5 had grown to over 25,000 targets. This resulted in a large "gap" between targets and available weapons, helping at least indirectly to generate pressures to increase the size of U.S. offensive nuclear forces in order to gain more warheads to fulfill targeting requirements.[59]

The Schlesinger Doctrine

Throughout the Nixon administration, the issue of nuclear doctrine was dominated by Secretary of Defense James Schlesinger and Kissinger, unelected aides, not by the president. Nixon had left the whole matter to Kissinger. Schlesinger eventually persuaded the president to be briefed on the SIOP, but Nixon sat quietly through the briefing and later complained about having been bored.[60]

It is an irony of history that Kissinger, for all of his efforts, was scooped by Schlesinger in announcing the new nuclear doctrine to the public. Schlesinger had been only peripherally involved in the studies and did not become secretary of defense until July 1973, just months before the policy was disclosed. Schlesinger had run a number of studies on the subject at the Rand Corporation, and was thought to be influential in the development of the concepts on which the new doctrine was predicated. He was especially supportive of the theories of intrawar bargaining articulated by Thomas Schelling and others. According to Welch, however, Schlesinger's contribution has been vastly overrated. "Very few people in the active, agitating military—of which I'm a card-carrying member—ever heard of Schlesinger" before he was appointed to the Nixon Cabinet, Welch claims.[61]

For many critics who believe that Kissinger spent his career taking credit for others' work, there was much satisfaction in seeing Kissinger "Kissingered" by Schlesinger's speech on January 10, 1974. It launched the misnomer of the "Schlesinger doctrine" for all time. Kissinger was reportedly furious.[62]

The decision to make the new doctrine public seems to have had much more to do with bureaucratic vanities than with compelling rationales of foreign policy or domestic politics. Certainly, there was an impetus, in the aftermath of the Vietnam War, to announce to the world that the United States had a strong nuclear deterrent. This was particularly true for Korea, which some thought might be the next target of Communist expansion. A perception of growing European doubts about the American defense commitment also influenced the decision to announce the policy publicly. Many had argued that the SALT I process, which was drawing attention to the demise of American nuclear superiority, was unsettling to NATO, suggesting a superpower stalemate that would keep the United States from going to the defense of Europe. Kissinger noted the appearance of a "long-dreaded condominium" between the two powers that could be seen as restraining not just the capabilities of arsenals but the American commitment to European security as well.[63]

The SALT process also had helped jell conservative opposition to the administration's détente policies, both from those who denounced the 1972 decision to repudiate defenses and from hawks who thought the administration was moving with undue haste to conclude SALT II. Kissinger's "back-channels" to the Soviets, especially, infuriated the Joint Chiefs and helped set off congressional criticism of the negotiations.[64]

The reassuring of Korea and of Europe was integral to the NSDM-242 exercise. But there was no internal agreement as to how or when to discuss the doctrine publicly, and considerable resistance to revelation of the new doctrine at all. Some on the NSC, concerned that the political consequences would be adverse, hoped to delay public discussion indefinitely. If there was a conscious public relations strategy, no record of it is available. The schedule seems to have been driven by Schlesinger's impatience. His first "posture statement," the document presented to the Congress annually by the secretary of defense to justify the defense budget, was in draft and had to be concluded by February 1. Since the annual budget included a long discussion of nuclear doctrine, the administration's hand was forced.[65]

The announcement, in a speech at the Overseas Writers Association, prompted instant public and congressional outcries. Particularly loathsome to the press and the public were such statements as "There has taken place . . . a change in the strategies of the United States with regard to hypothetical employment of central strategic forces. A change in targeting strategy as it were. . . ."[66] Kauffman, now Schlesinger's special adviser, was out of town but was instantly called back "to clean up the mess."[67]

One more time, a secretary of defense was discussing holocaust in cold-blooded terms. Schlesinger seemed to want to make nuclear war wageable and winnable; he seemed intent on providing a rationale for new MIRVs and a first-strike posture; and he seemed to be reducing the inhibitions on the use of nuclear weapons for the resolution of political conflicts. In sum, he was abandoning assured destruction. White House speech writers were put to the task of damage control. The speech given by Nixon a week later affirming NSDM-242 said, "These decisions do not constitute a major new departure in US nuclear strategy; rather, they are an elaboration of existing policy." It was an overt contradiction of the repeated use of the word "new" in Schlesinger's speech. But it was too late: the public image of a radical departure in nuclear strategy had already taken hold.[68]

The Congress hastened to take up the issue. A classified briefing of the Arms Control Subcommittee of the Senate Foreign Relations

Committee by the secretary, on the subject of counterforce, was scheduled on September 11, 1974. As spelled out in the letter from Senator Case to Schlesinger on July 25 requesting the meeting, the political sensitivities were clear:

> My object in asking for this information is to examine the apparent assumption that enemy attacks upon US military installations would, in the words of your defense report this year, result in "relatively few civilian casualties." . . . While it is generally known that all-out nuclear exchange between the United States and the Soviet Union would result in the destruction of our societies as we know them, I do not think there has been any comparable public discussion of the human cost of the limited nuclear exchanges you have postulated.[69]

In fact, Case was already furious with Schlesinger. Having requested an earlier briefing, he had essentially been informed by Schlesinger aides that his question was stupid. "I was told," Case charged, "that the 'anti-military' attacks you would consider likely would be so small in scope as to make their effects largely localized and therefore not be susceptible to analysis of their larger societal consequences." The staff later realized they had committed a serious political blunder.[70]

In addition to Schlesinger, the briefing was conducted by Lieutenant General John Elder, from the Joint Chiefs of Staff, and Lieutenant Colonel Howard Graves, Edward Aldrige, James Wade, and Terrence King, from the Office of the Secretary of Defense. "We have no desire to develop a unilateral counterforce capability against the Soviet Union," Schlesinger began. He went on to commit a truly unnatural act, conducting a detailed briefing to senators on nuclear attack options and the fatalities that would be likely under different contingencies, as well as on Soviet targeting plans and the preparation of the SIOP to reflect the new concept.

There was detailed discussion of the vulnerability of American missile bases, "acceptable" levels of American casualties, and the ability to retarget weapons flexibly. Schlesinger illustrated his arguments with graphs showing the effects of a Soviet missile attack on Whiteman Air Force Base in St. Louis, the hometown of one of his principal Senate critics on the committee, Senator Stuart Symington.[71]

The exchanges between the Pentagon analysts and the senators are sobering. At one point, Terrence King stated that a Soviet strike to knock out all American Minuteman silos would result in just

800,000 casualties. The calculation was based on a one-megaton air-burst on each silo, "a conceivable attack if accuracy is good enough," King stressed. Given the size of the Soviets' current missiles, and their rapidly growing MIRV program, it was not a very likely scenario in any case.[72]

When Senator Case countered that he could not conceive of an American president's not responding to such a provocation with an all-out attack, Schlesinger coolly pointed out that such a response would sacrifice an additional 95 million Americans. That was the whole point: the president "might well choose not to respond with an urban-industrial attack against the Soviet Union but rather to re-spond selectively." The doctrine was meant to ensure that "the use of nuclear weapons would not result in the orgy of destruction to which the Committee has referred."

In an exchange with Senator James Pearson, Republican of Kansas, Schlesinger was pressed about Soviet reactions to the new doctrine. He clearly revealed one of the motivations underlying the doctrine, the growing suspicion among hard-liners about Soviet objectives under Kissinger's détente policy:

> The change in the targeting doctrine is not so surprising to [the Soviets] .... They always assumed that we would target this way. Therefore, why do we say so, what is the purpose of all this fanfare? ... It has the benefit ... of forcing upon the Soviet Union ... the choice ... [of] whether they will come to a true accommodation with United States or whether the process of détente will come to be viewed by the Soviets as simply a means to shift the balance of power in their favor.[73]

Schlesinger was denounced variously as "Dr. Strangelove" and "the architect of Armageddon" in the media. The outcry was reminis-cent of the one that had followed McNamara's no-cities speech. But for all of the congressional and public furor, NSDM-242 was eclipsed by larger political developments. Détente was on the wane. SALT was moving at a snail's pace, in the aftermath of a failure to achieve a strategic accord at the 1974 Moscow summit. Conservatives were taking up the cause of Soviet military advancements and "Minute-man vulnerability." The Watergate scandal had destroyed the credi-bility of the president. Just a few months after Kissinger made his famous remark lamenting the absence of restraints on strategic weapons—"what, in the name of God, is strategic superiority?"—the Soviets deployed their first MIRVs.

The Politicization of Nuclear Authority

NSDM-242 aside, another development helped focus congressional attention on nuclear war during the Nixon administration: the placing of American strategic forces on heightened alert during the 1973 Arab-Israeli war. Heightening the alert status—to so-called DEFCON 3—was Kissinger's response to a letter from Leonid Brezhnev to President Nixon proposing joint intervention to enforce a cease-fire in the war and threatening a unilateral Soviet military intervention if this offer was rebuffed. Led by Kissinger, the president's senior advisers decided to put American forces on alert to "show resolve." The action would be detected by Soviet intelligence almost immediately, they reasoned, and would provide the clearest possible signal of U.S. determination. They took this action without seeking the president's advice. According to insiders present at the decisive meeting, Nixon remained in the personal quarters of the White House. He was drunk. The public service performed that evening by Alexander Haig, then White House chief of staff, was to entertain the president in order to prevent him from crashing into the Situation Room.[74] Although the alert affected mostly conventional forces and was meant only as a "signal," the domestic reaction focused on the idea that nuclear forces were being prepared to fight a war with the Soviets over a country that seemed remote from American security interests. Many criticized the move as a cheap political ploy to divert attention from the Watergate scandal; others saw in it the recklessness of Kissinger, the "nuclear cowboy." There was one point of agreement: the absence of the president from the chain of command was terrifying.

Watergate and the 1973 crisis accentuated congressional concerns about who had the authority to start a nuclear war. Senator Alan Cranston, Democrat of California, had become particularly concerned after a meeting with the president in 1974 to discuss the impending impeachment hearings:

> As he spoke, he got very emotional. His work for peace, he said, was more important than any "little burglary" at Watergate. And then, perhaps to emphasize the awesomeness of the power he had administered so wisely and so well, Nixon said a very strange thing. "Why," he said, "I can go into my office and pick up the telephone and in 25 minutes 70 million people will be dead."[75]

Cranston's concerns were shared by other colleagues and a number of House members, including Congressmen Jonathan Bingham, Les Aspin, and Richard Ottinger, who proposed legislation to prohibit the president from authorizing nuclear war without congressional consultation. The legislation never went anywhere, and there exists currently only the most cursory of mechanisms for Congress to gain access to information about nuclear operations even in peacetime.

Under the rubric of hearings on the policy of first use of nuclear weapons, the House Subcommittee on International Security and Scientific Affairs of the International Relations Committee took up the question of authority to launch nuclear weapons in March 1976.[76] The real issue was not the traditional concern that a psychopathic submarine commander could launch without authority, because the system to prohibit the unauthorized launch of nuclear weapons seemed well established. The question was what University of Maryland professor George Quester described as "the schemes of mad Generals rather than mad Majors."[77] Now it seemed that the centralized system itself, in the climate of growing doubts about the president's emotional stability, could result in war. The impeachment proceedings had proven so psychologically taxing that Americans were beginning to fear that the president himself could go berserk. The public's sacred trust in the "guardians" was suddenly in question.

Secretary of Defense Schlesinger reportedly shared these concerns, enough to issue a directive in 1974 demanding that any unusual orders emanating from the White House to the armed forces be referred back to him before action—perhaps an unconstitutional, but probably a prudent, move. Another press report alleged that the president had to be persuaded in the last hours of his presidency to give up the "football," the briefcase containing the codes for launching weapons, to the vice-president.[78]

The Doctrinal Legacy, Part 2

In 1974, in a secret Senate hearing, Schlesinger discussed the progress being made in the techniques of "flexible retargeting" needed to implement the new doctrine:

In the past we have taken 16 to 24 hours, say, to change a target tape on a missile. One had to enter the missile in the silo to change the tape. Now, we are installing what we call the Command Data Buffer System in all Minuteman III wings which permits us to change target set in the missile computer in 36 minutes remotely from the launch control center.

As a result of NSDM-242, Schlesinger emphasized, a single option "could be as few as one or two missiles." Individuals no longer had to climb down into a silo to change the direction of a weapon. And it would be possible to program missiles for different types of targets in advance.[79]

But Schlesinger's technological optimism was not matched by actions that actually resulted in major operational innovations. The military felt no more comfortable with limited options under Schlesinger than it had with those imposed by McNamara. Planners were still being asked to develop military contingencies in which they would have to withhold their "best" weapons for some chimeric political objective. And the command and control infrastructure was still too weak to command precision nuclear strikes in the inevitable chaos of nuclear war. In the end, Kissinger declared the effort to reform nuclear doctrine a failure:

> Some new targeting options were . . . produced. Unfortunately, by the time they were developed they had been overtaken by advances in technology. Achieving a more discriminating nuclear strategy, preserving at least some hope of civilized life, remains to this day one of the most difficult tasks to implement, requiring a substantial recasting of our military establishment.[80]

Curiously enough, Kissinger's own predictions in 1960 had been borne out. In his book *The Necessity for Choice,* he had argued:

> While it is feasible to design a theoretical model for limited nuclear war, the fact remains that 15 years after the beginning of the nuclear age no such model has ever won general agreement. It would be next to impossible to obtain a coherent description of what is understood by "limited nuclear war" from our military establishment.
>
> The Air Force thinks of it as control over a defined air space. The Army considers it vital to destroy tactical targets, which can affect ground operations. . . . The Navy is primarily concerned with eliminating port installations. . . . Since disputes about targets are usually settled by addition—by permitting each service to destroy what it considers to be its mission—a

limited nuclear war fought in this manner may well become indistinguishable from all-out war.[81]

In retrospect, Kissinger squarely blames the military for thwarting his innovations. Although Kissinger was mostly satisfied with the cooperation of the Joint Chiefs in the studies leading to NSDM-242, and in their formal acceptance of the new doctrine, he believes this occurred because the change was presented as demonstrably in the Chiefs' self-interest: "The Joint Chiefs cooperated because they understood that the doctrine of 'assured destruction' would inevitably lead to political decisions halting or neglecting the improvement of our strategic forces. . . ."[82]

Beyond formal adoption of the new doctrine, however, the military's cooperation declined substantially. Civilian intrusion into declaratory doctrine was one thing; such intrusion into operations, quite another. Even the authority of Kissinger could be ignored when it came to the actual plans for war:

> Since our military operations are planned by combined commands not subordinate to the military services, the various chiefs of staff are more heads of procurement enterprises than of organizations responsible for implementing strategy. They are deeply suspicious of any doctrinal formulation that later might interfere with their procurement decisions. So it happened that a specific Presidential directive of 1969 inquiring into the rationale of naval programs was never answered satisfactorily in the eight years I served in Washington. . . . Despite semiannual reminders it was listed as incomplete on the books when we left office.[83]

His summary observation of the bureaucratic intransigence of the military seems equally applicable to McNamara's experience: "The response [to directives] was always short of being insubordinate but also short of being useful." SIOP-5 was somewhat more successful than SIOP-63 in harnessing nuclear war plans to political objectives, providing the president for the first time with targeting options using several hundred weapons rather than several thousand, as had been the only alternatives in the past. At the same time, political rhetoric, dominated by popular pressures to "control the arms race," had diverged even more widely from the reality of nuclear operations, as large segments of the Congress were actively opposed to SALT and what they took to be the entire failed architecture of détente.

The Return of the Democrats

The defeat of President Gerald Ford by an almost unknown southern Democrat seemed to herald positive change to a country exhausted and discouraged by the travails of Watergate. Jimmy Carter ran on an anti-Washington, antigovernment platform, promising bold reforms in all areas of policy, including that of nuclear forces.

Carter's nuclear legacy is especially schismatic, a salient example of the structural dissonance that afflicts nuclear planning. Although he had served as nuclear officer in the navy, he had an almost evangelical hatred of nuclear weapons. An unparalleled proponent of arms control negotiations, he succeeded in concluding no agreements, instead presiding over the collapse of the decade-old SALT process. In the end, his visceral loathing of nuclear weapons gave way to a deep interest in the details of war planning. The man who had entered office promising "to banish nuclear weapons" left behind a rich legacy of plans for the conduct of protracted nuclear war, a subject of particular fascination to his national security adviser, Zbigniew Brzezinski.

"Banishing" Nuclear Weapons

The 1976 presidential election provided a former governor of Georgia an opportunity to attack the entire Washington establishment, especially its military policies. The country had shifted to the left in the aftermath of Vietnam and Watergate. The devastating experience of the war in Vietnam, the failure to conclude a SALT II accord, the proliferation of nuclear weapons in the Third World, the United States as the leading "merchant of death" in arms sales to the Third World, and the growing public fears of nuclear conflict were all central campaign themes.

Carter shared one trait with Kennedy: he looked for diversity of opinion in choosing his advisers. Culturally and ideologically, National Security Adviser Brzezinski and Secretary of State Cyrus Vance were worlds apart—one a hawkish Pole who had left his country after Soviet occupation, the other a preppie blue blood from

Wall Street, the quintessential member of the Council on Foreign Relations. In between the two was Harold Brown, a former nuclear weapons designer and an aide in the McNamara Pentagon who would serve as secretary of defense. The VBB, as the triumvirate came to be called, formed a microcosm of the varied views in the administration as a whole.

As Carter saw it, the hard-line views of Brzezinski would complement his own idealism and be a perfect counterpoint to the accommodationist spirit of Vance. Brown was the technical expert, who could temper their competing abstractions on world order with a sense of empirical reality. The chain of command was flexible, apparently in keeping with Carter's belief in intellectual "survival of the fittest." Through conflict, the best ideas would supposedly surface.

In practice, the divergences among his chief advisers were disastrous for Carter's leadership. His policies—from the conduct of arms control talks to the handling of Soviet incursions in the Horn of Africa—mirrored the divisions among his staff. To the detriment of coherent policy, senior aides and subordinates spent an inordinate amount of time in bureaucratic sabotage. Eventually, each part of the bureaucracy has its own press and congressional constituency, although no one could rival Brzezinski in zealous cultivation of allies in the media. Before long, the conservative arms control expert Richard Burt, a correspondent for the *New York Times,* was seen regularly meeting Zbig at Washington watering holes.

At bottom, the major policy disputes were over incompatible beliefs about the Soviet Union. Vance pressed for a panoply of instruments to expand and deepen Kissinger's policy of détente, eventually helping persuade the president to launch seven separate sets of arms control negotiations, ranging from antisatellite weapons to the regulation of armaments in the Indian Ocean. By contrast, Brzezinski was a serious hard-liner, a believer in containment, and viscerally hostile to the Soviet government. This doubtless had something to do with the fact that the Soviets had made him a victim of social downward mobility: having left Poland without social status, he had had to make his own way. He later described his relationship with Vance as follows:

> Our different backgrounds had produced substantially different conceptions of how the world works and consequently a different estimate of the proper balance between power and principle. . . . As a member of

both the legal profession and the once-dominant Wasp elite, he operated according to their values and rules. . . . In a striking historical coincidence, the decline of the Anglo-American hegemony in the world coincided with the decline of Wasp predominance in America. . . . Cy would have made an extraordinarily successful Secretary of State in a more tranquil age.[84]

Brown's views on world politics were more in tune with Brzezinski's, although the two often disputed in the earlier stages. Brzezinski later took some credit for having pushed Brown toward a harder line and higher defense budgets, and Brown became a forceful advocate, against Carter's resistance, for building up American military forces. Brown also skirmished with Carter early on for wanting to control presidential contact with the JCS. Ultimately, Brown played the role of the technical wizard, always better informed and impatient with the intellectual ramblings of his colleagues. Brzezinski expressed irritation with Brown's sense of superior knowledge: "I was particularly put off by his tendency to interrupt me in mid-sentence and to complete for me the argument that I was making before then plunging into his own rebuttal of it."[85]

The Carter administration created the political context for its defense policies through a series of early decisions that earned it a reputation for antimilitarism and naïveté. Aside from the array of arms control initiatives, Carter canceled the Air Force's new strategic-bomber program, the B-1, started but then reversed abruptly an effort to withdraw American troops from Korea, and offered a package of "deep cuts" in strategic forces, which the Soviets summarily rebuffed. By his own account, Carter was fighting a three-part war from the beginning: with the JCS, who hated his budget cuts and were suspicious of the arms control agenda; with the Congress, which thought he was weak on defense; and with the Soviets, who were habitually testing his will. He might have added his own advisers as the fourth source of friction.[86]

It did not help that the Soviets were expanding their military capabilities and engaging in relatively bolder military adventures in the Third World throughout the late 1970s. Eventually, it was Carter who was blamed for having emboldened the Soviets with his pacifist rhetoric. As had happened in the late 1960s, however, the president had inherited changes in the relative military balance that Americans found frightening. Over time, this led to clamors for new weapons and higher budgets and culminated in the "technological escapism" of the Reagan presidency.

Carter stressed that his one ambition in coming to office was a "much more dramatic reduction in the nuclear arsenals." He elaborated, "I wanted to build what I considered to be a penultimate arrangement, that is, a small number of single-warhead missiles, with the missiles all uniform in size, and deploy them in a totally invulnerable place."[87] He also wanted a comprehensive nuclear test ban to halt nuclear modernization and a ban on space weapons. Arms control was to serve as the engine of an overall reduction of global tensions.

Ironically, Carter presided over the most detailed restructuring of the American war-fighting apparatus since the time of McNamara. At Brzezinski's urging, Carter sanctioned an unprecedented number of studies on how to fight and prevail in nuclear combat, studies that resulted in hefty investments in the architecture of nuclear war fighting. It was Carter, not Nixon or Reagan, who contributed the most to the refinements of thinking about protracted nuclear war.

As one of his earliest ventures, Carter hoped to launch a fundamental reexamination of the utility of nuclear weapons. Although he probably knew more about nuclear weapons than any of his predecessors, he had a fundamental, Christian antipathy to nuclear issues. Shortly before his inauguration, in his first meeting with the JCS in Blair House, Carter got off on the wrong foot. Why couldn't the United States make do with a force of two hundred missiles? he asked. This was enough to destroy the Soviet Union in an unimaginable holocaust. Wasn't it a sufficient basis of deterrence?[88] His advisers, especially Brzezinski, were profoundly embarrassed at this wanton display of naïveté. They set about educating the president.

In March 1977, Brown was asked to provide the president with three items: (1) a statement of current nuclear doctrine, (2) the plan for conducting nuclear war after deterrence failed, and (3) a statement of the objectives sought through limited nuclear options.

In the interim, Brzezinski organized "drills" to learn about how to locate the president in seconds in the event of nuclear hostilities. These so-called command post exercises were not a great success and did not last much beyond the first year. One involved flying around in the National Emergency Airborne Command Post (NEACP), a Boeing 747 equipped with the necessary communications gear to let the president command the war from the air. An official who participated in one of these NEACP exercises claims the drill was stalled for over an hour because of engine trouble.

In another drill, Brzezinski is reported to have surprised the "man with the football," demanding that he act as if Zbig were the president and needed to be evacuated under emergency conditions. The Secret Service almost shot down the helicopter carrying the simulated "escape team" as it veered unannounced over the White House lawn. All the participants were completely befuddled. Why weren't we given any time to prepare for the exercise? they complained.[89]

According to Aaron, exercises of the "red phone," the secure line over which the president would conduct "missile conferences" to decide whether to authorize the launching of nuclear weapons, were no better: "There'd be twenty-three people on the line; the president didn't know any of them. It could be a psychopath, or a maniac or a fool on the other end; or the secretary of defense or CINCSAC [commander in chief, Strategic Air Command] could be drunk."[90]

The experience helped win Carter's approval for large increases in funding for "nuclear preparedness." The military adviser William Odom has given the president credit for his personal interest in the matter: "He really got into the procedures, ran through numerous scenarios. . . . He wanted to be awakened a three o'clock in the morning and not be confused, and understand what he was going to see . . . what the voice would sound like on the other end, that sort of thing."[91] Carter's almost childlike enthusiasm made him susceptible to Brzezinski's growing fascination with things nuclear.

Russian Russians

With a disingenuousness characteristic of new advisers, Brzezinski described his own motivation to recast doctrine in terms that have now become excessively familiar:

> Over the years, I had become increasingly concerned that our existing deterrence doctrine, based on the principle of mutual assured destruction, had been formulated largely in a setting of actual US nuclear superiority . . . . It might not deter an opponent capable of conducting both a major and a more limited nuclear conflict and significant conventional conflict.[92]

The anti-MAD stance seemed like old wine in new bottles, but Brzezinski had greater ambitions. Even more pointedly than General Welch, he wanted the Russians to know that U.S. nuclear forces were out to get them. There is a now famous story about Brzezinski's highly personal interest in targeting. "Where are the criteria for killing Russians?" he asked an aide who was briefing him on hypothetical targeting plans. When the aide responded that American policy did not target populations per se, but that economic targeting and general war would still kill millions of Soviet citizens, Brzezinski said, "No, I mean Russian Russians." He wanted the plans to reflect the understanding that Russians—not Ukrainians, not Armenians—were the elite scourge who should be targeted directly.[93]

Brzezinski went on to argue for a deterrence based on "the threat of counterviolence designed to negate the capacity of our opponent to compel us to fulfill his will." Eventually, this rather rococo formulation was to become the basis of a DIA study, given the task of operationalizing deterrence by targeting the way the Soviets target—a refinement of "denial strategy" that had some important consequences for force development during the Reagan administration.[94]

With Brzezinski's support, President Carter subsequently commissioned the so-called Comprehensive Net Assessment and Military Force Posture Review, known commonly as Presidential Review Memorandum (PRM) 10. The overall study was headed by the conservative Harvard professor Samuel Huntington and was to cover U.S. global interests and military forces. The analysis of strategic forces was chaired by a Pentagon aide, Lynn Davis, a deputy assistant secretary for policy planning and a protégée of Brown's. Much was made of the fact that she was a former professor of political science, new to government, thirty-three, and female.

PRM-10 seemed star-crossed from the start. Davis found bureaucratic opposition at every turn, familiar military resistance amplified by wholesale sexism. "They massacred her," said one participant. The clash of cultures was similar to the whiz kids' experiences of the 1960s, except this time the military was less reluctant to be blatantly uncooperative. "Lynn would chair these big interagency meetings full of lieutenant colonels and open with the greeting 'Okay, campers,'" recalled one participant. "When a young woman offends a two-star general, they don't forget it." The atmosphere was filled with open contempt.[95]

There are many reasons beyond personalities, however, that the

Joint Chiefs were violently opposed to the exercise. For one, they did not want targeting doctrine subjected to another interagency review. Like the whiz kids, these new civilian appointees thought it perfectly appropriate to discuss every vulnerability of the deterrent, as if it were a problem like housing policy or tax reform. "They were exceedingly academic. They didn't believe that if a government is seen to be officially examining an option, the mere fact of looking at it associates you with that option," said Welch. "If the government is being run by people who don't understand this point, heaven help us."[96] The PRM-10 analysts later admitted that some of the options "were wild and wooly, involving very, very large increases." And major decreases.

Second, there was the real fear that PRM-10, by trying to develop force options that met alternative doctrinal objectives, would be used to justify budget cuts. Force structures sufficient to achieve requisite damage levels could provide a basis for alternative structures of deterrence that justified smaller force levels. Joel Resnick, an aide to Davis, argued, "We were just trying to do real analysis."[97] But for the JCS, this was mucking around of the highest order. The exercises might end up formalizing one of these flaky postures.

Marrying forces with objectives was the most dangerous aspect of the study. It is the opposite of how the military was used to planning. "You can claim the objective of attack plans are identical to attack policy, but that's crazy," said one air force general who participated in the study, "because you can't manifest a plan except in the current environment, and you can't manifest objectives except in the future." This was the crux of the civilian-military dispute: civilians thought the SIOP should reflect policy objectives, but the military knew it should reflect only *current capabilities*—otherwise it would lock the nation into the existing force posture and codify the existing structure even as adversaries continued to move forward. At bottom was the question "How much is enough?" A document that connected political objectives to forces meant a budget blueprint that was bound to bring ceilings, if not outright cuts.[98]

The final draft of the strategic forces section of PRM-10, entitled "Military Strategy and Force Posture Review," outlined "about a dozen" options on how to deter, from "roll over belly up to nuke 'em till they glow," according to a participant. The options were extremely specific, radically so, according to some military analysts. In a climate of defense budget cuts and arms control, the lower options were bound to be exploited by civilians seeking strategic restraint, the Joint Chiefs feared, even though Davis reportedly had "promised" that the study would not affect procurement. (The promise had been exacted as the price of the JCS's releasing data needed for the study.) As the NSC staffer Roger Molander pointed out, the matching of force levels with criteria of desired destruction could have been a great instrument for arms control: "If you know how much deterrent you need, then you could do reductions."[99]

Apart from creating friction with the military, the study showed the fundamental incompatibility among Carter's advisers. The PRM-10 analysts had taken the president at his word when he said he wanted a thorough review of strategic forces and objectives. They produced a document that showed how force postures could be altered to reflect alternative beliefs about what should constitute deterrence. That was exactly what Brzezinski found absurd: the Soviets were striding forward with a war-fighting capability, and here were Americans talking about deterrence and self-restraint.

A more banal reason for rejecting PRM-10 was that it essentially recommended continuity with NSDM-242: "Zbig didn't like that; it wasn't good to be with Nixon. It wasn't a major departure," explained Leon Sloss, a former Nixon official who was soon to take over the task of reforming U.S. nuclear doctrine. In other words, it did not measure up as grounds for what should be remembered as the "Brzezinski Doctrine."[100] And so Brzezinski had the government try again, incorporating the findings of PRM-10 into a larger exercise known as PD-18. The directive from President Carter mandated two studies, one on targeting and one on a "secure reserve force," whose broad purpose was "to assure national entity survival against an all-out nuclear attack—at least as well as the USSR could survive."[101]

The targeting study, completed in December 1978, was huge; it featured a summary of 150 pages and six annexes, on subjects ranging from crisis management to ways to develop the SIOP. The key recommendation for reforming the SIOP was to identify smaller target sets for implementing flexible options for nuclear strikes, including ones for after a nuclear war had started. Two of the study's findings proved extremely significant for force planning. First, it identified major changes in the Soviet target base, suggesting a trend toward the hardening of key targets to a point that would make it much more difficult for the United States to conduct credible counterforce attacks. Second, it revealed the existence of a major Soviet civil defense program, with the potential to ensure that Soviet leaders and "key personnel" would be out of reach of U.S. weapons in the event of war.[102]

These conclusions were very similar to those of an earlier debate in which Odom had been centrally involved. At issue was the extent to which the Soviets really were planning to "survive as a society" after nuclear war. If this was a major factor in their resource allocation decisions, it might indicate a willingness to wage war. Evidence such as their preparations to reload silos with additional missiles following an attack suggested plans for a protracted nuclear exchange. The existence of evacuation plans for Soviet workers critical to postwar survival was also taken to support this assessment. The fundamental issue was whether the Soviets could ever be satisfied with the status quo, as was implied in the SALT objectives of "essential equivalence" and stability, or whether this was a dangerously sanguine view that overlooked the unrelenting Soviet drive for hegemony. Differing perceptions about whether the Soviets could ever be "a status quo power" form the leitmotif that runs through the controversies about U.S. nuclear policy going back to the 1950s, probably the most important determinant of attitudes about the merits of U.S.-Soviet accommodation.[103]

Sloss's study also highlighted major deficiencies in U.S. capabilities to command and control nuclear forces. Flexible options, still the cornerstone of American strategic objectives, were a fantasy in the absence of effective command and control systems to execute the limited strikes in a disciplined way in the midst of war. Sloss concluded that many of these "options" would not be possible without major investments in new technologies that could perform such functions as assuring communications among commanders "in the trans-attack and postattack" environment of a protracted nuclear exchange.[104]

The study also recommended changes in U.S. targeting plans, to take account of ongoing changes in the Soviet Union. In addition to the goal of "greater flexibility," Sloss urged less emphasis on economic recovery targets and more on the "effectiveness of our attacks against military targets." Recovery targeting was shifted back to "war-supporting industry," which narrowed the list of industrial targets and released additional weapons for pure counterforce missions. "There were 'high-quality' weapons assigned to economic recovery targets, which could be as stupid as a shoe factory," said one official, and these were reassigned "to higher-priority missions."[105]

The targeting changes were deliberately made in a manner that would not upset the military. Instead of cutting weapons to fit the shrinking target list, the study "kept the same number of weapons and allocated more to each target," according to one analyst. It justified this by raising the damage criteria, a more exacting standard imposed to determine what was needed to destroy the targets.

Sloss spent a great deal of time out at the JSTPS in Omaha and was personally close to General Richard Ellis, of CINSAC. "I didn't want to repeat the experience of PRM-10," he explained. "Personalities have so much to do with it. You don't change policy; you influence people."[106]

The final draft of the study was sent to the White House in December 1978. It recommended even more-limited options: "targeting packages," which could be "tailored" to different contingencies; a larger secure reserve force, which would be "withheld" in the first stages of war; explicit targeting of Soviet conventional forces; and a series of steps to improve the structure for "protracted war"—survivable communications and satellites to conduct a nuclear exchange of some duration. The latter would help targeting by aiding in the identification of new targets, like mobile forces, as war ensued.

The structural innovations recommended by Sloss also addressed civilian control. The key problem was to make sure that in crises the president had options he would understand. As Sloss observed, the resistance of SAC to concepts of limited strikes would endure unless there was more routine oversight. And the president himself needed to be kept informed of the plans.

As it was, the targeting review was caught up in the politics of the Carter administration and languished for eighteen months. While some in the NSC urged that a new strategic doctrine was an imperative, the "doves" claimed it would frighten people and derail SALT. Debate already was raging in Congress and elsewhere over Carter's policies. The Soviets were probing in the Horn of Africa and steadily building up strategic forces. The Europeans, still reeling from Carter's fumbling of the "neutron bomb" issue, were divided over how to respond to American pressures to accept new nuclear weapons on their soil. But it was SALT II that was the real lightning rod for opposition.

Beginning in 1976, the opponents of SALT II, led by Paul Nitze, who had established an extremely powerful lobby called the Committee on the Present Danger, was growing steadily. The lobby set untold precedents, followed in the 1980s, with its extraordinary energy, money, and relentless dedication to a single foreign policy objective. Its specific target was the SALT II Treaty still in negotiations, but the underlying agenda was the weakness of the United States in the face of the Soviet menace.

The media and Congress joined in the esoteric debate launched by Nitze about the vulnerability of American missiles to a Soviet first strike. "Minuteman vulnerability," demonstrated with calculations of the accuracy of Soviet missiles and with examples of Soviet evil intentions, was the subject of vivid controversies around the country. The United States under Jimmy Carter was in imminent danger of Soviet attack. The committee pulled out all stops: television ads, books, posters, and a stable of colorful speakers. "Everyone knows [ACDA Director] Paul Warnke is a paid Russian agent," one representative told a university audience.

The administration's rebuttals were an apt reflection of its internal inconsistencies. Officials from the State Department, ACDA, and the Pentagon—eventually, any able-bodied civil servants who could speak English—were sent on a far-flung "SALT sellers" circuit. They addressed Quakers, automobile manufacturers, and students at junior colleges in the Midwest—basically, anyone who asked. Courses in public speaking were offered in the State Department specifically to train pro-SALT speakers.

There was one problem. The White House, ever believing that only the truth can set you free, issued strict directives about what could and could not be said by officials stumping for SALT. No discussion of the effects of nuclear war; that was too lurid. No discussion of intelligence satellites, even though one of the key liabilities being assailed by Nitze was that SALT II could not be verified, because our "spy" capabilities were inadequate. And no denunciations of the opposition.

As Nitze and other activists disseminated terrifying maps of American cities being destroyed by a single Soviet SS-18 missile, dozens of bureaucrats went on the road with terse little statements about the contributions of MIRVs for ensuring U.S. hard-target kill capabilities. SALT could be verified, Americans were assured, by "national technical means," whatever that meant. SALT should be supported because it would provide for subceilings on heavy land-based missiles and functionally related observable differences on cruise missiles— another example of a stellar political argument.

Within a year of the Carter public relations strategy, even the Left was denouncing SALT II. It had no real impact on the arms race, argued some in the disarmament community. They were joined by Americans on the right who saw it as a plot to give away U.S. missiles to the Communists.

Meanwhile, Brzezinski was devising his own SALT strategy, based on the concept of "linkage." Unlike the arms controllers in the White House, including Jimmy Carter, Brzezinski thought it unconscionable that SALT or any accommodation with the Soviets not be part of a larger strategy to force them to behave better. "SALT was buried in the sands of the Ogaden in Ethiopia," he had argued in 1978 after the Soviets launched an invasion there. By 1979, linkage had won the day: the Soviets invaded Afghanistan, and the SALT II Treaty was never submitted to the Senate for ratification.

PD-59

Although Brzezinski recalls in his memoirs that he agreed with Brown in May of 1979 to "codify" their respective reviews of strategic modernization and targeting objectives, PD-59, the official document proclaiming the new U.S. nuclear doctrine, was not signed by the president until July of 1980. One reason was internal opposition. Vance and his successor, Edmund Muskie, thought the document ghoulish, and Brzezinski did what he could to exclude them from meetings. Muskie was not invited to the meeting in which the final details of PD-59 and its release were decided.[107]

The coordination of the Sloss recommendations with the JCS had also proven difficult. Headed by Jasper Welch, who was aided by an NSC analyst, Victor Utgoff, the study was not popular with the Joint Chiefs. SAC, needless to say, was no more comfortable with the idea of withholding forces in the first round of a war for *long* periods in an explicitly protracted war than with the idea of doing so for the shorter periods contemplated under earlier notions of flexible response. The Joint Chiefs claimed they still did not have the forces to execute these even more elaborate civilian fantasies.

As Welch said, there was no explanation of what these civilians really wanted to do with this doctrine. There was no strategy for the "endgame." And it did not help that the air force did not have either the MX or the B-1. Whereas Brown preferred to announce the new policy in a more discreet manner—drafting up a new NUWEP and including its principles in the posture statement—Brzezinski and Odom argued that more publicity would help Carter in the campaign.[108]

PD-59 was a curious document in several respects. It had limited targeting guidance or new target concepts. It was a political document, a domestic message sent to a beleaguered electorate in the misguided effort to reassure. Although much was made of its radical innovations, the thinking behind the document had been cemented well before. If there was a change, it was to say that American strategy was now one of *protracted* as well as flexible response. It was Kauffman who wrote the words "countervailing strategy," by which the policy came to be known. According to his account, he came up with them in the middle of the night because he was bored with every other formulation of this old chestnut.[109]

Jimmy Carter does not seem to like talking about PD-59. It is scarcely mentioned in his memoirs, and he skirts the issue in interviews. If he is not being disingenuous, his motivations for a new doctrine were to develop more flexibility in U.S. internal planning and to reassure China, with whom diplomatic relations were opened in 1978. As it was, Carter's contradictory legacy of a strategic buildup, including approval of two hundred MX "hard-target kill" missiles with ten warheads each, together with herculean efforts at major strategic restraints, left acrimony on both the right and the left. He was a victim of his own rhetoric, having presided over "a decade of neglect," according to the Right, and sacrificed arms control to plans to fight nuclear wars, according to the Left.

Unlike Kissinger, who was perhaps criticizing Schlesinger when he honestly assessed the limitations of NSDM-242, Brzezinski asserts that PD-59 was an unqualified success, with "acquisition policy being tied to employment policy, for the first time." In an act of rather self-serving obfuscation, Brzezinski wrote, "Till PD-59 was issued, American war planning postulated a brief, spasmic, and apocalyptic

138

conflict. *It was based on the assumption of a short war, a few days at the most* [emphasis added]."[110]

Whatever legacy there was to PD-59 was left to Ronald Reagan. Numerous "continuity in government" studies were contracted in 1980 but were not completed until the next administration. The highly detailed plans to target "Russian Russians"—including "miserable little buildings housing Communist party cells," as Aaron described Brzezinski's innovation—were not developed until after 1980. The warhead count to cover what was now over forty thousand targets was impeded by the controversy over the basing of the MX missile, still unresolved. Although a public outcry resulted from PD-59, no real change occurred. As it was, Reagan ordered a review of nuclear policy barely a year later, the National Security Decision Directive (NSDD) 13, which largely reaffirmed the familiar principles of its predecessor.

CHAPTER 4

Defenses Reincarnate

THE HISTORICAL DIVISION between the theater of public debate and the reality of plans for nuclear war came of age as a full-blown political drama with the birth of the Strategic Defense Initiative. Despite the cacophony of debate over the SDI, the strategic transformation promised by President Reagan was never taken very seriously even by the highest circle of defense decision makers. Officials paid obeisance in public to the SDI's high-minded goals and some capitalized on the SDI's glamour to advance other objectives, like dispensing with the ABM Treaty. But it was left to a relatively small number of true believers, largely outside the administration, to engage in the political battles that the president's rhetoric helped provoke. As the director of external affairs of the SDI Organization (SDIO) put it in 1987, "There are very few real supporters of the program in the administration."[1]

The SDI represents an episode in American nuclear doctrine in which an apparently radical innovation dominated headlines for the duration of a two-term administration. But the debate had far more to do with ideology and political partisanship—struggles for control of public perceptions and over basic American values—than with concrete decisions affecting nuclear war planning. In fact, there has been no real change in American nuclear doctrine, despite the histrionic disputes between supporters and opponents of this imaginary revolution.

The SDI's political profile has been vastly out of proportion to its influence over specific decisions about the nation's nuclear arsenal. Even the ABM restrictions that came under extreme assault remain more or less intact. In short, the SDI served as a metaphor for support of or opposition to a popular administration, but it was divorced from the significant developments undertaken in the 1980s on behalf of the nation's security. The nuclear arsenal has grown steadily, independent of the rhetorical excesses of the political arena.

The tension between public perceptions of nuclear weapons as "weapons of mass destruction which can never be used" and the military requirement to develop plans for their use in actual conflicts is an enduring problem of American politics. For President Reagan, this was precisely the point: if the public could see the bankruptcy of the plans that underlie deterrence, it would support radical change. This is exactly what the Roman Catholic bishops argued in their letter to the president, declaring that the waging of "nuclear war . . . in any form . . . is morally unjustifiable."[2]

The president's SDI speech prompted the public to "think about the unthinkable": the consequences of a failure of deterrence. He urged the public to examine the logical outcome of the dismal thinking of deterrent strategists and arms control advocates, that deterrence is a tenuous stalemate won by the threat to use nuclear weapons. Its supporters are not just myopic in believing that somehow deterrence will never fail, he implied, but are in fact openly dedicated to fighting a nuclear war in the event that their strategic house of cards collapses. Their moral shallowness is captured by their refusal to even consider an alternative basis for security, a system in which "we save lives rather than avenge them."[3]

But in rejecting the allegedly decadent logic of mutual vulnerability and assured retaliation, the president publicized the Achilles' heel of Western security policy—the belief that nuclear weapons ensure peace. Nuclear weapons have traditionally made up for shortages of more expensive conventional forces and are supposed to make war potentially so devastating as to be unthinkable. This "uneasy tacit armistice," as Henry Kissinger described it, is not a comfortable political concept. While trying to solve the fundamental conundrum of the nuclear age—how actually to apply this awesome power without incurring unacceptable consequences—politicians also have to shroud "war-fighting" plans in more publicly acceptable terms, like MAD, and to pursue diplomatic efforts aimed at reducing nuclear arsenals.

The central contribution of nuclear weapons to American security is not a principle most politicians like to dwell on in public, for obvious reasons, and it is traditional for every new president to enter office deploring the nuclear arms race. Denounced at political rallies and international forums, nuclear forces nonetheless remain explicitly valued in the centers of government as the cornerstone of security. As a result, antinuclear rhetoric tends to temper quite quickly in incumbency, as the new president faces the realities of nuclear force planning and the demands of the U.S.-Soviet strategic rivalry. As we have seen, even Jimmy Carter, who at first pledged to eliminate nuclear weapons, eventually presided over and publicly defended an increased emphasis on nuclear counterforce capabilities.

But Ronald Reagan's approach was genuinely radical, if ironic in the extreme. For the first time, an American president launched and sustained a wholesale public repudiation of the legitimacy of nuclear weapons as a way to gain support for an unprecedented buildup of the American nuclear arsenal and a rejection of arms control. The commitment to eliminate nuclear weapons did not fade over time, moreover, but remained an element of Reagan's public positions throughout his tenure. Even as the antinuclear rhetoric made its mark in the public consciousness, however, influencing the way in which some analysts and media commentators perceived future policy, its impact on real decisions about weapons' characteristics, requirements for new weapons, and plans for waging war was tangential, to say the least. Sadly, it will remain so for the foreseeable future. Nuclear weapons are still the cornerstone of American security policy.

The Reagan Revolution

How President Reagan was led to his personal crusade for strategic defense as a way of balancing competing political and military demands of nuclear force planning illustrates, in particular, how the influence of a few key individuals can fundamentally alter the course of policy, especially during the transition of a new president. The role of advisers with no prior experience in government is growing in the American political process, partly as a result of the longer periods and intensified demands placed on candidates striving for the presidency. There is a growing dissonance between what is required for a successful campaign and what may be required to govern, but it is axiomatic that new presidents will reward those who helped bring them to power with key government jobs: a president naturally wants his trusted advisers near him. Such advisers are increasingly more expert in public relations and fund-raising than in history or military policy.

With the exception of Robert McFarlane, the deputy national security adviser who was a veteran defense specialist and had served in the NSC under the Nixon administration, most of the individuals who initially encouraged the president to pursue the SDI were political strategists. Many were close to him personally and knew how to frame issues in a way he would find appealing—populist themes, which were relentlessly optimistic. Like the president, the men at the top of the White House hierarchy were "can-do" Americans who had an unshakable faith in entrepreneurship and innovation to solve problems; they infused a corporate mentality into government.

Having engineered one of the most overwhelming political upsets in history, based largely on a highly successful media strategy, these advisers knew about public relations. By design, campaign themes had been short on detail but had broad public appeal. This winning strategy was to find its way into White House policy-making. The "Reagan revolution" was not going to be impeded by an excessive sensitivity to either tradition or bureaucratic procedures.

The new administration also tended to show what one official described as a "we-they" mentality, a strong suspicion of the East Coast establishment and the entrenched government bureaucracy. The campaign had pushed a strident antigovernment platform that was not just popularly resonant but also reflected the actual beliefs of the key players. The "magic of the marketplace" was going to replace government intervention in economic policy. This view was part of a broader hostility to "big government" that soon permeated many other areas of policy, including foreign and defense affairs.

The antipathy to the status quo also derived from the latent populist ideology of the "New Right," the political faction of conservatives from which Reagan traditionally drew his support. "Populism" in the case of foreign and defense policy meant a deep distrust of and often overt resentment toward the "foreign policy establishment," the blue-blooded, blue-blazered men (and a few women) who had long dominated this sphere with their clubby elitism. In contrast to these experts who enjoyed polite debate over sherry in the confines of the Century Club or the Council on Foreign Relations, the architects of the New Right—more often attired in polyester and leisure wear than in Brooks Brothers broadcloth—had little interest in the nuances of international problems and relished the give-and-take of domestic politics. As Adam Garfinkle has described the leaders of the New Right,

> [They] are young and vigorous, are skilled in modern communications techniques, and have come on the political scene at a time when the appeal of liberal political philosophies has diminished, fatigued by Vietnam, social ills that have defied solution, an economy out of control, and an aggressive Soviet foreign policy. . . . They have also learned the craft of raising large sums of money. And they have profited from and helped bring together a series of traditionalist single-issue social movements that have been catalyzed by opposition to the political initiatives, or failings, of the dominant establishment over the past ten years.[4]

Reflecting the influence of the New Right, domestic political considerations—which entailed taking charge of public opinion—would always take precedence in the design of policy in the early years of the administration. The first priority was to dispose of remnants of what were considered the disastrous policies of the Carter administration. Anything associated with past administrations had to be changed, including the name and acronym for the strategic arms negotiations in Geneva (from Strategic Arms Limitation Talks, or SALT, to Strategic Arms Reduction Talks, or START).

This was not an environment in which career civil servants felt very welcome; many, indeed, were treated with profound suspicion and displaced. Even the under secretary of defense for policy, Fred Iklé, a nuclear strategist by training, was inspired by this ethos, described by one of his subordinates as "paranoidly hiding out in his office because he was convinced the Pentagon was full of liberals held over from the Carter administration."[5]

The administration's pursuit of the SDI reveals an unprecedented dislocation of those with expertise in diplomacy or defense. The Reagan administration had an unusual number of Cabinet positions filled with men who had never grappled with such issues before. Edwin Meese, who held the Cabinet-level title of counselor in the White House and had managerial authority for the National Security

Council, had been an aide to Reagan when he was the governor of California and previously had served in the Alameda County District Attorney's Office. National Security Adviser William Clark, former executive secretary to Governor Reagan and briefly a California supreme court judge, first came to public attention when, in Senate hearings on his appointment as deputy secretary of state, he could not answer simple questions about current events. Even Secretary of Defense Caspar W. Weinberger had experience only in domestic policy, having served as director of the Office of Management and Budget and as secretary of health, education, and welfare in the Nixon administration.

But even these men had little influence over the origins of the SDI. They were ignored initially in favor of Reagan's closest associates from previous times, including the conservative economist and campaign aide Martin Anderson, the domestic adviser Michael Deaver, and the "kitchen cabinet," a group of wealthy businessmen who had helped finance several of Reagan's campaigns and were his closest personal friends. Indeed, in considering how to frame the issue of strategic defenses, its initial advocates went to great lengths to keep it out of traditional bureaucratic channels. According to Anderson, "The Defense Department, being the largest bureaucracy, is the . . . worst bureaucracy. . . . Missile defense would be seen as a new idea and nothing threatens the bureaucracy like a new idea. If we asked the Defense Department to study the issue, we were pretty sure what the outcome would be—nothing."[6]

The President's Vision

Reagan's commitment to the SDI was born first of a strong personal belief that American technology could and should be challenged both to overwhelm Soviet military power and to thwart any nuclear threat. Many advisers have revealed that the president strongly believed that it is technologically possible to defend against all forms of nuclear attack—from a Soviet first strike to a terrorist's "suitcase bomb." He had an intuitive regard for the "common sense" of defenses. It was basic human instinct to protect against danger, whether personally or as a nation. In a rather sentimental response to a reporter's question about the SDI in 1985, he said, "It's like when in Geneva in 1925 all the nations of the world after World War I got rid of poison gas but everybody kept their gas mask. Well, [this is] the same thing—[the SDI] is like the gas mask."[7]

More important, Ronald Reagan had a deep mistrust of negotiations with the Soviet Union. Years of protracted efforts to achieve limitations on nuclear weapons had not only brought marginal results, he argued, but had also resulted in the legitimation of the Soviet Union as a superpower perceived as equal to the United States. Hiding behind the screen of treaties and cordial diplomacy, the Soviets were routinely cheating on agreements and advancing their hegemonic aims around the world. Yet they had never been brought to task for their violations, because of the American public's yearning to believe in the false promise of arms control. This massive public delusion had resulted in the permeation of the American electorate with active constituencies naïvely pushing for ever greater accommodation with the "evil empire." Those most "duped" by these beliefs were the increasingly vocal grass-roots organizations and their advocates in the Congress who supported a "freeze" on all further increases in the U.S. nuclear arsenals.

The president and many of his advisers had an intuitive dislike of the assured destruction paradigm that guided publicly articulated nuclear policy and that one new Defense Department official described as follows: "If the Soviets attack us or our allies, we promise to blow ourselves up."[8] Like arms control, existing doctrine was far too dependent on the belief that the Soviets accepted Western deterrence concepts, a belief challenged by analysts who concluded that Soviet military capabilities indicated a quest for military superiority and the ability to wage preemptive attacks against the United States and its allies.

A study conducted under the Ford administration, which came to be known as Team B, headed by the Harvard professor Richard Pipes, had come to this conclusion, helping to lend intellectual credence to the president's intuitive beliefs. The Soviets had never accepted MAD as the basis for planning, had never believed in the tenets guiding the ABM Treaty, and were far less deterred by the potential annihilation of their population than was the United States, they argued. This was revealed not only by the Soviets' inexorable offensive force buildup but also by their ongoing efforts in passive defenses to protect national leaders and key industrial workers in the event of war—planning to survive as a society after a war—and, according to some extremists, by the Soviets' having "less regard for human life."[9]

The president also came to feel strongly that the continuation of "business as usual" in nuclear planning was inevitably leading to an unacceptably dismal future, one at odds with the positive agenda he hoped to implement in all areas of American policy. There was no foreseeable end to the steady expansion of Soviet military power, while U.S. efforts to redress Soviet military advantages—advantages acquired during what Reagan officials came to refer to as "the decade of neglect"—would be forever impeded by an anxious electorate, a constraint virtually absent in the Soviet Union. The projection of the status quo into the future produced a grim picture—a continuous expansion of superpower nuclear forces, antinuclear movements throughout the West, an inevitable proliferation of nuclear weapons in other countries, and the growing threat of nuclear terrorism. In short, the president understood that nuclear weapons could no longer *assure* citizens of their security, a theme already widely touted by the antinuclear constituencies, whose language he was eventually to appropriate.

Underlying the president's views was a structural recognition among planners that the U.S.-Soviet nuclear rivalry had reached a point of technical exhaustion. The Soviets could match or exceed the United States in most categories of nuclear technology: there was nothing left that even suggested a basis for outwitting the Soviets. Shifting the focus from the dismal nuclear treadmill to a new arena—space—seemed to be the logical next step in the competition for military advantage. As Paul Nitze said of this view, "Some in the administration believed it would be nothing but disaster if we stuck to the competition with the Soviets in offensive forces. We had to change the rules of the game."[10]

The president's beliefs served as the backdrop for political calculations by a few advisers anxious to define and advance the Reagan agenda, whose foremost priority was promoting the largest increases in spending for defense in the nation's history, including a modernization program for nuclear weapons that called for the expenditure of $222 billion in five years. These budget increases had to be pushed through an increasingly fractious Congress, over the heads of a more and more disenchanted citizenry. Marked by growing public concerns over the steady deterioration of relations with the Soviet Union following the invasion of Afghanistan in 1979, the accompanying failure to submit the SALT Treaty for Senate ratification, the appearance of declining American global influence (symbolized by Americans held hostage in Iran in 1980), the spread of antinuclear movements in Europe, and domestic outcry over burgeoning nuclear arsenals, the public mood was seen as a political liability to the new administration.

Adding to White House concerns, an ill-advised comment by the new president in 1981, which seemed to imply that a nuclear war could be waged and "won" in Europe, had been seized on and distorted by the media and public critics as evidence that Ronald Reagan was cavalier in his approach to the nuclear menace—a "nuclear cowboy," as one senior administration official put it. And in November 1982, a highly classified document laying out the administration's plans for the development and use of nuclear forces, the so-called five-year defense guidance, was leaked to the *New York Times* and the *Washington Post*. Reportedly based on National Security Decision Directive (NSDD) 13, delineating the administration's nuclear doctrine, the document detailed plans for new strategic weapons capable of destroying Soviet military targets and ensuring that the United States would "prevail" in a nuclear war. Although NSDD 13 was not markedly different from the Carter administration's doctrine enunciated in Presidential Directive 59 in 1979, it prompted widespread commentary implying a radical departure. Many critics said the administration was intent on achieving the capability to launch a first strike against the Soviet Union and wage war—a perception exacerbated by the absence of any progress in the ongoing arms control talks with the Soviets in Geneva.[11]

A president working to establish his own historical legacy apparently took the public's preoccupation with nuclear issues far more seriously than many administration critics seemed aware of at the time. Advisers knew they needed a political home run to translate the Reagan mandate into a positive "Morning in America" foreign policy, helping defuse the antinuclear constituencies and providing a cover for the administration's reluctance to pursue arms control.

The Freeze and the MX Missile

Public attention to nuclear issues had been galvanized by the protracted debate over the SALT II Treaty signed with the Soviets in 1979. Viciously attacked by the Right and enjoying only lukewarm support by the Left, which characterized it as a "ratification of the arms race," the ill-fated treaty had helped create a broad public impression of the limits of arms control that was ripe for exploitation.

For the disarmament community, SALT II was the epitome of the failure of experts and bureaucrats who controlled the arms control agenda. Marginal limits on nuclear arsenals, tortuously negotiated over a period of years, were being vastly outstripped by the steady growth and modernization of both sides' nuclear forces. Even more galling, the price of a treaty was often a new weapons system, like the MX missile, a "sweetener" offered to defuse potential critics. Judged by its achievements as a step toward disarmament, arms control was increasingly seen as a propagandistic device to lull the peace movement into a false sense of security.

After 1980, grass-roots organizations rallied around the national movement in favor of a *freeze* on nuclear weapons—the idea that there would be no further developments or deployments of U.S. or Soviet nuclear missiles, the first step toward serious arms reductions. According to its staunchest supporters, the freeze was an alternative not just to the Reagan buildup but to all of the traditions of the establishment, especially the "arms controllers" who had failed miserably to harness the growth of nuclear arsenals.

It did not take Congress long to recognize the political importance of the freeze movement and to take appropriate action, either to support or to defuse its message. Senate Joint Resolution 163 on Nuclear Weapons Freeze and Reductions, known as Kennedy-Hatfield, was introduced in the Senate on March 10, 1982, and quickly attracted arms control activists and administration opponents.

Efforts to discredit the freeze movement came from many quarters, ranging from those who alleged that the movement was a Soviet front to the more moderate skeptics who feared it would undo congressional support for nuclear weapons and undercut the president in future arms negotiations. Appalled by public opinion data suggesting that over 70 percent of the public supported the freeze in 1982, the conservative senators John Warner, Republican of Virginia, and Henry

Jackson introduced their own resolution supporting the president in his efforts to negotiate reductions in nuclear arms.[12]

By any standard, the freeze's threat to the administration was vastly exaggerated by its opponents. Only after a series of legislative failures was a nonbinding and watered-down freeze resolution passed by a narrow margin in the House of Representatives in May 1983. Paradoxically, its passage reflected the declining political significance of the freeze movement as a force for arms control. Neither the administration nor the freeze advocates had anticipated that the resolution would help the administration garner votes for the MX missile in the House. In July 1983, the freeze provided a symbolic cover to over ninety congressmen who had voted in favor of the freeze resolution but who now voted to fund the MX. The activist disarmament lobby SANE noted, "The American people have been betrayed today by politicians who claim to support a nuclear weapons freeze but who have repudiated that idea by voting for the most deadly, destabilizing nuclear weapon system ever devised."[13]

Even more paradoxically, the freeze contributed to the political environment conducive to the SDI. It did so not just by sending administration strategists scrambling to thwart its momentum but also by helping alter the tactical setting for arms control. The disputes first over the SALT II Treaty and then over the freeze revealed a fundamental and growing split between the "activist" peace community, working to mobilize political support from citizens inspired by disarmament sentiment, and professional arms control groups—epitomized by the Washington-based Arms Control Association, made up of former government officials, journalists, and defense experts—who tried to influence government policy through establishment channels. In helping discredit the "arms control elite" as unresponsive to the basic interests of the American people, the freeze movement indirectly paved the way for the next "bumper sticker" nuclear policy, Star Wars.

The MX missile itself played a role in the resurgence of interest in defensive concepts, since it symbolized the decline of public support for the modernization of offensive nuclear forces. At one time the administration's highest priority, the MX had been mired in congressional dispute for several years. At issue was the problem of ensuring the survival of land-based missiles in the face of burgeoning Soviet capabilities to destroy fixed, land-based targets, such as missile silos. The vast increases in Soviet counterforce—antisilo—capabilities stemmed from the deployment of more-accurate missiles equipped with multiple independently targeted reentry vehicles (MIRVs).

Armed with ten warheads, the MX was far too attractive a target to be deployed in vulnerable silos. In a crisis, this vulnerability could invite a Soviet preemptive attack against the MX. Alternatively, the United States would have to adopt a "launch on warning" policy, launching the MX at the first sign of hostilities—a "use them or lose them" strategy that critics saw as potentially destabilizing.

The problems of ensuring the survivability of land-based missiles had been debated for years in countless government and private studies. The Reagan administration, which had come into office decrying the "window of vulnerability," inherited the fractious legacy. By 1982, thirty-three separate proposals for basing the MX had been considered, ranging from planes to trains and underground shelters. The problem was becoming a joke. It was suggested that maybe the best way to protect the MX was to put it on Amtrak, the notoriously unreliable American train system; the Soviets would *never* know where it was.

On the assumption that only mobility and deception could protect the MX, the Carter administration had put forward a scheme to deploy the missiles in "multiple protective shelters," frequently changing shelters to avoid Soviet detection. Virtually on assuming office, however, President Reagan canceled this plan—partly to separate himself from Carter, but also in response to the political opposition, led by his close friend Senator Paul Laxalt, Republican of Nevada, which had concerns about the potential by damaging environmental effects of the scheme.

In its place, after evaluating several alternatives, the administration advanced a basing mode called Densepack, basing the missiles so closely together that incoming Soviet warheads would supposedly destroy each other or be diverted, a phenomenon known as fratricide. Although no basing mode can be tested operationally for effectiveness, Densepack was strangely counterintuitive, since it ensured survivability only under attack. It had a "come and get them" message that did not sit well with critics. Absent any ongoing efforts to limit the expansion of Soviet missile forces through arms control, moreover, the idea of the MX's surviving against ever larger numbers of Soviet warheads, regardless of its basing, was hard to accept.

Densepack had been conceived and approved by Pentagon officials—including Richard DeLauer and Jasper Welch, at the time serving as deputy director of Air Force Research and Development—but had never gained the full support of the military service chiefs. Even more important, it lacked a compelling rationale. As one administration official complained, his effort to get DeLauer and Welch to present the case for the basing mode to Congress as part of an overall framework—"this is why we have deterrence, this is why we have a strategic triad"—was ignored. Whereas this individual wanted a political tactic that forced Congress to see Densepack as a vote for or against a strong deterrent, the basing mode was presented to Congress as a fait accompli. As such, it was debated on its own merits.[14]

It never passed the "Herblock factor," a reference to the Washington political cartoonist who quickly lampooned it, and was soon nicknamed Duncepack. In November 1982, the debate was essentially finished before it ever began when General John W. Vessey, chairman of the Joint Chiefs, revealed in Senate testimony that the JCS were divided over Densepack basing. Opponents of the MX seized on Vessey's revelations, and Densepack was soon history. The administration, like its predecessors, found itself with a homeless missile. By its own calculations, it was now glaring into a window of vulnerability of its own making, hoisted on its own rhetorical petard.

In January 1983, the administration established a senior panel of former officials and experts and charged it with defining the future of strategic, especially land-based, forces. The President's Commission on Strategic Forces, known more widely as the Scowcroft commission, after its chairman, began its work in early 1983. Although the establishment of the commission seemed to some to herald a new spirit of bipartisanship and professionalism on the part of the administration—the panel comprised the very type of "traditionalists" the administration most disliked, that "old SALT crowd," as Perle called them—it was actually to become a sideshow to the developing enthusiasm for strategic defense.

The Relegitimation of Defenses

Why strategic defense? As we have seen, the idea of building defenses to protect either nuclear forces or populations had been actively debated in the United States since the 1940s but had been repudiated by the mainstream of American strategic thought since the early 1970s, in recognition of the seemingly inexorable ability of offensive nuclear forces to counter any currently conceivable defense system. According to this logic, any defensive measure would prompt the other side to develop offensive countermeasures, leading to an upward spiral of competitive offense-defense deployments and no net gain in security. Even a highly capable defense, it was argued, could be provocative, suggesting a U.S. capability to launch a first strike. And defenses could lead to the unraveling of the NATO alliance, making possible a U.S. retrenchment behind its "shield" while leaving Western Europe as the nuclear and conventional battleground for U.S.-Soviet rivalry.

Nevertheless, the United States had invested heavily in research on defensive technologies for three decades and had steadfastly held out for provisions permitting a wide range of research activities on such technologies under the ABM Treaty signed with the Soviet Union in 1972. Research programs were being pursued in almost all the technologies that were to become showcases of the SDI, from nuclear-powered X-ray lasers to kinetic-kill vehicles. And although very few scientists believed a full-scale defense of populations to be feasible, a small number of defense intellectuals, some of them weapons designers and physicists, such as the "father of the H-bomb," Edward Teller, had long promoted comprehensive defense concepts, opposing in principle the ABM Treaty.

On the other hand, many individuals who played a role in the Reagan administration did not believe in "peace shields" but did recognize promise in emerging defensive technologies to improve U.S. nuclear retaliatory capabilities. Defensive concepts had begun to be discussed in the late 1970s as a possible way to close the "window of vulnerability," a colorful slogan referring to the vulnerability of U.S. ICBMs to a Soviet first strike. For example, the defense guidance in 1982 had suggested that the United States might seek a revision in the ABM Treaty to accommodate new types of basing for the MX missile.[15]

Advances in such technologies as that of directed-energy weapons that could be based in space were also being touted by some weapons designers and contractors seeking to promote their own programs. Such advocates and their supporters in the Congress had even persuaded President Carter to pursue more vigorous research for space-based lasers in 1979. Key to this technical momentum was an implicit recognition that security based on "traditional" nuclear weapons had reached an upper limit, that it was no longer technically challenging or strategically advantageous to keep adding more warheads to nuclear arsenals.

Prior to 1983, however, the idea of comprehensive defenses—to substitute for offensive nuclear missiles or to protect populations—was virtually taboo among mainstream defense specialists. Discredited in major establishment circles, strategic defense advocates had tended to be stereotyped as minor-league cranks and "strategic superiority nuts." They were not asked to speak at the Brookings Institution and were certainly never invited to cocktail parties at the Harrimans'. A number of these individuals were linked to an emerging space-defense lobby group known as Project High Frontier, founded by Lieutenant General Daniel O. Graham, the eccentric former director of the Defense Intelligence Agency. Graham was seen by most, including conservatives, as part of the "lunatic fringe," but he had served as a defense adviser to Reagan during the 1976 and 1980 presidential campaigns. His efforts to promote his ideas were utterly tireless. In less than a year, Graham had written to and lobbied dozens of administration officials on behalf of High Frontier. In a speech against SALT II during the late 1970s, he told his audience to stop worrying about nuclear war, because they already had the best defense against nuclear attack: "your feet . . . if you can run, you can get away and protect yourself."[16]

Leading figures behind the SDI were not widely known before 1983, especially in Washington. On a visit to the Lawrence Livermore National Laboratory in early 1983 to discuss strategic defense technologies, this author found a largely uninterested staff of scientists, with the notable exception of Lowell Wood, a protégé of Edward Teller's who was pursuing research on the X-ray laser. Wood and his program were about to become the cutting edge of the new administration's policy. But when other lab scientists heard about the scheduled appointment with Wood, they laughed derisively. One asked, "Why the hell would you see him?" Wood was located on the literal outskirts of the lab, in a house trailer on the perimeter of the lab's property, far removed from the main building, where the senior staff had offices.

Champions of strategic defense were frustrated by what they considered the reification of assured destruction theories among establishment thinkers. The president's personal attitudes, however, provided a newfound legitimacy for many advocates of strategic defenses who had been dispossessed politically after the signing of the ABM Treaty. Some had supported Reagan in the campaign, rising to positions that afforded considerable access, if not directly to the candidate, then to those who would help craft his policies. Later, the highly charged and diffuse environment that surrounded the implementation of the SDI, underscored by the vagueness of its objectives, gave ample latitude to competing proponents to push for their own interpretations of "what the president really meant."

Edward Teller claims to have made the first inroads into the president's thinking. As Teller has recounted on several occasions, Ronald Reagan was introduced to some of the concepts of strategic defense as early as 1967, when he was governor of California. Teller proudly describes the tour he conducted through the Livermore laboratory. Livermore, in northern California, along with the Sandia and Los Alamos nuclear laboratories, in New Mexico, is one of the key facilities charged with developing nuclear weapons; both Livermore and Los Alamos are formally parts of the University of California.[17]

Teller recalls he gave the governor a several-hour *tour d'horizon* of technological breakthroughs in nuclear concepts, including defenses, that were being pursued at Livermore. In an interview with William Broad, of the *New York Times,* Teller claimed, "We showed him all the complex projects. . . . He listened carefully and interrupted maybe a dozen times. Every one of his questions was to the point. He clearly comprehended the technology. And there was no skimping on time. He came in the morning and stayed through lunch." Some of the president's own advisers find this description of the meeting less than credible. "It doesn't square with a man who likes his briefings on three-by-five cards and believed you could recall submarine-based ballistic missiles after they were launched," said one.[18]

During Ronald Reagan's quest for the presidency, a number of individuals—some just free-lance "advisers" who had no formal role in the campaign—provided the candidate and his staff with materials about the promises of strategic defense. One notable article, "Opportunities and Imperatives of Ballistic Missile Defense," written by a staff aide to Senator Malcolm Wallop, Republican of Wyoming, is said to have actually been read by the candidate. According to the author, Angelo Codevilla, the paper was returned with Reagan's marginalia and commentary.[19]

Widely recognized as another key influence on the president's attitudes was a visit by the candidate Reagan to the North American Air Defense Command in Colorado Springs, Colorado, in 1979. Arranged by the screenwriter Douglas Morrow, a Hollywood acquaintance eager to impress the candidate, the trip was Reagan's first visit to a military base. Martin Anderson, the domestic political adviser who accompanied him, said Reagan was "deeply concerned" about what he had seen and heard in the briefings conducted by NORAD officials. Dramatically illustrated on the huge computer screens used to track Soviet missile flights, a version of which was used as the Hollywood set for the film *War Games,* a Soviet attack could leave barely fifteen minutes of warning time, with no recourse for those unfortunate enough to be within the target area. Anderson's depiction of the scene is quite dramatic:

> Carved deep down underneath a granite mountain, the nerve center of [NORAD] looks just like it does in the movies. A massive steel door, many feet thick, swings open to let you in. The command room has a two story high display screen showing the United States and the surrounding air space. Any attacking nuclear missiles show up as tiny, bright, blinking lights slowly moving across the screen. . . . I asked the general what would happen if the Soviet Union were to fire one nuclear missile at a US city. "Well," he replied, "we would pick it up right after it was launched and the officials of the city would be alerted that a nuclear bomb would hit them in 10 to 15 minutes. That's all we can do. We can't stop it."[20]

General James Hill, the commander of NORAD at the time, confirms the story, although he suggests it has been somewhat dramatized. Poetic license aside, the "discovery" of U.S. vulnerability to nuclear missiles—missiles launched as part of a deliberate strike or even accidentally—has served as a profoundly sobering moment in the life of all new presidents since Kennedy. Accounts of these personal epiphanies are fascinating illustrations of the psychology of presidential leadership—the moment of recognition of the immense responsibilities that accompany the sudden change from being a successful campaigner to being commander in chief.

Assuming responsibility for 250 million American lives—a reality first brought home in military "threat briefings" rife with technical jargon about "decapitation strikes," "collateral damage," and "circular error probables"—is a far cry from the campaign rallies in places like Cedar Rapids, Iowa, of just a few months earlier. Suddenly the message is, "It's you, Mr. President, who has his finger on the button."

The realization that the Soviet Union could destroy the United States and that the only recourse would be to destroy the Soviet Union in retaliation was clearly at odds with Reagan's optimistic view of the world. As he put it, "It is inconceivable to me . . . that the great nations of the world will sit here . . . each with a cocked gun, and no one knowing whether someone might tighten their finger on the trigger."[21]

Presidential attitudes toward the use of nuclear weapons provide an interesting perspective on the practical nature of deterrence. President Eisenhower expressed frustration with the inability to gain decisive military advantage from the U.S. nuclear arsenal during the Korean War. How is it, he asked, with all these missiles and all this money spent on defense, that we find ourselves with so few credible military options? President Kennedy, who presided over the expansion of overwhelming American nuclear superiority, did not believe that even this level of U.S. nuclear capability could permit the use of nuclear weapons during the Cuban missile crisis without the risk of unacceptable Soviet retaliation against American cities.

Decades later, Ronald Reagan expressed his own frustration at the limits of the American arsenal, this time in its failure to ensure the ability to protect against, rather than wage, war. Struck by the part of the briefing at NORAD that showed how the United States counted and identified the objects in orbit at any given time—not only satellites but also "space trash," ranging from bits of old shuttles to an astronaut's stray glove—he said,

> The thing that struck me was the irony that here, with this great technology of ours, we can do all of this, yet we cannot stop any of the weapons that are coming at us. I don't think there was a time in history when there wasn't a defense against some kind of thrust, even back in the old-fashioned days when we had a coast artillery that would stop invading ships.[22]

With the possible exception of Jimmy Carter, no president has come to office with experience in nuclear planning. As a result, new presidents are susceptible to the nuclear theories and attitudes of their advisers. Reagan's apparent despondency over America's nuclear vulnerability first prompted his campaign aide Anderson to try to find a means to capitalize on the candidate's sentiment to demonstrate his concerns for peace—and thus to defuse antinuclear critics—while advancing American military capabilities. Inspired by the soon-to-become-president's optimistic belief in technology, his profound distrust of the Soviets, and his interest in finding "a way out," Anderson thought a comprehensive defense scheme might prove to be the political panacea of the decade.

In a campaign memorandum written in 1979, Anderson argued that the idea of a "peace shield, if formulated properly . . . could become known in the press as 'Reagan's Peace Plan,' or some such nomenclature." He added, "That idea is probably far more appealing to the American people than the questionable satisfaction of knowing that those who initiated an attack against us were also blown away."[23] This formulation captured the essential linkage between the need for a bold public relations strategy and the strong influences being brought to bear on the president, including his own predilections, in favor of a new security paradigm. Defenses might help Reagan leapfrog the protracted controversies surrounding nuclear policy and forge new ground militarily, in the ultimate political-technical end run.

Anderson remembers the beginnings of White House discussions of missile defenses in mid-1981 among an informal "quadriad" of White House staff, consisting of himself, Richard Allen, Edwin Meese, and George Keyworth. Phone calls to outside advisers, including General Graham, began in September 1981, and the first formal White House meeting was convened on September 14. In addition to the four, Teller, Graham, and Edwin W. Thomas, Jr., assistant counselor to the president, were included. "I felt a rising sense of excitement," said Anderson, "as it became clear that not only did everyone feel we should pursue the idea of missile defense, but they also believed that it could be done." The outside advisers agreed to prepare a paper for the next meeting, scheduled for six weeks later.

The report, according to a participant, was "glowing and encouraging." It cited broad support for missile defenses, on the basis of interviews with individuals in the CIA, the air force, the Congress, NASA, and the DoD, although it identified none by name. The discussion hinged no longer on whether to go forward with defense but on when and how. Some time was spent on finding the right name. Graham's "Global Ballistic Missile Defense" was considered, as was "Protective Missile Defense," but no decision was made just then.[24]

High Frontier, E.T., and the Kitchen Cabinet

Coincident with the White House advisers' meetings, the president also received advice from a number of individuals whose support and friendship he had long valued, even prior to the presidential campaign. In addition to Teller, the president assembled his kitchen cabinet—a foursome of wealthy industrialists, all men in their seventies, including the retired chairman of the Champion International Corporation, Karl Bendetsen, who had been secretary of the army under Truman; the oil executive, rancher, and Reagan riding buddy William Wilson; the grocery magnate Jacquelin Hume; and the chief of the Coors brewery, Joseph Coors, a well-known Republican philanthropist. Meeting regularly in offices provided by the Heritage Foundation, a conservative think tank and lobbying organization in Washington, the kitchen cabinet, Teller, Wallop, and Graham began to discuss strategic defense.[25]

Behind the initial commonality of purpose in the group, however, were severe divisions as to how best to proceed. After several briefings by Teller and Lowell Wood, the president's friends began to be very attracted to the breakthoughs in highly advanced technologies being pursued at Teller's laboratory—state-of-the-art systems that could be deployed in space to kill missiles before they reentered the earth's atmosphere. The idea of war confined to space was extremely appealing, and Teller's enthusiasm helped create the impression that they were witness to the most significant revolution in warfare since the development of the atomic bomb.

But the futuristic concepts being promoted by Teller were not the High Frontier's or Senator Wallop's. Graham's blueprint for comprehensive defense was based on existing technologies, a "Global Ballistic Missile Defense" using ground-based interceptor missiles and earth-orbiting battle stations armed with what he called guns, systems able to fire millions of high-velocity pellets to destroy attacking missiles. These systems would be accompanied by civil defense shelters. This scheme could be readily deployed, Graham claimed, with hardware that was "off-the-shelf" and affordable—a mere $40 billion for a three-layered defense scheme that could be in place by 1990. Unlike Teller, Graham did not believe that one had to push the outer limits of physics to defend the country. He decried the euphoric technological revolution Teller kept touting and argued that the X-ray laser, Teller's pet concept, might be scientifically interesting but would not survive Soviet attack. Graham wrote of the dispute,

> Dr. Edward Teller, with whom we consulted frequently as High Frontier was being fleshed out, was particularly supportive of the X-ray laser option. The concept . . . was based on a nuclear device, a fact which appealed to Dr. Teller as one of history's most eminent nuclear physicists. I do not think, though, that he has ever forgiven me for attacking this concept with the lowly logic of an infantryman.[26]

Reflecting the views of his staffer Codevilla, Wallop also argued for technologies that seemed promising for near-term deployment, including space-based chemical lasers and ground-based interceptors, prototypes of which were being developed by a number of contractors—Boeing, Rocketdyne, TRW, and Lockheed. Several existing programs relevant to the chemical laser—code-named Alpha, Talon Gold, and Lode—were already being pursued by the Pentagon's Defense Advanced Research Projects Agency (DARPA) and the air force, and they could be accelerated. Wallop had between 1980 and 1982 sponsored several Senate amendments encouraging laser development, one of which succeeded in adding funds to the defense appropriation for fiscal year 1984.[27]

Like Graham, Wallop and Codevilla saw the promise of defenses not so much as a visionary transcendence of the nuclear dilemma but as the next logical step in the U.S.-Soviet strategic competition. This decision was driven not by technology—although many technologies had advanced over the years—but by a strategic imperative. These men saw defenses as the way to escape the growing threat of Soviet counterforce developments and the resulting constraints placed on U.S. capabilities, especially in light of the problems being faced in deploying the MX. In short, it was a way out of what arms control experts referred to as nuclear parity but what many conservatives believed to be a dangerous concession to Soviet military power. As Codevilla argued in a recent article,

> It is essential to reiterate that interest in strategic defense arose in the late 1970's not because of any millennial hope that technology just over the horizon would prevent any Soviet missile from reaching the U.S. Rather, it arose because there was no way out of our strategic predicament, and because the technology then in hand, if used, would have radically de-

creased the military and political usefulness of Soviet missiles while providing substantial protection to the American people.[28]

As Graham, Teller, and the kitchen cabinet continued to meet during 1981, their disagreements became increasingly acrimonious, with Graham and Teller intermittently turning to their respective supporters on Capitol Hill and in the media to air disputes. But Graham's influence with the administration was clearly on the wane by the end of 1981. Although he had already briefed Weinberger and General John W. Vessey, who was shortly to become chairman of the JCS, his initial appeal—that he had a blueprint promising "a way out" of existing doctrine—was ultimately his undoing. It was an easy target, as it turned out. An appraisal prepared for the Defense Department in September 1981 ruthlessly ridiculed and discredited the High Frontier proposal.[29]

Wallop and Graham could not compete with Teller's forceful advocacy of revolutionary technological breakthroughs. By Graham's own admission, High Frontier was "scientifically unaesthetic." Graham approached defenses with the perspective of a soldier, not a visionary. As Teller said in 1983, "[High Frontier] is very do-able. And very easily destroyed. It is much too simple to be effective in the way in which it has been proposed." By contrast, Teller had sweeping technological schemes. When asked by Norman Moss about the arms race, Teller said, "It's not an arms race, it's a competition in military technology. . . . It's not the deployment of weapons that counts, it's what goes on in the laboratories. By the time you see weapons being put into place, it's too late."[30]

The members of the kitchen cabinet in 1982 were much more concerned with finding the right political strategy than with finding the most effective technology, however, a subject in which they were not expert. Reflecting the sentiments of the president, they were looking for a major realignment in policy, a bold political stroke. Arguments from Graham or Wallop that defensive efforts were needed to add to U.S. military capabilities—such as Graham's statement "[High Frontier] is not a panacea for all national security problems. Spaceborne defense does not mean that our nuclear retaliatory capabilities can be abandoned or neglected"—were not hitting the right tone.[31]

The kitchen cabinet *was* looking for a panacea, not a plan that could be accused of bolstering American war-fighting capabilities. It began to worry that the concept of "early deployment" of partial defenses, supported by Graham and Wallop, might just end up looking like something from the ABM debates of the 1970s, a development the group specifically wanted to avoid. And Graham himself was beginning to pose image problems. One of his own consultants publicly broke with High Frontier in early 1984, charging that Graham had close ties with the Unification Church—the "Moonies"—including large financial contributions.[32]

By contrast, Teller was inspirational. He kept emphasizing the real possibility of a defense scheme that entirely redirected conflict from earth to space. Teller was adept at using bold language that had intuitive appeal, dramatizing both threats and promises. Teller typically argued that his favorite defense concepts, especially the "Excalibur" X-ray laser, "would end the MAD era and commence the period of assured survival on terms favorable to the Western alliance." On another occasion, he implored the president to fund Excalibur on the grounds that the Soviets already had this system and might soon be able to blackmail the United States: "It is now a question of life and death," he claimed in September 1982.[33]

By January 1982, Teller and the kitchen cabinet had openly broken with Graham and Wallop. Wallop's chemical laser was dismissed as not feasible: it was too heavy to be deployed in sufficient numbers and would be vulnerable as a target since it had to be placed in space before the onset of hostilities. Graham's "mature technology" concepts seemed both hopelessly optimistic and too prosaic.

After being kicked out of the president's advisory group, Graham established a permanent lobby group in Washington, the American Space Frontiers Committee. With support from a range of conservative luminaries, including Clare Boothe Luce, former chief of naval operations Admiral Thomas Moorer, and the science fiction writer Robert Heinlein, Graham set about to build constituencies in the Congress and the bureaucracy. His efforts extended to the financing of congressional candidates sympathetic to his views.

For his part, Wallop continued to promote chemical laser programs in the Senate and to seek support in the administration. Wallop and his staff aide Codevilla arranged a meeting with Weinberger in September 1982 to discuss space-based missile defenses, prompting an article by Clarence Robinson in *Aviation Week and Space Technology* that hailed Weinberger's backing "for a US space-based ballistic missile defense system for protection against intercontinental ballistic missiles." Also attended by Fred Iklé, Richard DeLauer, and H.

Alan Pike, acting director of directed-energy programs at DARPA, the meeting was apparently a lobbying session for the chemical laser. Wallop reported his side of the discussion: "There is no argument that the US could deploy within the next five years a 5-megawatt, 4 meter diameter chemical laser weapon in space that is capable of defeating the current inventory of Soviet weapons systems—ballistic missiles, hostile spacecraft, and bombers at high altitude."[34]

Robinson's depiction of Weinberger's reactions notwithstanding, the chemical laser did not gain a strong constituency in the administration. A Defense Science Board group that assessed space-based lasers (SBLs) in April 1981, a group constituted by the Pentagon in response to a Senate Armed Services Committee request, had been very negative in its evaluation of SBL capabilities for ballistic missile defense. Chaired by the former Pentagon official John Foster, the task force had concluded, "It is too soon to attempt to accelerate SBL development toward integrated space demonstration for any mission, particularly for ballistic missile defense."[35]

Even this largely negative conclusion soon aroused criticism. The Pentagon's inspector general, called on to investigate the panel's findings, alleged that the report's "favorable" conclusions—the panel had recommended an allocation of $50 million for SBL research— were the result of bias. The composition of the panel, including Foster, a senior executive for a company (TRW) that had substantial financial interest in the space-based laser, constituted a conflict of interest.[36]

Both Graham and Wallop and their respective supporters on Capitol Hill, in industry, and among the general public have gone on to become salient critics of the administration's SDI formula. The foundations of the disputes among strategic defense proponents, which were to prove anathema to the SDI, were thus first revealed in the offices of the Heritage Foundation. The group's split over technology reflects the long-standing struggle between advocates of applied and basic research, translated into a struggle over "early deployment" options and visionary technologies. The competition is a question of turf and funding, in addition to any disputes over strategic outcomes. On one side are the interests of weapons designers like Wood and Teller pushing the outer frontiers of science—activities conducted at nuclear laboratories, in universities, and "advanced concept" R & D sectors of defense companies. On the other are defense contractors and their supporters who promote emerging technological concepts that might actually be tested and deployed if given sufficient funding. This competition over "futuristic" versus "near-term" technologies is helping drive the current political wars over the SDI program discussed below.

The Joint Chiefs

On February 11, 1983, the Joint Chiefs assembled in the Roosevelt Room in the White House for a meeting with the president. The decision to hold frequent meetings with the Joint Chiefs was new to Reagan, apparently a reflection of his personal admiration for Vessey. But the Joint Chiefs were finding that these sessions were becoming increasingly tiresome. All they ever seemed to do was present the president with pessimistic assessments of eroding U.S. nuclear capabilities and continued Soviet inroads. After the defeat of Densepack, they were especially dispirited. Vessey felt personally vulnerable for having contributed to the disaster by his ill-advised remarks to the Congress.[37]

In preparation for the meeting on Saturday, March 9, the Joint Chiefs discussed the alternatives they might present to the president. Maybe there was something a bit more impressive and upbeat than improvements in readiness, or some such technicality. The chief of naval operations, Admiral James Watkins, had one possible innovation, derived from a secret navy "white paper" he had commissioned in 1982: strategic defenses. Watkins's idea and the ensuing discussion were modest and quite abstract, according to a participant. Watkins suggested that perhaps over time and in discussion with NATO allies, the United States might exploit its technological advantages and move to a "more moral" defense posture. The question "Wouldn't it be better to save lives than to avenge them?" is reportedly Watkins's, first revealed in this meeting. It reflects the rather philosophical nature of the discussion—not a remark typically heard in the "the Tank," the classified area in which the Joint Chiefs meet to hammer out policy.[38]

Meeting with the president over lunch at the White House, the Joint Chiefs simply presented "defenses" as one item on a list of possible priorities. This was understood simply to suggest that perhaps a study group might be established to investigate defensive alternatives and assess their feasibility, according to General E. C. ("Shy") Meyer, former army chief of staff. In truth, the Joint Chiefs went into the meeting with such an open-ended and inconclusive agenda that they were worried about the president's reaction. They were split on fundamental issues. As one senior official described it, "The Chiefs went over to the White House without any clear idea of what they wanted to achieve and prescribed no particular outcome." Worst of all, they had no solution to the pressing problem of basing the MX.[39]

The discussion with the president was desultory until they came to the subject of defenses. Although the president's account of the hour-long meeting later differed from theirs, participants reported that the president "perked up" when Watkins began his discussion, but that was it. They received no instructions and had little debate. According to a senior administration official, the Joint Chiefs were victims of their own disorganization and ended up completely blindsided. Unknown to them, Watkins's philosophical musings were reinforcing an incipient presidential crusade. The president later claimed that it was "after careful consultation" with his advisers, "including the Joint Chiefs of Staff," that he was embarking on the SDI. The lesson of this episode, the same official concluded, is "don't ever go into a meeting with the president with a briefing that doesn't have a bottom line. That was incredibly bad staff work for four very senior officers."

A Nuclear Event

The defense concept that won the support of the kitchen cabinet relied heavily on the promises of the X-ray laser, a system that Teller convinced the group made feasible the concept of intercepting incoming missiles far beyond the atmosphere. Since it could function only against space targets, not targets on the ground, it could not be accused of being offensive, Teller argued. It was also highly efficient: with a wavelength shorter than a chemical laser's it could achieve more "kills" for each unit of energy and at far greater distances. And it would be far more survivable, since it could be mounted on rockets or submarines and "pop up" at the sign of Soviet attack, not requiring predeployment in space. Its Achilles' heel, apparently not scrutinized by the president's friends, was that it required a nuclear explosion for its energy source.

At what point officials became aware that the nuclear-pumped X-ray laser directly contradicted the idea of the SDI as a nonnuclear defense is not clear, but it served as a key factor undermining the administration's credibility in the congressional and public debate. In an interview with William Broad, an administration official claimed that the president was completely unaware of this problem in 1983. On March 24, 1983, Weinberger reportedly asked DeLauer about the X-ray laser: "It's not a bomb, is it?" DeLauer suggested he refer to it as "a nuclear event."[40]

According to Bill Furniss, an analyst in the Pentagon's Office of Strategic Defense and Space Arms Control Policy, Weinberger would never accept that the X-ray laser was a nuclear-powered system. Richard Wagner, at the time assistant secretary for atomic energy, told Furniss of his repeated efforts to explain it to Weinberger, who simply refused to understand. "Like others who'd tried before, Wagner was finally reduced to saying, 'Cap, it go boom,' " said Furniss. But Weinberger preferred "to close his eyes to reality" and refer to the system with euphemisms like "an X-ray generating device."[41]

The X-ray laser was also subject to acrimonious dispute in the scientific panel appointed by the administration in 1983 to assess technologies for the SDI, according to one participant. "You didn't want to have nukes in space, and putting them on submarines meant we'd have to get the Canadians involved—it was a nightmare for all concerned," remarked another participant. Although it was not endorsed by the panel, and Teller was not a formal consultant, the program remained a key element of SDI funding and rhetoric. As a kind of "black sheep" program, it was kept under the Department of Energy budget and acknowledged by technical experts to be marginal to the SDI per se, but a potentially very significant antisatellite system.

The Excalibur program came to haunt the administration again in 1987, when allegations were leaked to the press that Teller and Wood had exaggerated its capabilities in order to ensure continued funding. A dispute over Excalibur had resulted in the resignation of Roy Woodruff, former head of weapons programs at Livermore, in late 1985. Woodruff accused Teller and Wood of falsifying data and undermining his authority. Woodruff's complaints reportedly led to his demotion and reprimand by the laboratory director, Roger Batzel, whom

Woodruff had also accused of being "fully aware" of the false claims about Excalibur and refusing to reveal "correcting technical data" to temper "overly optimistic, technically incorrect" information being put forward by Wood and Teller. The developments surrounding Woodruff's case underscore the belief among many at the laboratory that any criticism of SDI programs, however valid, was being suppressed.[42]

There were some clear reasons why the labs might discourage disparaging remarks about the SDI. The administration often referred to the "inspiration and excitement" that the SDI brought to young scientists around the country as one of its key achievements. Quite apart from any contribution to American security, it rescued scientists from the monotony of working on traditional nuclear technologies, which had become unexciting. William Lowell Morgan, a Livermore physicist who worked on the X-ray laser, expressed doubts about the SDI but said the science was "very interesting," especially compared with "just going on building warheads for missiles," which had "gotten very predictable and boring." If the technologies remained predictable, moreover, it would mean that continued testing of weapons would be harder to justify—an argument already seized on by advocates of negotiations for a Comprehensive Test Ban, the labs' greatest bête noire.

Having received more than $1 billion for its development between 1983 and 1988, however, the program appears at least on a political level to have done the SDI far more harm than good. As Gregory Herken has argued, the acceleration of Excalibur best exemplifies the description by the former Livermore director Herbert York of the SDI as a whole: "An instance of exceedingly expensive technological exuberance sold privately to an uninformed leadership by a tiny in-group of especially privileged advisors."[43]

The kitchen cabinet and Teller reportedly met with the president three times between January 1982 and March 1983 to discuss strategic defense, as a technical and as a political strategy. The group's recommendations to the president supported a comprehensive defense based on exotic technologies that might take years to develop. As a "futuristic" plan, it could be both politically visionary and less vulnerable to attack on its technical merits.[44]

According to a participant in the meeting of the kitchen cabinet on January 8, 1982, the president asked whether a defense system should protect civilians as well as military forces; Bendetsen argued that it could do both. While the two objectives differed substantially in cost and ambition, he said, "it was too early to make a distinction between city protection and silo protection and we ought to get on with it." The president reportedly responded, "You're right."

Treaty constraints, Bendetsen went on, like those of the ABM and the Outer Space treaties, were problems others could deal with: "So many people on your staff and State and committees on the Hill will be endlessly involved in those questions that it is more constructive for you to pursue the means involved." In response to Bendetsen's recommendation that the president announce a national challenge to develop defensive weapons, something akin to the Manhattan Project, the president said he would have to consult his secretary of defense. "No," said Bendetsen, "if it is going to come from the secretary of defense, you're going to have to talk him into it." Thus, the political strategy for the SDI—a bold announcement that swept aside criticism by ignoring constraints and avoiding consultations with other officials—got another solid boost.[45]

Since the group's optimism was fueled by the promises of the X-ray laser, it appeared that Teller had won a decisive victory. Teller had not just restricted his activities to the kitchen cabinet, moreover, but had engaged in numerous briefings around Washington. His discussions with Admiral Watkins are believed to have had a profound influence on Watkins's thinking. Teller had suggested to the admiral that there might be an augmented role for the navy in strategic defenses if the X-ray laser was placed on submarines. A devout Catholic, Watkins came to support defenses as a philosophical alternative to the immorality of assured destruction.[46]

But Teller was still frustrated that he had not met with the president privately. After many entreaties that were rebuffed by White House staff, he complained during an interview on William F. Buckley's television program "Firing Line" that the president was being denied information on major innovations that could transform American security. Watching the program at his ranch in California, the president had his staff schedule a meeting with Teller. The meeting took place on September 14, 1982, and was apparently cut short by National Security Adviser Clark when it turned into a shameless lobbying effort for the X-ray laser. But despite Clark's admonishments—he reportedly expressed concern that a shift in nuclear strategy of the type being urged by Teller could be so controversial that it would paralyze the bureaucracy—the president was by now committed. Just before giving his speech in the White House, Reagan reportedly turned to Teller—who, along with a small group of eminent scientists, had been invited to watch the speech on closed-circuit television—and said, "Edward, you're going to like it."[47]

Political Theater

Working on the final details of the nuclear freeze resolution about to be introduced in the House of Representatives, Douglas Waller, then an aide to Representative Edward Markey, Democrat of Massachusetts, got a call from his boss right after the president's televised speech on the evening of March 23, 1983. "What the hell is this all about?" asked Markey urgently. "Beats me," Waller responded. "I thought the president was just going off his rocker." But he promised to look into it right away.[48]

The next day, this scene was repeated in offices throughout the Congress. March 24, 1983, was a day for frantic phone calls and hastily assembled meetings as congressional staff struggled to prepare briefing memos on the meaning of the president's speech. Even members of the president's own party were caught in the whirlwind of confusion, and only a few, the members of the "laser lobby," had the slightest idea what the president was talking about.

It is an unwritten rule that the worst mistake a congressional aide can commit is to let the boss be blindsided by unforeseen developments. Members of Congress do not like political surprises. They especially do not like being being quizzed on television about their reactions to policy issues they have not even heard of. Few politicians will ever answer, "I have no idea," when asked an important question in public. The SDI bombshell was therefore not entirely appreciated by many members of Congress who felt they might have been given some warning. Only later did they find out that the secretary of defense had been almost as surprised as they.

No one in the administration now questions that it was a fundamental tactical error to invite the Congress to serve as the arbiter of American nuclear strategy. But this was the net effect of presenting the abstract vision of the SDI to an unprepared Congress. "This is the president's highest priority so just give us the money we ask for and shut up," is how one Republican supporter of defenses described the administration's attitude. But ultimatums have almost never worked in executive-congressional relations. Given the partisan storm already raging over the administration's defense policies, it was like taunting a band of armed guerrillas.

Other groups were quick to get into the act. Within seventy-two hours after the speech, a press conference was held at the Federation of American Scientists, a pro–arms control scientists' lobby in Washington, to denounce Star Wars. Two established arms control experts who had been active participants in prior debates over the ABM, the former SALT I negotiator Raymond Garthoff and the head of the federation, the physicist Jeremy Stone, ridiculed the president's notions. It is a reincarnation of the 1970s debate over defenses, with all of its familiar shibboleths, they argued, a technological pipe dream aimed at destabilizing the U.S.-Soviet nuclear balance. "The president just fell into our hands," said the FAS scientist John Pike, suggesting that the president was naïvely unaware that the national debate over defenses had already been waged and lost, leaving its armies of critics ready to do combat against any possible resurgence.[49]

But many critics badly underestimated the appeal of the president's vision; they assumed that the facts, the patent illusions inherent in the promise of a hermetic shield, would speak for themselves. It was quickly evident that the popular appeal of the astrodome concept, along with the overwhelming technical complexities associated with space defense, was a deadly combination for opponents. They had to explain why they were opposed to defending American lives, but they could do so only with hideously complex arguments about nuclear stability, missile flight trajectories, and Soviet countermeasures. This approach was no match at all for the simple appeal to self-preservation and patriotism in the president's address.

As in the late 1940s when the "atomic revolution" was said by the government to promise everything from cancer cures to a transformation of energy supply and public transportation, the administration's primary public strategy was to emphasize continually the peaceful and patriotic nature of the SDI. It was repeatedly compared to the Apollo program and the effort to put a man on the moon—the embodiment of Americans' greatest hopes and dreams.

As Paul Boyer discusses in an analysis of mass culture and popular attitudes about public policy issues, America was ripe for the SDI in 1983. Two signs were the popularity of video games that simulated exotic space weapons and the overwhelming fascination with the Manichaean values of George Lucas's 1977 film *Star Wars.* Such cultural phenomena carried an implicit message that nuclear war or any military combat could in fact be a matter of bloodless, high-tech battles carried out far beyond any nation's territory, and that the forces of good would inevitably triumph.[50]

It is perhaps not accidental that the same president who had referred to the Soviet Union as the evil empire in 1981 would arrive at a notion of nuclear strategy akin to the mythology of a struggle between the powerful and wicked Darth Vader and the innocent but ingenious hero Luke Skywalker. In fact, within a matter of months, the SDI debate seemed to invoke such a conflict, taking on the appearance of a mortal struggle over competing notions of good and evil and pitting those who "believed" against the doomsayers who questioned the capacity of the American spirit to overcome all things.

All over the country, headlines hailed or decried the president's speech: "Reagan Plans New ABM Effort," "Reagan's Defensive Shield: Hope of the Future," "Cap Hails ABM," "False Promise of Reagan's Star Wars Defenses." Whatever the viewpoint, the early public debate tended to draw on the concepts and arguments over ABM familiar from the 1970s, and it galvanized old struggles among traditional political factions. The Right and the Left mobilized in predictable patterns for a vitriolic debate, bringing in scientific opinion as each saw fit and deploring "the politicization of the scientific community" when competing viewpoints were put forward.

Although much of the public debate took place among experts and scientists—the science wars discussed in chapter 5—citizens' groups played an important role in sparking and sustaining controversies. The SDI prompted the coalescence of many preexisting pro– and anti–arms control groups, ranging from the Coalition for SDI, seventy-five organizations whose aims were identified as preventing "erosion in the SDI budget" and stopping "SDI being traded at the upcoming summit meeting," to the Coalition for the Peaceful Use of Space, a panoply of peace activists, politicians, and media stars who opposed the program as an additional step toward "the militarization of the heavens."

Although over time the debate moved further and further toward the political center, with the press, experts, and politicians increasingly engaged in more sober discussions, the "crazies" on both ends of the political spectrum persisted in their disputes over the SDI as the Apocalypse. A group known as Women for a Secure Future distributed a pamphlet in 1986 that implied Jesus' opposition to disarmament and implicit support for the SDI. Walter Mondale spent over a million dollars on television campaign ads that promised he would "draw a line at the heavens," an anti-SDI cartoon that his campaign manager, Robert Beckel, later admitted was so confusing that most people thought Mondale was brandishing a peace shield.[51]

What the President Meant to Say

The administration's effort to define the SDI program began in a meeting in the White House on March 25, 1983. Richard Bovery, an air force officer on detail to the NSC, was assigned to help Clark oversee the effort from the White House. Pentagon officials included Under Secretary for Policy Fred Iklé and Director of Strategic Forces Frank Miller. Weinberger and Perle were in Europe, discussing the planned deployments of intermediate-range nuclear missiles at a conference of West European defense ministers.

The organizational meeting produced the text for National Security Study Directive 6/83 (NSSD-6/83), signed by the president that day, which set out "the development of an intensive effort to define a long-term research and development program for ballistic missile defenses." The president clearly did not intend his initiative to be the prelude to a new era of conventional antiballistic missile development. He said to McFarlane and his staff in a meeting in the Oval Office to discuss the speech insert on March 21, 1983, "If there is one thing I do not mean by this, gentlemen, it is some kind of terminal defenses around this country." Caspar Weinberger, in remarks on "Meet the Press" on March 27, went further, insisting that the SDI was not for a partial defense but would even include cruise missiles and airplanes.[52]

The president clearly hoped to avoid the political liabilities of the ABM disputes of the 1950s and 1960s. ABM was morally fallible; without the promise of population defense, it would cede the high ground to the very critics he was trying to preempt. Politics aside, terminal defenses were limited to systems that could destroy missiles as they reentered the atmosphere, at the end of their flights. More expensive and technically difficult than simply adding warheads to offensive systems, terminal defenses could be demonstrated to be easily saturated or destroyed.

The appeal of emerging technologies, however, was that offensive missiles could, in theory, be attacked during all phases of their trajectory—boost, postboost, midcourse, and terminal—with each layer adding incrementally to the defense. And the first three phases could be intercepted entirely by space-based systems. The intercepting of missiles in their boost phase is most compelling technologically: at this stage, the missile has not yet dispersed its warheads; a single successful interception can thus destroy as many as ten warheads. The missile also can be tracked more easily and is moving at a slower pace than later in its flight.

Three to six minutes after launch, in the postboost phase, the missiles have begun to disperse warheads, but having left the atmosphere, the missiles become more vulnerable to attack by directed-energy weapons, which are refracted as long as the missile is inside the atmosphere. At midcourse, the major technological hurdle is discrimination: missiles could be armed with dozens, maybe hundreds of decoys that emit the same "signature," confusing and exhausting the defenses. The final, terminal defense layer would be designed to intercept only the few surviving warheads as they reentered the atmosphere and headed toward their targets.

The idea of a "layered" defense provided the technological underpinnings of a "peace shield." For most scientists, this was truly a leap of faith and left abundant technical gaps. The problems ranged from the survivability of the defenses themselves to the computer software required to manage such a complex system, to the achievement of integrated command and control for systems operating in space, to the enormous potential cost.[53]

As was discussed earlier, however, even the possibility that such a scheme might work someday was for Reagan a sufficient basis for a new doctrine. He believed that Americans could finally achieve the ultimate dream of perfect security, effectively disarming the Soviets with American technology or, barring that, deflecting nuclear combat from earth to the nether regions of space. As John Pike put it, "He wanted Americans to share his belief that if war occurred, Americans could go out on their porches with glasses of lemonade, watch an amazing laser light show, and then go back in and watch TV."[54]

From the outset, the discrepancy in the president's speech between a perfect defense that protected populations and a partial defense against ballistic missiles was an intellectual plague for proponents of the SDI. The one had to be total and infallible; the other, only a selective adjunct to offensive forces. This posed questions of technology, timing, and strategic intent. If a defense shield had to be "perfect," then all of its technologies had to be perfected before it was deployed, and it had to be demonstrably survivable, suggesting either remarkable advances in capabilities or a severely reduced offensive threat.

If, on the other hand, the system were designed only to defend the U.S. deterrent against ballistic missiles, then a "phased" deployment of defenses could occur while new technologies were being developed and efforts were made through new offensive developments to thwart additional threats from the Soviet Union. But since the resulting shield would then be imperfect, the Soviets would be expected to add to their offensive capabilities to hold the United States still at risk. This leads to concerns about "crisis stability." Alternatively, the transition to defenses might be linked to arms control, but many Reagan administration officials objected to that on political grounds.

These problems were papered over in NSSD-6/83 with two key decisions. The first was to characterize the enterprise as a long-term research project. Questions about objectives could then be deflected with the response "Until we complete the research . . ." And it sidestepped the question of treaty compliance or the role of arms control as well. Research was permitted explicitly by the ABM agreement and did not need to be discussed with the Soviets. The second decision was to insist on population defense as the only acceptable outcome, to deflect the accusation that the SDI was anything but a "peaceful" initiative designed to end the folly of nuclear vulnerability. Later, the concept of a "peaceful transition" was amplified with the idea that Americans would share their defense technology with the Soviets, moving together into the brave new world.

What the Hell Is Strategic Defense?

NSSD-6/83, signed on April 18, established requirements for two studies, one on policy and one on technology, to give contours to the president's rhetoric. The Defense Technologies Study Team, chaired by the former (and subsequent) NASA director James Fletcher and reporting directly to DeLauer, had sixty members and was charged with looking into the technical feasibility of ballistic missile defenses. The Future Security Strategy Study, chaired by Fred S. Hoffman, president of the defense consulting firm Pan Heuristics, was placed under Iklé's authority to investigate "strategic" implications—the effect of a change in strategy on a range of policy objectives.

The Miller panel, chaired by Frank Miller, also was established by NSDD-6/83 and reported to Iklé. This internal, interagency group was charged with assessing policy implications and coordinating the recommendations of the outside panels. In addition, Weinberger established an "executive committee," composed of Deputy Defense Secretary Paul Thayer, Vessey, all the defense under secretaries, the deputy assistant for directed-energy weapons, Donald Lamberson, Vince Puritano (assistant secretary in charge of the comptroller's office), and David Chu, director of program analysis and evaluation. Lamberson was later replaced by Brigadier General Robert Rankine.[55]

The appointment of outside panels had two prime motivations. First, there was little expertise assembled inside the Pentagon to conduct technical analyses. Some work did begin under Robert Cooper, the director of DARPA, who relied on Lamberson and a small staff, which reported to DeLauer. But this was thought insufficient, in terms of both staff size and the outside image that the analyses required. A blue-ribbon panel was needed to give the enterprise a serious boost and the imprimatur of the country's most-senior scientists.

Besides, some of the professionals inside the administration had already been criticized publicly by staunch defense advocates. Some NSC staff members, for instance, complained about Cooper's commitment to science over weaponry. Another critic accused him of having "striven to reduce pressure from Congress for strategic defense." DeLauer had also already made known his profound skepticism about the initiative. Just after the speech, on April 1, 1983, he was quoted in the *New York Times* as having said, "To think you can engineer them [theories] into a weapons system, with the same incredible pointing accuracy, and put it all into space—well, I think the difficulty of such programs has been understated."[56]

The reason for the second outside panel, according to a senior Pentagon official, was that Iklé wanted a panel of his own but thought his internal staff lacked the stature or vision to conduct a study that could compete with the Fletcher panel. Iklé was still concerned about the "Carter holdovers" and professional technocrats who might resist bold change. And he had tremendous regard for the "strategic genius" of some of his old friends from the Rand Corporation, including Hoffman and Albert Wohlstetter, a strategist who had developed the first theories of deterrence. It was an opportunity for Iklé to accord a role to his former colleagues, and he knew he could trust them.

In one of the earliest bureaucratic conflicts over the SDI, Iklé assumed that members of his staff would work for Hoffman, among them Deputy Assistant Secretary William Hoehn, Director of Strategic Forces Frank Miller, and his deputy, Bill Furniss. They confronted Iklé and refused, arguing that they did not believe that fundamental government policy decisions could be contracted out, conducted by consultants who make up a sector known in Washington as "beltway bandits." In any case, they stated, we work for the government, and can't provide staff support for contractors.[57]

The reliance on outside contractors to conduct studies was soon to become the mainstay of SDI analyses, as will be discussed below. The extent of the reliance bothered some professionals in the Pentagon, civilian and military, and was to become a more serious irritant over time. In Iklé's case, the decision to launch the Hoffman study reflected a fundamental misunderstanding of how the bureaucratic process works. One official remarked, "Just like there's matter and antimatter, there's bureaucratic skill and antibureaucratic skill. No matter what, Iklé instinctively always does the wrong thing."[58]

Since Iklé was to become a leading spokesman for the most ambitious goals of the SDI, his role in the Pentagon is important. Although he was an ultimate "true believer," he seems more often than not to have been at sea within the Pentagon mainstream. As one official close to him said, "Iklé is almost unique among Washington figures. He writes his own stuff. No one knows who he speaks for. He isn't close to Weinberger. And everyone knows that he was appointed as a payoff to [the conservative North Carolina senator] Jesse Helms for getting [Deputy Secretary Frank] Carlucci confirmed." (Carlucci, appointed secretary of defense to replace Weinberger in late 1987, is a career public servant who somehow won a reputation as being too liberal for the Reagan administration. Liberal, in this case, means "a closet pragmatist," in the words of one of his colleagues.) Asked why Iklé was so uncommunicative and isolated from his staff, a senior Pentagon official said simply, "He's Swiss."[59]

The conflict over the relative authority of "outsiders" and "insiders" persisted throughout the studies' lifetime. Furniss recalls that he repeatedly explained to Iklé that the internal review group had the final say on the coordination of the studies. On a day when Furniss and Iklé were to brief the Fletcher panel, they discussed this in the car on the way to the meeting. "Iklé made no objections. But as soon as he stepped up to the podium to address the Fletcher panel members, all he talked about was the Hoffman study and never mentioned his own staff." As the studies proceeded, Hoffman and Iklé met privately a great deal. "We never knew what they talked about," says Furniss, "but we had to force ourselves on him to give him briefings about our work."[60]

The Fletcher panel, which consisted of representatives from the entire defense R & D community, from government laboratories to private industry and universities, produced a twelve-volume classified report. The report was cautiously optimistic about some technologies—infrared chemical lasers, excimer lasers, neutral- and charged-particle beams, electromagnetic rail guns, and X-ray lasers. It was represented in White House and Pentagon briefings, however, as upbeat in assessing the possibility of developing a comprehensive defense. A "meaningful" level of defense, with terminal and midcourse layers, could be deployed by the 1990s, it concluded. A complete system, including a boost-phase layer, might be deployable in the year 2000 and would cost about $90 billion. The panel recommended a "technology-driven" research program—a program limited not by funds but by the pace of technical advancements—with an initial price of between $18 billion and $27 billion over five years.[61]

But the panel did not endorse the president's peace shield, which it called "not technically credible." In fact, the panel did not even address the question of defense against air-delivered Soviet weapons—bombers and cruise missiles—or more prosaic efforts for terminal defenses. And to the horror of near-term defense proponents, the

Fletcher panel had used a standard of 99 percent effectiveness as the basis for judging the viability of a comprehensive system.

The Fletcher report was attacked from both the Right and the Left. Supporters of "early deployment" of mature technologies argued that the report had made impossible demands on technology and had derailed the goal of strategic defense with an open-ended quest for futuristic technology. Defense critics claimed falsification of conclusions, arguing that the technical reports did not support the optimism of the unclassified summary report. As Theodore Postol, a former assistant to Watkins, described it,

> If you read volume seven [the classified concluding section of the Fletcher report], you wouldn't bother reading the rest of the report. It presents an overwhelming case against the possibility of a hope of mounting something useful. It quite unambiguously indicates the problem was insolvable unless certain things were solved that no one even knew how to address.[62]

The twelve-man Hoffman panel, meeting in offices in Rosslyn, Virginia, on the floor below the room where the Fletcher group often met, argued that defenses would be helpful to "retaliatory deterrence" and, unlike the more futuristic Fletcher panel, recommended phased deployment of defense systems. Deployments could begin with antitactical ballistic missiles in Europe, which the panel deemed urgent, to be followed by defense of the U.S. command and control infrastructure and some "intermediate boost-phase capabilities against large Soviet ICBMs." Although it was less exacting in its demands on technology, the Hoffman panel also repudiated the concept of perfect defenses, or even significant population defenses.[63]

The Hoffman report had little impact. It was appended to the Fletcher and Miller reports for White House transmission and sank quietly into obscurity. The Hoffman panel had been late in starting and was late with its report. More important, for whatever reason, it had strayed from its mandate of evaluating policy implications—issues like the political impact on the NATO allies of a shift in U.S. doctrine—and tried to be a mini-Fletcher technology group. Distracted by "technology-envy," according to one source, it did not measure up in this regard, either. As one panel member put it, "The study fell into the trap that went into the thinking about MIRV developments, asking, 'What happens if we deploy?' and holding the Soviet threat constant. It was unrealistic and unenlightening." Defenses always look good if measured against a static offensive threat, but this hardly provides a path to reality.[64]

Ideologues and Apparatchiks: The Phantom Report

The task of policy integration fell to the Miller group, comprising about ten midlevel officials from the Pentagon, the State Department, the CIA, DIA, and ACDA who examined the full range of policy questions raised by a defensive doctrinal shift. The State Department assessed foreign policy implications, ACDA the implications for arms control, the CIA and DIA looked at likely Soviet responses, DIA evaluated the impact on other nuclear states, including China, and the Pentagon examined the effects on deterrence and nuclear war plans. Together, the analysts conducted a dynamic analysis of the potential effectiveness of both U.S. and Soviet defenses, the impact of each side's perceptions of effectiveness, the real and perceived vulnerabilities of defenses and offenses, and the implications for the overall U.S.-Soviet military balance.

The report went into detail about potential ways to defeat defenses, including the potential increases in Soviet countermeasures and augmented deployments of systems not covered by defenses, about the problems of cost and technical feasibility if defenses prove more expensive and elusive than offenses, and about the need for arms control to bring about a stable transition from current strategy. It also explored very sensitive political issues, such as the uncertainties of allied nations resulting from a major shift in U.S. strategy, the absence of protection implied by the SDI for NATO and non-NATO allies like Japan, and the negative impact of some defenses on the U.S. strategy of "limited nuclear options."

At the end, the Miller report stated that defenses could augment deterrence by complicating the problems faced by a Soviet attack, but it offered nineteen cautionary conclusions about the implications of different ways to achieve this objective. "We said some defenses are good, some defenses are bad—you have to identify the context and resolve the stability problems before you can judge whether to go forward," said Furniss.[65]

The classified version of the Miller report was never released to the Congress, and Miller's report per se never had an unclassified version akin to those of the Hoffman and the Fletcher panels. This led to speculation that Miller's conclusions were extremely critical of the SDI and were therefore suppressed. The phantom Miller report has been the subject of great press interest, as if it were the hidden stake that could have been driven through the heart of the SDI at the outset. In fact, many of the conclusions of the Miller group appear in unclassified form in other documents, including the Pentagon report "Policy Implications of Defenses against Ballistic Missiles." According to one individual familiar with its conclusions, "It was by no means a diatribe against the SDI."[66]

Miller's group tried to integrate the bold rhetoric of the SDI into practical considerations of current policy—from existing U.S. offensive force modernization goals to the cohesion of the NATO alliance, which was then being sorely tested by the impending intermediate-range nuclear forces (INF) deployments, and the difficulties of maintaining strategic stability during a major realignment of the U.S. force posture. It represented the collective wisdom of the professionals who would actually have to implement the policy, reflecting their real-world biases and concerns. As such, it was a far more revealing document than the reports of the contractors' panels, which did not have the task of integrating technical and political objectives into the more prosaic reality of competing security priorities and international constraints.

When Furniss went to brief the Fletcher panel about the Miller group's work, in the summer of 1983, he raised hackles by stating categorically that they should forget about population defense. "This is about deterrence," he said, "how to complicate the task of the attacker and hopefully, one day, to deny an attacker's objectives." He also demonstrated that even near-perfect defenses left a world of MAD—even 1 percent "leakage" allowed sufficient warheads through to pose an unacceptable threat to populations. "I don't think I want that kind of defense, where the Soviets say, we can accept ten million deaths, can you?" Furniss told the panel. The irony of "perfect defenses" is that they really did create a world of MAD, where the only recourse either side had was to target populations, since military forces would be defended.[67]

Furniss also demonstrated the difficulties of transition: the most unstable world was one in which defenses were 50 percent effective, driving both sides to add to both offenses and defenses in order to offset the rapidly changing military calculus. "Why are you even showing this?" John Gardner, the executive secretary of the Hoffman group and later a key SDI official, scoffed. "We would never deploy anything of this low level of effectiveness." His words were to come back to haunt him.[68]

Fletcher and Jerry Yonas, later the chief scientist and acting director of the SDI, were aghast. Fletcher went immediately to complain to DeLauer that the policy people were way off base. "A hundred and eighty degrees from the president's vision," he said. Miller had to calm DeLauer down and assure him that his group was not trying to sabotage the SDI.[69]

But there was a clash of understanding about "what the president meant" and how best to implement it. The contractors had been hired to engineer the revolution, while the Miller report struck political officials as the product of disloyal "status quo" advocates. Iklé simply concluded that a report prepared by bureaucrats was of no consequence, and he was most instrumental in seeing that it was never considered seriously. "Since it didn't take a rosy view of BMD, there was something wrong with its patriotism," said Furniss in describing the reaction of some administration persons. Its principal conclusion, that defenses had as their major contribution the heightening of an attacker's uncertainty, was criticized as myopic. It was not what the president intended at all, critics maintained. Yet this anodyne conclusion, seen as heresy in 1983, is the main rationale offered for the SDI today. In fact, it is only the Miller group's work that has withstood the test of time and survived the ideological excesses of the initial years of the SDI's formulation.

The administration's depiction of the Miller report as an executive document, thus not releasable to Senator John Warner's Subcommittee on Strategic and Theater Nuclear Weapons, fueled the perception that the hard questions were deliberately being avoided. It was reported that for bureaucratic reasons—Iklé jealously guarding his turf—the Fletcher panel had been told repeatedly not to stray into the realm of policy questions. Some commentators concluded that the analysis was therefore entirely about technological feasibility but that no one had ever asked whether the enterprise itself was worth the risks. Michael MccGwire, a senior fellow at the Brookings Institution, described his impression as follows:

Arguments about costs and technological feasibility are inevitably spongy, because SDI research is still exploring new possibilities and operational deployment lies ten, twenty or even thirty years ahead. The fact that discussion focuses on these aspects reflects a bias in the Washington debate on defense procurement and does not denote their relative importance. Before one asks "Will it work?" or "How much will it cost?" there comes the question "Is it necessary or even desirable?"[70]

As it was, the hard questions were asked in the Miller study, but no answers could be provided, the study argued, until scientists had developed the technical foundations for the SDI. Only after the system's effectiveness and cost were assessed, and the likely Soviet reactions to it better understood, could any reasoned decision be made about the SDI's feasibility. As it was, the fundamental question "Is it desirable?" had already been answered on March 23.

Accordingly, the Pentagon concluded that a quest for new ballistic missile defense (BMD) technologies was a worthy objective. In November 1983, Weinberger announced the formal beginnings of the SDI. The findings of the reports got offical sanction from the president in NSDD-119 on January 4, 1984, and the first budget for a boosted defense effort was submitted to the Congress in February, a request for $1.99 billion, $250 million above the prior year's allocation.

CHAPTER 5

Star Wars: The Bureaucracy

"**S**DI is the label applied to a number of preexisting programs of the Defense Department which bear an arguable relationship to strategic defense," criticized Angelo Codevilla in 1986. In fact, the SDI Organization (SDIO), established in March 1984, was first based on an amalgamation of existing programs, about twenty-five current BMD-related programs from the air force, the army, the navy, the Defense Nuclear Agency, and DARPA. Five new program elements were defined for the SDI effort: surveillance, acquisition, tracking and kill assessment; directed-energy weapons; kinetic energy weapons; systems analysis and battle management; and support programs.[1]

According to the SDIO's plan, the program would have four phases. Phase 1 was to be the research phase, coinciding with the Fletcher panel's recommendations for the pursuit of futuristic technologies, and lasting into the early 1990s. On the basis of the phase 1 analysis, the next president could decide whether or not to begin full-scale engineering development of a defensive shield. Phase 2 would require the abrogation of the ABM Treaty to permit the development, testing, and production of defense prototypes. Phase 3 was to be the "transition" phase, in which the United States and the Soviet Union would both move toward greater reliance on defenses, and finally, in phase 4, both sides would have "highly effective" shields and negligible offenses.[2]

Phase 1 of the enterprise was to have a five-year budget of $26 billion, a figure that DeLauer improvised under pressure from the

Senate. "I tried to figure out what the hell we're talking about," he said. "Sam Nunn wanted a number and kept insisting on having a number. . . . OK . . . first year was $2.4 billion, and I figure, OK, best we could handle is maybe 20–25 percent per year growth."[3]

Underlying almost any policy debate over national goals and objectives is the impetus of competing self-interests. Different perceptions of gains and losses, in addition to belief systems, motivate individuals and organizations to interpret policy in a way that they find advantageous and that may sometimes be at odds with more abstract ideas of the national interest. With persistence and political skill, individuals can often exercise influence considerably out of proportion to their formal authority in the American political process, a phenomenon quite pronounced in the diffuse bureaucratic environment surrounding the SDI. Formal, Weberian models of bureaucracy simply do not explain the day-to-day struggles among government officials in this instance.

Competing interests often fall across institutional lines. As Morton Halperin has described it,

> When individuals in the American government consider a proposed change in American foreign policy, they often see and emphasize quite different things and reach different conclusions. A proposal to withdraw troops from Europe, for example, is to the Army a threat to its budget and size; to Budget Bureau examiners a way to save money; to the Treasury Department a gain in the balance of payments; to the State Department's Bureau of European Affairs a threat to good relations with NATO; and to the president's congressional advisers an opportunity to remove a major irritant in the president's relations with the Hill.[4]

The first to "win" as a result the 1983 policy shift seemed to be the reascending BMD community; the first to "lose" were members of the old-line establishment, caricatured as MAD advocates. A closer look at the SDI debate within the executive branch, however, and even just among individuals with responsibility for the SDI in the Pentagon, reveals a wide variance of perspectives about SDI goals. This was clearly aggravated by the policy vacuum created by the president's speech. The internal SDI debate became an exaggerated version of traditional rivalries—among the national laboratories, defense contractors, the services, and different components of the civilian bureaucracy. The real winners and losers are hard to identify in the maelstrom of shifting program objectives.

Star Wars: The Bureaucracy

The mandate of the SDIO was "to conduct research to determine the feasibility of an effective ballistic missile defense." The dissonance between the president's vision and the mandate of the SDIO was thus formally and explicitly laid out.

The policy did not even have a name until the fall of 1983. The State Department referred to it as DABM, Defense against Ballistic Missiles, after the decision memorandum. The press first called it ABM, then Star Wars, to the administration's chagrin. Finally, in September, in a meeting in the Pentagon, the name "Strategic Defense Initiative" was hatched. Perle had argued that "Star Wars" was just fine— "it was a great movie and the good guys win"—just the message they were trying to convey. But Weinberger thought this was too frivolous; he wanted a more prosaic title. Although many take credit for inventing the label "Star Wars," from Representative Tom Downey, Democrat of Massachusetts, to Art Buchwald, the term "Strategic Defense Initiative" was just the product of a bureaucratic process, hatched inadvertently by Miller and Furniss in a draft response to NSSD-6/83, in which they tried to avoid the awkward formulation DABM by referring instead to the "president's initiative" for strategic defense.

At first, the all-consuming nature of the SDI helped build coalitions among individuals who otherwise might have been at odds. A futuristic research program sidestepped the difficult issues of treaty compliance, the role of allies, and "all those other tacky political questions," as Furniss put it. Galvanized by the high priority given the program by the president, traditional proponents of strategic defenses found cooperation among those who were not at first enthusiastic but who saw defenses as a potential way to advance other objectives. To some, it suggested a way to challenge the Soviets in Geneva to gain arms control concessions; to others, it was a glamorous cover for achieving terminal defense deployments; to still others, it held the promise of an enhanced U.S. military space program.

Within a short time, however, the policy confusion led to feuds between White House and Pentagon officials, and among political appointees and professionals inside the Pentagon. The political attraction of the peace shield was its selling point as a public strategy. But the intellectual and strategic fragility of an all-encompassing astrodome defense made the enterprise seem ludicrous and might lead to its undoing.

Even as Pentagon officials were discussing ways to use defenses to "enhance deterrence" and possibly limit damage to population centers as a by-product, administration advisers like Abrahamson and Keyworth were touring the country decrying this goal and promising a hermetic seal. "The president was not talking about improving warhead exchange ratios," said Keyworth in 1984; "we're not trying to preserve nuclear deterrence in this program; we're trying to move away from reliance upon the nuclear deterrent." Each time administration officials engaged in this kind of exaggerated promise, it fell to career Pentagon professionals, like Frank Miller, to take them to task.[5]

Institutional lines were redrawn after the SDI became a subject in U.S.-Soviet arms control discussions. At first fairly oblivious to the SDI, the State Department and the NSC, along with officials in the Pentagon's Office of International Security Policy, took a far more active interest beginning in early 1985, and their disparate opinions, revealed publicly as if they were administration policy, were never again in sync.

In the effort to wrest control of the rhetoric, a National Security Decision Directive was signed in late 1985 requiring that all public pronouncements about the SDI go through clearance by the NSC. The inspiration of a special assistant to the national security adviser, Colonel Robert Linhard, it reflected the ascendancy of diplomatic sensitivities about the program. Ironically, the directive was not coordinated with anyone in the Pentagon who knew anything about the SDI. To some SDIO officials, it had the effect of stifling their "sales program," as one described it. It restricted who could speak for the program in public, as well as what could be said. "We called it the gag order," said a former SDIO representative, who claimed that it preempted the ability of SDIO spokesmen to take their case to the public.[6]

In the absence of clear objectives and in the face of growing public and congressional scrutiny, competing advocates soon found themselves at odds over the most basic rationales. Eventually, this led to bureaucratic sabotage. Too many contradictions were being papered over to discipline the competing interests of officials, while the prominent profile of the program invited the disaffected to leak their disagreements to the Congress and the press.

The tactic of shifting objectives, termed "bait and switch" by the former defense secretary Harold Brown, forever kept critics off guard. But it caused even more consternation among serving officials, especially those who thought that the only honest policy for the administration was to abrogate explicitly the ABM Treaty and thereby repudiate its intellectual origins in MAD doctrine, as had been the SDI's promise. Reflecting institutional biases, some thought this should be done through deployments of mature technologies, while others promoted demonstrations of futuristic technologies.

When the administration moved to "reinterpret" the meaning of the ABM Treaty in late 1985, both these factions thought they had won a decisive victory. But in bowing to political pressure and stating that it would still conduct the SDI program within the treaty's traditional boundaries, the administration fueled further internal dissent. To a growing number of officials tired of the "charade" of the ABM Treaty, the White House seemed gutless. As one official remarked, "The idea that you could pursue the SDI without abrogating the ABM Treaty is the bureaucratic analog of the zipless fuck."[7]

Sibling Rivalry

The struggle to define the program was influenced significantly by the military services, although the Joint Chiefs were virtually out of the formal policy-making process until quite recently. At the time the SDIO was established, the only "mature" BMD programs were under the aegis of the Army Ballistic Missile Defense Command in Huntsville, Alabama. The BMDC had two programs, the Advanced Technology Program, which had a space component, and the Systems Technology Program, largely built around ground-based, terminal concepts. The army's role in defenses has to be understood in the context of its historical struggle to gain a role in planning strategic nuclear war, a struggle motivated not just by prestige but also by the competition for funds. Since the army has been largely unsuccessful in gaining a part in strategic planning, it has jealously guarded its one prerogative, the previously unglamorous task of missile defense. As a result, the SDI had great appeal for the army. "The Army's tenacity in strategic defense paid off when the SDIO was formed," boasted Lieutenant General Robert D. Hammond, commander of the BMDC's stepchild, the Army Strategic Defense Command, established in 1985.

The army had a direct interest in ensuring that the SDI was not just a futuristic program but would lead to deployments in the near term.

The army at first had the least stake in emerging, meaning mostly space-based, technologies, with the exception of the free-electron laser. Over time, however, the army laid claim to a far broader role, not only capturing a third of the SDI's budget but also redefining its own technological interests to include space-based systems useful for army missions. "The Army of today and the twenty first century," argued Hammond, "must make the necessary mental adjustment to expand its thinking to easily encompass space capabilities."[8]

An initial effort to associate the SDI with the army's programs had been vociferously opposed by the other services. The opposition was quite straightforward: it was over money. As one official charged with briefing the Joint Chiefs about the conclusions of the Miller, Hoffman, and Fletcher panels described it, "All they wanted to know was where the money was going to come from." Reassured that the funds would come from future allocations for research and development—"funny money," as Shy Meyer put it—and not their own coffers, the other services still would not abdicate authority for the SDI to the army. The army–air force dispute over defenses in the 1960s, which revolved around air force opposition to having "its" missile silos protected by army ABMs and around concern that a commitment to silo defense would take money away from new missiles, was not forgotten. In addition, there was the SDI's promise of a greater U.S. role in space, an arena the Air Force planned to dominate fully.

The prospect of space defense poses inherent rivalries among the services. These were summarized colorfully by Daniel O. Graham in a letter to Weinberger in November of 1982:

> . . . A change of roles and missions among the services [is] a problem which runs shudders of apprehension through the JCS. The Army cannot retain the mission of strategic defense if its future is in space, and will therefore stoutly resist any spaceborne BMD concept. What makes the problem worse is that the Service which would have to accept the mission, the Air Force, doesn't want it. Air Force was born of strategic attack, not defense. Further, both Air Force and Army see the High Frontier concepts as threats to ongoing programs. . . . If one can see spaceborne defense even partially deployed, there is no need for high-capability, long-life, ground-based ABM systems. And the protection for MX can be provided without resort to expensive deployment schemes.[9]

Initial guidance from the Office of the Secretary of Defense called for the air force to assume the preponderance of responsibilities, including research into space-based lasers, continued activities in the detection and tracking of missiles, the survivability of satellite and communications links, and preparation for manned operations in space.

An effort by the army in 1983 to present its defense programs to the Congress as broader and more ambitious than silo defense, in the effort to get larger appropriations, had not succeeded, notwithstanding the lobbying by interested contractors. The army did succeed in subsequent years. Of the large, long-term SDI contracts awarded between 1983 and 1985, almost two-thirds went for army BMD projects, and the army was to take over significant responsibility for systems such as ground-based lasers. Overall, the funding profile for the SDI reflected a "split the difference" strategy to paper over the services' disagreements about whether the program was evolutionary, with a role for "traditional" technology, or futuristic and revolutionary.

The establishment of the U.S. Space Command, spurred by the SDI, also fueled service rivalries, as well as disputes with NASA. Although in title multiservice, the United Space Command is naturally dominated by the air force. Its purpose is to coordinate space activities of all the services and to provide the operational focus for strategic defenses. The Space Command was originally just an air force enterprise, and the establishment of the unified agency was strongly resisted by Secretary of the Navy John Lehman and has since been a source of chronic friction. The navy complains that air force control of the satellites on which it depends will result in cuts to its programs in favor of SDI activities preferred by the air force. "We don't want to have to sit around saying 'Get off the phone, we need to make a long-distance call,' " said one navy official. The army has weighed in with its objections to air force control of its Huntsville operations.[10]

The failure to resolve interservice rivalries is playing a key role in current factionalism over the direction of the SDI. Supported by the army, "Lockheed and MacDonnell-Douglas want to sell 'Sentinel' again, so they run around the Hill and brief their friends whenever they can," according to Bruce Jackson, an official in the Office of Strategic Defense and Space Arms Control Policy in the Pentagon. Lockheed put together a briefing on its "ERIS" ground-based ABM interceptors, which won wide support among early-deployment buffs, eventually becoming one of the first six systems approved for acquisition in an early deployment plan. But this and other related "terminal" concepts are subject to attack by the air force and civilian officials who see an emphasis on terminal defense as derailing the real objective of the SDI, to augment U.S. military capabilities in space.

The Star Czar

Given the less than unanimous support from the services, the idea of a central directorate for the SDI had been discussed off and on—by the Fletcher panel, among others. The Senate had faced the issue indirectly in the fiscal year 1984 defense authorization bill, when it defeated an amendment by Senator Wallop to shift responsibility for laser research from the air force and DARPA to the army's BMDC. In deference to Wallop, the subsequent House-Senate conference report recommended that a "single, senior official with overall responsibility for directed energy" be designated within the Pentagon.

The most important reason for having a new organization was the SDI's need for an institutional champion. Without it, the SDI could easily be shunted aside in intramural disputes among the service secretaries and the Joint Chiefs. The job was too great for the resources of DARPA. Jointly managed programs, such as the one implicit in the suggestion that the SDI be run by a coalition of representatives from the services and laboratories reporting to DR & E, had never worked well in the past. Some argued that what was needed was a separate office like the one Hyman Rickover had run to develop the navy's nuclear power program.

On the civilian side, no one seemed especially wild about taking over the SDI. The resignation of Paul Thayer as deputy secretary in 1984 removed one key individual who could have overseen the program. Perle and his deputy, Frank Gaffney, preoccupied with the Reagan arms control agenda, paid very little attention in the early stages and, according to several administration colleagues, thought it a liability to be too closely associated. Gaffney had earlier, as a Republican staffer for the Senate Armed Services Committee, "routinely slashed the army's ballistic missile defense programs by half or more," according to one of his former Capitol Hill colleagues. "Most senior people in the administration thought it was oddball, and didn't want to get tarred," said Furniss.[11]

The search for a "star czar" in early 1984 first faced the question of who would be willing to take a job in which he or she would be dependent on good relations with the armed services, while simultaneously encroaching on their turf. This would be difficult for a senior military officer—potential career suicide if he alienated those who would later determine his promotions. And the SDI still struck some as flaky and probably short-lived. Several individuals were reportedly offered the job and declined, including the former NASA deputy director Hans Mark and the retired air force generals Bernard Schriever and Samuel Phillips.[12]

Abrahamson, the associate administrator for space flight at NASA and formerly the manager of the F-16 fighter program, was no one's first choice. A quiet and affable man, he was of "no consequence," according to one official centrally involved in the search. Abrahamson came to Washington all but lacking any "in-house" constituency, just after overseeing the eleventh flight of the space shuttle *Challenger.*

Reflecting the institutional sensitivities surrounding the SDI—especially the potential drain on resources or clout coming from a new layer of bureaucracy—Abrahamson was designated a program manager, although he reported directly to Weinberger. The SDIO was considered a "technical program," not a defense agency. Abrahamson's title is now used by critical colleagues as a put-down, to indicate his limited authority and limited skills.

The SDIO's mandate sought to incorporate all of the potentially competing bureaucratic interests. Although Abrahamson reported directly to the secretary and was to have "overall responsibility for managing the program and reporting on its progress," several corollary groups were established to provide policy advice and coordination. An interagency group, known as the SIG-DP, chaired by the deputy secretary, included representatives from all executive branch agencies with an interest in security policy. An SDI executive committee, Excom, was to provide policy coordination within the DoD, including the services, military departments, defense agencies, and components of the Office of the Secretary of Defense. And there was to be an SDI advisory panel of outside consultants, "to provide important independent assessments of our plans and research efforts." For the most part, these institutional formalities have been irrelevant to the implementation of the SDI.[13]

The program aggregated significant new authority at the expense of existing bureaucracies and the services. Three "fundamental authorities" given the SDIO director, revealed by Abrahamson in April 1984, included (1) the right to ask each service and agency to designate an office responsible for the SDI, "to facilitate prompt response on the program"; (2) giving full responsibility for the overall policy directly to the secretary of defense; and (3) issuing task orders for SDI work, under SDI management, from relevant components of the Pentagon.

In response to a question from Senator Warner about how he planned to make sure that other agencies did not siphon off his funds or circumvent him, given his lack of experience in management in the Defense Department, Abrahamson replied,

> The process which we have come to agreement on is one that we think will provide a fully fenced budget, but also will make the SDI program a responsible part of the overall problems. They will be examined and the Secretary of Defense will be the only one that will make final apportionment. The way in which we go about that is that we will ask the services in the preparation of their budget . . . to estimate their programs, to rank them and to propose any initiatives in the area they think are important, *but they will only be able to keep those in any line item that is in the SDI line. They will not be able to trade those off for other service needs.*[14]

In other words, according to a Pentagon official, "every time Abe had a fight, he had carte blanche to go whining to Weinberger and circumvent normal channels."[15]

Abrahamson did develop a rather freewheeling management style, which drew on his access to the secretary and his implicit backing by the president. Policy coordination was not his strong suit. "When the JCS asked if they could go with him to a meeting with the president or the secretary, his staff would say, 'No, he's going as the head of a defense agency.' When someone from OSD would ask, they'd say, 'No, he's a military officer.' When he'd have direct contact with the NSC on a policy matter, his staff would claim he was part of the OSD," recalled a close colleague who was infuriated with the degree of autonomy granted Abrahamson.[16]

Abrahamson's failure to coordinate policy matters through routine channels had partly to do with the siege mentality that surrounded the SDI: "This is the jungle and we have no friends," one SDIO official noted. It was also consciously run as a "guerrilla operation," bent on circumventing the lumbering bureaucracy that might squelch its revo-

lutionary exuberance. Many SDIO officials talk about the SDIO as a
"unique culture" or "an attitude," specifically aimed at imposing innovation on the hidebound bureaucrats who are inherently wary of
change and mindlessly protective of the status quo.[17]

But it was also a matter of Abrahamson's personal pride. Even
though he had no policy experience and though his understanding of
nuclear strategy was embryonic—or "juvenile," as one of his colleagues claims—he insisted on being the chief spokesman for the
entire program, its strategic rationales as well as its technical feats.
"Instead of going to Perle and saying, 'Help me, I don't know anything
about policy, and I should be spending my time at the national labs
evaluating technology,' he insisted on being the president's spokesman. 'I have assistant secretary rank,' he'd insist," argued Bruce
Jackson. "The program fell victim to the Andy Warhol syndrome. The
general became surrounded by sycophants telling him he was a
star."[18]

Apparently, no civilians had sufficient clout to correct the excesses
and failing of his public diplomacy efforts. "Why should a general
listen to a twenty-nine-year-old bearded twerp?" asked one official,
referring to the deputy assistant secretary for policy, Frank Gaffney,
who had theoretical authority for SDI policy clearance. As a result,
no one reviewed Abrahamson's testimony or ever persuaded him to
bring his public relations rhetoric more in line with the realities of the
program.

As it was, Weinberger and Iklé also operated in a realm of unrelenting high polemics. According to colleagues, only Kathy Troia had
any success watering down Weinberger's excesses, partly because
she was the speech writer and partly because of her personal relationship with him. Iklé simply refused to hire additional people in his
directorate to handle policy control for the SDI and engaged in exten-
sive rhetorical profligacy of his own. As a result, the SDIO could fill
the policy vacuum largely as it saw fit, and could do so increasingly
independently of the agencies with whom it was supposed to work.

Thrown to the forefront of the debate before he had much time even
to read into the subject, Abrahamson became something of a human
microcosm of the SDI, reduced to using hyperbole and exaggerated
rhetoric when the answers to the litany of questions simply were not
there. He was also the ultimate incarnation of the "can-do" mentality,
full of boundless technological optimism, and never taking no for an
answer when a subordinate tried to tell him something was impossi-

ble. As was to become increasingly clear, however, even Abrahamson could not negotiate the laws of physics.

Abrahamson's first and enduring priority was to create a bureaucratic reality for the SDI—from a base of contractors developing "systems architectures" and answering technical and policy questions to a robust in-house staff capable of running studies, preparing testimony, rebutting critics, and generally defending the program against the onslaughts of critics. The staff grew quickly, drawing on lab scientists, military personnel, and sympathetic civilians. In 1985, Abrahamson announced plans to double the staff from 100 to 200 in two years: "You cannot spend billions of dollars of this kind of money with a 100-man team and do it in a responsible way," he told a congressional subcommittee. The Defense Department overall also doubled its SDI-related personnel in this time period, the largest increase going to the air force.[19]

The impulse to bureaucratize is the most frequently cited characteristic that Abrahamson's colleagues refer to in describing his stewardship of the SDI. This is ironic, since in public he had stressed the need to avoid bureaucratic protocol in order to impel radical progress. As a "program manager," however, he had the instinctive understanding that it is difficult to roll back policy initiatives once they involve people and money—constituencies that will resist being zeroed out.

This bureaucratic tendency is quite characteristic of NASA. Cloaked in the mantle of patriotism and the pioneering spirit of space exploration, NASA had enjoyed all of the benefits of nationalistic pride without any of the onus that results from controversial military policies, enabling it to resist funding cuts or program scrutiny virtually from its inception until the *Challenger* tragedy. It was very much the spirit in which Abrahamson tried to run his new bureaucracy: attacks on the SDI were viewed as attacks on the nation's boldest hopes and dreams.

Even physically, the SDI office in the Pentagon is quite a phenomenon. The Pentagon is one of the most decrepit and depressing buildings in the country—"like several dozen 1930s public high schools jammed together," according to one description—with literally miles of peeling-paint corridors housing tiny cubicle offices whose main features are cracking linoleum and gray safes. Hundreds of offices are nowhere near windows, prompting some—mostly the secretarial help—to cover the dingy walls with cheerful posters, including drawings of outside scenery. Inspirational messages are also a favored item—"Ziggy" posters saying "Have a Nice Day"—in bizarre contrast to the grim fluorescent lighting and government-issue desks covered with classified memos. Even some senior officials' offices, like Frank Gaffney's, sported gaping holes in the ceilings revealing old wiring and bits of asbestos, the result of lame efforts to remove this toxic material. One official in the JCS hates having meetings in his office because the sound of toilets flushing upstairs is so loud it interrupts conversation.

In the midst of this squalor, the SDIO occupies a large suite of newly renovated offices in the basement of the Pentagon, just next to the entrance to the Metro, convenient for its many guests. An official escorts those who do not have a Pentagon pass into the building and seats them in the "ACC" room, short for "access," while they wait for their meetings. Just beyond the bottom of the decaying stairs leading to the basement, a gray carpet extends to a set of glass doors with the SDIO logo—a sword and shield—blazoned on the front. The ACC room is much like the foyer of a modern, upscale motel: gray modular stuffed chairs, mauve carpeting, a coffee machine and cups neatly poised in the corner, and a desk like a large airline counter where the security officers inspect identification cards and punch out badges on computers for visitors.

The high-tech, sleek interior extends into the inside suites. Entry into the offices is guarded by a computer-operated security system. Employees hold up their picture IDs to a sensing device that verifies their validity. The machine registers the comings and goings of individuals and remembers where they are, so that an employee who enters through one door and exits through another cannot reenter the first door, because the machine has recorded him as still being inside. (The security officers routinely hand up their cards to assist employees in foiling the machine when this occurs. Since the system is meant to record all access, the logs must be odd indeed, showing Mr. Gonzales, security officer, entering the inner suite dozens of times and never coming out.)

The inside suite is decorated with elegant, abstract paintings, mostly of space objects, and modern furniture. An unofficial estimate of the cost of the furnishings is $13 million. The SDIO refuses to release cost numbers for the office decor. But the message intended is quite clear: we're special. Another interpretation, from those not so blessed with Pentagon largesse, is that the SDIO is squandering the taxpayers' money and has an attitude problem. It is odd that a program so controversial, especially in regard to cost, would so deliberately seek out such a high physical profile.

As it happens, the elaborate security system was among the first and most publicized of the SDI's technological failures. In April 1988, an air force major working on SDI kinetic energy programs entered the SDIO office at night and stole a personal computer and software, foiling the security system. Videotape cameras intended to track the goings-on in the offices did not detect the perpetrator, "because they weren't loaded," according to a source. Since the small computer that was stolen was linked to the SDIO's mainframe computer, there was concern about the compromise of sensitive information, through industrial or foreign espionage. An FBI investigation was launched. Now believed to be an instance of petty theft, the incident added to the ridicule already being heaped on the SDIO. As a reporter for WJLA television in Washington put it, "Even if it is the petty thief scenario, you have a thief who walked into one of the most secure offices in the Pentagon [and] stole something which he should have been able to find much easier at far less risk at Radio Shack."[20]

One of Abrahamson's former chief assistants, Simon "Pete" Worden, is highly critical of the SDIO, especially for its overbureaucratization. "They should have had thirty top-notch people." Instead, he claims, Abrahamson was unselective, and even missed the opportunity to hire very high-quality scientists because he was so rank conscious. "A major with a Ph.D. in physics, who was really excited about the program, would ask for a job, but Abe would say, 'Sorry, this position is for a lieutenant colonel.' " At the same time, he tended to hire former colleagues and friends. As Worden described it, "He hired old hacks. Some colonel would come in and say, 'I can't get a job, can you make me a director?' And Abe would hire him."[21]

Internally, the SDIO staff is severely compartmentalized. Individuals work on highly specified projects and are instructed to stay out of each other's way. Abrahamson believes he should review everything and is the ultimate "micromanager." "Only Abe could make a decision about anything," claimed one Pentagon official, and that stifled initiative. Preoccupied with selling the program around the country, moreover, Abrahamson is often simply not there to provide internal discipline. "You'd go and try to resolve a problem, but Abe would be off opening an Orange Julius or at the VFW."[22]

Without the "best and the brightest," the SDI foundered on both technical and policy grounds. "It was like trying to run a Manhattan Project without any Oppenheimers," said an official from the staff of the Joint Chiefs. Spokesmen to communicate program goals effectively were ever scarcer, as competent strategists and scientists either avoided the SDIO or resigned early. One colleague claims Abrahamson was "the most inept spokesman" he had ever seen. Worden blames the bureaucratic rigidities for the SDIO's failures. "Once the external affairs office was established for the SDIO, we couldn't carry on the battle. It was full of hacks. We needed to do something more than to pour oil on troubled waters. It was a theological argument, and we needed to get out there and convert the heathen," he said. Worden himself left the SDIO in 1986, partly because he thought he would be "more effective helping the program from outside."[23]

The ineptitude of the SDIO public relations operation was cited by one of SDI's leading critics, the FAS scientist John Pike, as one of the main reasons he developed media notoriety. The repeated failure of the SDIO to answer press questions or often even to return reporters' calls, Pike alleged, "created all this walk-in business for me from reporters who were just trying to get simple questions answered—like what does this acronym stand for or what's a rail gun?" On the basis of his steady reliability as a source of technical information, the rather shy scientist became a media star and eventually figured in a number of crucial political disputes between the Congress and the administration.[24]

The SDIO external affairs director, navy captain John Dewey, vehemently disputes that the SDIO is overbureaucratized and claims it is terribly understaffed. "It's not a bureaucracy at all," he stressed in an interview, yet later in the same discussion he referred with pride to the thousands of individuals working directly or indirectly for the program. "The number's inestimable," he said with satisfaction.[25]

Something for Everybody

In what was to become a standard method of SDI promotion, the SDIO held a conference for defense contractors at the American Institute for Aeronautics and Astronautics in August 1984, to explain the SDI and assure them that it was here to stay. Abrahamson soon became a highly sought-after speaker at such marketing events, which had titles like "The Military Electronics Market: Exploring the Opportunities of the SDI" and "Find Your Role in SDI Battle Management/C3." "Will you find a place in this state-of-the-art cornucopia expected to be a greater undertaking than the Apollo Program?" asked a brochure from the American Society of Mechanical Engineers in 1984. The promotion of SDI contracts spawned a cottage industry of newsletters and data bases designed to alert companies of SDIO business opportunities. The *SDI Monitor* was launched in 1986 with a promotional letter that said,

> The good news is the White House is still committed to the Strategic Defense Initiative. While many high-tech defense programs suffered cuts in the FY87 budget proposal, SDI emerged unscathed. . . . Will you identify opportunities to win contracts? . . . Get it first. Get it right. Get it all in the SDI monitor.[26]

A year's subscription, twelve issues of the newsletter, costs $587.

In December 1984, the SDIO awarded major contracts to ten contractors to begin the first round of what came to be known as architecture studies. Abrahamson promoted the concept of the "horse race," pitting contractors against one another to come up with the best scheme. Rather than laying out the Pentagon's specifications for needed technologies, the SDIO issued a blanket request for proposals. The firms selected were then organized to do parallel and competitive projects. Part social Darwinism, the concept was motivated by the understanding that the contractors would be impelled by a sense of competitive urgency to come up with appealing concepts in order to win future business. This was not an environment in which scientific uncertainties would receive much attention. The contractors were supposed to "work the problem"—that is, get something compelling together before the competitors did.

As Abrahamson told an industry audience, "Performance is the key to maintaining public support for the SDI. . . . We will not be able to do that without showing visual progress. We must get Congress to sit up and take notice." The buzzword became "speed in contract completion." In congressional testimony describing the development of a test facility for the SDI, Abrahamson said,

> By a horse-race, I mean we have selected four teams. Those teams will be
> going as fast as they can to reach their first objective. When they reach the
> first milestone, we will probably cut them down to two, pick the best ones
> and go forward. . . . I think you will find that you have a higher degree of
> competition in this program than any of recent history and, in fact, some of
> our contractors are beginning to say they are exhausted making proposals.[27]

Although Abrahamson saw the process as healthy competition and
believed this to be a selling point in the Congress, others argued that
it gave financial incentives to companies to produce politically upbeat, but scientifically mediocre, results. The "let a hundred flowers
bloom" strategy, as one military officer referred to it, was not only
expensive but scientifically suspect as well. Rather than focusing on
the solution to technical problems, the contractors "raced around the
country trying to make their case," according to one SDIO official.

Over time, the influence of contractors grew by leaps and bounds.
As Bruce Jackson put it, "Abe couldn't say no to anyone." Competi-
tiveness aside, Abrahamson was reluctant to discourage any contractor who was "trying to help." By contrast, criticism or questions
of the program elicited excoriation and a place on the informal black-
list. Under Secretary of Defense Donald Hicks stated openly in 1986
that he saw no reason why critics of the SDI should receive Pentagon
funds for research contracts. "If they want to get out and use their
roles as professors to make statements, that's fine, it's a free country," Hicks stated in an interview, "but freedom works both ways.
They're free to keep their mouths shut . . . [and] I'm also free not to
give them money."[28]

The program seemed to be pursuing every technological option at
once, without regard to cost or efficiency. In a Senate hearing in 1986,
Abrahamson discussed the "healthy diversity of opinion on how to
resolve the key issues" among the contractors doing architecture
studies. Under questioning from Senator Gary Hart, Abrahamson
admitted that there were fundamental disputes among proponents of
different technologies. "People who know and understand space-
based lasers have not given up on that idea. Some of the people who
know and understand space-based kinetic kill vehicles have not
given up on that idea," he said, going on to explain that although
ground-based lasers were preferred, he had "not made [the other
systems] zero in order to cut them out."[29]

Normal "clearance" channels in the Pentagon bureaucracy were short-circuited. One member of the staff of the chairman of the Joint Chiefs said of his experience,

> The whole program pits men of principle against men who are mouthpieces. A lieutenant colonel hands up his critique of a system, his supervisor sends it up the ranks, and before long the critic is branded a troublemaker. Whenever the SDIO wanted clearance on something, the timing would be reduced to twenty-four or forty-eight hours for a really complex subject—really outlandish. If they didn't like the answer, [the SDIO] would simply shop around for a contractor who would give them the answer they liked. We called it McThought.[30]

As of April 1987, the SDIO had signed 3,300 contracts, worth $10.9 billion. A panoply of policy consultants—the "beltway bandits"— came in to develop the intellectual underpinnings of the SDI. Policy-related contracts originated not just in the SDIO but in other branches of the Pentagon as well, including DR & E, and in the policy division of the Office of the Secretary of Defense. In a short time, many contractors had developed entirely new divisions just to handle SDI work and gave senior executives titles like "Vice-President for SDI Research."[31]

This resurgence of contracts was the industrial analogue of the huge increases in the weapons laboratories' budgets, which took place at the same time. As John Pike described it,

> For some defense contractors, if the SDI didn't exist, it would have to be invented. . . . There are no more large, expensive strategic, offensive weapons systems left to develop. . . . SDI is the only program currently in the pipeline which could prevent a sharp decline in funding for strategic forces in the mid-1990s.[32]

There was an explicit effort to distribute the contracts geographically and among sectors that might otherwise be expected to be critical, like universities. One estimate shows that over three-quarters of the prime contracts distributed in 1984 went to states and congressional districts represented by House and Senate members of the Armed Services Committees and Defense Appropriations Subcommittees, the true arbiters of congressional authority for SDI funding.[33]

For example, a letter from Abrahamson in April 1985 to Senator Hart, a member of the Armed Services Committee and an SDI critic, announced enthusiastically, "The Colorado School of Mines and

Martin Marietta Laboratories in Denver are among a consortium of eight universities, two government laboratories, and six corporations that will be funded to study novel composite materials for possible application in the . . . SDI." This was one of dozens of letters sent to Hart and other committee members, drawing their attention to SDI's economic promises for their constituents.[34]

University support was a key objective. An SDIO conference was organized in Washington in April 1985 for over 250 university representatives to reveal that $70 million in SDIO funds was earmarked for university research. The requirement for security clearances for researchers was suspended for most projects, and any remaining security requirements were liberalized so that only principal investigators, not their students, needed "secret" level clearances, the lowest Pentagon clearance granted.[35]

The existence of the university-earmarked funds was also revealed *prior* to approval by the Congress. The manager of the SDIO office spearheading the solicitation of university support, the director of the SDI Innovative Science and Technology Office, James Ionson, acknowledged that this was unusual. "It's probably something that's never been done, but this office is trying to sell something to Congress. If we can say that this fellow at MIT will get money to do such and such research, it's something real to sell," said the former astrophysicist, on leave from the Goddard Space Center.[36]

But the goal of eliciting university support proved to be more elusive. The announcement of a $15 million university consortium for SDI research to be headed by MIT prompted instant public rebuke. A week later, MIT and another university cited, the California Institute of Technology, accused the SDIO of misrepresenting their roles in the projects "in an effort to help sell the program to the Congress." Individual researchers had apparently been awarded grants, not the universities. The president of Caltech, Marvin Goldberger, accused Abrahamson of "gross misrepresentation" by implying university commitment to the SDI. MIT's president, Paul Gray, charged that the Pentagon was engaged "in a manipulative effort to garner implicit institutional endorsement for SDI" to help in its congressional lobbying. "The first time we learned we were in a consortium was when we read it in a newspaper," said Gray. "You'd think if an organization was going to be drawn into a consortium, the discussions would involve more than one researcher."[37]

University-sponsored criticism grew steadily. For example, 6,500 scientists at American universities signed a letter in May 1986 pledging not to accept SDI money: "as working scientists and engineers, we pledge neither to solicit nor accept SDI funds. We hope together to persuade the public and the Congress not to support this deeply misguided and dangerous program." In June of that year, 1,600 scientists from private and government laboratories, including over half of the nation's Nobel laureates, urged the Congress to limit SDI funds, criticizing the SDI as pursuing a chimera.

But for all its critics, the SDI was seen by many scientists and analysts as a positive opportunity. Thousands of researchers working quietly in nuclear laboratories, trying to push to the outer frontiers of physics for new weapons concepts, were suddenly thrust into the limelight. Many, in fact, were appointed to policy positions in the government, despite a lack of prior experience in government, in the effort to give scientific credence to the president's rhetoric. One senior scientist working in the SDIO in the Pentagon said of himself in 1984, "I'm one of the legions who was offered a job on March 24, 1983"—the day after the president's speech.

While only a few of these scientists shared the president's dream of a peace shield, they had every reason to welcome the new respectability of defense concepts; it enabled them to advance favored technologies and their own careers. A recent statement by the SDIO said the university boycott "had been absolutely no problem," citing 2,000 contracts and 10,000 scientists and engineers working for the SDI.[38]

Science Wars

Policy analysts also found a critical role in rebuilding the intellectual foundations of strategic defense. Given the voluminous literature that the SDI engendered in just four years, it is easy to forget how unfamiliar and embryonic its concepts were in 1983. A study commissioned by the Pentagon to "identify deterrent postures in a world of defense dominance" had analysts scrambling to find sources to develop an analytical framework. So little attention had been paid to defenses that many of the basic concepts were drawn piecemeal from the BMD debates of the 1950s and 1960s. Ideas that are familiar today, like "stable transition" and "ensuring extended deterrence under defenses," were crafted in 1983, adapting reincarnated debates over the Sentinel and Safeguard ABM systems to a world of space defense.[39]

Proponents of strategic defenses working in the "real world" of Washington policy-making were soon to discover the difficulty of articulating policy options in the highly charged political environment the SDI had helped create. Challenging orthodoxies in rhetorical flourishes is one thing; presenting serious plans for their implementation is quite another. As the Miller analysis had predicted, officials were suddenly forced into a world where they had to articulate revolutionary change in the language of orthodoxies, to marry fantasy and boldness with the grim realities of nuclear planning.

It was not just that many were unprepared for the task but also that the severe politicization of the program at its outset made the task extremely difficult. It was not an environment in which doubts or questions about program elements could be admitted or discussed publicly, because they would be seized on by critics determined to discredit the program as a whole. As an environment for scientific inquiry, it was wholly inappropriate.

The SDIO's chief scientist, Jerry Yonas, new to Washington from a job as a physicist at the Sandia National Laboratories, found this out through personal experience. In early discussions with congressional staff, Yonas sometimes strayed from his formal briefing to muse on possible ways in which seemingly intractable defense problems might be solved. Readily admitting that the most critical difficulty for the SDI was how to ensure the survivability of command and control systems—such systems could themselves be targeted and cause the complete collapse of "battle management" capabilities—he once suggested that the United States and the Soviet Union could just agree to have joint command and control. Amazed at the naïveté of the notion—a degree of optimism about possible U.S.-Soviet cooperation found not even among nuclear freeze advocates—this author asked how such an agreement could ever be devised. "Simple," he replied. "It's a matter of survival, and I'm sure the Soviets know that." His military escort, the SDIO Senate liaison Colonel Jon Anderson, paled visibly and tried to change the subject. But Yonas innocently continued to mention this notion in subsequent briefings and was soon the butt of jokes all over Capitol Hill.[40]

The justification for the multiple objectives of the SDI that developed over time was that it was a "seamless web." A smooth progression of R & D demonstrations would advance short-term objectives, like defending U.S. offensive missiles, as well as the grand design of eventually rendering missiles "impotent and obsolete." As a futuristic research program, the SDI's ultimate objectives could span the waterfront, including heightening attackers' uncertainties, limiting damage if deterrence failed, defending U.S. retaliatory capabilities, and, eventually, assuring survival. The administration argued that this meant no research activities should be restricted and no part of the program could be tampered with, because any cuts would undermine the coherence of the program as a whole. But the openendedness of the program's technological objectives fueled sharp disagreements among official and nonofficial analysts and forced the new SDIO employees into an intense public debate. Two key outside documents, a study conducted by the Union of Concerned Scientists (UCS) and a second study by Congress's Office of Technology Assessment (OTA), started what was to be a protracted series of technical controversies—so-called science wars—which mushroomed into political firestorms.[41]

The OTA report, written by Ashton Carter, a professor at Harvard who worked also as a Pentagon consultant, concluded that the prospect of a perfect or near-perfect defense was "so remote that it should not serve as the basis of public expectations of national policy about BMD." With full access to classified technical information, the OTA report explored the range of technologies under consideration by the SDI and found each one of them lacking as the basis for any major change in American strategy. The UCS report had arrived at similar conclusions.

The OTA report, seen as quasi-official and thus particularly dangerous in the Congress, was attacked by Abrahamson and the SDIO with ferocity. They argued that the report was full of "technical errors, unsubstantiated assumptions, and conclusions that are inconsistent with the body of the report." Gregory Canavan, a physicist at the Los Alamos nuclear laboratory, wrote most of the SDIO critique. In the guise of a technical dispute, it impugned even Carter's personal reputation. It suggested he was politically biased because he had worked for the 1984 presidential candidate Walter Mondale, a false allegation. Even more viciously, Canavan suggested that Carter had revealed classified national security information. Representative Henry Hyde, Republican of Illinois, threatened to launch an investigation into the alleged security breaches.[42]

In an unprecedented move, William Taft, deputy secretary of defense, asked the OTA to withdraw the report. The OTA appointed a bipartisan senior panel—including Lieutenant General Glenn Kent of the Rand Corporation, William Perry, former under secretary of defense for research and engineering in the Carter administration, and Charles Townes, a Nobel laureate and professor of physics at Berkeley—to reassess the report's findings. The director of the OTA, John Gibbons, wrote to Taft in July 1984 and said they stood by Carter's analysis: "Because of the extraordinary nature of your request . . . I took the unusual step of asking several distinguished outsiders to review the . . . paper and the critique which you enclosed with your letter. [On the basis of the panel's findings] I do not believe it appropriate to withdraw the paper."[43]

The battle lines were now firmly drawn. In its bitterness, the conflict was reminiscent of the the ABM debate, which had created permanent enmity among many scientists. The tactics were even more vicious, though; the 1960s debates had managed to avoid the McCarthyite charges of divulging classified information.

The UCS study fared less well, since it contained a critical mathematical error, a conclusion that 2,400 satellites would be needed for a credible defense, a number that was later drastically revised to 162. Even after the corrections were widely distributed, however, the acrimony persisted. As a key aide to Abrahamson, Worden found himself enmeshed in a public fight with the report's principal author, the physicist Richard Garwin. In a meeting on the SDI held at the University of Rochester in March 1985, Worden raised Garwin's hackles by offhandedly commenting, "You heard a lot of bullshit here tonight," after a speech by the UCS director, Kurt Gottfried. "It was a audience full of students and a rowdy atmosphere, and I was just trying to speak in their language," Worden said later. Nevertheless, the remark, which Garwin heard secondhand, prompted him to send letters to Abrahamson and Gabriel, the air force chief of staff, demanding that Worden be reprimanded.[44]

In what was to become a typical dynamic in such disputes, both sides revealed their rancor in detail. A private citizen who was to become a major volunteer spokesman for the SDI, Robert Jastrow, urged Abrahamson to come to Worden's defense. In a rather disingenuous statement for someone who was centrally involved in the SDI public relations campaign, Jastrow said, "[Garwin's] campaign against Worden seems entirely out of line. It is an ominous sign of the politicization of the scientific community that a critic of strategic

defense [who] refuses to admit the technical errors of his analysis
. . . instead tries to get rid of his opponents by blackening their
names."

Keyworth also came to Worden's defense and in a letter to
Abrahamson said, "Garwin's contribution to the understanding of
strategic defense is like the PLO's contribution to global stability."
Garwin called Jastrow a "hyena" in a public interview. And an article
by William F. Buckley, entitled "Dear Comrade," charged that the
UCS had "developed techniques of cooption that haven't been seen
since the heyday of the American-Soviet friendship league."[45]

This was not a debate in which informed but moderate skeptics
could play a salient role, at least at the outset. Under siege, Abrahamson found it ever more urgent to refute critics with claims of great
progress in the SDI program, describing technical progress as "incredible" and "genuine breakthroughs" and attempting to demonstrate that key program elements, like the X-ray laser, would be well
ahead of schedule. "There have been monumental breakthroughs
that have made us far more confident two and a half years later than
we projected in the original [SDI] speech," said Keyworth in an interview with the *Washington Times*. It became a war of competing
"view-graphs" and technical speculations, pitting "believers" in the
program against "naysayers" who refused to admit its implementation was just around the corner.[46]

Despite official pressure to support the program, a few government
studies still criticized the SDI. A Pentagon-appointed panel charged
with exploring the software requirements for the SDI was harshly
critical of the way in which Abrahamson had alloted money to the
architecture studies. Charging that current research was designing
systems that "demand excessively sophisticated software and cannot be adequately tested," the panel added to the cacophony of
technical questions about system feasibility. Its conclusion soon led
to yet another politicized scientific dispute. David Parnas, a computer
scientist from Vancouver University, resigned from the panel after
alleging that its members were biased in favor of the SDI. Elevated to media prominence, the diminutive, bespectacled Parnas was
soon a favorite witness at congressional hearings and arms control
meetings.[47]

A report by the OTA in late 1987, still classified ("It has more
stamps than I've ever seen," noted an author) but leaked to the press,
reveals a new kind of political dynamic betwen the technical commu-

nity and the SDIO. Highly critical of early-deployment plans and of the overall feasibility of an astrodome defense, this more recent OTA report has the added credibility of having been scrubbed repeatedly by the SDIO itself. As a critic of its conclusions argued,

> The OTA report reaches its negative conclusions by feeding in unrealistically high estimates of the Soviet "responsive threat" [the Soviet Union's capability to respond to U.S. defensive deployments with new missile programs and measures to attack or evade a defense]. It also uses poor system designs for the "star wars" defense itself. . . . The rub: the SDI office itself has accepted this highly debatable version of the "responsive threat." And the vulnerable cluster of satellites is the very model used by the SDIO.

In short, as SDIO technical asessments have moved closer to those of outside analysts, the program has come under attack by those who still construe analyses of technical constraints as lack of support for the program as a whole.[48]

As the SDIO moved into its third year, more and more funds were allocated to early demonstration projects. Originally termed BEACONS—bold experiments to advance confidence—these tests showed the growing pressure on the SDIO to suspend science in favor of public relations. Videotapes of a chemical laser burning a hole through a Titan booster rocket and a rail gun destroying a missile airframe were produced for consumption by groups ranging from Congress to Kiwanis clubs. These tests were quickly criticized on both political and scientific grounds: early demonstrations are expensive and tend to lock in the relevant technology, even if it is immature.

Politically, demonstration tests added to the momentum to break out of the ABM Treaty and move forward with early deployments. Not entirely without scientific merit—"They did help explain the phenomenology of missiles in important new ways," said one official—the tests were held primarily for reasons of public diplomacy, by Abrahamson's own admission. As he told a House Republican study conference in June 1985, "We have to be able to present results of true experiments . . . so that it will be apparent not only to you but to your constituents, to our populations and to the whole world and to the Soviet Union, as well, that this can be done."[49]

By 1986, the "schedule-driven" nature of SDIO research was undermining its scientific rigor, according to key SDIO scientists cited in a Senate staff report. Abrahamson himself said, "I tell people that the only way to save money is to do it faster." Speed and cost savings were political goals—to overcome congressional skepticism. The concern among scientists, however, was that promising long-term research goals were being overwhelmed by the schedule and that the demonstration projects were being diverted into what one scientist referred to as "a series of sleazy stunts." Moreover, the program had been constantly reoriented, with one year's top priority altogether disappearing the following year. Despite a tripling of its budget by early 1987, the SDIO still had not produced a framework for the required effectiveness of a defensive system measured against a realistic Soviet threat.[50]

As the objectives of the SDI moved more explicitly from an astrodome defense to a partial defense aimed at enhancing deterrence, the scope and cost of SDI technologies were increasingly subject to challenge. If these were the objectives, skeptics argued, there were far cheaper and more immediate ways to achieve them than a layered, space-based defense.

A critical appraisal of the SDI advanced by the former secretary of defense Harold Brown provided a detailed blueprint of the technologies one could exploit to achieve the more modest goals. Most important, Brown exposed a key flaw in the SDI's stated objectives: once you admit that you cannot have a perfect defense, then this is a program to permit more efficient counterforce targeting. As such, the SDI was vulnerable to charges that it was designing overly ambitious technology and wasting money. Although this was at odds with the beliefs of those supporting space deployments to "transform the strategic environment," no one disagreed that the administration had laid itself open to this charge by its own actions.[51]

Cost was another key issue that was never handled successfully. Although the projected budget for the SDI program was a relatively modest fraction of the overall defense budget, it reflected a disproportionate share of overall funds dedicated to military R & D, and it was clear that deployment of a multilayered system might absorb huge percentages of the defense budget. Senator Barry Goldwater, Republican of Arizona, said in frustration to administration witnesses at an Armed Services Committee hearing in 1984,

> This is probably the biggest project this country has ever been asked to fund. You don't know how much it is going to cost. We don't know how much it is going to cost. You don't even have an idea. . . . We are faced,

in my opinion, with a threat far more destructive than anything that Russia might throw at us in missiles and that is our deficit. . . .[52]

At first, the SDIO resisted all pressures to assess costs and denounced analytical efforts from outside experts. It was too early for any responsible estimates, it argued. But the SDIO did come up with a remarkable concept called should-cost. Taking current estimates of shuttle flights to carry SDI payloads, for instance, and recognizing that they might be prohibitive, Abrahamson would present the cost targets or should-cost parameters needed to make the SDI viable. For Abrahamson and his staff, there was never any question that these targets would be met, though he could not explain how it might be done. This prompted one critic to say, "I'm going to buy myself a Ferrari because even though it costs $45,000, it *should* cost $3,000."[53]

Paul Nitze helped craft the terms of the cost debate in 1985 by devising criteria for assessing the viability of defenses that stressed "cost effectiveness at the margin." Weinberger ridiculed the Nitze criteria in public: "I don't know what cost-effective at the margin means. It is one of those nice phrases that rolls around easily off the toungue and people nod approvingly because it sounds rather profound." The criteria, which were actually developed by Frank Miller and Furniss, came to serve as a key debating point for critics of the SDI. It helped temper initial pressures for early deployments, as these could too easily be demonstrated to be readily overwhelmed by cheaper Soviet countermeasures. After the explosion of the shuttle *Challenger* in 1986, more pronounced concerns were raised in the Congress. The space transportation costs alone for a national defense system seemed likely to exceed any conceivable parameters of affordability.[54]

The Learning Curve

To many, the real story of the SDI is centered in the Congress. The SDI's critics and proponents alike accord an unprecedented role to legislators in influencing its destiny. Unarguably, the debate over the SDI offered a vivid object lesson in partisanship and in the relative effectiveness of the Congress in adjudicating principles of national security.

The formal means for congressional influence over defense policy is money, the approval of the administration's defense budget request submitted every February. A multilayered scrutiny of the budget takes place in the House and Senate Budget, Armed Services, and Appropriations committees. By the time a defense budget is approved, dozens of members and staff aides have spent hundreds of hours debating controversial items. Countless witnesses, official and unofficial, have appeared before committees and subcommittees, and each chamber has logged days of debate over final passage of the various bills.

The open sessions—hearings and floor debate—are often pitched to the press and the public; sensitive discussions are held in closed sessions. Floor debate is especially coveted by members who are not on the relevant committees, for it is often the only opportunity these individuals have to participate in that year's national security controversies. Increasingly in recent years, members of Congress offer legislation on particular issues not so much because they know they will decisively influence policy but in order to raise their own public profiles and appeal to their constituencies.

The real work of the Congress, the decisions that end up altering executive branch policy, tends to take place away from the bombast of floor debates and public hearings. The testimony of experts rarely sways the opinion of a senator, and their colleagues' eloquence has not frequently been known to persuade members to change their votes. By the time an important issue is brought to the floor for debate, its supporters and opponents are generally already aligned. Except for policies on which there is broad consensus or that simply split members across party lines, ad hoc alliances worked out behind the scenes determine the outcome of a controversy.

In the case of the SDI, members initially lined up in support or in opposition strictly on the basis of their attitudes toward the administration. Even if there had been the inclination, there would never have been the opportunity to develop the intellectual and technical base to launch an informed, bipartisan debate, or to serve as the nation's forum for the most fundamental question: are defenses in the national interest? In the rush to recapture the initiative, members of Congress were forced to take sides, reflecting biases from prior disputes. This issue really brought out the worst tendencies in Congress:

its high political profile and amorphous objectives were easy targets for florid rhetoric and political opportunism.

Because of the sheer complexity of space defense concepts, most members could not be even modestly conversant in the technical issues raised by the SDI. Unlike those of earlier specific weapons systems, such as the MX, the characteristics of the program "couldn't be put on an index card," as John Pike put it. The objectives of the program were so open-ended, in any case, that its technical merits could never be discussed concretely. "The amount of evidence about the feasibility of the peace shield was so small one way or the other that there was no factual basis to be forming opinions," said William Hoehn, the former Defense Department official who had clashed with Iklé over the Hoffman report and now a senior aide on the Senate Armed Services Committee. "We knew that now and again you can hit a bullet with a bullet, but the question was how to shoot ten thousand 'bullets' in a cloud of a million objects."[55]

Even now, after six years of debate, there are few congressional "experts" on the SDI, just as there are few members of Congress who have ever had the time or the training to become knowledgeable about many other highly complex policy issues, such as the budget deficit, health care, or tax reform. This does not deter anyone from advancing forceful opinions, however. Once an issue becomes a test of partisan loyalty, moving the debate toward reasoned consideration of the national interest is always difficult. As the emotional confrontations over the SDI increased, it became clear that no amount of expert testimony or technical information could end what was increasingly a competition over belief systems.

The history of the SDI brings out the relative ineffectiveness of the Congress in coming to grips with technical issues. The democratic process is not well equipped to deal with questions of exceptional complexity. It was certainly not up to the demands put upon it by evolving SDI concepts and objectives. Indeed, how could it be? Presented with a "slogan in search of objectives"—a slogan infused with public sentiment—Congress had little choice but to treat the idea of space defense as a partisan event. "Show me the list of senators, and I'll tell you exactly how they'll vote on any part of the SDI," said Mark Albrecht, aide to Senator Pete Wilson.[56]

In the first two years of the program, the congressional debate on the SDI was almost entirely a battle of ideology. "It pitted the 'people' killers against the 'missile' killers," said Waller, referring to the polemic between critics and defenders of a perfect population defense. All competing advocates brought their cases to the congressional debate, which developed into "a stew of politics, physics, and metaphysics," as Senator Nunn put it, but never quite forged any durable policy guidance born of consensus.

The divisions created in 1983 have endured. Arms control liberals who denounced the initiative from the outset have sought to impose various types of funding and policy limits and oppose all aspects of the program except for a modest level of research. Defense advocates who rushed to hail the president's wisdom sustained a passionate effort to preserve the program's funding level and policy priorities against any incursions, and many urged the administration to move more quickly, through deployments or space tests of advanced systems that would abrogate the ABM Treaty. A number of these eventually split with the administration because of its failure to act more decisively. The rift was widened by the presidential ambitions of one of its chief spokesmen, Congressman Jack Kemp, Republican of New York.

Somewhere in the middle, various senators of both parties struggled to walk the line between outright criticism and support. Over time, they developed a sufficient political coalition, with enough technical credibility, to begin to question the program on its merits. But the politicized environment of "true believers" and "true naysayers" made this a difficult task. The first challenge, to move beyond the "activation" phase in the congressional debate—staunch advocacy or opposition—and build legislative vehicles that could elicit support beyond the predictable pro- and anti-SDI factions, took over two years.

Trying to craft a compelling story line for the SDI, Republican moderates, like Senator John Warner, repeatedly urged the administration to stop the absurd rhetoric and come up with some concrete goals tied to military requirements. Warner said to Fred Iklé in late 1985,

> One of the purposes of this series of hearings is to really try and remove some of the points from the overall record of the SDI that we in the Congress frankly feel to be somewhat incredible. This program has suffered, if I may say respectfully, from a credibility gap. The thing that bothered me from the very earliest has been the representation that through this program we could, and I quote your testimony today, eliminate the awful threat posed by ballistic missiles.[57]

Warner's concerns were not helped by the fact that the same administration officials who were postulating the elimination of the missile threat were also asking the Congress to approve funds for the MX, Midgetman, and Trident II missile programs.

Another key reason cited for the program was that the Soviets were ahead in defensive programs and were thus threatening the United States' nuclear deterrent. This rationale put into question the notion that a "defense dominant" world was a welcome development. Why should we be encouraging the Soviets to move toward defenses if defenses were destabilizing? At the same time it was pointing to the perils of Soviet defense programs, the administration tried to suggest that the Soviet response to U.S. defense deployments, whether defensive or offensive, would not be that serious a problem. Patently contradictory, this position prompted Nunn to comment that some SDI advocates were "trying to convince us that we are in a contest with the Little Sisters of Mercy rather than the Evil Empire."[58]

Even more roundly ridiculed was the president's suggestion that we would "give the Soviets our peace shield," sharing U.S. technology with the Soviets as we went along. "We will make available to everyone this weapon," said Reagan in reference to the SDI in 1985. "I don't mean we'll give it to them. They're going to have to pay, but at cost." For an administration that had initiated one of the strictest "technology security" programs ever devised, specifically to keep American technology from the Warsaw Pact nations, this proposal was too absurd even to be contemplated.[59]

Opponents had their own problems in articulating objections to the SDI. From the outset, it was immensely difficult to make a case against the noble ideal of protecting American lives. Extolling the virtues of nuclear vulnerability and questioning the capabilities of American technology were not popular themes with constituents. Senator Goldwater, for example, played up this political liability in an Armed Services Committee hearing in 1985. Reacting to a press report on the difficulties of designing computer software adequate to the task of coordinating the "battle management" of the SDI, he said,

> I began to wonder what would have happened if the Washington Post had been with us forever. I think we would not have automobiles. We would never have had a man on the moon. We would not have penicillin. We would not have modern day panty hose. . . . So I came to this meet-

ing this morning just to have my confidence refreshed in the ability of Americans to do almost anything they want to, the Washington Post notwithstanding.[60]

Many opponents exaggerated the dangers of the SDI and found themselves in a logical trap. Any defenses were destabilizing, they argued, since they could prompt responses from the Soviets, including a preemptive strike by them if they perceived their retaliatory capabilities to be diminishing. But this argument clashed with the simultaneous allegation that the SDI would never work. If it wouldn't work, why would the Soviets see it as such a threat? Opponents also had the larger problem of explaining what should be done about Soviet defenses—including the deployment of a phased-array radar at Krasnoyarsk, in clear violation of the ABM Treaty.

The Congress is perceived by some to have served as a tempering influence on the more obvious excesses of SDI program objectives but by others as unnecessarily intrusive. In truth, from the start, members worried constantly about engaging in "micromanagement." They decided as a matter of deliberate policy to set only broad funding limits and not to look too closely at specific programs in the first two years.

Partly this was a practical matter: who knew the difference between an electromagnetic rail gun and a free-electron laser? When the senior staffer for strategic programs on the House Armed Services Committee, Tony Battista, for example, tried to explain that "Talon Gold" was a reincarnation of an old laser system and "a real turkey," he drew blank stares from committee members. How could they hurl their limited technical understanding against the assessments of the battalions of technical experts in the Defense Department? As it was, the hundreds of line items in the SDIO budget meant nothing to most members of Congress, who would not have known a space-based kinetic-kill vehicle if it had landed on their desks. It was unrealistic to expect even a very interested senator to make critical judgments about the relative contribution of neutral-particle-beam weapons to a boost-phase defense, although, remarkably enough, discussions of this topic did go on.

As a political matter, moreover, opponents in Congress were reluctant to micromanage because they did not want to be blamed in retrospect for the failure of population defenses, preferring that this unrealistic goal implode of its own accord. As it was, those who questioned even minor aspects of the SDI were already accused of being antiprogress, antitechnology, and even anti-America.

Imposing binding legislation on the SDI to redirect its focus or to prohibit certain activities created two other political problems. The first was the sensitive issue of imposing limits on the president when the SDI became a key bargaining chip in arms negotiations. Tinkering with programs of domestic importance is one thing, but "undercutting the president and U.S. negotiating strategy" is a gambit that gives pause to even the most vocal critics. Thus, when the second Reagan-Gorbachev summit was announced suddenly, in late 1986, the House Democratic leadership withdrew a series of amendments to the defense authorization bill that had had a good chance of passing, including one to enforce adherence to the ABM Treaty.

The second problem was the question of political clout. Forcing a vote on a resolution that affirmed the viability of the ABM restraints, for instance, if unsuccessful, would have disastrous consequences. Unsure of their strength if it came to a showdown, SDI opponents thus hesitated to confront the White House directly. As a result, countless "nonbinding" amendments were advanced in both Houses, expressing concern over a variety of SDI issues. These "educational devices" sought to raise the consciousness of other members and send signals to the administration. But no major efforts to modify program elements or significantly alter the direction of the program were successful until 1986. Lacking the strength to challenge the program with any certainty, the Congress fell back on familiar terrain—that of funding cuts.

The congressional debate on the SDI was never really a debate over nuclear doctrine. The legacy of congressional oversight was preoccupation with budgetary levels, and a virtual Kama Sutra of funding amendments in which members tried to express policy grievances. Wielding the power of the purse is, of course, Congress's primary constitutional role. But whereas in domestic issues legislative conflicts can be resolved successfully through "split the difference" budgetary strategies, for the SDI a similar approach resulted in the worst of all worlds—enough money to keep programs going, but no guiding rationale or consensus for the budget level selected. Reduced to chiseling away at the SDI budget, congressional critics of strategic defenses never did manage to force a referendum on the basic question of whether defenses were in the national interest.

Pressure for Early Deployment

By 1985, public pronouncements on SDI goals were increasingly out of sync with the SDI program and funding patterns. As had been mandated in 1983, the SDI was to focused predominantly on the advanced technologies required for the development of a full-scale "layered" defense based primarily in space. Although administration officials had made numerous contradictory statements as to when deployment would be considered—initially, only when a comprehensive system could be fielded credibly—the budget requests submitted to the Congress reflected a steady deemphasis of long-term goals in favor of more mature technologies that might be deployed sooner.

One example was the space-based kinetic-kill vehicle, a system that was to become the centerpiece of one near-term deployment plan. In late 1986, SDIO directors had urged a deceleration of this program, a cutting of its funding in favor of "more promising technologies." According to one report, Abrahamson had considered scrapping the program entirely, a proposal discussed among SDIO officials and alluded to in congressional testimony earlier that year. But the interest of senior officials in developing possible deployment options led instead to the addition of $10 million for kinetic-kill systems in the subsequent budget. This was accompanied by a decision to scale down the program's technical requirements, like sensor technologies, in order to meet an early-deployment deadline. Colonel Raymond Ross, director of the kinetic program in SDIO, revealed that a conscious decision had been made to eliminate certain specifications identified earlier, with potentially serious consequences for the capability and survivability of the system that might be deployed.[61]

Beginning in 1986, Abrahamson claimed that congressional budget cuts had forced a reorientation of the program toward more immediate goals, at the expense of futuristic concepts. This was a political, not a budgetary or military, decision, however. It had become increasingly clear within the SDIO that the program had to be institutionalized so that it could survive beyond the Reagan administration. Key Republican members of Congress were pushing the administration in this direction, and the possibility of a Democratic victory in the Senate in 1986 heightened their sense of urgency. In a meeting in Iklé's office in late 1985, some officials had urged that the program be given a more up-front definition of its goals. It could not remain a "research forever" effort, they argued, because of the growing criticisms and the short time left of Reagan's incumbency.

By mid-1986, Weinberger had accepted in principle and publicly alluded to the concept of developing near-term technologies and going ahead with the first round of an admittedly limited defensive system. There was lengthy discussion of what to call it: Weinberger passed over the terms "incremental" and "sequential" in favor of "phased." But there was a widening split among proponents as to how to proceed. Advocates of early deployment, especially in the Congress, wanted Lockheed's exoatmospheric reentry vehicle interception system (ERIS) missile and other terminal programs, while most administration officials insisted on a space-based element and a prior schedule for a space-testing program.

In the summer of 1986, White House officials received a briefing from proponents of terminal systems. Based largely on the ERIS, supported by the army, it represented the views of an increasingly vocal congressional lobby, including Representatives Jack Kemp and James Courter and Senators Wallop, Wilson, and Quayle. The briefing was essentially a reincarnation of High Frontier, vanquished, the SDIO had thought, in the early 1980s.[62]

During the mid-1980s, attacks on the SDIO by High Frontier champions had grown vitriolic. One of them proclaimed in a June 1986 article entitled "Fish or Cut Bait," "We are no closer to a defense against ICBMs than we were in March 1983. . . . If you scratch someone in the SDI Office, he bleeds RESEARCH. . . . The emphasis on RESEARCH ONLY has played into the hands of strategic defense opponents. . . . The administration must make an unequivocal decision in favor of deploying defenses."[63] Weinberger was at first opposed to the concept of early deployment because he believed terminal systems to be the only technical option. He worried that a deployment plan would divert from the futuristic objectives for the SDI and undercut the popularity of the president's grand design, triggering a debate like that over ABM. All the officials in the policy office of Fred Iklé agreed. "Ground-based defense of U.S. offensive forces is all bad and contrary to the objectives of the SDI," argued Bruce Jackson. The chairman of the Joint Chiefs, Admiral William Crowe, was also critical, remarking, "We probably could not have early deployment in the field before the mid-1990s," and stressing that decisions about weapons would have to come well before then. Even contractors complained. "The whole thing is being pushed too fast for other-than-technical reasons," said an executive quoted in *Business Week.* Also resisted by National Security Adviser Carlucci and Secretary of State Shultz, the decision was deferred.[64]

With encouragement from some individuals in the Pentagon's Office of International Security Policy, Abrahamson began to study the possibility of a near-term defense scheme that included greater reliance on space systems, a scheme that would be more appealing technically and politically but that could also be tested and deployed in the early 1990s. Until this point, Abrahamson had resisted pressures to propose plans openly violating the traditional interpretation of the ABM Treaty. Treaty compliance was in every discussion the key issue for the Congress, which sought assurances from Abrahamson that the program would not violate the 1972 accord. A component of the Office of the Secretary of Defense, headed by Assistant Deputy Undersecretary Lee Minichiello, worked tirelessly to show that each SDI program element was consistent with the treaty.

Some officials had urged Abrahamson to put forward a noncompliant experiment. "We needed a real contradiction between the optimum research program and the constraints of the restrictive interpretation to bring the issue to a head," said Jackson. The effort to justify each step in the SDI was becoming more and more tortuous, and it infuriated the "test-early" supporters. But Abrahamson resisted. He wanted to avoid conflict with the Congress because he was worried about a loss of funding. Jackson urged him on a number of occasions to put the full testing program before the Congress: "We advised General Abrahamson that the Democratic Congress was going to cut the SDI in any case. Without fully capable tests, he sacrificed his one political asset, a credible engineering development program. We argued that he couldn't please everybody and so should stick to the technical merits."[65]

In the summer of 1986, Abrahamson relented, instructing his program directors to make proposals for a "phase 1 architecture" that could form the basis for moving the program from research to acquisition. William Furniss found out about the meeting by accident and does not believe that his office, which has coordinating authority for all "space policy," would have ever been informed.

Furniss crashed the meeting. As Abrahamson went on about "phase 1," a concept Furniss had never heard about, Furniss raised the point that no decision could be made about any systems until there was an adequate understanding of likely Soviet countermeasures. It was clear that Abrahamson was under pressure. The usually mild-mannered general "got completely pissed off and started yelling." The realization that time was running short was the main reason for the sense of panic, according to the chief scientist Alan Mense. "Like it or not, we saw a political reality staring us in the face. If we don't come up with something specific, people are not going to let us play in the sandbox for ten years."[66]

A briefing on a possible defense system was assembled and run through Weinberger's office four or five times. In December 1986, Abrahamson and Perle took the plan to the president. This time, they were able to demonstrate a scheme that seemed far closer to the president's vision. Describing a shield made up of space sensors, orbiting battle stations with kinetic-kill vehicles, and ground-based rockets, Abrahamson convinced the president that this could be the first round of his astrodome. The plan had the strong backing of Weinberger. The president expressed no concern that the plan lacked lasers or particle beams or any of the other futuristic systems that had first helped convert him to defenses.

The SDI Counterthrust

Moving beyond the hardened factions mobilized for or against the SDI and away from mindless votes on funding levels had by 1986 become key priorities for a number of concerned congressmen. Previously, the fractionation over funding levels had undercut any effective opposition. The Senate debate over the fiscal year 1985 defense authorization bill had been particularly appalling. The five separate unsuccessful efforts to cut the proposed SDI budget ranged from a funding "freeze" at $1.4 billion proposed by the liberal Democratic senator John Kerry, of Massachusetts, to the offer of $2.7 billion by the centrist Democrat John Glenn, of Ohio. Democrats were divided over these initiatives and garnered only modest Republican support at the highest level. Glenn was hard pressed to explain his amendment: "I feel better at $2.7," he said in a meeting of Democratic senators.

It fell to two moderate southern Democrats, Senator Lawton Chiles, of Florida, and Senator J. Bennett Johnston, of Louisiana, along with their liberal colleague from the Budget Committee, Senator Proxmire, to start an "education" campaign on the SDI. Proxmire had begun his effort in 1985 when he tried to give some empirical backing for his funding amendment, offering an "alternative SDI" with a $1.8 billion budget. Reducing funds for near-term options and early demonstration tests, the Proxmire proposal argued for an emphasis on long-term technologies and specific programs to hedge against the possible threat of a Soviet breakout.[67]

According to Proxmire's staff assistant, Douglas Waller, this amendment was not expected to win, and it did not. Its purpose was to establish the precedent for more activist congressional oversight. "We were saying there are alternative ways to look at the program," Waller said. "People didn't want to get into the issue, because they didn't understand the technologies, and the SDI guys were these men in white coats who knew everything. We were arguing that you could responsibly oppose the program on its merits."[68]

Waller began organizing a series of SDI briefings for congressional staff, inviting SDIO officials and outside experts to informal meetings. Aside from their educational value, the briefings helped develop a network of staffers who focused on the SDI. In the fall of 1985, Waller, along with the Johnston staffer Jim Bruce and the Chiles staffer Doug Cook, organized a trip to several major SDI installations and had meetings with over fifty scientists associated with the program.

One of the main questions they asked was, "Have you had 'tremendous progress' in your programs, as Abrahamson was claiming?" To their surprise, they heard a resounding no from the majority of SDI scientists they interviewed. Expecting to be lobbied about the miracle of defenses, they were surprised to find profound technological skepticism among those working on the program. Scientists scoffed at the exaggerated promises being made in Washington. More and more of them resented the politicization of their scientific pursuits. Some feared that, however valid, their research would be the victim of political whims, with funds suddenly slashed in the backlash against the SDIO.

On the plane ride home, the three Senate staffers decided to draft a report on their findings. They spent months on a detailed, technical assessment of the program, a very unusual event. Staffers generally lack the time to write long reports, and these three were not even on the Armed Services Committee. "It consumed an inordinate amount of time," said Waller, "and our bosses didn't know what we were doing or what to do with it when we were done."[69]

The senators approved the report, however, and decided to send the draft to Abrahamson to get his comments and have him coordinate its declassification among the several agencies that would have to review it. To the authors' astonishment, the report was declassified almost in its entirety, within three weeks. One possible explanation for the ready cooperation—it was expected that the SDIO would either squelch the report or drag the process out for several months—was that two of the senators were on the Appropriations Committee. The report had arrived at the SDIO right in the middle of the deliberations over the defense budget by the Defense Appropriations Subcommittee.

The report was the opening salvo in what became a far more active debate over the SDI's technical merits. Although the Waller report was dismissed as biased and ill informed by SDI supporters, the SDIO never officially released its rebuttal but leaked it to the magazine *Aviation Week and Space Technology* instead. The report was distributed widely, however, and had the imprimatur of three respected senators, two of them moderate southern Democrats. A series of studies was subsequently commissioned by the General Accounting Office, laying out the details of the SDI budget, and growing numbers of outside studies from reputable organizations, like the American Physical Society, joined them. "It was part of our 'Chinese water torture' strategy," said one staffer, "keeping up a steady deluge of technical critiques to debunk SDIO exaggerations."[70]

By the time the fiscal year 1987 defense authorization bill was considered in the Armed Services Committee, in 1986, an increasing number of moderates were willing to voice reservations about the SDI. For the first time, the Senate Armed Services Committee passed a binding amendment that channeled funds from the SDI to other military programs. The so-called Balanced Technology Initiative underscored the sentiment that the SDI was absorbing funds from the U.S. technology base far out of proportion to its relative contribution to U.S. security. The most pressing area for attention was that of conventional forces in Europe, and it thus seemed promising to emphasize the SDI's technological spin-offs applicable to conventional technologies. A piece of the SDI budget was transferred for this purpose, under the jurisdiction of a separate Pentagon agency.

Debate on the amendment was acrimonious; it passed only because of the support of the Republican William Cohen, of Maine, in the face of great pressure from his Republican colleagues. How could he commit the unconscionable act of breaking party lines on behalf of what was seen as a clear rebuke to the administration and the SDIO? they demanded. In one moving moment, Cohen expressed his dismay at the apparent accusation from Goldwater that his patriotism was in question because of his refusal to place party loyalty over conviction.

Failing with Cohen, Republican members and their staff tried furiously to sway one Democrat to break ranks and vote against the amendment. Glenn was the logical choice, since he tended to favor the SDI. "We even bribed Glenn with the promise of additional B-1 bombers," said a senior Republican staffer, alluding to aircraft supported by Glenn because their engines were produced in his state.[71] But Glenn chose party loyalty over pork, probably a sound decision in light of the fact that the Balanced Technology Initiative was the brainchild of Senator Sam Nunn, the committee's ranking minority member and soon to be its chairman. The amendment established another precedent: the SDI could now be assessed against other defense priorities. It was no longer a sacred cow.

In the final stages of the Reagan administration, the Congress succeeded in passing an amendment that restricted a specific SDI technology, space-based interceptors, "fencing" the SDIO budget to limit expenditures on its development. The success of this amendment, intended to slow the pace of technologies that were being pushed for near-term deployment, marked a precedent in congressional activism. Partly because of the intrusiveness of this initiative, the president vetoed the defense authorization bill in which it was contained, setting off a new round of confrontation between the executive branch and the Congress.

Congressional Prerogative

The administration committed its greatest tactical blunder with respect to the Congress in late 1985. In a decision that one official admitted "dwarfed in stupidity all the other mistakes" it had ever made, the administration announced a "new" interpretation of the

ABM Treaty, seeking to overturn twelve years of common understanding of the treaty's constraints on the testing and development of futuristic technologies. The administration argued that it could now move forward with space tests of technologies based on "other physical principles." These technologies had previously been understood to be prohibited by article V and agreed statement D of the treaty.

Announced on television by Robert McFarlane on October 6, 1985, apparently inadvertently, the decision prompted instant hostility in the Congress. The idea that twelve years of treaty constraints could be overturned unilaterally by a legal brief prepared by a lawyer on contract to the Pentagon was a procedural outrage. All those who had alleged that the SDI was simply a cover to destroy arms control felt suddenly vindicated. The administration's subsequent refusal for over a year to release to the Senate the records on which it had based the analysis created new rifts in executive-congressional relations. The administration had finally given members of the Congress something they could rally around: constitutional prerogative.

The issue provoked a feud in the Cabinet as well. In a meeting in the White House on October 11, 1985, Secretary of State George Shultz persuaded the president to preserve the treaty's limits, in deference to the allies and the Congress. In what was described as a "knock-down, drag-out meeting," which also included McFarlane, Weinberger, and ACDA Director Kenneth Adelman, Weinberger and Shultz were almost literally at each other's throat. Backed up only by Special Arms Control Adviser Paul Nitze, who sent documentation of negative allied reactions and argued that the decision would severely complicate U.S.-Soviet relations on the eve of the first summit, Shultz reportedly had to threaten to resign before he won the argument.[72]

In what was to become the formulation of NSDD-172 in late 1985, Shultz crafted the compromise position to lessen congressional outrage. The United States would continue to conduct the SDI program "in accordance with the restrictive interpretation" but was fully justified in moving to the "legal" interpretation when it saw fit. The SDI program would thus continue to comply with the "traditional" interpretation for the foreseeable future. This papered-over conflict soon gave rise to other disputes, not just about the SDI but about the whole future of arms control. Those in the administration and the Congress who were happy to scrap the treaty, no matter what the costs, and who had lauded the administration for its creativity and courage, felt that the White House had once more copped out.

In January 1987, Nunn became chairman of the Armed Services Committee as the Senate returned to Democratic control. The ongoing dispute over the ABM Treaty threw the new chairman into the forefront of the SDI debate, in which he had previously been very conservative, always voting for the upper limits of funding requests and avoiding association with contentious amendments.

After gaining access to the treaty's negotiating record, Nunn launched into an assessment of the administration's legal analysis. It was ironic for Nunn to be playing a central role in this realm. His political style was to avoid congressional-executive confrontations wherever possible, especially over foreign policy, which he believed to be rightfully the business of the president. Even more pointedly, he was no great fan of the ABM Treaty, recognizing that the technological realities at the time of its signing had changed markedly.

Housed in a classified area in the dome of the Capitol, the treaty records were accessible to all senators but to only six staffers—two representatives of each party from the Armed Services and the Foreign Relations committees and one from the majority and minority leaders. Many cynically expected that the staffers would simply reach conclusions that coincided with partisan positions. Nunn's staffer, however, Robert Bell, a former defense analyst for the Congressional Research Service and a veteran of the Foreign Relations Committee under Charles Percy, the former Republican senator from Illinois, took his job seriously. Virtually alone, he spent days in the windowless room, amazed at the awesome responsibility he had inherited. Abraham Sofaer, the State Department's legal adviser who had prepared the administration's case, had dozens of lawyers; under the rules, Bell could discuss his analysis only with Nunn. And there was obviously no "smoking gun." Like any legal document, this one presented endless complexities and nuances. Bell developed a great respect for the sophistication of Sofaer's arguments.

Nunn's final, four-part report refuted the Sofaer interpretation in painstaking detail. But even before he had had a chance to discuss it with the administration, another skirmish occurred. Leaked to the conservative reporter Gregg Fossedal, the minutes of an NSC meeting on February 3 indicated that Reagan was ready to move out with the "broad" interpretation of the treaty. The meeting had begun with Weinberger's argument that the decision to deploy was obviously correct. Nothing comprehensive was available yet, but something "integral to the whole system" should go forward, he maintained.

National Security Adviser Frank Carlucci asked if the deployment, though desirable militarily and strategically, was correct politically. The chairman of the Joint Chiefs, Admiral William Crowe, responded, "The chiefs support SDI and support phased deployment. But we don't have enough in hand to decide now." Weinberger retorted, "But we need to make some decisions now."

Secretary of State Shultz argued that the decision was premature. Weinberger disagreed and mentioned the plan devised by the SDIO for kinetic-kill vehicles: "We've made great progress for kinetic kill vehicles for boost-phase. Do we deploy incrementally or all at once?" He went on to argue for the deployment of sixty vehicles that could destroy 2,000 warheads, to be validated in an upcoming test called Delta 181. Shultz, stating that the 1993 deployment target date was "Abe's view" and probably unrealistic, urged deferral of the decision. Although Shultz supported the phased deployment in principle—it might help as leverage with the Soviets in Geneva—he was opposed to adopting the broad interpretation and pointed out that the existing testing schedule for the next year was already compliant, so why borrow trouble?

Weinberger kept pressing, reminding the president of the December briefing where these issues had been discussed. "It is an area defense, and not a point defense, and it is stabilizing," he said. In increasingly strained tones, Shultz replied,

> I didn't know we made any decisions in December, but I have talked to Abe twice and all the chiefs individually, and am impressed by what I heard. . . . The chiefs have been skeptical on going back on the ABM Treaty. . . . [You shouldn't deploy] unless you have some idea on where you're going beyond. I agree with Crowe that we're not in a position to confront that decision.

Arguing that the decision should wait to give the United States the opportunity to assess the likely Soviet reaction, Shultz was reprimanded by Weinberger, who said, "We shouldn't debate with the Soviets what can and can't be prohibited."

Reagan was at first extremely cavalier about the possible consequences. Urged by Shultz to think about the Soviet reaction, Reagan said, "Don't ask the Soviets. Tell them . . . I see the price tag and I'm willing to pay."[73]

"Whoever thought they were helping the cause by leaking to

Fossedal really got it wrong," said an aide to Nunn. "I've never seen him so mad." Nunn fired off a letter to the president, telling him that the adoption of this policy before reaching consensus in the Congress would face "severe problems." The SDI would be subject to "much deeper cuts than would otherwise occur." More important, the refusal to accept the interpretation of the ABM treaty that had been presented to and ratified by the Senate in 1972 "would provoke a Constitutional confrontation of profound dimensions."[74]

The battle lines were now drawn. Repeated efforts by Nunn to get the administration on record as agreeing to the constitutional principle that the Senate had a role in interpreting treaties were not successful. Again uncharacteristically, Nunn then joined the liberal Democratic senator Carl Levin, of Michigan, in sponsoring a sweeping amendment to the defense bill, prohibiting funds for tests or technologies that violated the narrow interpretation of the treaty. It was the first binding amendment of its kind to pass any part of the Senate. It was remarkable that the amendment originated in the conservative Armed Services Committee and that it had Nunn's name on it all, let alone as a principal sponsor.

In the second week of February, the president and his senior advisers met again. They evaluated three options: to proceed with deployments, including some ground-based systems that could go forward before the end of Reagan's tenure; to proceed with the new interpretation of the treaty to permit a series of noncompliant space tests; or to defer the decision for several months in order to gauge the Soviet reaction. The decision was made to move forward with the phase 1 design, but to look into the impact of restructuring the SDI program under the "broad" interpretation. NSDD-261 in February 1987 approved the plan. Negotiators in Geneva were instructed not to discuss any interpretation of the treaty other than the "broad" one, and several internal studies were commissioned.

Sofaer was asked to reinvestigate the negotiating record, to see if an even stronger case could be made for what was now called within the administration the "legal" interpretation. A DoD study was commissioned to prove the legality of deploying the space-based kinetic-kill vehicle, renamed the space-based interceptor (SBI). The issue of the SBI had already been investigated several times, once by an outside contractor. The question was whether it could be demonstrated to be a "new" system permitted under the broad interpretation or, as many argue, whether it would be prohibited in any case because it is an interceptor based on traditional rocket technologies. Traditional interceptors cannot be tested in space under any reading of the treaty. And the Pentagon's Office of International Security Policy investigated what programs could be accelerated or changed if the administration moved to the broad interpretation, partly in response to an amendment Senator Wallop attached to the fiscal year 1987 defense authorization bill.

The DoD completed its evaluations in April 1987. The decision was made to move the program into the formal acquisition process, subjecting the plan to a "milestone 1" review by the Defense Science Board, to inform subsequent decisions by the Defense Acquisition Board. The general consensus was to move into phase 1 deployment as soon as possible, with a balanced program of mature and advanced technologies. After protracted negotiations with the Congress, the decision to move to the broad interpretation of the treaty was once more sidestepped. The fiscal year 1988 defense authorization bill prohibited funds from being used to test or produce systems that violated the restrictive interpretation of the treaty.

In July 1987, a report by a task force of the Pentagon's Defense Science Board—a standing committee of scientists who advise the Defense Department—was leaked to the *Washington Post*. The draft report was extremely critical of the early deployment of strategic defenses. Arguing that the SDI was not ready for a deployment decision, the task force, chaired by Robert Everett of the Mitre Corporation, approved of the phased deployment concept but cautioned, "Much remains to be done before a confident decision can be made to proceed with the initial implementation of an initial phase of a ballistic missile defense." It questioned the survivability of SBIs, posed questions about software, and cast doubt on the SDIO's cost estimates, "which greatly exceed the amounts currently under discussion in the Congress."[75]

Some Pentagon officials claim the panel's report was mishandled by the new acquisition under secretary, Richard Godwin. "One guy on the panel took a walk—Bill Perry. He was pushing language for the report which any House subcommittee could have used to justify an SDI funding cut. It was Washington dirty pool." Perry, it is claimed, advanced arguments about the system's feasibility that were too exacting and premature "for phase 1." Perry responded that the evaluation was an honest one, but he refused to comment on any personal involvement in its leak to the press.[76]

In preparing for the milestone 1 review, the Joint Chiefs had been brought in to develop an agreed "threat assessment" and generate requirements to develop a "20–30 percent defense effectiveness." The JCS did not go into the process with great enthusiasm, since they were again worried about the proposed costs of the system and its potential drain on resources. Under direction of the former commander in chief of NORAD and current vice-chairman of the JCS, General Robert Herres, the JCS identified a series of modest requirements to achieve a notional defense by the mid-1990s. The requirements were developed against a threat assessment that held Soviet defensive developments constant. As the task force pointed out, "the requirements process should be broadened to include an analysis of the desirability of deployment which includes a consideration of two-sided BMD deployment." The document forced a fragile consensus on the JCS that belies their intense disagreements over program goals and even the desirability of the defenses themselves.[77]

The Defense Acquisition Board in July 1987 nevertheless recommended that six systems be studied for possible deployment, including space-based interceptors, the ground-based rocket interceptor ERIS system, the boost surveillance and tracking system, a satellite to track missile launches, command and control architecture, and the space surveillance and tracking system, a second type of satellite to find Soviet missiles in the middle of their trajectory. A phase 1 program director, Jack Donnigan, was appointed to oversee the effort. As these systems move into testing and validation, the process will be conducted in a manner compliant with the "old" ABM Treaty. When the system is "ready," it will be evaluated on the basis of cost, survivability, and other criteria and a decision made whether it should be moved forward into deployment.

The plan notably lacked any laser or particle beam weapons. As one critic said, "It's like digging up 'Safeguard' and hurtling it into space." Among the casualties in the future may be the laser programs, which will have to be cut to accommodate the deployment plan. A JCS official expressed the view that the main effect is to derail and potentially undo the twenty years of solid scientific progress on lasers, "crippled by the ambitions of political zealots."[78]

The study of options to reorient the program toward more advanced technologies under the broad interpretation, the so-called Wallop report, is revealing on several counts. Most important, it suggests that the SDI program has been so conditioned by political pressures that its own commitment to rapid progress has been stymied. When first approached by Furniss, who was asked to be the study director, the SDIO program directors balked. "They didn't want turbulence in their programs, and didn't want to have to change them," said Furniss. After the excruciating effort of designing their programs to be compliant with the treaty, they were very protective and conservative. At first, they offered minor modifications, which Furniss found unsatisfactory.

Furniss went to Abrahamson, to tell him to "lay down the law." "All of a sudden, Abe is pulling ideas out of the air, writing them down as he thinks of them on the chalkboard," Furniss recalled, before turning to his directors and saying, " 'You go fill in the details.' " SDIO officials were running around frantically. "The technical people would come in saying, 'We can't do this,' Abe would insist, and back they'd go." The result was the design of "four broad options," with a deployment date that is classified "but not inconsistent with the early 1990s deployment date for phase 1." For the most part, the Wallop report had only one main conclusion, which was already well known: it would be cheaper and easier to conduct space tests if the treaty constraints were removed.[79]

By November 1988, faced with a fractious Senate controlled by the Democrats, continued fiscal pressures, and the election of a moderate Republican to the White House whose enthusiasm for defenses seemed in doubt, the SDIO had submitted a revised blueprint for an initial deployment scheme. The new SDI was a pale shadow of its former self, a plan that savaged space systems and emphasized terminal defense even more, especially the ERIS. As further evidence that the enthusiasm for astrodomes had finally been died down, a White House Science Council panel made up of many members of the defensive revolution, including Teller, Yonas, and Canavan, submitted a report urging the president to deploy a limited defense. Although still clinging to the distant prospect of a more comprehensive scheme, the panel squarely supported the push for prosaic technologies for "earliest possible deployment at minimum risk."[80]

Renewed Warfare on Testing Limits

Since the end of 1987, much of the debate inside the administration over the SDI revolved around arms control. Finding the way out of the Soviet refusal to bargain on central strategic systems without an agreement on the future of the ABM Treaty has been the key challenge. The disputes were mostly between the State Department and the Defense Department, although some officials in the NSC and the State Department were violently opposed to any trade on the SDI. The ascendancy in the administration of "arms controllers" like Paul Nitze was far worse in the eyes of many SDI proponents than anything the Union of Concerned Scientists could ever have dreamed up. As one said, "The salient threat to the SDI comes from those who continue to view it as a potential sacrifice on the altar of arms control."[81]

In April 1987, the Soviet Union proposed that it and the United States work out a list of permitted space tests under a ten-year extension of the traditional interpretation of the treaty, including a list of thresholds dividing prohibited and permitted testing of SDI technologies in eight categories. The constraints would impede the technological range of tests—reducing the velocity of kinetic rockets, for instance, or the intensity of laser beams. The proposal was fervently attacked by the Pentagon, which saw it as a direct assault on the broad interpretation of the treaty. There is no need to have thresholds or any other limits on tests under the broad interpretation, which would limit only deployments. In the Pentagon's view, the Soviet proposal and its support by the State Department amount to an underhanded way of relegitimizing the ABM regime.

This led to a brutal struggle in the administration between those who reject the ABM paradigm, and all of its implications, and the "traditionalists," who, critics allege, cannot stand to give up their atavistic intellectual legacy of deterrence. The fight is between those who want to force the Soviets to accept the SDI as a inevitability, using it to "beat the ABM paradigm to death," as one official put it, and those who believe that negotiations to limit tests of space systems are a necessary and desirable precondition for reaching a broader agreement. One Pentagon official describes Shultz's and Nitze's efforts in Geneva as driven by the belief that "if they just wait long enough, they will be able to resurrect the respectability for the ABM framework." The effort to negotiate testing limits is also opposed by many congressional SDI proponents, who argue that the limits themselves will cripple the SDI. More important, the critics see test limits as one more delay in the effort to scrap the ABM Treaty, in deference to outmoded ideas about the importance of arms control.

The dispute prompted personal attacks on Paul Nitze, the leading figure of the administration's Geneva negotiations. One of his colleagues compared him to Lieutenant Colonel Oliver North, the NSC official disgraced for running covert sales of arms to Iran: "He's the Ollie North of arms control and defense; he thinks he knows better than the president." "Nitze doesn't belong in this administration," said another; "he doesn't represent the arms control principles of the administration." Other officials have fueled allegations in the press that Nitze had set up a "back channel" with the Soviets through a committee of scientists in the National Academy of Sciences. This group of private experts, which meets regularly with Soviet counterparts to discuss arms control, briefed administration officials before and after its meeting in October 1987. Press accounts sparked a firestorm on Capitol Hill by falsely charging that the committee, with Nitze's explicit support, helped develop the Soviets' proposals and encouraged them to "hang tough" against administration ideologues. This latest round of acrimony represented a last-ditch effort to seize the SDI from the jaws of arms control.[82]

Advocates of the "test and break out" school have stepped up pressures to conduct noncompliant tests in order to render the debate irrelevant. A test scheduled for 1989, Delta 181, in which two missiles collide, has been portrayed by these advocates as a deliberate violation. Without a robust testing schedule, they fear, the SDI will be chiseled away in negotiations and by opponents. "Let's say we're looking at thirty tests," said an SDI proponent on Capitol Hill.

> . . . They aren't scheduled until 1993, 1994—all we have to do is put them off for a couple of years to stay within the treaty for that length of time. Another five tests or so—maybe the Soviets don't object to these. And another five or 10—maybe these can be broken down into smaller, inefficient tests. Soon you're down to maybe five tests which are simultaneously important, timely, and disputed by the Soviets. And Nitze will say, 'Mr. President, you can get a 50 percent cut in nuclear weapons in exchange for those measly tests, which the Senate may kill anyway.' "[83]

In May 1987, Weinberger urged the approval of four tests that violated the traditional interpretation of the ABM Treaty. These experiments, he held, were needed to permit the deployment of defensive systems by 1994. The tests would be conducted in 1989 or 1990, although some in the Pentagon were arguing they should be conducted earlier. Asked about the basis of these tests, Furniss said, "Abe just pulled them out of the air."[84]

On November 23, the Pentagon announced it would be conducting a test of a chemical laser in the early 1990s. Although it is supposed to be "compliant," officials conceded this would require serious realignment of the test to downgrade the capabilities being explored. For the first time, the administration is proposing to test a highly sophisticated interception system based on lasers, a system that a recent report by the American Physical Society said would not be possible until well into the next century.[85]

In the closing months of his administration, virtually on the day of the initialing of the INF Treaty, President Reagan promised workers at an SDI contracting firm, Martin Marietta, "You are not working to build a bargaining chip. . . . It will not be traded away." Standing in front of the mock-up of the laser "Zenith Star," the president once more seemed oblivious to the activities of his own administration. The speech must have been a great surprise to the negotiating team in Geneva.

The disputes over SDI's future became increasingly desperate as the administration drew to a close. The debate seemed to have come full circle, culminating in the accusation that Paul Nitze, the former head of the Committee on the Present Danger, the organization that fanned the frenzy over American strategic weakness that helped bring Ronald Reagan to power, was soft on the Soviets. There seemed to be no mercy in the struggle for the definition of the SDI.

In the end, the strategy for the SDI—an appeal to lofty goals without a concrete plan for their implementation—engendered a level of controversy that plagued the effort to carry it out as something short of a technological fantasy. Even though more than $12 billion was allocated to the scheme and some important scientific breakthroughs have been reported, the program achieved no concrete alteration in American strategy. It has proved instead to be a major obstacle to consensus and may yet end up turning strategic defenses into a casualty of partisan politics, political forces the scheme itself helped set in motion.

CHAPTER 6

Mediators and Gladiators:
The Enduring Schism

I N JANUARY 1988, Senator Sam Nunn stunned the audience at a meeting of the Arms Control Association in Washington by suggesting that it might not be a bad idea to look into technologies for a partial defense. The newly anointed hero of arms control, about to be lionized by the association for his leadership in thwarting the administration's attempt to revise the ABM Treaty, had just dropped a bombshell.

To those familiar with Nunn's style, the proposal was typical of his political pragmatism and general common sense. If we're going to spend a few billion dollars on defenses every year—and not even the most liberal of his colleagues quarreled with that—we might as well assign to defenses a compelling mission. Given the state of existing technology, maybe a "thin" defense of ground-based systems could be deployed, in conjunction with an agreement with the Soviets about limitations on more elaborate defenses. Nunn argued that such a system, meant to protect the country from an accidental or third-country attack, could be pursued with only slight modification of the ABM Treaty.

As it was, Nunn's articulation of a limited-defense scheme did not even amount to a real endorsement. Analysts at the Rand Corporation had been thinking about it, and Nunn had recently returned from several days of briefings in Santa Monica. He presented the hypothetical accidental launch protection system, or ALPS, as it was called, in a few conditional sentences, a small part of a speech that included almost a dozen different proposals for accelerating progress in U.S.-Soviet arms limitations.[1]

But to the members of the Arms Control Association, who had paid $250 for dinner and the chance to revel in the triumph of having "saved the ABM Treaty," the substance of Nunn's speech was eclipsed in that one moment of extraordinary bad taste. The new champion of arms control had just committed an act of ultimate heresy. Defenses? No way. Nunn's a captive of the Right.

Across the river at the Pentagon, officials who had been advocating space-based systems were equally appalled when they heard about Nunn's diabolical scheme. "A gambit to force a premature debate on BMD systems," charged Bruce Jackson. As he saw it,

> It's a politically inspired challenge to space defense, which will undercut any prospects for pursuing space options. As soon as you start talking about terminal systems, you recapitulate the 1970s ABM debate and lose the battle. This is a struggle for the future of American strategy, and the fate of the old ABM paradigm. Nunn and his staff have joined the Left.[2]

The response to the speech shed light on where the political debate over defenses was headed. The Left rushed to oppose any deployment of defenses, railing about the instability and high costs of even the most modest concepts. The space advocates joined in the repudiation of a limited ground-based defense, pointing out that it neither overwhelmed the Soviets nor moved the country beyond the atavism of the ABM regime. A few Pentagon officials went so far as to hastily prepare for the secretary of defense a briefing demonstrating that ALPS would violate the ABM Treaty—the treaty they themselves had been trying to bury.

For those who remembered the McNamara legacy, Senator Nunn's speech sounded a very familiar note. But what was Nunn really up to? Was he proposing a modest deployment of defenses as part of a deliberate effort to emasculate the SDI program, revitalize the ABM Treaty, and discard the rhetoric of technological supremacy touted by administration extremists? Or had he actually "sold out," suggesting, as some analysts at the Heritage Foundation claimed, that "opposition to the SDI is beginning to crumble"?[3]

Only the senator can say how calculated his strategy may have been, and to what end. But once again, the result was that a proposal for a limited defense contributed to the demystification of the notion that defensive technology promised strategic superiority. Along with the technical uncertainties and prospective high costs of an SDI system, the idea of a partial defense helped underscore the point that defenses were not a panacea for the problems of nuclear deterrence. Just as the limitations of the Safeguard system had demonstrated the modest contribution that defenses could make in the early 1970s, the 1980s version, though much more robust technically, had essentially the same effect. ALPS was something tangible, mere machinery whose capabilities and costs could be weighed against other security requirements. It ensured that the SDI, divested of its glamour as a way "to escape the prison of mutual terror," as the president put it in 1985, would now have to be considered on its merits.[4]

By portraying critics as the true reactionaries and the president as the visionary seeing beyond a world of nuclear peril, the SDI had proved itself a brilliant domestic political gambit. It is what political advisers spend their lives trying to invent, a real triumph of Orwellian "spin control," as the media experts call it. As the foundation for a major shift in military doctrine, however, it failed. Its unorthodox logic and blatant contradictions posed formidable challenges to those charged with implementing American nuclear strategy.

Like each of its antecedents, the doctrinal revolution promised by the SDI joined the ranks of bold initiatives tempered by bureaucracy, technological realities, and the resilience of the status quo. For all of the loose talk about peaceful transitions to defenses, no real alteration in war plans had ever been considered. Indeed, the one possibility for reducing offensive forces—progress in the START negotiations with the Soviets—had foundered on the Soviet objection to the administration's insistence on the right to test futuristic, defensive technologies. In this regard, the SDI served as the political wedge ensuring continuation of the status quo—expansion of offensive forces by both superpowers.

Ever sensitive to political tides, Lieutenant General Abrahamson gave an interview to the *New York Times* in September 1988 to publicize a much simplified version of the SDI. Presenting it as a scheme to cut costs, the general insisted, "We are not trying to restructure the program." But the proposal included major changes in the way in which space-based interceptors would be designed and deployed, and it vastly downgraded the requirements for space-based systems altogether.[5] The interview took place only days before Abrahamson was forced to retire early and was replaced by an air force lieutenant general, George Monahan, handpicked by Secretary of Defense Carlucci with apparently no discussion with anyone associated with the SDIO. It was not the graceful exit the remaining loyalists had planned. "We were hoping to give him the Medal of Freedom," lamented one of them, "or at least say good-bye."

"Killing Cossacks from Space"

The peaceful public cast of the SDI has always belied the more hardheaded motivations of the strategists who have been thinking about the use of space for offensive military operations. The SDI helped generate a technological and political push for new military concepts in space. This "innovative" thinking, which has gone on at the Space Command and in think tanks around the country working under contract to the Pentagon, has its intellectual roots in previous efforts to "quietly remove the stifling concept of retaliation," as the so-called Project Control study conducted by the Air War College had tried to do in the early Cold War period.[6] Virtually since the development of the first atomic bomb, frustrations among strategists and weapons designers about the straitjacket of a retaliatory strategy have encouraged steady efforts to find alternatives.

As in all former shifts in doctrine, the latent recognition of obsolescing weapons—in this case, silo-based ICBMs—has spurred the effort to discover new and more ingenious ways to compete. The current environment is ripe for technological change.

For those pushing the "high frontiers" of technology to advance the U.S.-Soviet rivalry, the next, urgent step is acceleration of military activities in space. As Pete Worden and others have argued, there is a critical synergism between offensive space capabilities—kinetic- and directed-energy weapons, for instance—and forces needed for conventional engagements. To their advocates, space systems are "force multipliers" that could provide the key to fixing "the correlation of forces" between East and West, greatly improving NATO's ability to fight wars.[7]

Given the growing interest in the late 1980s in "improving conventional deterrence," a clarion call by both Democrats and Republicans, the political impetus for modernizing conventional forces could be the unwitting catalyst space advocates have been seeking to advance their concepts of strategy. Whether space developments will ever involve a radical paradigm shift, with an explicit commitment to eliminate or vastly reduce reliance on nuclear weapons in favor of weapons and other systems in space, or whether they will rather involve incremental changes that over time render traditional nuclear deterrent concepts obsolete, is the key question for future leaders. If the experience of the SDI is any indication, decisions will be driven by politics as much as by strategy. To those who are pressing for a "nonnuclear world," however, a word of warning: advocates of the "next frontier" have developed some rather advanced ideas for how to get to such a world, and they do not entail disarmament.

The Real Legacy: Prevailing in Nuclear War

In September 1988, the U.S. ambassador to West Germany, Richard Burt, stated that Western leaders had the responsibility to explain to their public that there was no alternative to the strategy of flexible response.[8] Although he aimed his criticism at those who believed that improved conventional forces could eventually replace nuclear weapons, he inadvertently confirmed the utter irrelevance of the metamorphosis in doctrine promised by the SDI five years earlier. Twelve billion dollars and five years of debate later, Burt's remarks highlighted how little the administration had moved from the tired jargon of "credible deterrence."

Every president and secretary of defense since McNamara has tried to solve the fundamental conundrum of nuclear operations: how to design forces that can both deter a first strike and survive one if it occurs, and how to do so within fiscal constraints and the logic of "stability." If there is one constant, it is the failure of each new administration to recast nuclear doctrine in its own image. No innovation has ever been fully implemented, and no political leader has ever "undone" the nuclear infrastructure of his predecessors. Instead, the evolution of American nuclear doctrine reflects the growing schism between the rhetoric of nuclear policy—what some people candidly call the marketing side—and the operational doctrine for actually fighting a war.

The real doctrinal debate has not taken place in the public or in the Congress. It has gone on quietly in the Pentagon among a few civilian officials, the Joint Chiefs, and weapons planners. Even internally, the activities of the SDIO in the Pentagon have had little bearing on the planning of the force structure, except to impart some political momentum for breaking out of the constraints of the ABM Treaty and to lend indirect impetus to a new bureaucracy trying to design space doctrine. As the tactics and capabilities of the nuclear targeteers have grown more complex, the planning community has expanded accordingly. And it has done so largely on its own terms. Let political leaders fuss about the public image of our nuclear posture, they argue; we targeteers have a job to do.

The struggle between advocates of MAD and advocates of mutually assured survival, as it was publicly called, is an intellectual struggle over the future of nuclear doctrine and the structure of American nuclear forces. But for now it is a struggle firmly grounded in the technological reality of the supremacy of offensive forces. "Prevailing" strategy, as revealed in NSDD-13 early in the Reagan administration, is the logical and almost cosmetic extension of Jimmy Carter's "countervailing" strategy, enunciated in 1979. The key challenge during the Reagan administration was to formulate justifications for the continuing major additions to U.S. counterforce capabilities, especially with regard to the modernization of ICBMs. As the 1980s draw to a close, American strategic doctrine continues on the steady course it has followed for forty years.

The Open Window

The main impetus for American nuclear force planning over the last decade owes much of its political and technological energy to the "window of vulnerability"—the "discovery" of an emerging Soviet capability to destroy U.S. land-based missiles in a successful first strike. Although the theoretical vulnerability of American ICBMs had been a subject of mounting concern for over fifteen years, as a result of the Soviets' steady expansion of highly accurate, multiple-warhead missiles, the issue did not peak politically until the SALT II disputes in the late 1970s and the presidential campaign of 1980. Partly to discredit the Carter administration's policies of accommodation with the Soviet Union, Soviet nuclear advances were seized upon by administration critics as evidence of the bankruptcy of the Western notions of "parity" and "stability," which guided the pursuit of mutual, negotiated arms reductions.

The vulnerability of American ICBMs is the 1980s version of the bomber and the missile gaps of the 1950s. Like every prior episode of change in Soviet technological capabilities, Soviet deployment of highly accurate, MIRVed land-based missiles, such as the SS-18, provided the impetus for domestic political controversy about declining American power.

Even though the authors of the grimmest scenarios of Soviet attacks on U.S. missile fields acknowledged that surviving American bombers and submarine missiles could devastate the Soviet Union in retaliation, the idea that the Soviets could place the core of American counterforce capabilities at risk had tremendous political repercussions. In its most extreme version, the "window" represented a de facto return to the paralysis of massive retaliation. According to proponents of this view, the Soviets could destroy U.S. ICBMs with only a portion of their forces, while the United States would be left with insufficient "hard-target kill" capability to destroy Soviet military targets. With only bombers and submarines remaining, the only recourse would be attacks on Soviet cities, prompting Soviet retaliation against American cities—in other words, surrender or suicide.

Countless critics dismissed the credibility of the "window," arguing that the execution of a Soviet first strike was a technical flight of fancy and that the United States retained more than enough nuclear capability, including counterforce capability, in its bomber and submarine force to deter or retaliate against a Soviet strike. The prevailing view, though, among moderates as well as conservatives, was that once fixed ICBMs became vulnerable, there was no alternative but to develop missiles that could thwart even the hypothetical threat of a Soviet surprise attack. A Soviet capability to hold U.S. missiles at risk, however remote, had sufficient political significance that it had to be countered by commensurate U.S. modernization programs.

The Carter administration had begun development of a ten-warhead, land-based MX missile, to be deployed in a mobile multiple protective shelter (MPS) scheme. Moving toward mobility in deployment, it was reasoned, would be stabilizing because it would make forces both more survivable and less attractive as first-strike targets.

For purely political reasons, the Reagan administration canceled the MPS deployment plan and was lukewarm in its support for the Midgetman. Despite the bipartisan compromises recommended in 1983 by the Scowcroft commission, which reinforced the reasoning of the Carter administration and called for a mixed force of one hundred MX missiles and deployment of the single-warhead, mobile Midgetman missile, deep political divisions about the objectives of missile modernization persisted. After considering and rejecting countless basing proposals for the MX, the Congress imposed a ceiling of fifty missiles in 1985, pending the development of a compelling deployment scheme that could be seen as survivable and could justify a larger force. But the administration's solution presented in 1987—MX on rail-mobile launchers, and a deceleration in the Midgetman program—proved just as controversial. At the end of 1988, the best the Congress could do was to keep funding for both the MX and the Midgetman at levels sufficient to forestall any decisions until the next administration.

The enduring issue in this controversy is the degree to which the United States needs the capability to launch quick, effective attacks against the Soviet Union's vital military assets—in particular, on the land-based ICBMS that form the mainstay of Soviet forces. In traditional deterrence logic, highly accurate, fixed ICBMs are anathema to stability. Their inherent vulnerability, combined with maximum lethality, represents the worst of all worlds: systems that have to be launched first to be truly effective and that therefore, according to some, encourage both sides to place their forces on ready alert, resulting in the so-called hair trigger. Despite the seemingly insuperable difficulty of assuring the survivability of such systems, the tremendous military, political, and social problems associated with finding an acceptable basing mode, and more fundamental questions about the continued utility of a triad in the late twentieth century, the administration stood firm in its conviction that ICBMs were still the best way to conduct effective counterforce operations against hardened Soviet military targets. The administration's preoccupation with ICBMs reflects a deliberate choice about nuclear strategy consistent with SAC's enduring philosophy of war fighting. According to SAC, ICBMs are the only systems with the speed and flexibility to execute "time urgent" attacks against Soviet missile silos. Deployed on land, they are readily available to national command authorities for rapid launch in crisis. They are, in other words, the linchpin of a nuclear strategy that aspires to have a demonstrable ability to hit Soviet silos before Soviet missiles are launched. Submarines may be more survivable, but the perception of potential difficulties of communicating with submarines in crisis has led planners to see submarines as potentially less responsive, and thus less reliable, for these kinds of operations.

While politicians engaged in endless debates about survivability, stability, and hair triggers, war planners pursued a more practical agenda: pushing urgent new "requirements" for forces to close the gap in "time-urgent/hard-target kill capability." The systems that the administration emphasized most were the MX and the submarine-launched D-5 missiles, to be used against a target base consisting of an estimated 1,400 Soviet ICBM silos, 700 leadership "bunkers," and assorted other hard-point targets. And new "earth penetrating" warheads were approved for development for the specific purpose of targeting bunkers the Soviets had been building even deeper underground, in the apparent belief that this could ensure the survival of Soviet leaders during nuclear combat.[9]

According to one estimate, the number of prompt, hard-target kill warheads in the U.S. arsenal could be as many as 4,000 by the end of the 1990s, up from a mere 1,000 in 1988. As one analyst claimed, "If Trident II, Peacekeeper [MX], and Midgetman are actually procured in substantial quantities and perform as advertised, the US would attain for the first time . . . the theoretical ability to destroy most Soviet ICBMs simultaneously."[10]

In addition to improved capabilities to destroy hardened targets, U.S. plans also call for additional flexibility in targeting, assuring that forces could be used in a responsive way during a nuclear engagement. So-called requirements for nuclear weapons increased by almost 50 percent during the Reagan administration in support of these goals, from about 8,000 strategic warheads to more than 13,000.

These trends in U.S. nuclear forces reflect the administration's real thinking about strategy, the need to have improved "maximum options" for counterstrategic attacks and the ability to fight protracted nuclear wars. Although ICBMs still predominate, major efforts are being undertaken to improve the ability to retarget submarine missiles flexibly and to improve the air-breathing leg of the triad—with air-launched cruise missiles (ALCMs), the B-1B bomber, and the advanced-technology ("Stealth") bomber (ATB). Significant investments in command, control, and communications are being made, too, to ensure the survival of the infrastructure that commands nuclear forces, including the nation's political and military leadership.

The increasing mobility of Soviet military targets also has guided force planning. So-called relocatable targets—including mobile missiles and command and control capabilities—were assigned a higher priority in war plans in the middle to late 1980s. Relocatable targets provided the basis for according even greater importance to the manned bomber and the improvement of intelligence capabilities through the use of real-time sensors in space. General John Chain, commander in chief of SAC, said in July of 1987,

> With regard to manned bombers, I consider the human presence in the manned bomber crucial to detecting, identifying, and attacking the growing number of Soviet relocatable targets. . . . The capability of the manned bomber to penetrate enemy airspace and search out and destroy relocatable targets, particularly the highly threatening mobile ICBMs, is essential.[11]

These investments are a long way from the "peaceful transition to defense dominance" that was still being discussed in the White House in late 1988. But the direction of nuclear programs in the 1980s reflects a deeper contradiction than the obvious disparity between the mammoth buildup in nuclear forces and the lofty rhetoric of peace shields. It stems from the enduring tensions between the traditional logic of credible deterrence, which relies on the ability to retaliate against a Soviet attack, and the deployment of forces whose capabilities suggest plans to conduct counterforce attacks with such a degree of promptness that they approach preemption. Although preemption is not an operational objective of official U.S. strategy, some analysts argue that the structure of U.S. nuclear forces—particularly, the continued development of highly accurate, hard-target kill ICBMs—clouds the real objectives of national strategy. The premium put on accuracy, promptness, and hard-target kill capability, they argue, can be justified only as a means for destroying Soviet military forces before they are used, and this threatens the distinction between initiation and retaliation.

Administration officials disagree that the structure and content of U.S. forces imply an intent or capability to preempt. Highly accurate counterforce weapons, they argue, are needed to threaten Soviet forces that might be withheld in the first round of a nuclear exchange: Surviving Soviet forces if left intact, would give the Soviets an advantage in a "postexchange" environment. As such, highly accurate, hard-target kill U.S. ICBMs are fully consistent with a strategy aimed at deterring incentives for a Soviet first strike.

This is an enduring dispute that is likely to intensify as the U.S. continues to modernize its arsenal. In an article in the trade journal *Air Force Magazine* about the future of American nuclear modernization, for example, Robert Dudney posed the following rhetorical question:

> Some analysts assert that the current US military build-up, if fully implemented, could turn tables on Russia in the decade ahead. The Peacekeeper, the single warhead ICBM, and an expanding force of D-5 submarine launched missiles, they say, may confront a threat to their fixed ICBM force, which represents roughly sixty-five percent of their strategic striking power compared to twenty percent for the United States. *Why would the United States desire such a capability even though the first strike is not an option?* (emphasis added)

The author goes on to explain that it has to do with perceptions. Unless the United States can threaten Soviet land-based missiles with the same ferocity that the Soviets can threaten U.S. land-based missiles, he reasons, the Soviets will see the United States as weak— even if U.S. land-based missiles make up less than a third of the total number of weapons that would survive to destroy the Soviet Union in return. More colorfully put, "the existence of large numbers of superaccurate arms in the US force would drive home to the Soviet Union the dangers of nuclear bullying on Moscow's part."[12] That said, the author shows no apparent concern that such a force structure might signal other messages as well, such as a U.S. intent to deny the Soviet Union its capacity to retaliate—a direct contravention of the most sacrosanct tenets of stable deterrence.

Defenses in Left Field

The high profile the administration accorded the SDI contributed to its relative inability to articulate its rationale for modernizing nuclear forces. The Pentagon never made a serious effort, senior officials say, to coordinate offensive and defensive modernization objectives; it allowed the two realms to stay essentially separate. A study was undertaken in 1985 under the direction of the under secretary of defense for policy, Fred Iklé, with the purpose of "integrating strategic defensive capabilities" with offensive forces and to "update nuclear employment plans and guidance for the transition from offense to defense in the 1990s." According to one participant in the effort, ten substudies were commissioned as part of this initiative, but only one, on offensive targeting, was ever completed.[13]

The lack of coordination is explained in part by the difficulty of assessing hypothetical defensive capabilities against real Soviet threats, or against the tangible capabilities of offensive forces. But it is also a reflection of the abstract and largely political nature of the SDI and the concrete modernization priorities for nuclear forces. The goals of the SDI remain at odds with offensive programs in both strategic objectives and budget priorities.

A number of inherent contradictions in current doctrine could have been exacerbated by SDI developments. One is the survivability of U.S. communications and early-warning satellites in the event the Soviets develop effective antisatellite capabilities. The U.S. ability to retaliate against a Soviet attack, and particularly the coordination of flexible options, depends on a complex network of communications and intelligence satellites.

The Reagan administration planned major improvements in the command, control, communications, and intelligence infrastructure, alloting over $22 billion to rectify weaknesses in the defense budgets for the fiscal years 1982–86. The plans focused on shoring up land communications, which could be directly targeted by Soviet offensive nuclear forces. The administration gave far less attention to the threat to satellites, on which the United States relies disproportionately in peace and wartime relative to the Soviet Union.[14] Since the technologies for intercepting missiles and attacking satellites are quite similar, the Soviet development of effective strategic defenses could also provide the capability to threaten U.S. space assets in distant orbits and would be a source of serious concern. The SDI's promised acceleration of a competition in space systems, premised on a rejection of the ABM Treaty, thus seems to be a contradiction. It is as if the administration, by promoting strategic defense, were deliberately laying the groundwork for the defeat of its own nuclear war plans.

The administration's overall approach to protracted nuclear war included more specific plans for the survival of the National Command Authority, including the president, the secretary of defense, and the commander in chief of SAC, among others. These plans are said to ensure "continuity in government" after a nuclear attack. Although they may strike most Americans as reminiscent of scenes from *Dr. Strangelove* and as surrealistic, they are critical to nuclear war planning.

For example, at the onset of a crisis suggesting an impending nuclear attack, leaders would take refuge in various command posts—Fort Ritchie, in Maryland, is one possibility—if the Pentagon was destroyed. There are two airborne command posts: the NEACP, a specially equipped Boeing 747 that would be used by the president, and an EC-135 aircraft known as Looking Glass, which is provided for the SAC commander. Looking Glass, which is used in peacetime for surveillance and training and kept airborne twenty-four hours a day with a SAC general aboard, would provide the environment for the postattack command and control system—directing nuclear strikes against the enemy and, when desirable, trying to negotiate the termination of hostilities on terms favorable to the United States.

These types of postattack structures were a key modernization priority of the Reagan administration but were undertaken without regard to their future viability in a world of space warfare. Testing credulity in any case, the alternative command posts would be even more useless if the satellites they relied on for communications were destroyed.

In early 1984, administration analysts alleged that the Soviets could achieve a 20 percent efficiency rate in defenses by 1987—enough to force a change in U.S. targeting plans in the SIOP. They based this conclusion on Soviet efforts to upgrade the systems deployed around Moscow and on the belief that the Soviets were achieving significant improvements in laser and particle beam technology, which could be used for BMD.[15] Some administration officials actually charged publicly that the Soviets had imminent plans to break out of the treaty, suggested by the construction of the Krasnoyarsk phased-array radar in violation of the treaty, and the alleged covert manufacture of additional components of the ABM-X-3 missile defense system for the rapid deployment of a nationwide defense.

If the conclusions were true, there was reason to be very concerned that the SDI was shifting resources away from BMD options that the

United States could deploy in the near term to counter a Soviet breakout, in favor of embryonic concepts that might provide the basis for area defenses only in some future decade. According to one estimate, the funding levels for near-term BMD technologies were lower under the SDI than they would have been if incremental annual additions to the Carter level budget had been pursued quietly, without the political scrutiny engendered by the SDI.[16]

Even so, many in the administration continued to lobby for the United States to abrogate the treaty. This campaign was not based on a sound analysis of technical realities. As Harvard professor Albert Carnesale noted sarcastically in early 1988, "If we break out of the ABM Treaty today, the Soviets will deploy defenses and we'll deploy viewgraphs."[17]

The JCS's assessment in late 1987 of their requirements for milestone 1 of the SDI produced the first technical document evaluating operational needs for defenses against a measured Soviet threat. The exercise forced the JCS to agree on basic threat parameters and gave the SDI its first concrete goal for defining the desirable characteristics of a specific system. Like previous assessments, however, the document assumed that Soviet offenses and defenses remained constant. It estimated that the United States would need to have a 20 to 30 percent defensive capability against a range of Soviet attacks, but it did not examine the effect of any potential change in Soviet capabilities undertaken in response to U.S. deployment of missile defenses. As a result, and in line with the MIRV debates of the 1960s, the architecture for an "early deployment" scheme commits "the fallacy of the last move"—setting up a transitory strategic posture that does not take into account inevitable changes in the opponent's forces.[18]

Over time, the Joint Chiefs began to demonstrate more open hostility to SDI programs, which loomed as potential drains on the "real" budget, diverting funds from favored weapons systems. For space defense advocates, the greatest frustration has come less from the public's anti-SDI sentiment than from what Pete Worden called "the JCS mind-set." After finally succeeding in arranging a SIOP briefing for Abrahamson in 1986, Worden was dispirited by the JCS's lack of understanding or appreciation of the promises of defense: "The chiefs' goal is to destroy 60 percent of the Soviet military, and they view anything which helps as automatically good, anything which hinders as automatically bad."[19]

The Joint Chiefs participated in the milestone 1 exercise with some reluctance; and the services duly exploited this new civilian artifice, as they had prior doctrinal innovations, on behalf of their respective, traditional force goals. The split between the high polemics of the nonnuclear world heralded by the president and the realities of nuclear force planning had already served one purpose, inadvertently or otherwise, by diverting potentially adverse political attention from the offensive weapons modernization programs that were determining the real future of U.S. nuclear strategy.

The air force, for one, made it clear that even in the fantasy world of a "transition to a peace shield," it would need more, not fewer, nuclear weapons. "I submit [that] the most dangerous period of time in the next twenty years will be the period [in which] we begin to put a space defense in orbit and it becomes effective," said the air force deputy chief of staff, Lieutenant General Harley Hughes. "To continue to deter, it is obvious we need to maintain the triad."[20] The navy, for its part, pointed to the urgent need to counter Soviet submarine missile developments, which, according to one naval officer, would actually become more of a threat if the United States deployed defenses:

> Possible Strategic Defense Initiative weapons such as the railgun could force the Soviets to further develop their wide-ranging, sea-based strategic forces, forcing us, in turn, to increase our ability to find and kill Soviet Typhoons and other submarines armed with nuclear cruise missiles in the open seas, the Arctic ice, and off our coasts.[21]

If defenses ever become a technological reality, some familiar tensions might arise over what SAC considers to be its sacred mission—prompt attacks on military, including strategic, targets—and over the notion of "riding out" an attack by relying on defenses. By suggesting that the United States would actually absorb a Soviet strike before launching its forces, strategic defenses, no matter how capable on paper, might prove no more palatable to military commanders than prior notions of "assured second strike." Yes, there would be some putative capability to intercept incoming missiles, but would a prudent military commander ever have enough confidence in untested defense technologies to be willing to ride out an attack? There is a certain irony in the idea that the SDI is the natural heir of SAC's continuing scorn for civilians' follies.

The Quiet Revolution

In March 1985, Frank Miller was divested of his responsibilities for strategic defense policy; they were taken by Frank Gaffney, an un-abashed conservative ideologue. Miller retained responsibility for offensive forces policy. The split gave institutional reality to the schism in the administration's thinking about nuclear doctrine. As the SDI moved to the center of the political sphere, Miller—the civil servant—was left out. Many observers thought Miller had been rele-gated to bureaucratic purgatory. Like apparatchiks in the Soviet Union who are being removed from their jobs for resisting the tides of *perestroika,* Miller was left to preside over a fiefdom—offen-ses—that seemed destined to become a relic, part of the "old think-ing," as the Soviets now call ideas and practices discarded in the wake of Gorbachev's reforms.

To those who knew better, Miller's reassignment was fortunate. Unhampered by the chore of having to defend the peace shield in the hostile glare of the political spotlight, Miller set out to work on what he considered the most urgent business of American security: the rationalizing of nuclear strategy. A veteran of the analytical efforts in the Carter administration that had led to PD-59, Miller is a disci-plined strategist who understood the challenges of flexible response all too well. Two key problems identified in PD-59, which had been left to languish by the change of administrations, were the develop-ment of concrete targeting plans to provide for limited nuclear op-tions and of the need for clear procedures for civilian policy oversight to ensure that nuclear war plans reflected the strategy accurately. The problems faced by McNamara's whiz kids had not changed: how to achieve real flexibility in nuclear options, how to ensure the conso-nance of the SIOP with this policy, and how to make sure those with policy authority are kept in the loop in the planning for use of nuclear forces. In short, the enduring struggle has been over who determines the content of nuclear plans and controls their execution in a crisis.

As Miller stresses repeatedly, nuclear policy is the rightful domain of the president. If his decisions are to be effective, they must be reflected faithfully in plans and operations. Anyone who believes in deterrence and flexible response, Miller would argue, understood that the most dangerous situation would be one in which the president and secretary of defense believed they had options, but discovered they really did not.

Despite three decades of efforts by prior administrations to synchronize the various elements of nuclear doctrine, planning the details of nuclear strategy has resisted major interference from civilians. If only because of their complexity, the details of weapons employment are beyond the competence of all but a handful of individuals outside of JSTPS and the nuclear commands, and the military does not extend a warm welcome to persons who express an interest. As General Jack Merritt, who served on the NSC under Nixon and later was the director of the Joint Staff in the Reagan administration, put it, "You start talking about targeting or strategic command and control to the JCS and, baby, that's the family jewels. Anyone outside the uniformed military who tried this, the chiefs told them to jump in the lake."[22]

In 1985, there was no well-established mechanism to ensure routine attention to nuclear operations by policy officials, and access to the plans within the Department of Defense is strictly controlled. Outside the Pentagon, morever, access is even more constrained. Congress, for instance, has no formal channels to examine nuclear plans or to exert any influence over the way in which forces are organized to fight nuclear wars. Although congressional briefings are arranged by SAC upon request, at least "for those individuals with a strict need to know" (meaning only members of relevant committees and the small minority of staffers who hold security clearances), the briefings are superficial, covering only "the overall policy and approach for the planning and employment of nuclear forces," as SAC's official policy puts it.[23]

As it is, the subject is so arcane that no politician can be expected to be up to the task of challenging basic planning precepts, even if this were appropriate. Technical complexity is lethal in politics. As one military officer put it, "The price of admission is just too high" and the subject too brain-numbing not just in its moral but its in its technical dimensions as well. The jargon and what one observer dubbed the "acronymphomania" of the discipline do not make for good stump speeches or press releases. The whole subject, in the words of a JCS official, is "technically dull as dust."

There is a far more important reason why the details of nuclear strategy, especially the possible fallibilities in American nuclear plans, are carefully protected from broader discussion. That is the fear that leaks would inevitably occur and aid the decision making of the Soviets, help them in their own nuclear planning, or even encourage military ambitions. There is also an implicit concern that leaks about the character of nuclear war plans could be exploited by the Soviets for political propaganda.

This is not to minimize the importance of the procedures for providing civilian guidance to military planners that have evolved over the past four decades. Since the time of NSDM-242 in 1974, which authorized the secretary of defense to draft the so-called Policy Guidance for the Employment of Nuclear Weapons (NUWEP), guidance is provided directly from the secretary to the Joint Chiefs of Staff. The JCS prepare "Annex Charlie," part of the Joint Strategic Capabilities Plan (JSCP), which consists of highly detailed instructions to the unified and specified commanders and to the JSTPS about how to match existing forces to targets to build the SIOP. The JSCP is the key document for the preparation of the SIOP, and is conducted by the JSTPS. This process includes preparation of the target list, frequent updates to reflect changing intelligence estimates, and allocation of specific weapons to designated targets.

In theory, the extraordinary sophistication of the process, with its highly routinized procedures through which political authorities can dictate their intentions to military planners, suggests the basis for coherent planning. Indeed, there seem to be ample checks and balances and a reasonable division of labor. As the commander in chief of the armed forces, the president retains the formal authority for determining the content of nuclear plans, which are to be derived strictly from civilian guidance. More detailed guidance is to flow from the secretary of defense, who, by law, occupies a place in the chain of command between the president and the military commanders. The chiefs of the military services, in fact, have no legal role in the operational command of the armed forces or in the planning of their missions; even the chairman of the Joint Chiefs, who has a special responsibility as the principal military adviser to the president, is placed in the chain of command only at the direction of the secretary of defense. These legal distinctions are considered essential to protect the nation's 200-year tradition of civilian control of the armed forces.

By definition, therefore, the SIOP should be a blueprint that reflects national political and military objectives. Any significant deviations from the policy guidance must be cleared by the president or, at least, by the secretary of defense; to do otherwise would, quite simply, be unconstitutional. There are procedures to make this coordination happen. The former assistant secretary of defense for command and control Donald Latham argues, "Revisions to the SIOP . . . result in periodic briefings on the changes to the secretary and his staff. These processes provide assurance, through civilian oversight, that the final military operational plans conform to national objectives, strategy, and policy."[24]

When Miller assumed the responsibility for nuclear plans as the secretary's principal representative, however, he discovered a process that makes Latham's sanguine depiction little more than a formal fiction. The complex procedures for civilian-military cooperation notwithstanding, the secretary's directives and actual nuclear war plans remained worlds apart. The instruments for providing civilian guidance, especially the NUWEP, were so vague and confusing that the JSTPS was arguably justified in viewing them as "advisories," not as directives. "PD-59 had introduced lots of options into the SIOP, but they were paper options," said Leon Sloss, who had chaired the National Strategic Targeting Study, which became part of the new directive. Aside from ignoring the procedural reforms recommended in PD-59, the NUWEP that was produced in 1982 made no serious effort to cause highly selective options to be included in the actual SIOP.[25]

Miller had been appointed by Richard Perle in 1981 to direct the Strategic Forces Policy Office in the Pentagon. In this capacity, he had responsibility for all areas of strategic policy, including annual budgetary reviews and the weapon acquisition and procurement issues that required policy direction. He also had authority for formal declaratory policy, the official statements made about nuclear strategy that coexisted alongside the competing rhetoric of the SDI. Miller was responsible for everything except targeting policy, which came under the aegis of Iklé's deputy at the time, Richard Stillwell.

Stillwell and his staff had drafted the 1982 NUWEP and had attempted to revise it in 1984. The draft produced in 1984 was nineteen pages long, a detailed document that vastly altered the emphasis and content of its predecessor. Largely ignoring political questions, it focused on the military aspects of targeting, including extremely precise details about how and where to allocate weapons to specific targets. It provoked a harsh response from the uniformed military, who did not see that details of targeting should fall under the purview of the staff of the secretary of defense. Their reaction was entirely predictable.

Jack Merritt, serving then as the director of the Joint Staff, led a concerted effort to scuttle Stillwell's initiative. "Penny ante civilian bureaucrats getting involved," said Merritt. "It made me mad." Merritt took his case to Iklé, and the two men huddled behind closed doors in Iklé's office, emerging several hours later with a vastly revised document of just seven pages. "The original version was at an unbelievable level of detail," said Merritt. "It was full of targeting packages, options, how to do targeting, even where and when to launch. It was all just done in the interest of imposing bureaucratic will. We got it much abbreviated, to get at least some of the baloney out."[26]

The clash over NUWEP-84 was a classic flare-up of civilian-military tensions about authority for nuclear operations. Merritt, a career military officer, was wary of what he saw to be the "bureaucratization" of nuclear planning. The point was clear: These people are not legitimate arbiters of national security, are not expert enough to be players, and are interested mainly in personal aggrandizement. "Every political appointee in the Pentagon sees himself as *the* civilian authority," Merritt said. "The secretary of defense and the president are the civilian authority, not some third-rate deputy assistant secretary who's been anointed by the president for some ridiculous reason, like because he's the biggest used-car salesman in Southern California."

Moreover, Merritt argued, the system was not seriously flawed. "Each revision in the SIOP was laid out in excruciating detail. We briefed the chiefs, briefed the secretary of defense, and the chiefs briefed the president," he claimed. Asked if he thought political authorities were aware of and understood the problems in the SIOP, Merritt responded, "If you want options, you're accepting complexity. In every revision, we would work to make packages, withholds, automaticity of launch, and political concerns consonant. There are simplifying portrayals for all of this. But whether politicians understand—I think you're expecting too much."[27]

The clash between Stillwell and Merritt exasperated Miller. He was already very concerned that a lack of focus and outright bureaucratic ineptitude on the part of Stillwell's organization were resulting in a complete diminution of civilian control over nuclear war plans.

The lack of political oversight was not prompting any effective action from Iklé and was occuring without knowledge of the secretary of defense. Miller finally convinced Perle that it was crucial they take control of targeting policy. With Stillwell's fortuitous departure from the Pentagon in early 1985, Iklé was persuaded, albeit reluctantly, to give responsibility for targeting to Miller and his staff.

Miller began by preparing a list of specific areas where civilian control over nuclear planning had obviously broken down and where civilian guidance was not being followed. He and Perle took the list to the secretary of defense and made their case for new procedures to increase political oversight. According to a participant in the discussions, Weinberger was supportive from the outset and Miller proceeded on the assumption that he had the full backing of the secretary, despite vehement opposition from the chairman of the Joint Chiefs, Vessey, as well as from countless midlevel military officials.

Vessey was the first to try to block Miller's intrusion, as did the chief of staff of the army, General John Wickham, who remembered the disastrous consequences of intrusive civilian control of military operations in Vietnam. Weinberger overrode his military advisers, however, and agreed to sign several directives prepared by Miller, outlining problems in the substance and procedures of SIOP planning and giving Miller the authority to look into them.

In 1987, Iklé decided it was once again time to revise the NUWEP. Miller saw this as an opportunity to address all the problems in the planning apparatus, from defining the constitutional authority of the secretary of defense and his staff to developing the means for political authorities to examine nuclear employment plans on a regular basis. The key issue for Miller was making sure that the NUWEP did its job. If the NUWEP did not interpret political goals in a way that provided clear directives, Miller would argue, then it fell to the JSCP officers to make the interpretation. This meant that the exercise of civilian authority was simply academic. "The planners were getting no feedback," said one civilian involved in the process. "To do that, someone had to sit down and look at the actual plans."

As it turned out, NUWEP-87, drafted by Miller and his staff, was approved almost verbatim by Weinberger.

Miller's "quiet revolution" focused largely on establishing routine procedures for civilian involvement to provide the secretary of defense an independent source of advice about the degree to which operational plans reflected political guidance. Miller spent countless days at the JSTPS and with SAC and Joint Staff officers hammering out policy. Miller's preoccupation was to ensure that the plans really had options that "could actually be seen as limited by the Soviets" and that would serve a president in crisis. As always, this was the most difficult task: making operational the concept of flexible options and getting military commanders to take the specific steps to implement national strategy even though most of them might disagree with its logic.

Over strenuous objections, Miller demanded access to planning documents; a number of them had never been seen by a civilian before. In several key instances, he would not have known to ask for a particular document—and no one would have volunteered to show it to him—if it had not been for the assistance of a young military officer on his staff who could clue him in. Having worked previously on naval nuclear operations, the staff aide had been given access to planning documents the secretary of defense had never even heard of.

Miller was reportedly appalled at what he saw to be a serious breakdown in civilian control. The means by which civilians had been excluded from examining plans were often subtle, and not necessarily the result of blatant military subterfuge. For the most part, it was simply the banality of bureaucracy. Targeting is dull stuff, and senior officers and officials have more pressing and interesting things to do than go over technical charts about damage expectancies. "Sure, this is about the fate of the earth, but I have to testify in the Senate tomorrow," is how one military officer bitterly described the attitude of senior officials whom he had tried to interest in the subject.

According to a military official who had primary responsibility for preparing the JSCP, for instance, there was "criminal negligence by senior officials" when it came to oversight. "We would just cut deals as junior officers [of the different services] in allocating weapons. Sometimes this resulted in remarkable changes in the guidance, which should have been reviewed at the highest level—even the presidential level," he claimed. Instead, disagreements would be worked out in compromises among lower-level service representatives; rarely, if ever, were they sent to the Joint Chiefs for adjudication, let alone to civilian authorities.

Miller also sought to establish a more active dialogue with the planning community, to explain the meaning of the *political* criteria being imposed on nuclear policy to the targeteers. The absence of regular interaction had led to a troubling lack of understanding between the two spheres. "Most people in the nuclear business are from SAC and have an Omaha view of the world. They spend a few years sitting in a missile silo and then go to SAC. They have no concept of strategy. You say 'non-SIOP option' to them, and they say, 'That's crazy.' The trouble is when they become generals . . . ," observed a long time observer of the process. Leon Sloss tends to agree: "The JSTPS view of the president is like a switch in the system, just a function that gives the 'go' order. They don't think of him as a political actor."

In fact, guidance provided by political appointees had typically been seen by the targeteers as so out of sync with reality, or so vague, that there was little to be done but to ignore it. "I was in sympathy with those guys in Omaha," said one official who was deeply involved in the NSDM-242 exercise. "They say, 'You keep telling us to do things we can't possibly do. We don't have the tools.' " Indeed, in the 1960s and 1970s, it is claimed, officers at the JSTPS were reduced to reading public statements made by the president or the secretary of defense to try to divine what they were supposed to be doing with the weapons being introduced into the arsenal at a rapid rate.

Few outside of the JSTPS had ever bothered to learn enough about the planning process even to understand how weapons are allocated to targets, let alone how to provide new guidelines. As a result, they were not equipped to prepare guidance that could prove useful to military planners. Nor were they prepared to ask questions about changes in the SIOP even when those plans were presented to them upon completion. The process was one of acquiescence by inattention.

One of the more serious examples of dysfunction in the system was the discovery that copies of the "revisions reports"—the changes in the SIOP that require approval by the secretary of defense or even the president—had never actually been provided to political authorities. "For Frank to see the revision report was historic," said a military colleague. "It happened just because of the serendipity of some young guy on his staff who knew where the skeletons were buried." The reports are supposed to be the means to explain to civilians why changes in the SIOP have taken place and to assess their compatibility with political guidance. More often than not, the revisions were simply expansions of the target list, with no clear rationales other than to accommodate or request new weapons.

One officer noted, in describing these "reporting shifts," that no one before Miller had challenged the criteria upon which the changes had been made, the so-called damage expectancies, which specify the level of destruction needed for particular targets. Damage expectancy criteria used at the JSTPS "were never examined outside of Omaha," according to one target planner. As he saw it, this had led to serious distortions, which were compounded as the plans became more complex:

> The damage expectancies don't adequately show the consequences of targeting. The DEs are a good tool for laying down weapons; but they're unrelated to what goes on in the real world. No one ever goes back to the machine to say, did the machine do something smart? Like, if this weapon has already destroyed this target, why do we have two or three more allocated to it?

Ted Postol, a technical analyst who served as a special assistant to Admiral Watkins in the early 1980s, agrees: "The tendency is to treat all targets as equally valuable, instead of looking at objectives and assessing targets for their criticality to national objectives."[28]

Another concern is that the methodologies for allocating weapons to targets do not take into account any secondary effects of nuclear strikes, such as fire, radiation, or dust. They are static measures. One officer tried to demonstrate this point by assessing how current criteria would guide an attack mission against Hiroshima, whose entire territory was destroyed by less than 20 kilotons of atomic energy, compared with 200 kilotons carried by a single Minuteman warhead. As one example, he cited a gas plant in Hiroshima that had been demolished entirely by secondary effects. The equivalent target would be considered to absorb only "moderate" damage according to current SIOP calculations, even though it could have several strategic warheads assigned to it. The SIOP, moreover, does not take into account the forces available to the regional CINCs to carry out nuclear operations.

Critics claim that the process used to prepare targeting plans deliberately underestimates damage in order to justify new weapons. Indeed, the technique of targeting helps explain the steady growth of the target base, as well as the resistance of the SIOP to significant change. Three decades of effort have gone into forging clear demarctions among targeting objectives, to demonstrate how to "withhold" forces and control escalation during a crisis. But the basic categories and types of targets are startlingly similar to those extant in the 1950s. As one targeteer explained it,

> Allocation of weapons in the SIOP is theoretically a winnowing process. You have x number of targets and x number of weapons, and you decide on the basis of the guidance and intelligence assessments which of the weapons are "SIOP eligible." But in fact there's always a backup list. If more weapons were there, we'd have more targets. The guidance, which is supposed to determine the mix of targets and weapons, was useless. When the "economic recovery" targets were dropped from being SIOP-eligible (after PD-59), fewer targets should have meant fewer weapons, but we changed the mission to "war-supporting industry" and there was no change in the weapons-to-targets mix.[29]

Aside from generating a demand for new forces, such planning practices resulted in the design of "limited options" that were no-where near what political authorities were likely to find acceptable for execution. Postol is convinced that a president could never choose a planned SIOP option for a limited strike. "You think you're execut-ing a limited option, but 300 warheads will land in Poland," he claimed. "You wouldn't choose any canned plan unless you believe the world is over."

The most troubling indication of the possible consequences of civil-ian laxity has to do with providing the president with a range of limited options. Miller would always argue that since you cannot predict with certainty what the crisis will be, or how a president will react, the system needs to be fully prepared for all contingencies in order to be able to give the president any option he wants. Some military officials, however, have been quoted as arguing that the president should not be given the option to 'screw up,' " meaning any option which is unacceptable to SAC, according to a former targeting official. "This is the deliberate withholding of information from the president, the total destruction of civilian authority," he argued.[30]

The most critical disjuncture between Washington and Omaha stems from this enduring dispute about flexible response. As a politi-cal matter, the assurance that the United States has a range of options for using nuclear weapons in crises is the right message to send to allies and adversaries. And it is vital to ensure that the president know how to act in crisis, that he not be paralyzed with horror at being presented only with staggeringly large "attack options" that would result in millions of civilian casualities.

To operators, however, the formidable technical problems and dubious military effectiveness of carrying out controlled, limited strikes makes the strategy suspect. Aside from fearing that political leaders will not understand the military dangers of "withholds" or "limited options," planners abhor the uncertainties associated with such concepts. "From an operator's viewpoint," according to Henry Rowen, "a nuclear exchange in which the politicians try to mastermind the conflict while keeping the commanders from carrying out what they regard as necessary military options could be a frightening prospect."[31]

There is a chronic tension between the military's need for certainty and politicians' need for calculated ambiguity. "Options" are needed for the political management of deterrence, but for the military this need poses two major problems. First, limited options draw down forces from the central plans, reducing capability and potentially undercutting their coherence. Second, these options are at odds with the targeteers' efforts to plan for prompt, effective countermilitary operations before the other side has inflicted damage. By delaying the execution of the SIOP, limited options potentially give the Soviets time to launch a massive attack and preclude any effective U.S. response. For military commanders, delays in executing war plans when the country may be under attack border on treason.

Sloss summarized the situation as follows:

> Lots of options makes planning more difficult, the military doesn't believe that limited nuclear options will ever be executed, and they fear losing forces before they launch them. The air force really believes that the only way to survive is to launch weapons quickly. That's why they hate limited options.

The former CINCSAC general Thomas Power had put it more colorfully in 1960. At a whiz kid who had just presented the case for "limited options," Power shouted, "Why do you want us to restrain ourselves? Restraint! Why are you so concerned with saving their lives? The whole idea is to kill the bastards. . . . At the end of the war, if there are two Americans and one Russian, we win."[32]

The greatest challenge in the implementation of "flexible response" stems from the uncertainties associated with the command and control of nuclear forces in crisis. To a number of analysts, the weaknesses in the command and control structure have contributed to a strategic force posture and organizational arrangements that rely so heavily on promptness to be effective that political authority would simply be vitiated in a climate of crisis. As John Steinbruner argued,

> Command vulnerability has produced powerful incentives within the US military planning system to conduct full-scale strategic operations at the outset of any serious crisis. . . . Once the use of as many as 10 or more nuclear weapons against the USSR is seriously contemplated, US strategic commanders will likely insist on attacking the full array of Soviet military targets. . . .[33]

In other words, the sheer destructiveness of the weapons and the speed with which they can be delivered place a premium on preparations for preventing the other side from going first. In such an environment, the formal distinction between retaliation and initiation "thus reduces to a few minutes, and under the pressure of intense crisis it is questionable whether that distinction could be preserved."[34]

Bruce Blair is more direct in his charge that the formal doctrine of assured retaliation, the stated policy that the United States would launch nuclear weapons only under attack, is a fiction in practice. Blair argues that the military has finessed the tension between its desire for promptness and preemption and its recognition that such an explicit policy would never be acceptable politically by adopting a doctrine of "launch on warning"—according to which forces are kept on high alert for prompt launch at the first sign of an impending Soviet attack.[35]

Defining the point at which the "sign" occurs is the crucial question. Theoretically, it could range from the impact of Soviet missiles in the United States to satellite warnings of an attack and to intelligence gathered from a human source that such an attack was being contemplated. Indeed, the meaning is blurred even in official definitions. The *Dictionary of Military and Associated Terms* published by the Joint Chiefs in 1986, for instance, defines "launch under attack" as follows: "Execution by National Command Authorities of Single Integrated Operational Plan forces subsequent to *tactical warning* of strategic nuclear attack against the United States and prior to first impact."[36] For most policy analysts, launch under attack occurs when the United

States has unequivocal information that a strike is already under way. For some, it means the United States has already absorbed some kind of strike. But these political debates about the dangers of "shifting to a policy of launch on warning," which are a mainstay of congressional controversies, may already be obsolete.

For Blair, the relative neglect of improvements in command and control, in favor of new prompt counterforce weapons, and concerted efforts since the 1960s to draw up procedures providing for delegation of authority to the military in the event of a breakdown in the chain of command are decisive indicators of a rejection of national policy by the military, including any notions of "limited options." Institutional imperatives, especially in a crisis environment in which there is little warning time, Blair argues, are simply too powerful for political authorities ever to be decisive.

Obviously, these assertions are controversial. Blair himself has been scarred for his efforts to call attention to the weaknesses of the U.S. command and control structure. A report he prepared for Congress's Office of Technology Assessment in 1984 was considered so sensitive that all of its copies were confiscated by the Joint Chiefs and classified at the highest levels. It remains buried in a safe somewhere in the Pentagon. Shortly thereafter, just as he was about to testify in a classified hearing of a congressional subcommittee, Blair, a former ballistic missile officer and a technical analyst in the Pentagon, was abruptly informed he no longer held active security clearances.

Miller says that Blair's depiction is inaccurate and that the statements of generals in peacetime about what they would like to do in wartime are not likely to determine how a decision to launch nuclear weapons would be made. In a panel discussion with Blair at the Wilson Center, in Washington, in September 1988, he remarked,

> You can't expect a commander to tell his guys that the missiles they're in charge of would ride out an attack, that they're essentially useless. You'd have a morale problem. Anyway, it's not the policy of OSD to dictate attitudes. It's to make sure that where plans and procedures exist, they are consistent with national policy. You can't change mind-sets, but you can make sure operational plans reflect presidential choice.[37]

In other words, competing beliefs and even the appearance of competing doctrines can be indulged as long as there is confidence that political authorities—especially the commander in chief and the secretary of defense—would indeed be in charge. Conversely, if political officials provide guidance based on only limited knowledge about the operational environment, and pay no attention to how the instructions are implemented, then, yes, the system will break down. Miller believes that significant improvements in command and control and changes in internal Pentagon procedures ensure that any contemplated use of nuclear weapons would occur only in consonance with presidential policy. The days of vague civilian directives that provided ample latitude for SAC and the JSTPS to interpret policy as they saw fit, he maintains, are over.

The current NUWEP, prepared in 1987, is cited as an example of the newly effective civilian oversight. Written in such a detailed manner that it would no doubt infuriate General Merritt, now provides, according to both civilian and military officials, a formal mechanism that provides for political oversight of nuclear targeting. And there are now options, very small options, in the nuclear plans.

Among the most important changes in the planning process is the personal involvement of the secretary of defense. Everyone who has participated in it agrees that a strong role by the secretary is the linchpin of civilian control. "The secdef needs to monitor the plans personally. He should know about all the objectives and problems, and he should receive a report every six months," argues Sloss. Otherwise, there will be no informed senior political authority who can during a crisis articulate the consequences of actions to the president—in which case, "civilian authority" may devolve simply as a practical matter on those who can: nuclear commanders.

Among the innovations of the latest SIOP plan, SIOP6-E, which became effective in October 1988, is a renewed emphasis on flexible targeting, and the JSTPS is trying to reduce the time it takes to produce a SIOP—at present, months—and to be more responsive to "changes in policy, threat, and forces." According to Major General Richard Goetze, the deputy chief of staff for strategic planning at SAC, "The bottom line is that we can expect today's rigid preplanned SIOP, requiring months to build and change, to be a thing of the past."[38]

Lessons for the Future

To skeptics, the importance of civilian access to war plans is marginal, at best. As one put it, "What possible significance is there of a shift in targeting policy when there are thousands and thousands of warheads, and no one knows how to execute a limited nuclear strike anyway? Who cares?" Without doubt, there are far more significant issues for civilian oversight, including the structure, size, and organization of nuclear forces and the extent to which these support national political objectives.

But those who dismiss the importance of greater civilian participation in the review of nuclear plans should keep in mind how difficult it proved to achieve even these recent, modest revisions in planning. The recognition of that difficulty is sobering. Those who advocate more dramatic change have the greatest stake in understanding and appreciating the challenges and constraints of small steps. Moreover, control of targeting is a prerequisite for broader authority over nuclear strategy, a point missed time and again by successive administrations.

Given the total disregard for nuclear strategy among senior appointees in the Reagan administration—everyone in the "in" group was promoting peace shields or assailing the Soviets in Geneva—it is a minor miracle than anyone cared at all about the politically maligned policy of flexible response. Absent Frank Miller and the events that provided him the time to pursue his mission, the last eight years could easily have seen a continued inaction.

Clearly, the role of the secretary of defense and his staff in nuclear war planning should not have to depend on circumstances that may have been unique to the mid-1980s. Innovations like those that have been undertaken in the last four years by Miller and others should be part of an enduring institutional structure, which can survive changes in administrations and the vagaries of partisan politics. Realistically, achieving this will not be easy. The conduct of political oversight of nuclear planning requires a kind of personal commitment at odds with the existing incentive system that senior political appointees in government take for granted. It is technically arduous, politically adversarial, and anonymous. It requires time and painstaking attention. It promises to win few friends and countless enemies and to have no publicly demonstrable result.

Miller is not likely to win a MacArthur "genius" award, let alone a Nobel Peace Prize. (The category is hard to imagine: "in recognition of outstanding service in achieving effective and coherent civilian oversight of plans for limited nuclear options.") And even those who might be expected to be grateful—the president or the secretary of defense—are not necessarily predisposed to thanking individuals for developing "better" nuclear options or, for that matter, dragging them into yet another fight with the uniformed services.

Most important, under current arrangements, there is the perpetual threat of career suicide. However much backing persons may receive privately from senior officials, it is their head that will roll if adversaries succeed in discrediting them through bureaucratic or political sabotage. The American system discourages controversy, and the individual who is seen to have provoked conflict, however legitimately, tends to be penalized in the end.

Putting Civilians in the Loop

Like policy in every other agency of the U.S. government, nuclear doctrine suffers from a chronic tendency among officials to relish new initiatives but to tire quickly when it comes to implementation. "The weak link between policy formulation and implementation is a general phenomenon of government which is especially acute in nuclear war planning," Sloss maintained. "There's never any follow-up."

It is also an axiom of bureaucracy that the difficulties of implementing policy are directly proportional to the numbers of competing agencies involved. Almost any policy initiative, from the most trivial to the most dramatic, is subject to friction and turf wars as it goes through "the interagency process." As a result, the task of "clearing" a new initiative through multiple levels of bureaucracy can get to be an end in itself. Remembering the pains it took to get the NSC and the Defense Department to approve drafts of PD-59, Sloss said, "There was so much bureaucratic effort, there was a great sense of relief just to get the report done. You heave a sigh of relief and go away."

"War plans are far too important a task to be left to the military or, God knows, to amateur politicians," remarked one official. Then who should be in charge? Only the president and the secretary of defense are formally authorized to examine war plans, and both are more often than not amateurs in these matters.

As a first step, it is obvious, there should be a senior staff in the Pentagon with clear authority for nuclear planning, a staff that enjoys the full backing of, and access to, the secretary of defense. The recommendation put forward during the Carter administration to create a "targeting czar," a senior official with a direct line to the secretary, suggests one approach. The sensitivity of the subject, however, and the special skills required to understand the problems involved argue against a political appointment. A more effective solution would be to create a permanent staff of career civil servants not associated with a particular party or administration, who, in combination with representatives from each of the military services, would provide analytical support and advice to the secretary and to the chairman of the Joint Chiefs. The problems are too complex to be undertaken by individuals with short tenures and perhaps political agendas.

They should not be whiz kids. As we have seen, frontal assaults on military prerogative do not succeed, and in any case there is no need to put the military under indictment. Many military officers—at least privately—would welcome an effort to make targeting policies more coherent and to reach some understanding about the different perspectives that political authorities and planning specialists bring to bear.

The establishment of a career staff that has the mandate routinely to provide feedback to targeteers and keep the secretary of defense and the chairman of the Joint Chiefs informed about targeting matters may seem excessively prosaic to those who consider the entire system corrupt. There is no substitute for quiet perseverance and a low profile in the conduct of highly sensitive policy changes. It is equally clear that midlevel officials cannot be left to take on the battles alone. Ultimately, it is up to the president and his most-senior representatives to ensure harmony between military and political objectives in nuclear forces. If heads roll, they must be the right heads, not those of the individuals who are carrying out public duties faithfully.

The Targeteers

On the operational side, it seems past time to move some of the functions of the JSTPS into the Pentagon, or at least nearer to Washington, such as Fort Ritchie. The gap between policy and planning is widened significantly by the targeteers' physical separation from the policy community. This is not to say that the "culture" of the JSTPS, which strongly resists outside interference, is entirely the product of its physical remoteness. But it helps. Putting individuals four stories underground in Omaha guarantees that they will have at best limited exposure to the policies that their techniques are meant to be implementing. Short of moving to Omaha and taking over an office, no policy official will have the routine access to the construction plans that real oversight requires.

Security concerns inevitably would be raised in objection to such a move. But the JSTPS was put in Omaha in 1960 because that is where the only computer large enough to carry out targeting analysis was located, not necessarily because of a careful decision to centralize its functions with SAC or for security reasons. In fact, as LeMay recalled, it was not a considered decision at all:

> It was a hurry-up thing. The [air force] headquarters was at Andrews Field in Washington. But they already had orders to move to Offutt, and my first reaction was this is a helluva place to be going because there wasn't anything out there except an Indian fighting post. I wondered how it came about. . . . I think it was to a large extent political.[39]

It is obviously possible to ensure secrecy from Washington, or else the Joint Chiefs and the president would have to be moved to Omaha as well. As a first step, perhaps part of the JSTPS staff could move into the newly renovated offices likely soon to be vacated by the SDIO.

The main argument apt to be mounted against the separation of the JSTPS from SAC, however, would be the one LeMay used in the 1950s when he successfully fought against letting the Joint Staff review targeting plans. LeMay recalled, "I insisted that we get into war planning the people that actually had the responsibilities for destroying the targets. So the plan they would use was in part their plan and not some concoction some desk soldier thought up for them."[40]

LeMay's point is legitimate when it comes to detailed, operational mission planning. It is the people who would actually have to fly B-2's through Soviet air space, for example, who should have the dominant voice in planning those missions—allocating targets to individual aircraft, identifying flight paths and schedules, coordinating with refueling tankers, and so forth.

The problem is that with the remoteness of the JSTPS from Washington, its integration as part of SAC, and past neglect by civilians of its activities, bomber pilots and air force missile commanders have come to dominate not only these operational matters but also far broader questions, including the number and types of nuclear weapons "required" to fulfill targeting plans. These decisions have a strong, if indirect, influence over force acquisitions and, by implication, over arms control policy. They exert subtle pressure against the consideration of arms reductions that would force an alteration in target coverage; or, put differently, targeting "requirements" serve as a powerful instrument to demonstrate why radical changes in the force structure are inadvisable, providing an empirical and graphic demonstration of the target coverage "shortfalls" resulting from such policy.

If the objective is to harmonize nuclear plans with national policy, it would make sense to have the JSTPS function under the direction of the chairman of the Joint Chiefs and the secretary of defense, as part of the Washington-based Joint Staff. The relocation of the JSTPS should not be undertaken in a manner that interferes with the operational mission planning of the nuclear commands, which should retain normal planning activities like any other unified and specified command. Only elements of the JSTPS that conduct target identification and weapons allocation and application would be moved.

Obviously, there is no completely clear line of demarcation between operations and planning, and some overlap is inevitable and even desirable. As a first step, a detachment of JSTPS planners could be incorporated into the Joint Staff to see how the innovation works. A precedent for this occurred in the establishment of the Rapid Deployment Force during the Carter administration. Part of the RDF was retained in Washington to ensure that it stayed in close touch with policymakers while its operational missions were being defined.[41]

Placing the JSTPS under the authority of the Joint Staff in Washington, and ensuring that the Joint Staff exercise that authority, would serve a number of purposes. It would make it much easier for the policy staff to work with uniformed officers in carrying out target planning. Moreover, the chairman of the Joint Chiefs could have more direct input and involvement in planning, enhancing his ability to fulfill his legal responsibilities as the president's principal military adviser in the event of crisis. The secretary of defense would also benefit from more routine exposure to these matters than can be expected from a reliance on episodic briefings from officers flown in from Omaha.

Furthermore, an organizational relocation of the JSTPS could make it easier to improve coordination of nuclear plans among the nuclear commands. In addition to SIOP forces under SAC's control, the United States maintains nuclear weapons under the unified commanders in Europe, the Atlantic, and the Pacific. Plans for the use of these so-called theater forces, including munitions that would be launched from strike aircraft and, increasingly, nuclear cruise missiles based on submarines and warships, are drawn up by the staff of the relevant CINCs. In the past, civilian input into plans for theater operations was quite rare, and little effort was made to ensure that theater plans were compatible with overall nuclear objectives. Coordination of the respective CINCs' plans with one another and with SAC's is conducted by the chairman of the Joint Chiefs, to whom the CINCs report. But to date, there is more coordination in principle than in practice.

The problem of coordination is complicated by the role of the military services in the respective commands and, until recently, by the disproportionate involvement of the service chiefs in operational matters that resulted from their membership in the Joint Chiefs. Although in theory these commands are "unified" (meaning that the commander controls units from more than one service), the Atlantic and Pacific commands have traditionally been dominated by the navy, while the European command is an army fiefdom. The result is a natural service bias in the perception of missions. CINCPAC, for example, has always been preoccupied with fighting a naval war in the Pacific, and it plans its targeting accordingly, focusing on the destruction of enemy naval forces and the ports, airfields, and industrial facilities necessary to support them. The execution of such plans in a crisis could undercut national policy if not closely tied to central strategic force plans and political expectations about the consequences of alternative launch decisions.

There is no reason why theater commands' nuclear plans should not be subject to the scrutiny given the SIOP, to ensure their coherence with the same policy assumptions and overall national targeting objectives that pertain to SAC. The relocation of the JSTPS therefore should be accompanied by a more direct and routine involvement of the policy-oriented "targeting oversight" staff in this element of planning, as well as providing for more direct coordination between the JSTPS and the theater planners.

Putting the JSTPS under the Joint Staff could also help ease tensions over what is now a strong air force bias in strategic planning and, by implication, over nuclear "requirements." The domination of the JSTPS by SAC, and therefore by the air force, has been a long-standing source of resentment among the other services, not least because of the air force's resulting ability to capture the lion's share of strategic nuclear resources. As part of the Joint Staff, the JSTPS would be expected to reflect a more "joint" perspective and to plan its requirements accordingly.

Many observers agree that a compelling case can be made for not having strategic targeting plans under the dominant control of CINC-SAC. It is clearly a potential conflict of interest to have a simultaneous interest in planning and in competing for budgetary allocations for strategic forces. This, of course, is why a divestment of planning functions from SAC would very likely be resisted, by the air force in particular. Aside from the interference of the other services, SAC could be expected to cringe at the idea of policymakers using targeting criteria to demonstrate why fewer strategic forces were needed to achieve requisite levels of destruction to fulfill national policy.

The Phantom Commander

The most difficult question, the hardiest of perennials, is the role of the president in managing nuclear matters. As the commander in chief, he must ultimately authorize or delegate authority to launch nuclear forces. But actual political authority derives from information, and the acquisition of real information takes time and attention. It is not realistic to expect a president to become an expert on targeting or to devote large amounts of his schedule to briefings on the subject.

But it is critical to recognize that the exercise of genuine political authority is possible only if the president knows what he is doing. If he is genuinely unaware of how and when nuclear weapons might be used, he will not be able to make decisions effectively, especially in a climate of crisis.

There are two reasons to be concerned about presidential ignorance about nuclear operations: the possibility of a complete devolution of authority in a crisis, his abdicating the decision to others intentionally or by default, or outright paralysis. As was seen during the Cuban missile crisis, the level of American casualties from a Soviet response to a U.S. first strike that was "acceptable" to the military did not agree with the president's notions of what he could bring himself to do.

The differences in perspectives are likely to be stark. As General Dougherty argues,

> The nation's nuclear commanders are all senior, experienced military professionals. Assuming that these commanders have made peace with their own consciences (and tenure would indicate they have), the morality of war, even nuclear war, is not an issue with them. . . . Fighting wars, with the equipment and weapons issued them, is their job.[42]

But this is not so with presidents. Their feeling is more akin to what one military officer described as "you lose New York City and you're going to get lynched."

A crisis is not the right time to be sorting out competing philosophies of nuclear deterrence, not least because of the potential for ambiguity in the chain of command. It is not exactly clear what General Dougherty means, for instance, when he says, "Execution orders for nuclear strikes that are spawned in protracted and acrimonious debate at the NCA level, schisms with congressional leaders, and vitriolic internal cabinet debate are sure to stretch military discipline to the limit."[43] What exactly does stretching military discipline consist of, in practice? Could this be a veiled allusion to the need to supersede incompetent civilian leaders if they fail to act?

However compelling in the abstract, the record of presidential involvement in nuclear planning is dismal. Other than Jimmy Carter, every president since Franklin Roosevelt has expressed only passing interest in the subject. And even though some officials claim that President Reagan was briefed by Secretary Weinberger on the SIOP periodically, a former chairman of the Joint Chiefs has a different view: "His last briefing was in 1981, and it lasted twenty minutes."

Turning away from the subject is perhaps a natural reaction. Having personal responsibility for millions of lives is not something the president wants to be reminded of too often. As a former national security adviser put it, "Presidents are awed by their power when it comes to nuclear war. They really don't want anything to do with it." And, as always, absent a crisis, boredom is a factor. The briefing book kept at the White House on the SIOP is two inches thick, especially daunting for presidents who do not like to read.

Routine presidential briefings on nuclear plans are critical, however unwelcome they may be. It is especially important that presidents be encouraged to get involved personally in crisis simulations. They can never play themselves in these games, for fear of leaks that would divulge what an actual president might do in a particular situation. But participation in such exercises could at least help give some foundation to the formal status of commander in chief. During the Eisenhower administration, the president and the entire cabinet routinely practiced their response to nuclear crises; it would be good to revive the tradition. It is critical to deterrence, as well as to civilian control.

How Much Deterrence Is Enough?

During his time as secretary of defense, McNamara thought he could control strategy by controlling force levels. As he saw it, if he was able to prevent the military from acquiring the forces it wanted to sustain a credible preemptive strategy, he could control their ambitions.

But the opportunity for averting the development of forces that contravene the declaratory policy of assured retaliation is long gone. McNamara himself failed to achieve this goal during his tenure. By approving additions to the nuclear arsenal in excess of the ceilings he himself had set, including the development of MIRVs, he helped ensure that his successors would never have a chance.

The most important reason for civilian authorities to understand the workings of nuclear operations is for them to be able to develop more coherent guidelines for bringing about changes in the force posture. Real civilian authority over nuclear strategy requires decisive control over the acquisition and reduction of nuclear forces. This, in turn, requires a better grasp of how targeting requirements influence the pace and content of nuclear modernization and the limits of arms control.

The ultimate civilian abdication has been the failure to define reasonable, practical parameters for deterrence, a set of agreed guidelines against which forces could be measured and choices made. Without a national basis for determining "how much deterrence is enough"—a question that admittedly can never be answered with precision—"deterrence" has served simply as an open-ended justification for multiple and often patently contradictory objectives.

The former air force general John Toomay would seem to agree. In an article on ICBM modernization in 1987, Toomay wrote,

> Our failures seem to arise from an erosion of the discipline that has governed both our acquisition and our operation of strategic nuclear forces for more than a quarter century. This discipline came about when the doctrine of deterrence, already characterized by demanding and unrelenting operational procedures, was given an analytic underpinning, which ensured that force level requirements and new system needs would be determined by rigorous criteria. Without this discipline, our justification for acquiring new land-based strategic nuclear missile systems has not been sufficiently compelling to overcome military, political, economic, and social issues which create cross-currents in the decision-making process.[44]

Toomay goes on to argue that "discipline" requires "estimates of Soviet perceptions," calculating what the Soviets value the most and making sure they know we can destroy those assets, "the 'worst-on-worst' analyses" condemned by some as resulting in "overkill," as he puts it. It is this kind of reasoning, more than any other, that makes deterrence most difficult to define. Discipline based on perceptions is an oxymoron. Perceptions of "what deters the Soviets" vary so widely in the United States because they derive from untested, and untestable, criteria. For some, the Soviets are deterred only by a U.S. capability to hold their entire military at risk, while others believe that the Soviets, having experienced devastation in World War II, are inherently cautious and far more fearful of war than are Americans. How can such widely divergent points of view be reconciled?

An artificial reconciliation of views has been imposed on the planning process by the practice of "worst-casing," to which Toomay refers. Since we can never know for sure what will deter the Soviets, it is reasoned, we should spare no measures to make sure they are "maximally deterred." Since Soviet forces do not remain static, and U.S. intelligence about potential force changes is never "certain," the United States must continue to modernize its own nuclear capabilities. The perpetual need to "hedge" against even improbable threats provides the compelling rationale for continued additions and improvements to the nuclear arsenal. The former under secretary of the navy James Woolsey put it most succinctly:

> In strategic modernization, we are dealing, in a sense, with a major insurance policy against an admittedly unlikely eventuality. But it is insurance against the most catastrophic of imaginable losses, and it is a curious kind of policy—one where paying the premiums can make the catastrophe less likely.[45]

For a strategy to be coherent, it must have operational meaning. But deterrence is now all things to all people and is generally useless as a guideline. Efforts actually to impose discipline on forces and plans have foundered on the abstract nature of its objectives. As it is currently defined, no amount of deterrence is ever enough.

Where as General White excoriated intellectuals for trying to mask the real purpose of nuclear weapons in 1962, contemporary commanders know better. Deterrence is a great concept, from their perspective, akin to patriotism and motherhood. As General Welch said in response to criticism that the B-2 bombers would cost over $450 million each, "What you're buying is deterrence. I can't put a value on deterrence."[46]

Imposing greater coherence and discipline on strategic planning requires the linkage of political concepts of nuclear strategy to actual operational requirements. As John Steinbruner put it, the task is to answer the question "How many and what types of targets must be threatened in order to achieve the desired deterrent effect?"[47] The question is not just about resources. The content and organization of the nuclear force posture sends powerful signals to allies and adversaries and is thus a far more important indicator of strategy than are statements by politicians. If the forces being developed and deployed are at odds with stated political objectives, the system of political authority has obviously failed.

Targeting plans today do not provide the basis either for making tough choices among alternative systems, however, or for calculating the utility of additional increments of accuracy or hard-target kill capabilities. To the contrary, as currently organized, targeting plans do not serve to enforce discipline at all.

Early in the Reagan administration, Admiral Watkins tried to calculate how many Trident submarines he would need to buy on the basis of strict targeting criteria—damage expectancies, warhead yields, and so forth. But he quickly realized this was impossible without knowing how many B-2 bombers and MX missiles would be operating at the same time. But the air force calculated its "needs" separately. Watkins started to agitate on behalf of joint criteria for strategic requirements but became discouraged when it grew apparent that this would serve only to fulfill the air force's long-standing hegemonic ambitions. Given the disproportionate influence of air force officers in SAC planning, a joint process would essentially give them control of the navy's strategic assets. The effort was quickly abandoned.[48]

Creating joint criteria for strategic procurement is obviously easier said than done. As part of the reorganization of the Defense Department mandated by the 1986 Goldwater-Nichols bill, however, there is a new planning process that could provide the basis for more coherence. By giving authority to the chairman of the Joint Chiefs, rather than to the service secretaries, for setting overall requirements for the military, the legislation aimed to create mechanisms to impose national rather than service-based criteria for justifying new forces. In the past, the individual services simply provided the chairman with weapons "wish lists" that were neither constrained by budgetary realities nor coordinated with the other services. In the future, the chairman and his staff, working with the secretary of defense, will prepare force postures in line with budgetary levels provided them by civilian authorities, forcing trade-offs among the different service interests at the outset.

The history of nuclear strategy is rife with missed opportunities to enhance the coherence of institutional arrangements for planning nuclear strategy, as in the early 1970s, when nuclear strategy captured for a fairly long time the attention of both the secretary of defense and the secretary of state. One mechanism that might be considered today is a standing committee of senior officials, to include the national security adviser, the secretaries of state and defense, and the director of the CIA, to review strategic options and provide periodic advice on such matters to the president. Its main purpose would be to develop sufficient expertise among policy advisers to help shift the burden of proof for opposition to national policies, whether these are changes in doctrine or arms control negotiations, to those who are resisting change.

The World's Greatest Deliberative Body

The absence of any firm criteria for determining strategic requirements is even more manifest in Congress's inability to influence the structure and direction of strategic forces. The decisions by elected officials about funding for nuclear weapons are not linked in any systematic manner to what is "needed" to carry out targeting policy. Why a *hundred* MX or a *hundred* B-1's? Congress never has the chance to understand, let alone influence, the calculations that result in appropriations requests. By the time a weapons development or procurement program reaches Congress for budgetary approval, it has developed such powerful constituencies—from the military-technical community, military officials, and even legislators who have a stake in its development—that it is considered on grounds often wholly unrelated to strategy, ranging from pure economic interests to a general perception that modernization is almost always a good idea. The countless examples of failed congressional efforts to cancel weapons systems demonstrate the weakness of the legislative process once a weapon has emerged as a "requirement" for development or production.

Congress's willingness to defer to the military and to "experts" when it comes to questions of how nuclear forces will actually be used reflects in part a deliberate avoidance of a "no-win" subject. Few legislators want, or are equipped, to engage in detailed discussions of force planning. Decisions about weapons are instead driven by the need to forge compromises between proponents and critics and to come up with halfway measures wholly unrelated to strategic criteria: fifty instead of a hundred MX, a lower level of funding for the SDI, or "continued research and development" for systems that prove most controversial.

Similarly, arms control proposals have been supported or decried without regard to the operational implications they might entail. A reduction of 50 percent of the nuclear arsenal, for instance, a proposal that has been on the negotiating table in Geneva for several years, is entirely a political concept. It will gain meaning only when these cuts are allocated among strategic missions, but this is not why most legislators will be for or against it.

The debate over the MX missile over the last decade is a good example of the discontinuity between politics and operations. The debate appeared to prove remarkable congressional involvement in questions of nuclear strategy, but this is misleading. The main reason why legislators supported the idea of modernizing land-based missiles was to preserve the strategic triad, the configuration of land, air, and naval forces that make up the deterrent. They never seriously considered shifting the U.S. nuclear posture to a *dyad,* despite the improvements in submarines and bombers that demonstrated to some analysts the basis for a deterrent far more consonant with the objectives of stability and survivability.

There are some compelling reasons to retain the flexibility and redundancy of forces afforded by land-based systems. But the political sanctity of the triad does not rest on strategic considerations. It is a shibboleth. It has long been forgotten that the triad was an intellectual artifice developed in the 1960s to provide a framework for nuclear forces allocated among the three major services. "I was there at the creation of the triad," said Bill Kauffman with some sarcasm. "Ivan Selin [a young analyst working for McNamara] made it up."[49]

For two successive administrations, it has proved impossible to demonstrate with any credibility that the ten-warhead MX missile can be based in a mode that is both survivable and politically acceptable. Over thirty basing proposals have been considered and rejected, ranging from underground railroads to airborne dirigibles. General Vessey, expressing his frustrations about the endless congressional debates over the MX, finally stormed, "We need those warheads on the MX so bad, I'd put them in the Pentagon parking lot." But few legislators thought to ask him why on earth the air force would want a missile that even arch-conservatives thought would be vulnerable to a Soviet first strike.

"Survivability," it seems, is in the eye of the beholder. It derives from an individual's or organization's belief about what American nuclear strategy really is. Survivability of the MX is not a critical issue to the air force, because the idea of riding out a Soviet attack is so implausible to commanders that the whole question about whether the missile would survive such an attack is academic. They believe that the MX will be survivable by virtue of its intrinsic mobility—prompt launch on warning, or in anticipation, of an attack. As General John T. Chain, the current CINCSAC, put it in early 1989, civilians' assumptions that U.S. land-based missiles would not be fired until after a Soviet first strike are "unrealistic."[50]

A former CINCSAC explained that the whole point of the MX was to convince the Soviets that the United States would launch quickly, knowing that otherwise these missiles would be useless. According to a prevailing view in Omaha, too much survivability could in some cases actually be a liability, since it could persuade a president not to act quickly. A missile that has to be launched fast to survive, however, could be a catalyst to getting him to overcome reluctance about granting the military the authority to launch.[51]

This is not to say that Congress should engage in prolonged discussions about "damage expectancy" criteria or that its 535 members should be granted access to the SIOP. But if Congress is to carry out its constitutional responsibility to appropriate public funds judiciously, at least some members need a better awareness of the consequences of their votes. Even more to the point, that the Speaker of the House and the president pro tempore of the Senate are in the chain of command in the event of war argues on both constitutional and practical grounds that they be better equipped to discharge their responsibilities. As Louis Henkin has argued, "When Congress appropriates funds for particular weapons, it approves or acquiesces in the strategy which those weapons imply."[52]

The question of congressional access to operational plans typically causes panic in the defense community. Congress is a security sieve, some argue. Or congressmen are interested solely in making headlines. Or they are just plain incompetent and will never devote enough time to the subject to be able to exercise competent authority.

In fact, there are already mechanisms to provide extremely sensitive and technical intelligence and security information to a select number of members of Congress who have relevant jurisdictions. On the whole, these procedures have worked well. The Senate and House Select Committees on Intelligence have routine oversight not just over covert operations and intelligence gathering but, increasingly, over the details of arms control treaties. Similarly, the Armed

Services Committees have jurisdiction over the funding for highly classified R & D programs for weapons—so-called black programs. All of these activities are conducted under strict security procedures; breaches are rare.

A panel of the Armed Services Committee or the Intelligence Committee could arrange to have regular briefings on operational nuclear matters. It is a question not of "micromanaging" the plans but of heightening legislators' awareness of the actual application of the forces they are being asked to buy. At present, Congress derives its information almost entirely through ad hoc briefings at the JSTPS and SAC arranged by request. Few members ever take advantage of them, and even fewer are able to ask intelligent questions when they get there. Not surprisingly, these briefings have been made into a fine art by SAC. It is sometimes even arranged for the commander of Looking Glass to say, "Hello, Senator——!" from his airborne command post.

Congress should have a more serious way of learning about these issues. If the matter were given sufficient political priority, it would not be difficult to recruit and train the analytical staff needed to help legislators stay informed. Technical experts, including those with substantial military experience, are already employed in Congress by the dozens.

Those in the military who could be expected to resist such congressional involvement should not overlook the possibility that the establishment of a small group of legislators to review nuclear planning, with whom they could establish a rapport, may be in their self-interest. Given the steady politicization of all other areas of national security, the immunity of nuclear operations is an anomaly and is not likely to be permanent. As a result, a select group of more expert members of Congress who see themselves as the legitimately constituted channel of communication about operations would be preferable to a sudden surge of demands for information from legislators who may not even have appropriate jurisdiction. Such institutional mechanisms have helped in the past to temper the excesses of colleagues. The Arms Control Observer Group, for instance, a standing oversight committee granted access to the negotiations in Geneva, has worked very effectively in this way, going to great lengths to discourage politicization of its activities. In turn, it serves as a effective bipartisan channel between the executive branch and the legislature for directing the debates about arms control.

As long as the spheres in which civilians debate and influence nuclear policy are removed from the realm of actual operations, disciplined debate about force requirements and strategy is impossible. Partisanship on such issues will never disappear, of course, but this does not diminish the importance of encouraging the legislature to be better equipped to deal with issues of national survival.

The Arms Control Card

The prospect of reducing strategic forces to 6,000 warheads, the current proposal pending in START, offers an opportunity to begin the process of evaluating the missions to which strategic forces are assigned. As John Steinbruner has argued, this could be the chance to conduct a serious evaluation of how our forces are designed to be used in war. If choices must be made in the allocation of weapons to targets because of negotiated reductions, this could bring more scrutiny of the relative "legitimacy" of alternative target missions.

Counterforce, for instance, which absorbs the largest share of forces, "has the most doubtful legitimacy, the most questionable effectiveness, the fewest domestic advocates, and the greatest Soviet resistance," according to Steinbruner. In effect, it contradicts the stated policy of deterrence through retaliation. By contrast, attacks on "other military forces"—the military infrastructure of the adversary—"do not require preemption, or a rapid reaction that is nearly equivalent . . . [and] can be the focus of strict retaliation."[53] Six thousand warheads, along with the counterforce emphasis of ongoing modernization programs, leaves a comfortable margin to allow for business to continue more or less as usual. But the idea of linking arms control proposals to the examination of target sets is intriguing. This is what the Joint Chiefs do to resist cuts they believe to be excessive.

If political authorities are serious about having a "rational" nuclear strategy, this is exactly the kind of analysis that would have to be elicited from senior officials. If Congress and the public pay more attention to the subject, moreover, the prospects for "operationalizing deterrence" could actually create credible coalitions of informed political authorities who could begin to answer the question "How much deterrence is enough?"

It is safe to say that by the time arms control proposals for reductions in particular types of forces have been put on the table, however, measures will have been taken by weapons planners to counteract the effects of the potential reductions. Sometimes these are entirely new technologies, or adaptations of technologies, which have demonstrated capabilities for far greater lethality than the weapons being bargained away.

Political authorities must examine more carefully the powerful influence that technological innovation exerts over force plans and strategy. There is no ready answer to the enduring, "chicken and egg" question about which comes first, technological innovation or weapons requirements. But it is quite obvious that the ability or the potential to produce a new weapon influences political decisions. The national nuclear laboratories—Sandia, Los Alamos, and Lawrence Livermore—promote their findings in the Congress and the executive branch. With notable exceptions, weapons concepts almost always find constituencies well before senior political authorities are even aware they exist. The SDI is no exception, except that the weapons designers got to the president first, rather than to officials in the Pentagon. One analyst described the "selling" process as follows:

> It is the creative energy of the weapons designers in the laboratories that drive the system forward in its unceasing search for new devices. . . . It could hardly be otherwise. If you assemble a team of scientists and engineers selected for their creative energy and drive, give them access to vast resources, and reward them for design initiatives, they will respond quickly. As new design ideas and systems concepts emerge, weapons laboratory representatives can hardly be ignored by defense officials who understand that new technologies may significantly affect force balances.[54]

Efforts to control the pace of technological change in nuclear weapons have taken place largely as part of negotiations for a treaty banning the test of nuclear devices, the so-called Comprehensive Test Ban. A priority in every administration from Kennedy's to Carter's, the CTB has been resisted successfully by the nuclear laboratories, as well as the Pentagon and the Department of Energy. Opponents argue not only that the reliability of the deterrent will erode if nuclear weapons cannot be tested but also that such a prohibition will stifle the scientific enthusiasm of the labs trying to invent weapons that will make the world "more stable." The briefings that the labs typically give Congress emphasize the extent to which their research efforts have permitted the development of "safer" and "cleaner" weapons, portrayed as distant cousins of the weapons of mass destruction with which we would have been saddled if a test ban had been imposed in the 1960s.

The degree of desirable innovation in weapons technology is not currently based on conscious political choice. Politicians tend to portray the march of technology as if it had a life of its own; this is not an accurate depiction. Weapons concepts do not become reality only because "the technology is so sweet," as Oppenheimer put it, but also because of very prosaic activities by lab representatives, activities that fall well outside the realm of science and are more commonly known as marketing.

Nuclear War Plans and Democracy

The American political debate about nuclear war planning has three fundamental characteristics: naïveté, fatalism, and a profoundly ahistorical perspective. The naïveté is best illustrated by the refusal to acknowledge that nuclear policy is grounded in plans for the execution of war. A modest minority of experts or political leaders consciously think beyond the superficial explanation that nuclear weapons are for deterring wars. What happens after deterrence fails—the launching of weapons to their designated targets, in elaborate plans for targeting and execution of nuclear strikes—is not accorded nearly the attention that "strengthening deterrence" or "assuring stability" has received over the years.

For most of the public, in fact, nuclear war is purely and simply a suicidal spasm. Even as the targeting of nuclear weapons has developed its own scientific discipline—a technical and even political culture unto itself—most observers pretend that this is not the case. Just conceding that these plans exist seems to besmirch the observer, making him suspect in the eyes of the civilized world.

The second feature is fatalism. Everyone in and out of the government familiar with the subject of nuclear doctrine can offer a host of reasons why nuclear war plans cannot be subject to active political scrutiny. Quite apart from security considerations, even critics of the rift between formal strategy and the infrastructure of war fighting will say it is hopeless to think about wresting greater control over the targeteers. The subject is too arcane, too sensitive, too complex. More important, it is controlled by an impenetrable group of "guardians" who have successfully resisted interference and will always thwart attempts to penetrate their inner sanctum. Those who think otherwise are politically naïve, "outsiders" with quixotic hopes.

Third is the absence of a historical memory or any apparent appreciation of how similar the strategic issues of the present are to those of prior decades. The weapons have changed, the people have changed, and the rhetoric has changed, but the challenges have not. Forty years of expert debate seem to provide peculiarly little guidance for the future. Highly opinionated pundits, largely without constructive proposals, have roamed academe, think tanks, and the media, harassing each other and engaging in endless acrimonious exchanges. They, too, tend to have a culture unto themselves, too often more interested in besting a colleague with a clever remark than in influencing policy. One is reminded of C. Wright Mills's excoriation of the bankruptcy of intellectuals in 1960: "Smug conservatives, tired liberals, and disillusioned radicals have carried on a kind of discourse in which issues are blurred and potential debate muted, the sickness of complacency prevails, and reasoning collapses into reasonableness. Its sophistication is of tone rather than ideas."[55]

It is customary in almost every discussion of nuclear strategy to end with a proposal for an alternative force posture. Having discussed whatever failings are found in the current configuration of forces, analysts typically advance one they deem better. These can take many forms, from virtual disarmament to "assured second strike" forces that eschew any prompt counterforce weapons to strategies for "denying Soviet war aims," often a euphemism for nuclear superiority.

Such analyses, however, are seldom accompanied by suggestions about how to implement change, radical or otherwise. It is somehow assumed that the reasoning that underlies the design of a new posture is so compelling that it will be seized upon by decision makers and implemented with dispatch. This is obviously misleading. The extraordinary divisions just within the government about *existing* nuclear strategy make it difficult to see how any innovation would fare better without a more coherent institutional foundation.

To many, the idea that nuclear war planning is subject to bureaucratic politics, institutional rivalries, and the petty ambitions of individuals competing for influence is so appalling that they refuse to acknowledge the "legitimacy" of such dynamics. Even discussing the political dimension of nuclear policy somehow trivializes the subject, and so it is discounted. Better to spend time refining moral exhortations or improving the exactitude of new quantitative models for force balances than to stoop so low.

For many antinuclear activists, in particular, discussing ways to make nuclear strategy more coherent is totally off the mark. It begs the real question about nuclear weapons: their fundamental illegitimacy as instruments of war or diplomacy. It is politically and morally bankrupt to talk about making strategy more coherent, they argue, when the real imperative is to get rid of these weapons altogether. "Reform" is just rearranging the deck chairs in the war-fighting bureaucracy that is leading the world in its inexorable march to Armageddon.

The illegitimacy of nuclear weapons is without doubt the source of the most enduring political problems in American security. Few politicians are ever willing to state publicly that they believe that nuclear weapons preserve peace or that a war-fighting strategy is the cornerstone of credible nuclear deterrence. These positions are accepted privately by many, of course, and discussed openly among the cognoscenti.

To many who argue for radical revisions in nuclear forces, the main problem is the fundamentally antidemocratic manner in which nuclear policy is undertaken. It is only because it has been hidden from the public view that the current character of nuclear strategy has survived. Almost everyone interviewed for this book was asked about this key assumption. Should nuclear doctrine be a subject for a national referendum? Should the American public exert influence on our war-fighting posture?

To a man (they were all males), the advocates of strategic defenses said yes. As Martin Anderson put it, "Absolutely. If you have the right strategy, the people will support you." Gregory Fossedal, a former *Wall Street Journal* editorial-page writer and now a media fellow at the Hoover Institution, echoed these words: "Reagan, Martin Anderson, and I are populists. We're governed by the people, not by the

Harvard faculty or the Brookings Institution. You change elite opinion through popular opinion."

An unacknowledged political alliance exists between the Right and the Left on this issue. Nuclear war plans, they both argue, would not stand up to public scrutiny. Though they could not be more divided in their goals, the two schools agree that the public needs to be informed about the Faustian bargain that the architects of flexible response have provided as the basis for American security.

But ask most officials with responsibilities for nuclear forces the same question, and you will draw laser glares. Those who are working on the actual implementation of war plans blanch at the thought of public or congressional intrusion into the private realm of strategy.

After examining the experience of four decades of policies about nuclear weapons, one is struck by the tremendous role that secrecy has played in holding the system together. Even the most modest efforts to be "candid" about real policy, like James Schlesinger's, proved disastrous. The public genuinely believes that nuclear weapons are illegitimate and does not want to be reminded of their existence.

As we have also seen, the public's concern about nuclear weapons can be readily turned to fear. And this kind of public sentiment helped spawn the industry of nuclear deceit, of which the SDI is simply the most recent example. Calls to public activism with unspecific objectives may thus not be the best approach. Frightened Americans looking for solace are a great constituency for clever political strategists.

There is no question that current nuclear strategy cannot sustain the glare of public attention. The whole concept of limited nuclear war has no political constituency. But, as Frank Miller is fond of saying, flexible response is the worst alternative—except for all the others. Not even the military, trained to be inured to the consequences of its dire responsibility, can "support" nuclear doctrine. General Dougherty has said,

> I consider raw, deliberate population attacks immoral as well as unlawful, and I know of no US nuclear planning force that has as its targeting objectives cities, civilian populations, noncombatnts, civilian objects, schools, or hospitals *that have no relation to the objective of preventing nuclear aggression from succeeding.* As proof, one has merely to look at the US nuclear inventory, which is clearly unsuited for optimum use in city

destruction or mass noncombatant kill. A commander planning deliberate attacks on cities ... would have a major morale problem on his hands with his command and combat crews.[56]

One of the key concerns in this book has been to demonstrate how democracy's failure to determine a nuclear strategy has impeded the implementation of policies that reflect commonly supported political objectives. It is clear that those who have ultimate authority for determining the structure of nuclear forces, beginning with the president, have neglected their constitutional responsibilities. The blatant contradiction between the abstract political beliefs of leaders about nuclear weapons, on the one hand, and the pragmatic realities of war planning, on the other, has created a fundamental lack of political accountability in the formulation of the nation's nuclear posture—in short, a failure of democracy in this vital area.

But this is not an immutable condition, or one that has to endure indefinitely. Indeed, the SDI, in its populist fervor, may have left an unintended legacy by breaking the taboo about more open discussions on the character of nuclear war plans. When the president says that deterrence based on war fighting is immoral, people pay attention.

The "illegitimacy" of nuclear doctrine should not be brought to the public for formulation, however, until the foundations for responsible change are in place. Those who argue that public opinion is the only power that can bring about change would be well advised to examine the history of the SDI. Overwhelming public support for population defense, backed by the president, could not change the reality of deterrence, disarm the Soviets, or negotiate the laws of physics.

For now, this argues for a more robust meritocracy for the examination of nuclear policy, a decision-making process that is more representative of the country's objectives and can subject nuclear plans to far greater opportunities for political, as well as technical, judgment. This is an elitist idea, not a clarion call to citizen action. It is in line with Robert Dahl's concept of a "minipopulus," of individuals whose technical competence and judgment earn them the ability to influence complex matters. As Mills argued in 1958, "Democracy requires that those who bear the consequences of decisions have enough knowledge to hold decision-makers accountable. . . ."[57]

This is not to discount the importance of public opinion, which has changed the tides of history on innumerable occasions. The challenge, however, is to sustain public attention for enduring change. Public opinion was crucial in overcoming obstacles to the recent ratification of the INF Treaty by the Senate. In turn, though, the success of the INF Treaty set of such waves of arms control euphoria among the public that its limited accomplishments—control of less than 4 percent of the world's nuclear forces—were virtually overshadowed; and the public once more receded into quiescence, basking in the afterglow of superficial success.

The key to any successful and responsible public strategy is an informed constituency that is not very vulnerable to political diversion. If the effort to change current nuclear doctrine relies on exhortation rather than on analysis, or seeks to discredit the entire defense establishment as part of its exorcism, it will fail again. The response to ill-conceived campaigns of this kind has always been to circle the wagons. And the establishment is still far more capable of thwarting unwelcome ventures than activists are capable of bringing down the walls of Jericho.

BIBLIOGRAPHICAL
NOTE

THE FAILURE of succcessive administrations to subject nuclear war plans to careful oversight is paralleled by the neglect of nuclear operations by academic analysts. This is partly because of the shroud of secrecy surrounding the formulation of nuclear targeting and employment policy, admittedly daunting. But it is also evidence of an unmistakable bias among strategic analysts, who have chosen to focus on more abstract matters of nuclear strategy. The use of nuclear weapons in the conduct of war is a subject that most observers find too arcane, technically arduous, or emotionally discouraging to examine closely. It remains the phantom dimension of policy making that largely has been kept from the public eye. Needless to say, academics bear some responsibility for helping to create the system of "guardianship" that this book tries to portray.

There are important exceptions, pathbreaking work conducted by a handful of analysts whose dedicated efforts to dissect this extremely difficult subject are invaluable. The most notable of these authors is David Alan Rosenberg, whose careful compilations of declassified government documents provide the empirical groundings for understanding the decisions about nuclear operations in the early postwar period that set the stage for current nuclear strategy. His works include "The Origins of Overkill: Nuclear Weapons and American Strategy, 1945–1960," *International Security* 7 (Spring 1983); "American Atomic Strategy and the Hydrogen Bomb Decision," *Journal of American History* 66 (June 1979); and "Reality and Responsibility: Power and Process in the Making of United States Nuclear Strategy, 1945–1968," *The Journal of Strategic Studies* (March 1986).

Fred Kaplan's *Wizards of Armageddon* (New York: Simon and Schuster, 1983), the story of the individuals who shaped the origins of American nuclear strategy, is also an excellent work, as well as a rich bibliographical resource, based on dozens of documents that Kaplan arranged to have declassified and then generously donated to the National Security Archives for use by other scholars. Marc Trachtenberg has also made important contributions. The most interesting of these for this book is his analysis of the transcripts of the meetings among President Kennedy and his advisers on the Cuban missile crisis, "The Influence of Nuclear Weapons in the Cuban Missile Crisis," *International Security* 10 (Summer 1985).

Desmond Ball's work on nuclear targeting and strategy is also an important source of both historical and technical information, including "The Development of the SIOP, 1960–1983," in Ball and Jeffrey Richelson, eds., *Strategic Nuclear Targeting* (Ithaca: Cornell University Press, 1986); and "Targeting for Strategic Deterrence," *Adelphi Paper* no. 185 (London: International Institute for Strategic Studies, 1983). A common criticism of Ball's work is that it is impossible to describe nuclear operations accurately at this level of detail without access to classified plans, a criticism that has to be weighed against the alternative, which is not even to try.

Details of the history of decisions about nuclear operations can be culled from personal statements, memoirs, biographies, and oral histories of participants. Oral histories such as those conducted by the Air Force Oral History Project (housed at Maxwell Air Force Base), for instance, provide insight into the personal opinions and recollections of senior military officers. Interesting, if often biased, accounts of nuclear decisionmaking appear in the memoirs of presidents and their advisers. Among the more notable in the latter category are Walter Millis, *The Forrestal Diaries* (New York: Viking, 1951); a fascinating account of the McNamara years by William Kauffman in *The McNamara Strategy* (New York: Harper & Row, 1964); the comprehensive analysis of strategic policy contained in Raymond Garthoff's *Detente and Confrontation: American-Soviet Relations from Nixon to Reagan* (Washington, D.C.: Brookings Institution, 1985); Morton Halperin's monograph on the politics of the ABM decision, "The Decision to Deploy the ABM: Bureaucratic Politics in the Johnson Administration" (Washington, D.C.: Brookings Institution, 1973); Henry Kissinger's three-volume *White House Years* (Boston: Little, Brown, 1979); Gerard Smith's account of the SALT I negotiations, *Doubletalk: The Story of SALT I* (New York: Doubleday, 1980); and Zbigniew Brzezinski, *Power and Principle* (New York: Farrar, Straus & Giroux, 1983), whose anecdotes are not only of substantive interest but provide a wealth of insight into the dynamics of petty bureaucratic ambitions.

One cannot exaggerate the importance of the declassification of government documents, largely the result of the 1974 amendments to the Freedom of Information Act (FOIA), in generating source materials for research about nuclear operations. During the heyday of the FOIA, from 1974 to 1981, hundreds of national security documents were released. The pace has slowed, but efforts continue. The Washington-based National Security Archives, in particular, is assisting in this endeavor. The archives serve as a repository of historically significant government documents, provide bibliographical resources, and help to train researchers in the art of penetrating the maze of government bureaucracy in the quest for original and accurate information.

Among the most important of the documents released about nuclear planning under FOIA were the Draft Presidential Memoranda (DPMs) prepared by Robert McNamara during his tenure as secretary of defense, detailed analyses of strategic priorities that McNamara once referred to as the equivalent of his memoirs. Along with the dozens of other declassified internal memoranda available from the Kennedy and Johnson administrations, the DPMs provide a record of key decisions that have had a lasting influence on nuclear strategy. This is particularly important since McNamara himself has since disavowed or reinterpreted many of the decisions that are detailed in the memoranda. Documents from subsequent administrations are more limited, a problem somewhat offset by more aggressive and informed media reporting of national security issues over time. The continued efforts to develop historical archives by such organizations as the National Security Archives and the recently established Nuclear History Program at the University of Maryland should help generate additional primary sources as declassification allows. Other sources include presidential libraries, the files on the Joint Chiefs of Staff housed at the National Archives, the historical office at the Strategic Air Command in Omaha, Nebraska, and the *Declassified Documents Index,* available at the Georgetown University library.

The preponderance of the literature on nuclear operations is extremely technical, focusing on the techniques of nuclear force planning, problems in the command and control of nuclear forces, and the technological dynamics of nuclear employment. Among the most informative of these, by far, is Ashton B. Carter, John D. Steinbruner, and Charles A. Zraket, eds., *Managing Nuclear Operations* (Washington, D.C.: Brookings Institution, 1987), a compendium of analyses on virtually every aspect of nuclear operations. The authors of the various chapters, many of which are extremely revealing, represent a broad spectrum of expertise. General Russell Dougherty's "The Psychological Climate of Nuclear Command," for instance, is a startlingly frank account of the differences in the way that civilian authorities and military planners perceive the goals of nuclear strategy. Other technical assessments of operational issues include Bruce Blair's *Strategic Command and Control* (Washington, D.C.: Brookings Institution, 1985), a detailed assessment of the implications for strategy of vulnerabilities in the U.S. command and control structure; Paul Bracken, *The Command and Control of Nuclear Forces* (New Haven: Yale University Press, 1983); and William C. Martel and Paul L. Savage, *Strategic Nuclear War: What the Superpowers Target and Why* (New York: Greenwood, 1986).

The disjuncture between political beliefs about nuclear strategy and operational assumptions in nuclear planning is replicated in the literature: technical experts rarely discuss the political and bureaucratic dimension of nuclear planning, and most historians, political scientists, and journalists aspire only to the most rudimentary assessment of technical issues. There are exceptions, including several books by Richard Betts about various aspects of nuclear policy, notably *Nuclear Blackmail and Nuclear Balance* (Washington, D.C.: Brookings Institution, 1987), which analyzes the role of nuclear weapons in a series of U.S. decisions taken during crises. Strobe Talbott's books about arms control policy, including *Endgame* (New York: Harper & Row, 1979), *Deadly Gambits* (New York: Knopf, 1984), and his most recent work, *The Master of the Game: Paul Nitze and the Nuclear Peace* (New York: Knopf, 1988), combine a readable journalistic style with technical substance. John Newhouse's *Cold Dawn: The Story of SALT* (New York: Holt, Rinehart and Winston, 1973) is also an enlightening examination of decision making during the Nixon administration which is grounded in a solid understanding of nuclear strategy and force planning.

From a more theoretical standpoint, this book owes a lot of its inspiration to Robert Dahl, whose elegant essay on political guardianship, *Controlling Nuclear Weapons: Democracy Versus Guardianship* (Syracuse: Syracuse University Press, 1985), discusses the tension between secrecy and openness in a democracy.

Some of the most important sources for a book of this kind are government publications, including unclassified technical reports from the Defense Department, the military services, and defense contractors, as well as "trade" publications, all of which tend to present an unvarnished view of what nuclear weapons are all about. There is a wealth of material to be found in congressional publications as well, including hearings, debates, and special reports. Hearings, in particular, are a source of technical detail as well a basis for gauging how political influences are brought to bear in shaping nuclear decisions. Most books about the Congress impute far too much formalism to the analysis of congressional decisions, however. One of the few exceptions is Alton Frye's *A Responsible Congress: The Politics of National Security* (New York: McGraw-Hill, 1975). For a more recent appraisal, the forthcoming *The Congress and U.S. Defense Policy from Vietnam to the Persian Gulf* by Barry Blechman is also helpful.

The central problem examined in this book—how and why there is a schism between political and operational assumptions about nuclear strategy—required going beyond published sources. It is not a subject that has been discussed much, and those who are expert on these matters have been privy to sensitive information about which they are necessarily discreet. The research conducted for this book would not have been possible without the help of these experts, the dozens of individuals—many of them from the military—who shared the common concern that the separation between politics and operations impedes the formulation of policy. Their anonymity has to be protected, but this should not diminish the importance of their generosity and dedication.

This book is written with the public in mind. Writing a book about nuclear strategy for public consumption in considered by many to be an oxymoron. In the view of this author, that is part of the reason that operational planning, the central determinant of nuclear policy, has remained so remarkably immune to decisive influence by political authorities. Discussions of these matters are usually so arcane that they cannot be grasped even by most experts. This book is admittedly a sketch of some extremely complicated problems that warrant far more detailed, technical examination. It is meant as a point of departure for a broader debate on these problems, a debate which is aimed at assuring that nuclear policy reflects considered choices about the nation's security which are consonant with a democratic system of government.

NOTES

Chapter 1

1. Flora Lewis, "Citizens Want to Know," *New York Times,* November 17, 1987, p. 35.

2. Text of speech by Reagan, March 23, 1983, *Public Papers of the Presidents of the United States, Ronald Reagan, 1983, Book I, January 1–July 1, 1983* (Washington, D.C.: Government Printing Office, 1984), pp. 437–43.

3. See, for instance, John Newhouse, "The Diplomatic Round," *New Yorker,* July 22, 1985, p. 41; Sidney Blumenthal, "Perle and the Diminished Dream," *Washington Post,* November 25, 1987, p. C2; Frank Greve, "Out of the Blue: How Star Wars Was Proposed," *Philadelphia Inquirer,* November 17, 1985, p. 1; and Greve, " 'Star Wars': How Reagan's Plan Caught Many Insiders by Surprise," *San Jose Mercury News,* November 17, 1985, p. A1.

4. From interviews with Pentagon officials, March–September, 1987. For a detailed discussion of the history of Reagan's arms control policy, see Strobe Talbott, *Deadly Gambits: The Reagan Administration and the Stalemate in Nuclear Arms Control* (New York: Knopf, 1984).

5. Interview with an NSC official, April 12, 1987.

6. Interview with William Furniss, Office of Strategic Defense and Space Policy, the Pentagon, Washington, D.C., December 29, 1987.

7. William J. Broad, "Reagan's 'Star Wars' Bid: Many Ideas Converging," *New York Times,* March 4, 1985, p. 22.

8. Memorandum prepared by Martin Anderson, August 1979, excerpt reprinted in Anderson, *Revolution* (San Diego: Harcourt Brace Jovanovich, 1988), pp. 85–86.

9. Interview with Martin Anderson, Palo Alto, Calif., December 3, 1987.

10. Ibid.

11. Quoted in Robert Scheer, *With Enough Shovels: Reagan, Bush, and Nuclear War* (New York: Random House, 1982), p. 18.

12. Interview with Douglas Waller, office of Senator William Proxmire, Washington, D.C., October 26, 1987.

13. Interview with Anderson, restated in *Revolution,* pp. 93–94.

14. Interviews with Pentagon officials, April–December 1987.

15. Based on interviews with NSC and Pentagon officials, March–September 1987. For other accounts of the genesis of the Annex, see Anderson, *Revolution,* pp. 94–99; Jim Drinkard, "SDI Shoots beyond Concept, McFarlane Says," *Washington Times,* May 18, 1988, p. 6; and Gregory Herken, "Technological Exuberance, Domestic Politics, and Strategic Vision: The Earthly Origins of 'Star Wars' " (unpublished paper, 1986).

16. Anderson, *Revolution,* pp. 90–91.

17. Interview with a Pentagon official, October 23, 1987.

18. *Report of the President's Commission on Strategic Forces,* April 6, 1983, p. 9.

19. See, for instance, Angelo M. Codevilla, "How SDI Is Being Undone from Within," *Commentary,* May 1986, p. 24, and Herken, "Technological Exuberance," p. 20.

20. Quoted in Leslie H. Gelb, "Vision of Space Defense Posing New Challenges," *New York Times,* March 3, 1985, p. 10.

21. Cited by James Schlesinger, testimony before the Senate Armed Services Committee, *Department of Defense Authorization for Appropriations for Fiscal Year 1986,* pt. 7, *Strategic and Theater Nuclear Forces,* 99th Cong., 1st sess., March 19, 1985, p. 4192.

22. For a list of anti-SDI organizations, see the attachment to the letter sent to Senators Goldwater and Nunn by Senators Johnston, Chiles, Proxmire, et al., May 22, 1986. See also E. J. Dionne, " 'Star Wars' Criticized in the Vatican: Pope Avoids Firm Stand on Study," *New York Times,* July 8, 1985, p. A6.

23. Testimony of Richard N. Perle, in Senate Armed Services Committee, Subcommittee on Strategic and Theater Nuclear Forces, *Strategic Defense Initiative,* 99th Cong., 1st sess., November 6, 1985, p. 72.

24. Quoted in "First Strike Weapons at Sea: The Trident II and the Sea-Launched Cruise Missile," *Defense Monitor* 6 (1987): 5. For a more detailed discussion of the Reagan offensive nuclear modernization program, see chapter 6.

25. *Report of the Secretary of Defense Caspar W. Weinberger to the Congress on the FY86 Budget, FY87 Authorization Request, and FY86–90 Defense Programs* (Washington, D.C.: Government Printing Office, February 4, 1985), pp. 51–52.

26. Quoted in George C. Wilson, "New U.S. Strategy for Nuclear War," *Washington Post,* July 20, 1975, p. C1.

27. See, for instance, Scott D. Sagan, "SIOP-62: The Nuclear War Plan Briefing to President Kennedy," *International Security* 12 (Summer 1987): 22–51; David Alan Rosenberg, "Origins of Overkill," *International Security 7* (Spring 1983): 3–71; and Desmond Ball, "The Development of the SIOP, 1960–1983," in Ball and Jeffrey Richelson, eds., *Strategic Nuclear Targeting* (Ithaca: Cornell University Press, 1986), pp. 57–83.

28. Russell E. Dougherty, "The Psychological Climate of Nuclear Command," in Ashton B. Carter, John S. Steinbruner, and Charles A. Zraket, eds., *Managing Nuclear Operations* (Washington, D.C.: Brookings Institution, 1987), p. 418.

29. Interview with Curtis LeMay by John T. Bolen, U.S. Air Force Oral History Program, interview no. 736, March 9, 1971, Maxwell Air Force Base, p. 29.

30. Dougherty, "Psychological Climate," pp. 413–17.

31. Thomas D. White, "Strategy and the Defense Intellectuals," *Saturday Evening Post,* cited in *Congressional Record,* May 7, 1963, pp. 7885–86.

32. Bill Gulley, *Breaking Cover* (New York: Warner, 1980), cited in Paul Bracken, *The Command and Control of Nuclear Forces* (New Haven: Yale University Press, 1983), p. 226.

33. Robert Dahl, *Controlling Nuclear Weapons* (Syracuse: Syracuse University Press, 1985), p. 7.

Chapter 2

1. Walter Millis, ed., *The Forrestal Diaries* (New York: Viking, 1951), p. 538.

2. John Foster Dulles, "A Policy of Boldness," *Life,* May 19, 1952, p. 151.

3. Transcript of interview with Andrew Goodpaster by Barry M. Blechman, Washington, D.C., April 14, 1988.

4. Dwight D. Eisenhower, *The White House Years: Mandate for Change, 1953–1956* (Garden City, N.Y.: Doubleday, 1963), p. 445.

5. Ibid., p. 181.

6. The context, content, means, and possible impact of President Eisenhower's nuclear threats to end the Korean War are described in detail in Barry M. Blechman and Robert Powell, "What in the Name of God Is Strategic Superiority?" *Political Science Quarterly* 97 (Winter 1982–83): 589–602.

7. Interview with Goodpaster.

Notes

8. The text of the note from the Soviet Ministry of Foreign Affairs of November 27, 1988, can be seen in *Department of State Bulletin* 40 (January 19, 1959): 81–89.

9. Townsend Hoopes, *The Devil and John Foster Dulles* (Boston: Little, Brown, 1973), p. 470.

10. David Rosenberg, "American Atomic Strategy and the Hydrogen Bomb Decision," *Journal of American History* 66 (June 1979): 77–79.

11. For a thorough and fascinating account of Paul Nitze's legacy, see Strobe Talbott, *The Master of the Game: Paul Nitze and the Nuclear Peace* (New York: Knopf, 1988).

12. Fred Kaplan, *The Wizards of Armageddon* (New York: Simon and Schuster, 1983), p. 140.

13. Richard G. Hewlett and Francis Duncan, *Atomic Shield, 1947–1952* (University Park: University of Pennsylvania Press, 1969), pp. 525–29.

14. Charles Hurd, "Expansion at Once Asked in Air by Policy Board," *New York Times*, January 14, 1948, pp. A1, A20. The report is summarized on p. A21.

15. See C. P. Trussel, "Taft Moves for GOP Accord on All Defense," *New York Times*, May 6, 1948, p. A1; and "Air Groups Called Barely Sufficient," *New York Times*, May 2, 1949, p. A15.

16. For contemporary accounts of the Symington hearings, see Anthony Leviero, "General LeMay Fears Soviet Lead in Air by 1960," *New York Times*, May 1, 1956, pp. A1, A12; Anthony Leviero, "$1.1 Billion More Voted Air Force by Senate Group," *New York Times*, June 19, 1956, pp. A1, A14; Anthony Leviero, "Senators Charge Wilson Misleads Nation on Might," July 4, 1956, pp. A1, A10; and Charles V. Murphy, "The New Air Situation," *Fortune*, September 1955, p. 221.

17. Dwight D. Eisenhower, *The White House Years: Waging Peace, 1956–1961* (Garden City, N.Y.: Doubleday, 1965), p. 456.

18. *Public Papers of the President, 1956* (Washington, D.C.: Government Printing Office, 1958), p. 236.

19. *Public Papers of the President, 1955* (Washington, D.C.: Government Printing Office, 1959), p. 303.

20. Donald A. Quarles, "How Much Is Enough?" *Air Force Magazine*, September 1956, pp. 51–52.

21. Elie Abel, "Dulles Suggests Soviets May Favor Cuts in Arms Cost," *New York Times*, March 1, 1956, pp. A1, A6.

22. Interview with Goodpaster. The Gaither report was published ten years later, as *Deterrence and Survival in the Nuclear Age (the "Gaither Report" of 1957)* (Washington, D.C.: Government Printing Office, 1976).

23. Millis, ed., *Forrestal Diaries*, p. 458.

24. Anthony Leviero, "Truman Declares Russia Forces U.S. into Bomb Security," *New York Times*, July 25, 1948, pp. A1, A4.

25. Millis, ed., *Forrestal Diaries*, pp. 460–61.

26. Hewlett and Duncan, *Atomic Shield*, pp. 521–25, 585–86.

27. JCS, "Decision on J.C.S. 2056/81: A Report by the Joint Strategic Plans Committee on Joint Chiefs of Staff Atomic Weapons Reserve," JCS 2056/81, February 1, 1956, JCS 1954–56, CCS 471.6 (8-15-45), sec. 75, box 155.

28. JCS, "Utilization of Atomic Weapons," SM-663–54, July 21, 1954, JCS 1954–56, CCS 471.6 (4-18-49), sec. 13, box 151; "Report of the Joint Strategic Plans Committee to the Joint Chiefs of Staff on Dispersal of Weapons," JSPC 902/605, November 2, 1955, JCS 1954–56, CCS 471.6 (8-15-45), sec. 71, box 154.

29. JCS, "Decision on J.C.S. 2019/208: A Report by the Joint Strategic Plans Committee on Authorization for Use of Atomic Weapons in Air Defense," JCS 2019/208, December 14, 1956, JCS 1954–56, CCS 471.6 (8-15-45), sec. 88, box 156.

30. Arthur Radford, "Memorandum for the Secretary of Defense: Authorization for the Expenditure of Atomic Weapons," November 14, 1956, JCS 1954–56, CCS 471.6 (8-15-45), sec. 87, box 156; David Alan Rosenberg, "The Origins of Overkill," *International Security* 7 (Spring 1983): 48–49.

31. Radford, "Memorandum."

32. What little is known publicly about operational nuclear planning is the result of painstaking work by a handful of historians and political scientists, including David Rosenberg, Desmond Ball, John Prados, and Fred Kaplan. Rosenberg, especially, has painted a vivid and disturbing picture, based largely on declassified documents, of nuclear planning during the Truman and the Eisenhower administrations.

33. NSC, "U.S. Objectives with Respect to the USSR to Counter Soviet Threats to U.S. Security," NSC 20/4, November 23, 1948, cited in Rosenberg, "Overkill," p. 14n31.

34. Rosenberg, "Overkill," pp. 16–17.

35. Interview with Curtis E. LeMay by John T. Bolen, U.S. Air Force Oral History Program, interview no. 736, March 9, 1971, Maxwell Air Force Base, p. 43.

36. Quoted in Rosenberg, "Overkill," pp. 34–35.

37. Ibid., p. 55.

38. Ibid., pp. 61–64.

39. The declassification of McNamara's DPM has provided an invaluable data source for force plans during this period. McNamara also introduced detailed, unclassified posture statements for the benefit of Congress. For an overview of the latter, see "Literary Merits of Robert S. McNamara as Revealed in His Posture Statements," *Army*, March 1967, pp. 22–24. See also top-secret letter to Thomas Power, CINCSAC, from Thomas White, air force chief of staff, February 1, 1961, in Collections of the Manuscript Division, Library of Congress, Washington, D.C., box 48, file 39.

40. William Beecher, "Pentagon's 'Whiz Kids': They Make Some Gains amid All the Controversy," *Wall Street Journal,* September 24, 1963, cited in *Congressional Record,* September 25, 1963, p. 17978.

41. Thomas D. White, "Strategy and the Defense Intellectual," *Congressional Record,* May 7, 1963, p. 7885. The air force's rejection of "flexible response" is also revealed in a memorandum from White to General Power in 1961 expressing concern that U.S. strategic targeting policy was being misrepresented by William Kauffman. See cable from Power to White, February 27, 1961, White Papers, 1961–75, Collections of the Manuscript Division, Library of Congress, Washington, D.C., box 48.

42. Interview with Dean Rusk in Michael Charlton, *From Deterrence to Defense: The Inside Story of Strategic Policy* (Cambridge: Harvard University Press, 1987), p. 6.

43. *Newsweek,* April 9, 1962, p. 32, cited in Desmond Ball, *Targeting for Strategic Nuclear Deterrence,* Adelphi Paper no. 185 (London: International Institute for Strategic Studies, Summer 1983), p. 13.

44. Quoted in Walter Isaacson and Evan Thomas, *The Wise Men* (New York: Simon and Schuster, 1986), p. 610.

45. Ibid. For a detailed discussion of the Berlin crisis, see Richard K. Betts, *Nuclear Blackmail and Nuclear Balance* (Washington, D.C.: Brookings Institution, 1987), pp. 92–109; Robert M. Slusser, *The Berlin Crisis of 1961: Soviet-American Relations and the Struggle for Power in the Kremlin, June–September 1961* (Baltimore: Johns Hopkins University Press, 1973); and Gregg Herken, *Counsels of War* (New York: Knopf, 1985), chap. 14.

46. Memorandum from Karl Kaysen to McGeorge Bundy, July 3, 1961, cited in Kaplan, *Wizards of Armageddon,* p. 296.

Notes

47. Quoted in Michio Kaku and Daniel Axelrod, *To Win a Nuclear War* (Boston: South End Press, 1987), p. 140.

48. For a more detailed discussion, see Kaplan, *Wizards of Armageddon*, pp. 298–300.

49. In Arthur Schlesinger, Jr., *A Thousand Days* (Boston: Houghton Mifflin, 1965), pp. 587–88; quoted in Betts, *Nuclear Blackmail*, p. 95.

50. Quoted in Isaacson and Thomas, *Wise Men*, p. 613.

51. Kaplan, *Wizards of Armageddon*, p. 298.

52. See Betts, *Nuclear Blackmail*, pp. 96–97. Information about NSAM-109 appears in Richard J. Barnett, *The Alliance: America, Europe, Japan: Makers of the Postwar World* (New York: Simon and Schuster, 1983), p. 231.

53. Interview with Leighton Davis by Lyn R. Officer and Hugh Ahmann, U.S. Air Force Oral History Program, interview no. 668, April 26, 1973, p. 105.

54. Interview with William Kauffman, Washington, D.C., June 1988. See also Kaplan, *Wizards of Armageddon*, pp. 260–61.

55. Memorandum to Thomas D. White announcing visit by McNamara to SAC, January 25, 1961, White Papers, January–June, 1961, Chief of Staff Memos, box 49.

56. See *Briefing for the President by the Chairman, Joint Chiefs of Staff on the Joint Chiefs of Staff Single Integrated Operational Plan 1962 (SIOP-62)*, September 13, 1961, reprinted in *International Security* 12 (Summer 1987): 41.

57. McNamara directive, "Assignment of Projects within the DoD," March 1, 1961, National Security Archives, 846T.

58. Memorandum from David Bell to Bundy and McNamara, January 30, 1961, p. 4, John F. Kennedy Library, International Security Meetings Folder, box 313.

59. John Prados, *The Soviet Estimate* (New York: Dial, 1982), pp. 122–24.

60. Quoted in Kaplan, *Wizards of Armageddon*, p. 134.

61. Bundy memorandum to McNamara, January 30, 1961, Declassified Documents Index, 81 610A.

62. Cited in Kaplan, *Wizards of Armageddon*, pp. 278–79.

63. Interview with Jasper Welch, Washington, D.C., May 18, 1988.

64. Lemnitzer memorandum to McNamara, " 'Doctrine' on Thermonuclear Attack," April 21, 1961, declassified November 19, 1980, OSD FOIA, JCSM-252 61.

65. See *Briefing to the President,* and Scott Sagan, "SIOP-62: The Nuclear War Plan Briefing to President Kennedy," *International Security* 12 (Summer 1987): 22–40.

66. For additional discussion of SIOP-63, see Desmond Ball, "The Development of the SIOP, 1960–1983," in Ball and Jeffrey Richelson, eds., *Strategic Nuclear Targeting* (Ithaca: Cornell University Press, 1986), pp. 62–70.

67. Speech by McNamara, cited in William W. Kauffman, *The McNamara Strategy* (New York: Harper and Row, 1964), p. 116.

68. Ibid., p. 75.

69. Interview with a former Kennedy official, discussed in Kaplan, *Wizards of Armageddon*, pp. 307–11. Rusk was also a supporter of civil defense, as is indicated in a memorandum to Bundy urging additional funding for fallout shelters in the 1962 defense budget. Rusk argued, "Our effort must be large enough manifestly to provide for the survivability of significant portions of our population, war-making potential and second-strike force." Rusk to Bundy, October 29, 1961, John F. Kennedy Library, National Security Meetings Folder, box 275.

70. See, for instance, David Boyer, *By the Bomb's Early Light* (New York: Pantheon, 1985), epilogue. A compilation of "atomic culture" can be seen in the 1982 documentary film *Atomic Cafe*.

71. Kaplan, *Wizards of Armageddon*, pp. 313–14.

72. From transcripts of Cuban missile crisis meetings, October 16, 1962, afternoon, cited in Marc Trachtenberg, "The Influence of Nuclear Weapons in the Cuban Missile Crisis," *International Security* 10 (Summer 1985): 148. Excerpts of the text of the audiotapes of meetings relating to the Cuban missile crisis are reprinted in "White House Tapes and Minutes of the Cuban Missile Crisis," ibid., pp. 164–203.

73. Cited in Trachtenberg, "The Influence of Nuclear Weapons," p. 152.

74. Interview with Curtis LeMay by Robert F. Futrell, Thomas G. Belden, and J. Van Staaveren, U.S. Air Force Oral History Program, interview no. 592, June 8, 1972, Washington, D.C., p. 3.

75. Interview with McNamara in Charlton, *From Deterrence to Defense*, pp. 17, 19.

76. Schlesinger, *A Thousand Days*, p. 841, aptly cited in Marc Trachtenberg's introduction to the transcripts of the White House Cuban missile crisis meetings in "White House Tapes," p. 168. For a further analysis of the Cuban crisis, see Raymond Garthoff, *Reflections on the Cuban Missile Crisis* (Washington, D.C.: Brookings Institution, 1987).

77. Interview with Welch.

78. Interview with McNamara in Charlton, *From Deterrence to Defense*, pp. 9–10.

79. Cited in Alton Frye, *A Responsible Congress: The Politics of National Security* (New York: McGraw Hill, 1975), p. 10.

80. See, for instance, the memorandum from McNamara to Kennedy recommending against appropriations for additional bombers, October 7, 1961, John F. Kennedy Library, National Security Meetings Folder, box 275, and the president's acceptance of the recommendations in Bundy memorandum to McNamara, October 28, 1961. See also Richard Fryklund, "McNamara View Dooms Bomber," *Washington Star,* February 14, 1967, p. 15, and Ted Sell, "McNamara Defends Role of Missiles," *Philadelphia Inquirer,* January 26, 1966, p. 1.

81. Memorandum from Kaysen to Bundy, November 14, 1962, John F. Kennedy Library, National Security Meetings Folder, box 275.

82. Interview with Kauffman, discussed in Ball, *Targeting for Strategic Deterrence,* p. 162.

83. Testimony of McNamara, in House Appropriations Committee, Subcommittee on Department of Defense Appropriations, *Department of Defense Appropriations for 1964,* pt. 1, 88th Cong., 1st sess., February 7, 1963, p. 328.

84. December 3, 1964, DPM, "Recommended FY66–70 Programs for Strategic Offensive Forces, Continental Air and Missile Defense Forces, and Civil Defense," p. 48, OSD FOIA, record no. 539. The point is restated in the subsequent year's DPM, which argues, "Feasible improvements in missile accuracy and the use of MIRVs where applicable can greatly increase the efficiency of our offensive forces against hard Soviet targets." "Recommended FY 1967–71 Offensive and Defensive Forces," November 1, 1965, p. 20, OSD FOIA, record no. 541.

85. November 9, 1966, DPM, "Recommended FY68–72 Strategic Offensive and Defensive Forces," p. A3. See also Kaplan, *Wizards of Armageddon,* p. 364.

86. Memorandum from Spurgeon Keeny to Bundy, November 9, 1965, Lyndon Baines Johnson Library, National Security Meetings Folder, DoD FY 1967 Budget.

87. Senate Armed Services Committee, Preparedness Investigating Subcommittee, *Status of U.S. Strategic Power,* September 27, 1968, cited in Senate Committee on Foreign Relations, Subcommittee on Arms Control, International Law, and Organization, *Briefing on Counterforce Attacks,* 93d Cong., 2d sess., September 11, 1974, p. 4.

88. Interview with McNamara in Charlton, *From Deterrence to Defense,* p. 25.

89. Interview with David Aaron, Washington, D.C., May 9, 1988.

90. Quoted in Ball, *Targeting for Strategic Nuclear Deterrence,* p. 15.
91. Interview with Kauffman.
92. McNamara quoted in Charlton, *From Deterrence to Defense,* p. 18; interview with Kauffman.
93. See *Department of Defense Appropriations for 1964,* pp. 313–27, 338–39; and *Congressional Record,* June 25, 1963, p. 11466.
94. Frye, *Responsible Congress,* p. 11.

Chapter 3

1. "Damage Limiting: A Rationale for the Allocation of Resources by the US and USSR," prepared for DR & E, Department of Defense, January 21, 1964.
2. Memorandum from L. J. Legere to Bundy on McNamara's memorandum for the president entitled "Ballistic Missile Defenses," dated November 20, 1962, November 26, 1962, John F. Kennedy Library, National Security Meetings Folder, box 275, DoD FY 1964 Budget, vol. I.
3. Memorandum from Rusk to McNamara on the 1966–70 DPM, November 28, 1964, p. 5.
4. For a full discussion of Lyndon Johnson's decision to deploy the ABM, see Morton Halperin, *The Decision to Deploy the ABM: Bureaucratic Politics in the Johnson Administration* (Washington, D.C.: Brookings Institution, 1973). For a discussion of the congressional ABM debate, see Alton Frye, *A Responsible Congress: The Politics of National Security* (New York: McGraw-Hill, 1975), chap. 2.
5. See Halperin, *Decision to Deploy,* esp. pp. 83–84, 93.
6. Interview with McNamara in Michael Charlton, *From Deterrence to Defense: The Inside Story of Strategic Policy* (Cambridge: Harvard University Press, 1987), p. 4.
7. Halperin, *Decision to Deploy,* pp. 85–86.
8. Speech reprinted in Robert S. McNamara, "The Dynamics of Nuclear Strategy," *Department of State Bulletin,* October 9, 1967, pp. 443–51.
9. Informal discussion with ACDA staffers, Washington, D.C., November 1977.
10. See, for instance, Joint Committee on Atomic Energy, Subcommittee on Military Applications, *Scope, Magnitude and Implications of the United States Antiballistic Missile Program: Hearings,* 90th Cong., 1st sess., November 6–7, 1967.
11. Cited in Henry Kissinger, *White House Years* (Boston: Little, Brown, 1979), p. 207. For a discussion of the scientific disputes over ABM, see Anne Hessing Cahn, "Eggheads and Warheads: Scientists and the ABM" (Ph.D. diss., MIT, 1971).
12. *New York Times* editorial, February 7, 1969, cited in Kissinger, *White House Years,* p. 205.
13. Ibid., p. 208.
14. Ibid.
15. Angelo Codevilla, *While Others Build: A Commonsense Approach to the Strategic Defense Initiative* (New York: Free Press, 1988), p. 54.
16. Frye, *Responsible Congress,* p. 45.
17. Codevilla, *While Others Build,* p. 54.
18. Cited in Fred Kaplan, *The Wizards of Armageddon* (New York: Simon and Schuster, 1983), p. 366.
19. Nixon's speech to Congress is cited in Desmond Ball, *Targeting for Strategic*

Nuclear Deterrence, Adelphi Paper no. 185 (London: International Institute for Strategic Studies, Summer 1983), p. 18.

20. Kissinger, *White House Years,* p. 215.

21. Frye, *Responsible Congress,* pp. 51–52.

22. Ibid., p. 52.

23. Interview with Larry Smith, September 11, 1987, Washington, D.C. See also Frye, *Responsible Congress,* pp. 61–63.

24. Frye, *Responsible Congress,* p. 68.

25. Ibid., p. 69.

26. Ibid., p. 70 n.

27. Ibid., p. 71.

28. Ibid., p. 78.

29. Ibid. *White House Years,* p. 212. Kissinger summarized his opposition to the Senate MIRV critics in his memoirs: "We were being pressed to take two momentous steps: first, to abandon our ABM without reciprocity; and second, to postpone our MIRV deployment as a unilateral gesture. . . . Our unilateral restraint would be an incentive for the Soviets not to settle but to procrastinate, to tilt the balance as much in their favor as possible while we paralyzed ourselves."

30. Frye, *Responsible Congress,* p. 76.

31. Interview with Smith.

32. Frye, *Responsible Congress,* p. 76.

33. Interview with Smith.

34. Interview with Aaron.

35. Frye, *Responsible Congress,* p. 80.

36. Kissinger, *White House Years,* p. 217.

37. Interview with Nixon NSC official.

38. Interview with Jasper Welch, Washington, D.C., May 18, 1988.

39. Ibid.

40. Ibid.

41. Ibid.

42. Ibid. For an analysis of the "economic recovery" mission, see Michael Kennedy and Kevin N. Lewis, "On Keeping Them Down; or Why Do Recovery Models Recover So Fast?" in Desmond Ball and Jeffrey Richelson, eds., *Strategic Nuclear Targeting* (Ithaca: Cornell University Press, 1986), pp. 194–208, and Scott D. Sagan, *Moving Targets: Nuclear Strategy and National Security* (forthcoming, 1989), draft manuscript, pp. 48–56.

43. For further discussion of NSDM-242, see Leon Sloss and Marc Dean Millot, "US Nuclear Strategy in Evolution," *Strategic Review* 12 (Winter 1984): 22–23; Senate Committee on Armed Services, *Department of Defense Authorization for Appropriations for Fiscal Year 1981,* 96th Cong., 2d sess., April 17–18, 1980, pt. 5; and Ball, "The Development of the SIOP, 1960–1983," in Ball and Richelson, eds., *Strategic Nuclear Targeting,* pp. 70–75.

44. Interview with Welch.

45. Cited in *Annual Defense Department Report for Fiscal 1978* (Washington, D.C.: Government Printing Office, 1977), p. 68.

46. See Ball, "Development of the SIOP," p. 74.

47. Interview with William Kauffman, Washington, D.C., June 1988.

48. Interview with Aaron.

49. Ibid.

50. For more detailed discussions of NATO nuclear policy, see David N. Schwartz,

Notes

NATO's Nuclear Dilemmas (Washington, D.C.: Brookings Institution, 1983); John Steinbruner and Leon Sigal, eds., Alliance Security and the No–First Use Question (Washington, D.C.: Brookings Institution, 1983); and Lynn Davis, Limited Nuclear Options: Deterrence and the New American Doctrine, Adelphi Paper no. 121 (London: International Institute for Strategic Studies, Winter 1975).

51. Kissinger, White House Years, p. 218.

52. Richard Nixon, First Annual Report to the Congress on United States Foreign Policy for the 1970s, February 18, 1970, in Public Papers of the Presidents of the United States, Richard Nixon, 1970 (Washington, D.C.: Government Publishing Office, 1971), pp. 116–90; and Kissinger, White House Years, p. 222.

53. Interview with Aaron.

54. Ibid.

55. Ibid.

56. Ibid.

57. Ball, "Development of the SIOP," p. 73.

58. For a detailed discussion of the problems of flexible response, see Desmond Ball, Can Nuclear War Be Controlled?, Adelphi Paper no. 169 (London: International Institute for Strategic Studies, Autumn 1981). Targeting guidance is discussed further in chapter 6.

59. See Ball, Targeting for Strategic Nuclear Deterrence," pp. 25–26.

60. Interview with Nixon NSC official.

61. Interview with Welch.

62. Interview with Aaron.

63. Kissinger, Years of Upheaval (Boston: Little, Brown, 1982), p. 136.

64. For a full account of the politics of SALT I, see John Newhouse, Cold Dawn: The Story of SALT (New York: Holt, Rinehart and Winston, 1973), and Gerard Smith, Doubletalk: The Story of SALT I (Garden City, N.Y.: Doubleday, 1980).

65. Interview with Aaron.

66. James R. Schlesinger, "Remarks to the Overseas Writers Association," January 10, 1974, reprinted in Public Statements of the Secretary of Defense, James R. Schlesinger, 1974, vol. I (Washington, D.C.: Office of the Secretary of Defense, 1975), pp. 17–33.

67. Interview with Kauffman.

68. See, for instance, James M. Wesley, "Schlesinger's Legacy: Limited Nuclear War?" Inter Dependent (United Nations Association), December 1975, pp. 1, 7.

69. Senate Committee on Foreign Relations, Subcommittee on Arms Control, International Law, and Organization, Briefing on Counterforce Attacks, 93d Cong., 2d sess., September 11, 1974, p. 1.

70. Ibid., p. 2.

71. Ibid., pp. 3–19.

72. Ibid., p. 24.

73. Ibid., pp. 42–43.

74. Interview with Nixon NSC official. For discussions of the 1973 Middle East crisis, see Barry M. Blechman and Douglas Hart, "The Political Utility of Nuclear Weapons: The 1973 Middle East Crisis," International Security 7 (Summer 1982): 589–602; Henry Kissinger, Years of Upheaval (Boston: Little, Brown, 1982), pp. 587–89; and Richard K. Betts, Nuclear Blackmail and Nuclear Balance (Washington, D.C.: Brookings Institution, 1987), pp. 123–29.

75. Cited in a press release from the office of Senator Alan Cranston, February 11, 1976.

76. House Committee on International Relations, Subcommittee on International Security and Scientific Affairs, *First Use of Nuclear Weapons: Preserving Responsible Control: Hearings,* 94th Cong., 2d sess., March 16, 1976, pp. 16–17. See also Phil Stanford, "Who Pushes the Button?" *Parade,* March 28, 1976, p. 6.

77. George H. Quester, "Presidential Authority and Nuclear Weapons," cited in *First Use,* p. 217.

78. *New York Times,* August 10, 1974, cited in *First Use,* p. 219.

79. *Briefing on Counterforce Attacks,* p. 22.

80. Kissinger, *White House Years,* pp. 217–18.

81. Henry Kissinger, *The Necessity for Choice,* cited in George C. Wilson, "New U.S. Strategy for Nuclear War," *Washington Post,* July 20, 1975, pp. 61, 64.

82. Kissinger, *White House Years,* p. 217.

83. Ibid.

84. Zbigniew Brzezinski, *Power and Principle* (New York: Farrar, Straus & Giroux, 1983), p. 43.

85. Ibid., p. 46.

86. Interview with Carter in Charlton, *From Deterrence to Defense,* p. 72.

87. Ibid., p. 71.

88. Thomas Powers, "Choosing a Strategy for World War III," *Atlantic Monthly,* November 1982, p. 84.

89. Ibid., p. 95, and interview with Aaron.

90. Interview with Aaron.

91. Odom quoted in Powers, "Choosing a Strategy," p. 95.

92. Brzezinski, *Power and Principle,* p. 455. See also Brzezinski's discussion of doctrine in *Game Plan* (Boston: Atlantic Monthly Press, 1986), p. 177.

93. Powers, "Choosing a Strategy," p. 86.

94. Interview with Edward Warner, Washington, D.C., May 20, 1988. For further discussions of "denial" strategy, see Sagan, *Moving Targets,* pp. 56–65, and Walter Slocombe, "The United States and Nuclear War," in Barry Blechman, *Rethinking the U.S. Nuclear Posture* (Boulder: Aspen Institute Press, 1982), pp. 17–41.

95. Interview with Carter NSC official.

96. Interview with Welch.

97. Telephone interview with Joel Resnick, Washington, D.C., June 1988.

98. Interview with a retired air force general, October 1987.

99. Powers, "Choosing a Strategy," p. 86.

100. Interview with Leon Sloss, May 4, 1988. See also Brzezinski, *Power and Principle,* p. 177.

101. See Brzezinski, *Power and Principle,* p. 456.

102. Powers, "Choosing a Strategy," p. 96, and interview with Sloss.

103. See Odom's remarks in Charlton, "From Deterrence to Defense," pp. 12–13.

104. Interview with Sloss.

105. Interview with former JSTPS official.

106. Interview with Sloss.

107. Brzezinski, *Power and Principle,* pp. 458–59.

108. Interview with a Carter NSC official, February 11, 1988, discussed in Charlton, *From Deterrence to Defense,* pp. 70, 86–89.

109. Interview with Kauffman. For a further discussion of PD-59, see Committee on Foreign Relations, *Nuclear War Strategy: Hearing,* 96th Cong., 2d sess., September 16, 1980.

110. Brzezinski, *Power and Principle,* p. 459.

Chapter 4

1. Interview with John Dewey, Washington, D.C., January 15, 1988.

2. The pastoral letter of the U.S. bishops on war and peace is printed as "The Challenge of Peace: God's Promise and Our Response," *Origins* 13 (May 19, 1983).

3. From the text of the president's March 23, 1983, printed speech, in *Weekly Compilation of Presidential Documents* 19 (March 28, 1983): 447–48.

4. Adam M. Garfinkle, *The Politics of the Nuclear Freeze* (Philadelphia: Foreign Policy Research Institute, 1984), p. 55.

5. Interview with Pentagon official, March 11, 1987.

6. Martin Anderson, *Revolution* (San Diego: Harcourt Brace Jovanovich, 1988), pp. 93–94.

7. Interview with foreign broadcasters, November 12, 1985, *Public Papers of the Presidents of the United States, Ronald Reagan, 1985, Book II, June 29–December 31, 1985* (Washington, D.C.: Government Printing Office, 1988), pp. 1369–75.

8. Meeting with T. K. Jones, McLean, Va., April 1983.

9. For further discussion of the Team B exercise, see William Beecher, "High Level Study Says CIA Understates Extent of Soviet Threat," *Boston Globe*, December 17, 1976, p. 1. Reagan expressed his own reservations about Soviet morality in his first news conference as president. See *Public Papers of the Presidents of the United States, Ronald Reagan, 1981, January 26–December 31, 1981* (Washington, D.C.: Government Printing Office, 1982), pp. 55–62.

10. Interview with Paul Nitze, Washington, D.C., November 21, 1988.

11. See, for instance, Richard Halloran, "Pentagon Draws Up First Strategy for Fighting a Long Nuclear War," *New York Times*, May 30, 1982, p. 1; and Jack Anderson and Dale Van Atta, "Secret Plan for Winning Nuclear War," *Washington Post*, April 6, 1988, p. E17.

12. For the text of congressional amendments on the nuclear freeze, see Garfinkle, *Politics of the Nuclear Freeze*, appendices C–F.

13. SANE press release, June 13, 1983, cited in Garfinkel, *Politics of the Nuclear Freeze*, p. 204.

14. For further discussion about Densepack, see Richard Halloran, "Reagan Urges Congress to Weigh Missile Plan with Sympathy," *New York Times*, November 23, 1982, p. 41; Charles Corddry, "Reagan Approves MX Basing," *Baltimore Sun*, May 19, 1982, pp. 1, 8; and Ira Nerken, "Dense Unpacking," *New Republic*, December 27, 1982, pp. 10–11.

15. Cited in Halloran, "Pentagon Draws Up Strategy."

16. Interview with Albert Pierce, Washington, D.C., January 10, 1989.

17. Teller's early visits with Reagan are discussed in Gregg Herken, "The Earthly Origins of Star Wars," *Bulletin of Atomic Scientists* 43 (October 1987): 20–28.

18. Interview with Teller in Broad, "Reagan's Star Wars Bid: Many Ideas Converging," *New York Times*, March 4, 1985, p. A1; interview with Pentagon official, June 11, 1987.

19. Malcolm A. Wallop, "Opportunities and Imperatives of Ballistic Missile Defenses," *Strategic Review*, Fall 1979, pp. 13–21. Its submission to Reagan is discussed in Angelo Codevilla, *While Others Build: A Commonsense Approach to the Strategic Defense Initiative* (New York: Free Press, 1988), pp. 66–67.

20. Martin Anderson, "An Insurance Missile Defense" (reprint of speech given to the Commonwealth Club of California, January 31, 1986) (Palo Alto: Hoover Institution, 1986), pp. 1–2.

21. Steven R. Weisman, "Reagan Says Plan On Missile Defense Will Prevent War," *New York Times,* March 26, 1983, pp. A1, A4. A transcript of the president's news conference appears on p. A4.

22. Quoted in Robert Scheer, *With Enough Shovels: Reagan, Bush, and Nuclear War* (New York: Random House, 1982), p. 104.

23. Anderson, Policy Memorandum no. 3, Reagan for President Campaign, Los Angeles, August 1979, excerpts reprinted in *Revolution,* pp. 85–86.

24. Interviews with Pentagon official, April 8, 1987, and with Martin Anderson, Palo Alto, Calif., December 3, 1987.

25. For further discussion of the kitchen cabinet, see Frank Greve, "Out of the Blue: How 'Star Wars' Was Proposed," *Philadelphia Inquirer,* November 17, 1985, p. 1.

26. Daniel O. Graham, *We Must Defend America: A New Strategy for National Survival* (Chicago: Regnery Gateway, 1983), p. 57.

27. For further discussion of Wallop's role in the genesis of the SDI, see Codevilla, *While Others Build,* chap. 4.

28. Angelo M. Codevilla, "How SDI Is Being Undone from Within," *Commentary,* May 1986, pp. 21–29.

29. Documents pertaining to the 1982 air force analysis of the High Frontier's Global Ballistic Missile Defense concept were provided to Senator J. Bennett Johnston by Lieutenant General James A. Abrahamson in March 1987. An even more critical appraisal was conducted in 1981 for General Richard Stillwell by Herbert Reynolds, an official in the Office of the Under Secretary of Defense, and was circulated in the White House Office of Science and Technology Policy in early 1982. Memorandum from Reynolds to Stillwell, "BMD Concept Proposal by Bud Redding," September 28, 1981.

30. Norman Moss, "It's Not an Arms Race; It's a Competition in Military Technology," *The Listener,* June 13, 1985, p. 1.

31. Graham, *We Must Defend America,* p. 114.

32. Henry Epstein, "Freeze Folk: The High Frontier Wants YOU," *Nuclear Times* 3 (May–June 1985): 12.

33. Greve, "Out of the Blue."

34. See "Washington Roundup," *Aviation Week and Space Technology,* September 20, 1982, p. 15; Clarence Robinson, "Defense Dept. Backs Space-Based Missile Defense," ibid., September 27, 1982, pp. 14–16. The meeting is also discussed in Codevilla, *While Others Build,* p. 87.

35. Memorandum for the chairman of the Defense Science Board from John S. Foster, Jr., "Final Report of the Space-Based Laser Task Force," April 30, 1981, and memorandum for the secretary of defense and deputy secretary of defense from Norman R. Augustine, "DSB Report on Review of the DoD Space-Based Laser Weapon Study," May 1, 1981.

36. "DSB Space Laser Panel Omitted Skeptics' Views, OSD Auditors Say," *Aerospace Daily,* December 7, 1983, p. 185.

37. For further discussion, see Greve, "Out of the Blue."

38. Interviews with Pentagon officials, April 11, 1987, May 2, 1988, June 10, 1987.

39. Ibid.

40. Greve, "Out of the Blue," and interview with Pentagon official, April 8, 1987.

41. Interview with William Furniss, Office of Strategic Defense and Space Arms Control Policy, the Pentagon, December 29, 1987.

42. Allegations about Teller's exaggerations about the Excalibur actually preceded the president's speech. A letter from the Livermore physicist Hugh E. DeWitt to David Saxon, president of the University of California, on October 3, 1982, charged, "The promise of a wonderful new nuclear defense against ballistic missile attack as de-

Notes

scribed by Teller is misleading and dangerous. . . ." For further discussion of the Excalibur controversy, see William J. Broad, "Beyond the Bomb: Turmoil in the Labs," *New York Times Magazine,* October, 9, 1988, pp. 23–93. See also Strategic Defense Initiative Program, *Accuracy of Statements Concerning DOE's X-ray Laser Research Program,* Briefing Report to the Honorable George E. Brown, Jr. (Washington, D.C.: General Accounting Office, 1988), which cites letters written by Teller to administration officials in support of the Excalibur's capabilities.

43. York is quoted in Herken, "Earthly Origins of Star Wars," p. 22; the weapons designer is quoted in Robert Scheer, " 'Star Wars: A Program in Disarray," *Los Angeles Times,* September 22, 1985, p. 4.

44. For further discussion, see Anderson, *Revolution,* pp. 90–97.

45. Quoted in Greve, "Out of the Blue."

46. Interview with Theodore Postol, December 3, 1987.

47. Greve, "Out of the Blue."

48. Interview with Waller.

49. Interview with John Pike, Washington, D.C., December 21, 1987.

50. Paul Boyer, "How SDI Will Change Our Culture," *Nation,* January 10, 1987, pp. 15–20.

51. Meeting with Robert Beckel, Washington, D.C., February 1987. The discussion of Christ and the SDI appears in Jonathon Moseley, *Deploying the Peace Shield with Space Based Missile Defenses* (Arlington: Women for a Secure Future, May 1986), pp. 44–47.

52. Weinberger repeated these remarks in a press conference at the Pentagon on March 29, 1983, in which he argued, "What is ultimately desired is a total defense," cited in *Star Wars Quotes* (Washington, D.C.: The Arms Control Association, 1986), p. 17.

53. Representative analyses of the technical and policy issues associated with a "layered defense" can be found in, for example, Ashton Carter and David Schwartz, eds., *Ballistic Missile Defense* (Washington, D.C.: Brookings Institution, 1984); *Strategic Defense Initiative: Defensive Technologies Study* (Washington, D.C.: Department of Defense, March 1984); Harold Brown, ed., *The Strategic Defense Initiative: Shield or Snare?* (Boulder: Westview, 1987); and Steven W. Guerrier and Wayne C. Thompson, eds., *Perspectives on Strategic Defense* (Boulder: Westview, 1987).

54. Cited in "SDI: A Prospect for Peace," film by the American Defense Preparedness Association, 1987.

55. For further discussions of the study panels, see R. Jeffrey Smith, "Star Wars Panels Highlight Uncertainties," *Science* 224 (April 6, 1984): 33; Donald L. Hafner, "Assessing the President's Vision: the Fletcher, Miller, and Hoffman Panels," *Daedalus* (Spring 1985): 91–107; Patrick J. Garrity, "The United States: The Politics of Strategic Defence," *World Today,* January 1985, pp. 6–7; and Codevilla, *While Others Build,* pp. 96–114.

56. DeLauer quoted in Richard Halloran, "An Under Secretary With a Rare Bent for Candor," *New York Times,* April 1, 1983, p. A14.

57. Interviews with Pentagon officials, December 12, 1987, and August 12, 1988.

58. Interview with Pentagon official, November 20, 1987.

59. Ibid.

60. Interview with Furniss.

61. *Defensive Technologies Study;* unclassified excerpts of the Fletcher Panel's recommendations can also be found in Senate Foreign Relations Committee, *Strategic Defense and Anti-Satellite Weapons: Hearing,* 98th Cong., 2d sess., April 25, 1984, pp. 94–175.

62. Cited in Tina Rosenberg, "Washington: The Authorized Version," *Atlantic Monthly*, February 1986, pp. 26–30.

63. See "Ballistic Missile Defenses and US National Security," Summary Report of the Future Security Strategy Study prepared for the Future Security Study Group (Alexandria: Institute for Defense Analysis, October 1983).

64. Interview with a member of the Hoffman panel, July 1987.

65. Interview with Furniss.

66. See *Defense against Ballistic Missiles: An Assessment of Technologies and Policy Implications* (Washington, D.C.: Department of Defense, April 1984). Miller also provided unclassified testimony about strategic defense, in House Committee on Armed Services, *Department of Defense Authorization for Appropriations for Fiscal Year 1985: Hearings*, 98th Cong., 2d sess., pt. 6, March 8, 1984, pp. 948–59, and in Senate Armed Services Committee, *Department of Defense Authorization for Appropriations for Fiscal Year 1985*, 98th Cong., 2d sess., pt. 6, March 22, 1984, pp. 2948–59.

67. Interview with Furniss.

68. Ibid.

69. Interview with Pentagon official, March 1987.

70. Michael MccGwire, "The Ultimate Umbrella," *Times Literary Supplement*, October 31, 1986, pp. 1214–21.

Chapter 5

1. Angelo M. Codevilla, "How SDI Is Being Undone from Within," *Commentary*, May 1986, p. 26. For the SDIO mandate, see memorandum for the secretary of defense et al., "Management of the Strategic Defense Initative," April 24, 1984.

2. For a full discussion of the SDI's plans for phased development, see the testimony of James Abrahamson before the House Committee on Appropriations, Subcommittee on Defense, *Department of Defense Appropriations for FY 1985*, 98th Cong., 2d sess., pt. 5, May 9, 1984, pp. 672–83.

3. Quoted in Robert Scheer, " 'Star Wars' Program: Scientists Scramble to Fulfill Plan," *Los Angeles Times*, September 22, 1985, p. 1, confirmed in an interview with a former aide to DeLauer, October 12, 1987.

4. Morton Halperin, *The Decision to Deploy the ABM* (Washington, D.C.: Brookings Institution, 1973), p. 65.

5. Quoted in R. Jeffrey Smith, "Weapons Bureaucracy Spurns Star Wars Goal," *Science* 224 (April 6, 1984): 32–34.

6. Interview with Simon Worden, Washington, D.C., December 15, 1987. See also Robert C. Toth, "US officials May Be Ordered to Clear 'Star Wars' Statements," *Los Angeles Times*, May 30, 1985, p. 6.

7. Interview with Pentagon official, December 15, 1987.

8. Robert D. Hammond and William M. Congo, "The Army as a Major Player in SDI," *Army 1988–89 Green Book*, October 1988, pp. 201, 202. For further discussion of the army's role in BMD, see Jack Cushman, "Army Envisions New Tasks for BMD," *Defense Week*, March 28, 1983, p. 1.

9. Letter from Graham to Weinberger, November 11, 1982.

10. Quoted in Fred Hiatt, "Military Considers Unified Space Command," *Washington Post*, August 27, 1983, p. 11. For further discussions of the establishment of the U.S. Space Command, see *United States Military Posture for FY1988*, Joint Staff, Office of

Notes

the Joint Chiefs of Staff, pp. 87–88; Iver Peterson, "U.S. Activates Unit for Space Defense," *New York Times,* September 24, 1985, p. A28; "President Authorizes US Space Command," *Defense Daily,* December 4, 1984, p. 167; and letter from Michael C. Kerby, director of U.S. Air Force legislative liaison, to Senator Gary Hart discussing the structure of command for the Air Force Space Command, September 10, 1986.

11. Interview with Furniss, November 20, 1987.

12. See "Washington Roundup: Strategic Initiatives," *Aviation Week and Space Technology,* December 19, 1983, p. 17; "Congress Generously Funds Beam Wars, But Awaits Plan," *Defense Week,* August 22, 1983, p. 1.

13. See SDIO mandate, Clarence A. Robinson, Jr., "Strategic Defense Group Speeds Effort," *Aviation Week and Space Technology,* June 11, 1984, pp. 16–18; and testimony of James A. Abrahamson, "Statement on the President's Strategic Defense Initiative," in *Department of Defense Appropriations for FY 1985,* 98th Cong., 2d sess., pt. 5, May 9, 1984, p. 680.

14. Abrahamson testimony to Senate Armed Services Committee, "The Strategic Defense Initiative", in *Department of Defense Appropriations for FY 85,* 98th Cong., 2d. sess., pt. 6, April 24, 1984, p. 3036, emphasis added.

15. Interview with a Pentagon official, September 26, 1987.

16. Interview with a Pentagon official, November 14, 1987.

17. Interview with an SDIO official, July 10, 1987.

18. Interview with Bruce Jackson, December 12, 1987.

19. See "Star Wars Staff Will Double," *Defense Week,* September 23, 1985, p. 4.

20. Transcript of WJLA-TV report by Renee Poussaint, "Investigation of Security at SDI Office," June 23, 1988, reprinted in *Current News,* Special Edition, August 24, 1988, pp. 2–4.

21. Interview with Worden.

22. Interview with Jackson.

23. Interview with Worden.

24. Interview with John Pike, Washington, D.C., December 21, 1987.

25. Interview with John Dewey, Washington, D.C., January 15, 1988.

26. Advertisement for *SDI Monitor,* 1986.

27. Testimony of James A. Abrahamson, in Senate Armed Services Committee, *Department of Defense Authorization for Appropriations for Fiscal Year 1987,* 99th Cong., 2d sess., pt. 4, March 26, 1986, p. 1618.

28. Quoted in R. Jeffrey Smith, "Hicks Attacks SDI Critics," *Science* 232 (April 25, 1986): 444.

29. Testimony of Abrahamson, in *Defense Authorization . . . 1987,* p. 1644.

30. Interview with a JCS official, May 11, 1988.

31. For a discussion of contractor-SDIO relations, see Katherine Magraw, "SDI: Fading Fantasy or Fait Accompli?" *Spacewatch,* May 1988, and "SDI and Corporate Contractors: Momentum, Ambivalence, and a Push for Early Deployment," *FAS Public Interest Report* 40 (April 1987): 1–12.

32. Quoted in Fred Kaplan, "Star Wars: The Ultimate Military-Industrial Compact," *Boston Globe,* September 14, 1987, p. 13.

33. Figures cited in *The Strategic Defense Initiative: Costs, Contractors and Consequences* (New York: Council on Economic Priorities, 1985).

34. Letter to Gary Hart from James Abrahamson, April 30, 1985.

35. R. Jeffrey Smith, "Star Wars Grants Attract Universities," *Science* 228 (April 19, 1985): 304.

36. Quoted in ibid.

37. The announcement is in SDIO "Memorandum for Correspondents," May 17, 1985. University response is reported in Michael Weisskopf, "Universities Say Pentagon Misstated Role in SDI," *Washington Post*, June 7, 1985, p. A11.

38. See "SDI Research Boycott Apparently Ineffective," *Defense Daily*, August 10, 1987, p. 221.

39. Study conducted by author for Science Applications International Corporation under contract to DR & E, "Deterrence under Defense Dominance" (series of briefings to Pentagon officials, January–December, 1983).

40. Meeting with Yonas, U.S. Senate, April 1984.

41. The two studies are Ashton Carter, *Directed Energy Missile Defense in Space* (Washington, D.C.: Office of Technology Assessment, April 1984), and *A Space-Based Missile Defense* (Cambridge, Mass.: Union of Concerned Scientists, March 1984).

42. See "Technical Review of Ashton Carter's Background Paper 'Directed Energy Missile Defense in Space,' " submitted to the Subcommittee on Defense, House Appropriations Committee, May 9, 1984. For reports on allegations against Carter, see editorial, *Wall Street Journal*, December 10, 1984; letter from Ashton Carter to the editor, *Wall Street Journal*, January 2, 1985; letter from William J. Barletta to Morris K. Udall, alleging security infringements by Carter, May 18, 1984.

43. Letter from William Taft to John H. Gibbons, 4 June 1984, and response from Gibbons, July 13, 1984.

44. Interview with Worden; letter to James A. Abrahamson from Richard Garwin, March 11, 1985.

45. The Worden incident and the controversy over the OTA and the UCS studies are discussed in "IBM Scientist Complains about Opponents," *Military Space*, September 16, 1985, p. 1. See also Robert Jastrow, "The War against Star Wars," *Commentary*, December 1984, pp. 19–25; letter from George Keyworth to Abrahamson, April 21, 1985; William F. Buckley, Jr., "Concerned Scientists Pen Hysteria," *Daily Camera*, February 2, 1985; Simon P. Worden, "Summary of Principal Errors in Criticisms of SDI" (paper prepared for the director of the SDIO, March 1985); "Star Wars and the Scientists" (letters to the editor), *Commentary*, March 1985, pp. 4–22; "SDI Critics, Defenders Fight, Round 2," *Military Space*, March 4, 1985, pp. 5–7; and memorandum for correspondents, an analysis of the OTA and the UCS studies released by the Department of Defense, September 25, 1985.

46. George Keyworth is quoted in Douglas Waller, James Bruce, and Douglas Cook, "SDI: Progess and Challenges" (staff report submitted to Senators Proxmire, Johnston, and Chiles, March 17, 1986), p. 13.

47. *SDIO Panel on Computing in Support of Battle Management. Summer Study 1985: A Report to the Director, Strategic Defense Initiative Organization* (Marina del Ray: Eastport Study Group, April 1985). For discussions of Parnas's role, see, for instance, David Lorge Parnas, "Software Aspects of Strategic Defense Systems," *American Scientist* 73 (September–October 1985): 432–40; Parnas's letter of June 28, 1985, to James H. Offutt, assistant director of SDIO, on resigning from the SDIO panel; and Experts Claim Battle Management Paramount to Missile Defense," *Aviation Week and Space Technology*, January 13, 1986, pp. 22–23.

48. Gregory Fossedal, "SDI Targeted in Critical Report," *Washington Times*, November 13, 1987, p. F1.

49. Transcript of House Republican study conference, June 1985.

50. For further discussion, see Waller et al., "SDI."

51. See, for instance, memorandum from Harold Brown to George P. Shultz, August 1, 1986, and Harold Brown, "The Strategic Defense Initiative: Defensive Systems and the Strategic Debate," *Survival* 27 (March–April 1985): 55–65.

Notes

52. Goldwater's statement is from hearings before the Senate Committee on Armed Services, Subcommittee on Strategic and Theater Nuclear Forces, "Strategic Defense Initiative," 99th Cong., 1st sess., October 30, 1985, p. 2.

53. Interview with a Republican Senate staffer, June 11, 1987.

54. Weinberger quoted in testimony before the Senate Foreign Relations Committee, October 31, 1985, quoted in the *New York Times,* December 15, 1985, as cited in *Star Wars Quotes* (Washington, D.C.: The Arms Control Association, 1986), p. 60; interview with Furniss. For further discussion of potential SDI costs, see Barry M. Blechman and Victor A. Utgoff, "The Macroeconomics of Strategic Defenses," in Harold Brown, ed., *The Strategic Defense Initiative: Shield or Snare?* (Boulder: Westview, 1987), pp. 139–81.

55. Interview with William Hoehn, Washington, D.C., December 21, 1987.

56. Interview with Mark Albrecht, Washington, D.C., December 9, 1987.

57. John Warner, opening statement, Senate Committee on Armed Services, Subcommittee on Strategic and Theater Nuclear Forces, *Strategic Defense Initiative: Hearings,* 99th Cong., 1st sess., October 30, 1985, p. 16.

58. Speech by Nunn before the Arms Control Association, Washington, D.C., January 19, 1988, reprinted in *Arms Control Today* 18 (March 1988): 3–7.

59. Ronald Reagan, interview with foreign broadcasters, November 12, 1985, cited in *Star Wars Quotes* (Washington, D.C.: The Arms Control Association, 1986).

60. Goldwater from the Senate Committee on Armed Services, Subcommittee on Strategic and Theater Nuclear Forces, "Strategic Defense Initiative," 99th Cong., 1st sess., October 30, 1985, p 2.

61. The decision is discussed in Waller et al., "SDI," p. 49.

62. Interview with Bruce Jackson, November 14, 1988. See also Melissa Healy and Dennis Mullin, "Reaganites at War over Star Wars," *U.S. News and World Report,* February 9, 1987, p. 30.

63. Thomas G. Moorer, "Fish or Cut Bait," *High Frontier Newswatch* 4 (June 1986): 4.

64. Interview with Jackson; Admiral Crowe is quoted in "SDI Deployment Is Years Away," *Washington Post,* January 22, 1987, p. 45; the defense executive is quoted in Dave Griffiths and Evert Clark, "Rushing Star Wars Could Send It Right Back to Earth," *Business Week,* March 2, 1987, p. 43.

65. Interview with Jackson.

66. Interview with Furniss, November 20, 1987; Mense, remarks to the Institute for Foreign Policy Analysis and Atlantic Commission conference, The Hague, October 10–12, 1987.

67. Alternative Strategic Defense Initiative Budget for FY 1986, bill cosponsored by Senators Proxmire, Mathias, Bumpers, and Chafee, July 1985.

68. Interview with Waller.

69. Ibid.

70. See Waller et al., "SDI"; "Analysis of Congressional Staff Report: SDI Progress and Challenges" (review conducted by Department of Defense, March 31, 1986), excerpts published in Paul Mann, "Congress, Pentagon Clash on Report Citing SDI Technical Problems," *Aviation Week and Space Technology* (April 7, 1986): 27–29, and the rebuttal submitted to the DoD by Waller and Bruce, April 1986; interview with Senate staffer, Washington, D.C., December 7, 1987.

71. Interview with Albrecht.

72. For further discussion, see "Resolving a Star Wars Skirmish: The President Papers Over a Heated Dispute on Weapons Testing," *Time,* October 23, 1985, p. 45.

73. Minutes of meeting printed in Gregory Fossedal, "NSC Minutes Show President

Leaning to SDI Deployment," *Washington Times,* February 6, 1987, p. 1. For further discussion, see "Speeding Up Star Wars," *Newsweek,* February 16, 1987, pp. 28–29.

74. Letter from Nunn to President Reagan, February 6, 1987.

75. Memorandum from the Defense Science Board task force to Under Secretary for Acquisition Richard Godwin, July 1987, excerpts published in David Lynch, "Deployment of SDI Found Premature," *Defense Week,* August 3, 1987, p. 5.

76. Interview with William Perry, Rosslyn, Va., January, 1988.

77. See "SDI Gains Milestone I Approval," news release, Office of Assistant Secretary of Defense, Washington, D.C., September 18, 1987.

78. Interview with a JCS official, Washington, D.C., January 22, 1988.

79. Interview with Furniss, December 29, 1987.

80. Trish Gilmartin, "White House Panel Recommends Missile Defense Scheme," *Defense News,* November 7, 1988, p. 3.

81. David Rivkin, "What Moscow Thinks," *Foreign Policy* (Summer 1985).

82. See Gregory Fossedal, "Nitze on the Dark Side?" *Washington Times,* October 26, 1987, p. D3, and Warren Strobel, "FBI Agrees to Investigate Nitze Role with Scientists," *Washington Times,* November 24, 1987.

83. Cited in Fossedal, "Nitze on the Dark Side?"

84. Interview with Pentagon official, December 22, 1987. See also R. Jeffrey Smith, "Weinberger Report Recommends Four 'Broad' SDI Tests," *Washington Post,* May 11, 1987, p. 10.

85. For further discussion of planned SDI space tests and the ABM Treaty, see Matthew Bunn, "ABM Treaty Compliance: Star Wars Tests on Shaky Ground," *Arms Control Today* 18 (April 1988): 11–20.

Chapter 6

1. Speech by Nunn to the Arms Control Association, Washington, D.C., January 19, 1988, reprinted in *Arms Control Today* 18 (March 1988): 3–7.

2. Interview with Bruce P. Jackson, February 27, 1988.

3. "Welcome Aboard, Sam Nunn (Or, SDI *Can* Protect America)," *National Security Record* (Heritage Foundation newsletter), February 1988, p. 1.

4. Quoted in testimony by Fred Iklé before hearings of the Senate Armed Services Committee, Subcommittee on Strategic and Theater Nuclear Forces, "Strategic Defense Initiative," 99th Cong., 1st sess., October 30, 1985, p. 8–9.

5. John H. Cushman, Jr., "Pentagon Official Proposes Cost Cut for Space Weapon," *New York Times,* September 8, 1988, p. 1.

6. Tami Davis Biddle, "Handling the Soviet Threat: *Project Control* and the Debate on American Strategy in the Early Cold War Period" (paper for the Conference of the Society for Historians of American Foreign Relations, June 9–11, 1988), p. 3.

7. Interview with Simon P. Worden, Washington, D.C., November 22, 1987. See also Simon P. Worden and Bruce P. Jackson, "Emerging Determinants of National Power" (draft of paper, August 13, 1987), and Fred Hiatt, "Air Force Manual Seeks Space Superiority," *Washington Post,* January 15, 1985, p. A13.

8. Richard Burt, article in *Die Welt,* September 7, 1988, cited in *European Media,* SHAPE Public Information Office, September 9, 1988.

9. For further discussion, see, for instance, Jeffrey Richelson, "PD-59, NSDD-13 and the Reagan Strategic Modernization Program," *Journal of Strategic Studies,* June 1983, pp. 125–46; Desmond Ball, "The Development of US Nuclear Weapons Employment

Notes

Policy" (memorandum, 1988); and Tim Carrington, "Carlucci Orders Move for Development of 'Earth Penetrating' Nuclear Weapon," *Wall Street Journal,* September 13, 1988, p. 5.

10. Robert S. Dudney, "Strategic Forces at the Brink of START," *Air Force Magazine,* February 1988, p. 42.

11. From Ball, "Employment Policy," p. 4.

12. Dudney, "Strategic Forces," p. 42.

13. Interview with an official in the Office of the Secretary of Defense, the Pentagon, July 1988.

14. For additional discussion, see Paul B. Stares, *Space and National Security* (Washington, D.C.: Brookings Institution, 1987), and Bruce G. Blair, *Strategic Command and Control* (Washington, D.C.: Brookings Institution, 1985).

15. Quoted in Carnes Lord, "Taking Soviet Defenses Seriously," *Washington Quarterly* (Fall 1986): 96.

16. Estimates of spending on BMD absent the SDI appear in Douglas Waller, James Bruce, and Doug Cook, "SDI: Progress and Challenges" (staff report submitted to Senators Proxmire, Johnston, and Chiles, March 17, 1986), p. 11.

17. Albert Carnesale, "SDI: The First Five Years" (remarks on panel discussion at Institute for Foreign Policy Analysis conference, Shoreham Hotel, Washington, D.C., April 1987).

18. Interview with an official in the Office of the Secretary of Defense, November 1987; see also R. Jeffrey Smith, "Pentagon Scales Back SDI Goals," *Washington Post,* March 27, 1988, p. A1.

19. Interview with Worden.

20. Address by Harley Hughes, deputy chief of staff for plans and operations, to Air Force Association symposium, Colorado Springs, June 1987, cited in *Spacewatch,* July 13, 1987, p. 3.

21. P. Kevin Pepper, "SDI and the Sub Threat," *Proceedings,* September 1988, p. 28.

22. Interview with Jack Merritt, Arlington, Va., July 27, 1988.

23. See Richard H. Ellis, "The Joint Strategic Target Planning Staff" (memorandum from JSTPS), pp. 6–7, and Thomas Powers, "What's Worse than the MX?" *Washington Post,* March 31, 1985, p. K.

24. Donald C. Latham and John J. Lane, "Management Issues: Planning, Acquisition and Oversight," in Ashton B. Carter, John Steinbruner, and Charles A. Zraket, eds., *Managing Nuclear Operations* (Washington, D.C.: Brookings Institution, 1987), p. 643.

25. Interview with Leon Sloss, May 4, 1988.

26. Interview with Merritt.

27. Ibid.

28. Interview with Theodore Postol, April 2, 1988, Palo Alto, Calif. For more detailed discussions of the techniques of targeting, see Desmond Ball and Jeffrey Richelson, eds., *Strategic Nuclear Targeting* (Ithaca: Cornell University Press, 1986); William C. Martel and Paul L. Savage, *Strategic Nuclear War: What the Superpowers Target and Why* (Westport, Conn.: Greenwood, 1986); and Richard Lee Walker, *Strategic Target Planning* (Washington, D.C.: National Defense University Press, 1983).

29. Interview with a former navy targeting official, September 19, 1988.

30. Ibid.

31. Henry S. Rowen, "Formulating Strategic Doctrine," in *Report of the Commission on the Organization of the Government for the Conduct of Foreign Policy,* vol. 4, appendix K, pt. 3 (Washington, D.C.: Government Printing Office, 1975), p. 233.

32. Interview with Sloss. Power is quoted in Fred Kaplan, *The Wizards of Armageddon* (New York: Simon and Schuster 1983), p. 246.

33. John S. Steinbruner, "Nuclear Decapitation," *Foreign Policy* 45 (Winter 1981): 22–23, and "The Prospect of Cooperative Security" in Steinbruner et al., *Restructuring America's Foreign Policy* (Washington, D.C.: Brookings Institution, 1989), p. 95.

34. Steinbruner et al., *Restructuring America's Foreign Policy,* p. 95.

35. Interviews with Bruce Blair, Washington, D.C., July–November 1988.

36. DoD, *Dictionary of Military and Associated Terms* (Washington, D.C.: Joint Chiefs of Staff Publication, January 1986), p. 204.

37. Frank Miller, panel discussion at the Woodrow Wilson Center for Scholars, Washington, D.C., September 14, 1988.

38. Richard B. Goetze, Jr., quoted in Ball, "Employment Policy," p. 7.

39. Interview with Curtis LeMay by John T. Bolen, U.S. Air Force Oral History Program, interview no. 736, March 9, 1971, Maxwell Air Force Base, p. 32.

40. Ibid., p. 35.

41. Telephone interview with Harold Brown, October 20, 1988.

42. Russell E. Dougherty, "The Psychological Climate of Nuclear Command," in Carter et al., eds., *Managing Nuclear Operations,* p. 420.

43. Ibid.

44. John C. Toomay, "Strategic Forces Rationale—A Lost Discipline?" *International Security* 12 (Fall 1987): 194.

45. R. James Woolsey, "American Strategic Force Decisions for the 1990's" (unpublished paper, July 27, 1988), p. 2.

46. Quoted in George C. Wilson, "Stealth Called Nuclear Deterrent," *Washington Post,* May 17, 1988, p. 10.

47. John S. Steinbruner, "The Effect of Strategic Force Reductions on Nuclear Strategy," *Arms Control Today,* May 1988, p. 3.

48. Interview with a former Pentagon official.

49. Seminar at Brookings Institution, November 1988.

50. R. Jeffrey Smith, "Bush Will Miss Deadline on Land-Based Missile Pick," *Washington Post,* February 15, 1989, p. A17.

51. See, for instance, Lynn Eden, "Obliteration Is Not Enough; or, Why the Air Force Wants the Missiles It Does" (presentation at Social Science Research Council Conference for Fellows, Morelos, Mexico, January 9–13, 1988).

52. Louis Henkin, "Foreign Affairs and the Constitution," *Foreign Affairs* 66 (Winter 1987–88): 301–2.

53. Steinbruner, "Effect of Strategic Force Reductions," pp. 4–5 n. 48.

54. Les Paldy, Review of *Making Weapons, Talking Peace: A Physicist's Odyssey from Hiroshima to Geneva,* by Herbert York, in *Friday Review of Defense Literature,* April 29, 1988, p. 6.

55. C. Wright Mills, *The Causes of World War Three* (New York: Ballantine, 1960), pp. 145–46.

56. Dougherty, "Psychological Climate," p. 423.

57. Mills, *Causes of World War Three,* p. 185.

INDEX

Abbreviations are explained on pages *ix–x*.

Index